Confessional Diplomacy in Early Modern Europe

Confessional Diplomacy in Early Modern Europe examines the role of religion in early modern European diplomacy. In the period following the Reformations, Europe became divided: all over the continent, princes and their peoples split over theological, liturgical, and spiritual matters. At the same time, diplomacy rose as a means of communication and policy, and all powers established long- or short-term embassies and sent envoys to other courts and capitals. The book addresses three critical areas where questions of religion or confession played a role: papal diplomacy, priests and other clerics as diplomatic agents, and religion as a question for diplomatic debate, especially concerning embassy chapels.

Roberta Anderson, FRHistS, is a retired Senior Lecturer in Early Modern History, Bath Spa University, Co-Director of the Premodern Diplomats Network (PDN), and is on the editorial board of *Legatio*, the online journal of PDN, and the advisory board of the *Royal Studies Journal*.

Charlotte Backerra is Assistant Professor of Early Modern History at the University of Göttingen. She has held positions as researcher and lecturer at the universities of Mainz, Stuttgart, and Darmstadt since 2009, and is Technical Editor of the *Royal Studies Journal* and a board member of the International Intelligence History Association.

Routledge Studies in Renaissance and Early Modern Worlds of Knowledge

Series Editors:

Harald E. Braun (University of Liverpool, UK) and Emily Michelson (University of St Andrews, UK)

SRS Board Members:

Erik DeBom (KU Leuven, Belgium), Mordechai Feingold (California Institute of Technology, USA), Andrew Hadfield (Sussex), Peter Mack (University of Warwick, UK), Jennifer Richards (University of Newcastle, UK), Stefania Tutino (UCLA, USA), Richard Wistreich (Royal College of Music, UK)

This series explores Renaissance and Early Modern Worlds of Knowledge (*c.*1400–*c.*1700) in Europe, the Americas, Asia and Africa. The volumes published in this series study the individuals, communities and networks involved in making and communicating knowledge during the first age of globalization. Authors investigate the perceptions, practices and modes of behaviour which shaped Renaissance and Early Modern intellectual endeavour and examine the ways in which they reverberated in the political, cultural, social and economic sphere.

The series is interdisciplinary, comparative and global in its outlook. We welcome submissions from new as well as existing fields of Renaissance Studies, including the history of literature (including neo-Latin, European and non-European languages), science and medicine, religion, architecture, environmental and economic history, the history of the book, art history, intellectual history and the history of music. We are particularly interested in proposals that straddle disciplines and are innovative in terms of approach and methodology.

The series includes monographs, shorter works and edited collections of essays. The Society for Renaissance Studies (www.rensoc.org.uk) provides an expert editorial board, mentoring, extensive editing and support for contributors to the series, ensuring high standards of peer-reviewed scholarship. We welcome proposals from early career researchers as well as more established colleagues.

15 **Embodiment, Expertise, and Ethics in Early Modern Europe**
Entangling the Senses
Edited by Marlene L. Eberhart and Jacob M. Baum

16 **Confessional Diplomacy in Early Modern Europe**
Edited by Roberta Anderson and Charlotte Backerra

17 **Travel and Conflict in the Early Modern World**
Edited by Gábor Gelléri and Rachel Willie

For more information about this series, please visit: www.routledge.com/ Routledge-Studies-in-Renaissance-and-Early-Modern-Worlds-of-Know ledge/book-series/ASHSER4043

Confessional Diplomacy in Early Modern Europe

Edited by Roberta Anderson and
Charlotte Backerra

Routledge
Taylor & Francis Group

LONDON AND NEW YORK

First published 2021
by Routledge
2 Park Square, Milton Park, Abingdon, Oxon OX14 4RN

and by Routledge
52 Vanderbilt Avenue, New York, NY 10017

Routledge is an imprint of the Taylor & Francis Group, an informa business

British Library Cataloguing-in-Publication Data
A catalogue record for this book is available from the British Library

Library of Congress Cataloging-in-Publication Data
Names: Anderson, Roberta, editor. | Backerra, Charlotte, editor.
Title: Confessional diplomacy in early modern Europe / edited by Roberta Anderson and Charlotte Backerra.
Description: Abingdon, Oxon ; New York, NY : Routledge, 2020. |
Series: Routledge studies in Renaissance and early modern worlds of knowledge |
Includes bibliographical references and index.
Identifiers: LCCN 2020027667 (print) | LCCN 2020027668 (ebook) |
ISBN 9780367532260 (hardback) | ISBN 9781003080992 (ebook)
Subjects: LCSH: Diplomacy–Religious aspects–Catholic Church–History. |
Diplomacy–Religious aspects–Christianity–History. | Diplomacy–Europe–
History. | Catholic Church–Foreign relations–Europe–History. | Christianity and international relations–Europe–History.
Classification: LCC BX1793 .C566 2020 (print) | LCC BX1793 (ebook) |
DDC 261.8/7094–dc23
LC record available at https://lccn.loc.gov/2020027667
LC ebook record available at https://lccn.loc.gov/2020027668

ISBN: 978-0-367-53226-0 (hbk)
ISBN: 978-1-003-08099-2 (ebk)

Typeset in Sabon
by River Editorial Ltd, Devon, UK

Printed in the United Kingdom
by Henry Ling Limited

Contents

Contributors

Roberta Anderson, FRHistS, is a retired Senior Lecturer in Early Modern History, Bath Spa University, Co-Director of the Premodern Diplomats Network (PDN) and is on the editorial board of *Legatio*, the online journal of PDN, the editorial board of the *Handbook of Early Modern Diplomacy* (2022), and the advisory board of the *Royal Studies Journal*. She has a PhD in *Foreign Diplomatic Representatives to the Court of James VI & I* (UWE, 2000) and Mas in *The English Renaissance: Politics, Patronage and Literature* (Reading, 1993) and *Church History* (Nottingham, 2016). Roberta has published on early modern diplomacy, focusing on the Catholic ambassadors at the Court of St James, 1603–1625, and has given papers on the subject at various conferences, including several of the Splendid Encounters series. Roberta has also published two medieval history sourcebooks and is currently working on the biography of an order of English Benedictine nuns, 1598–1975.

Charlotte Backerra is Assistant Professor of Early Modern History at the University of Göttingen. She has held positions as researcher and lecturer at the universities of Mainz, Stuttgart, and Darmstadt since 2009. Based on her PhD in Imperial-British Relations, she has published *Wien und London, 1727–1735: Internationale Beziehungen im frühen 18. Jahrhundert* (Vandenhoeck & Ruprecht, 2018). Her projects include the economics and culture of dynastic rule, monarchies and dynasties in the context of politics, gender, and culture, premodern international relations, and intelligence and espionage of European powers. Charlotte is Technical Editor of the *Royal Studies Journal* and a board member of the International Intelligence History Association.

Martin Bakeš received his PhD at the Institute of History of the Faculty of Arts and Philosophy at the University of Pardubice in 2018. His study deals with imperial diplomats in the Kingdom of Sweden (1650–1730) and was published as a book (Academia, 2020). Martin has also written articles on the imperial legation chaplains in Stockholm (2016) as well as on the diplomatic missions of Anton Johann von Nostitz and of Adolf Wratislav von Sternberg to Sweden in the 1680s and 1690s

(2014, 2015). Martin is one of the co-authors of *V zastoupení císaře: Česká a moravská aristokracie v habsburské diplomacii 1640–1740*, a new book on Czech and Moravian aristocracy in the diplomatic service of the Austrian Habsburgs, which was published in Czech in 2018.

Katharina Beiergrößlein is a historian and archivist. She works as a research fellow at the City Archives of Stuttgart. Her main research interests lie in the field of early modern English and German history, the history of migration, and the history of alchemy and natural law as a university subject. She teaches early modern history at the Ludwig Maximilian University of Munich. Katharina recently co-authored a monograph with Jürgen Lotterer on transatlantic migration, *Die Reise der Frau Lotter aus Herrenberg nach America in den Jahren 1786 bis 1787* (2019).

Cristina Bravo Lozano is Tomas y Valiente fellow at the Madrid Institute for Advanced Study (MIAS – Universidad Autónoma de Madrid). She obtained her PhD at the Universidad Autónoma de Madrid (2014). Her research interests include Spanish–Irish relations in the seventeenth century, the diplomatic and cultural activities of the Spanish embassies in Protestant courts, and the confessional politics of the Spanish monarchy in Northern Europe. She is the author of *Spain and the Irish Mission, 1609–1707* (Routledge, 2019).

Rubén González Cuerva is Permanent Scientist in the Spanish National Research Council (CSIC). He completed his PhD at the Autonomous University of Madrid (2010) on the biography of the Spanish statesman Baltasar de Zúñiga (1561–1622). Thereafter, he has been a postdoctoral fellow at the National University of Salta (Argentina), Marie Curie Fellow at the German Historical Institute of Rome, associate lecturer at the Autonomous University of Madrid, and Juan de la Cierva Postdoctoral Researcher in the CSIC. He specialises in early modern diplomacy and political communication. Rubén is currently working on network interaction between the Habsburg courts and on intercultural Habsburg diplomacy. His recent works include *Baltasar de Zúñiga: Una encrucijada de la Monarquía hispana* (Ediciones Polifemo, 2012) and *A Europe of Courts, a Europe of Factions: Political Groupings at Early Modern Centres of Power* (Brill, 2017).

Dorota Gregorowicz is Adjunct Professor of Early Modern History in the Department of Humanities at the University of Silesia in Katowice, Poland. She completed her PhD at the University of Eastern Piedmont, Italy, in 2017, entitled *The Holy See and the Interregna in the Polish–Lithuanian Commonwealth in the Second Half of the 16th Century (1572–1589)*. The study is published in Polish as *Tiara w grze o koronę: Stolica Apostolska wobec wolnych elekcji w Rzeczypospolitej Obojga Narodów w drugiej połowie XVI w.* (Polska Akademia Umiejętności,

2019). Her current research interest is the history of diplomacy and political communication, especially regarding the papal diplomatic service, published, for example, in an article on 'La Santa Sede nei confronti dell'istituzione della libera elezione nello Stato polacco-lituano della seconda metà del XVI se-colo,' *Rivista Storica Italiana*, CXXXI/3, 2019. Her current research project is *The Holy See and the Crisis of Sovereignty of John Casimir Vasa and Michael Korybut Wiśniowiecki's Election (1660–1669)*, project no. 2018/28/C/HS3/00176, financed by the National Science Centre, Poland, 2018–2021.

Gábor Kármán is a research fellow at the Institute of History, Research Centre for the Humanities (formerly part of the Hungarian Academy of Sciences). He received his PhD at Eötvös Loránd University, Budapest, in 2009 and another one at Central European University, Budapest, in 2010. He has published widely on the history of Transylvania in various contexts, on seventeenth-century confessional politics, and on the history of Ottoman tributary states. His recent works include *A Seventeenth-Century Odyssey in East Central Europe: The Life of Jakab Harsányi Nagy* (Brill, 2015) and *Confession and Politics in the Principality of Transylvania, 1644–1657* (Vandenhoeck & Ruprecht, 2020).

Jiří Kubeš works at the Institute of History of the Faculty of Arts and Philosophy at the University of Pardubice. He received his PhD at the University of South Bohemia in České Budějovice in 2006 and defended his habilitation in 2011. He works on the history of the early modern Austrian Habsburg monarchy, as well as the history of the nobility and their lifestyle. He has written books on the grand tours of the Czech and Austrian nobility (2013), on elections and coronations in the Holy Roman Empire in the seventeenth and eighteenth centuries (2009), and edited the travel diary of the Silesian nobleman Christoph Wenzel von Nostitz from his journey to the Netherlands in 1705 (2004). Since 2013, he has dealt mainly with the history of imperial diplomacy, published several articles, edited a monothematic issue of the journal *Theatrum historiae* dealing with imperial diplomacy (2016), and organised the Splendid Encounters V conference in Prague in 2016. In summer 2018, a new book by his project team on Czech and Moravian aristocracy in the diplomatic service of the Austrian Habsburgs, 1640–1740, was published in Czech; it will be expanded and published in English in 2021.

Béla Vilmos Mihalik is a historian of early modern Hungary. He earned his PhD at the Eötvös Loránd University, Budapest, in 2014. He was the Director of the Hungarian Jesuit Archive between 2011 and 2019. He has been a research fellow of the Institute of History, Research Centre for the Humanities (formerly part of the Hungarian Academy of Sciences), since 2012, and the scientific secretary of the institute since

2019. He studies the Catholic renewal in Hungary in the seventeenth and eighteenth centuries, and the diplomatic relations between the Holy See and the Viennese Habsburg court.

Steve Murdoch is Professor of History at the University of St Andrews. His research interests include Scottish and British relations with Scandinavia and Northern Europe, 1560–1750. He is also deeply interested in Scottish history in a British context, and currently directs the Scotland, Britain and the Wider World Project. Steve recently co-authored a monograph with Alexia Grosjean, *Alexander Leslie and the Scottish Generals of the Thirty Years' War, 1618–1648* (Pickering & Chatto, 2014). His present research concentrates on women, widows, and their dependents during the Thirty Years' War.

Ernesto Oyarbide Magaña has a dual *Licenciatura* in Spanish philology and journalism from the University of Navarra, Spain, and a master of studies in literature and arts with distinction from the University of Oxford. He is also on the last stages of a DPhil in history at the University of Oxford. Ernesto is interested in the study of early modern diplomacy, Anglo-Iberian relations, Renaissance libraries, print culture, and intellectual history.

Foreword

Anna Kalinowska

POLISH ACADEMY OF SCIENCES, TADEUSZ MANTEUFFEL INSTITUTE OF
HISTORY, WARSAW

This edited collection is the outcome of the annual conferences of the
Premodern Diplomats Network (PDN). This group was founded by
Dr Roberta Anderson and myself in 2012, with the first conference held
at the Polish Academy of Sciences, Institute of History, Warsaw, in 2013,
with the aim of encouraging further research into the history of early
modern diplomacy. It is staffed by volunteers and operates through
a website, social media, and our open access journal *Legatio*. The network has some 150 members worldwide, and harnesses the expertise of
scholars, students, and others through their willingness to share their
knowledge of this growing historiography. The annual Splendid Encounters conference brings together some of the membership and newcomers
to hear the latest scholarship.

Charlotte Backerra and Roberta Anderson have had the task of editing this
collection of chapters around the theme of confessional diplomacy. Most of
the chapters were originally papers presented at one of the Splendid Encounters conferences, while others were especially commissioned; the result is the
work of an impressive array of the international scholars who study religion
and diplomacy in the UK and across Europe. What is abundantly clear from
all the chapters is that confessional diplomacy is an under-researched field,
particularly in the area of Protestant clerics.

The collection begins with a brief introduction by the editors that will give
readers food for thought and discussion. It reviews the existing research and
introduces the topic in the context of diplomatic history, as well as the 'confessional age' as a continuous feature in early modern Europe. The chapters
and their main questions are presented.

The following chapters are empirically rich and offer a wide range of historical approaches with which to interrogate material from the archives. During
the final years of the War of the Spanish Succession, the subject of Irish Catholics was included in discussions during the first diplomatic negotiations at The
Hague. In this context, the papal mission of Fr Bonaventure Burke in

1708–1710 sought the support of the Catholic sovereigns to help find a solution to the *quaestio hibernica*, examined by Cristina Bravo Lozano in her chapter. We move east with Dorota Gregorowicz as she illustrates the confessional politics of papal diplomats in the Polish–Lithuanian Commonwealth during the periods of interregna in the sixteenth and seventeenth centuries. Next, Béla Vilmos Mihalik analyses how papal and imperial diplomatic networks interacted in the anti-Ottoman Holy League organised by Pope Innocent XI (1676–1689), which played a decisive role in the expulsion of the Ottoman Empire from Central Europe, especially from the Kingdom of Hungary. Ernesto Oyarbide Magaña focuses on a usually disregarded figure at the Spanish embassy who nonetheless played an important role in Anglo-Spanish relations: the embassy's confessor, Friar Diego de la Fuente, and his role as chargé d'affaires *ad interim* during the Spanish ambassador Diego Sarmiento d'Acuna's leave of absence to Spain from 1618 to 1620. Katharina Beiergrößlein addresses the complicated position of the heretical former prior of the Cambridge Augustinians, Robert Barnes, who found himself sent on several delicate missions to the princes of the Schmalkaldic League and Christian III of Denmark to seek support for Henry VIII's 'Great Matter'. Rubén González Cuerva points to the ways in which the Capuchin confessor of Maria Anna of Austria, Diego de Quiroga, was able to act as her spokesman in the environment of the male courtier. His spiritual prestige and political talent enabled him to develop a double role as theologian and diplomat. Roberta Anderson takes us back to the Court of James VI & I to examine the problems presented by Catholic ambassadors and the perennial embassy chapel question. Moving to Lutheran Sweden, Steve Murdoch discusses the problems encountered by Scottish Calvinist ambassadors conducting diplomatic business in a fully Lutheran confessional state. Charlotte Backerra, moving into the eighteenth century, and using London and Vienna as case studies, examines the different ways in which diplomats cared for the spiritual life of their household and supported their religion as a whole in such a diaspora, especially in times of need or persecution. Martin Bakeš and Jiří Kubeš sum up, in the first place, the most recent research focused on the chapels of the Emperor's envoys in Lutheran Saxony and the Scandinavian kingdoms during the reign of Leopold I. They focus on a particular group of Catholic chaplains, mainly members of the Society of Jesus, who took care of the embassy *devotio domestica*. In concluding, Gábor Kármán brings together the subjects covered in the chapters. The conclusions will help future researchers to better understand the vital role of religion in early modern diplomacy, even after the so-called 'age of confessionalisation'. Historians of confessional diplomacy will find this edited collection a fine addition to the growing critical scholarship on diplomacy, and it will feed the thinking of scholars who wish to examine the imbrication of diplomacy and religion with social and cultural change.

1 Confessional diplomacy
A short introduction

Roberta Anderson and Charlotte Backerra

In the period following the Reformations, Europe became divided: no longer connected by Rome and its orthodoxy, all over Europe, princes and their people polarised along confessional lines.[1] At the same time, diplomacy rose as a means of communication and policy, so all powers, monarchies as well as republics, established long- or short-term embassies and sent envoys to other courts and capitals.[2] Diplomatic links expanded to incorporate Russia, the Ottoman Empire, Morocco, and several South Asian polities.[3] Strategic concerns encouraged states to forge alliances that cut across confessional boundaries, engaging in cross-confessional diplomacy with polities that observed several different Christian and Muslim confessions, many of which were considered heretics or infidels.[4] Fundamental problems also arose when each ruler or state sought to protect the interests of its co-religionists who formed a minority living under the rule of another.[5]

Our book argues that the confessional and religious divide was a key element in the diplomatic affairs of premodern Europe, and as such should be addressed accordingly. Building on the 'new diplomatic history,' the essays included here focus on intermediaries in European cross-confessional diplomacy.[6]

Based on the recent historiography of early modern confessional diplomacy, this analysis demonstrates the importance of religion in defining not only the collective identity of international actors, but also their foreign policies, choice of alliances, and more generally their international outlook.[7] The present volume engages with the recent shift in focus of diplomatic history from high politics and the figure of the ambassador to a diverse range of individuals who engaged in diplomatic relations on the ground.

We are therefore addressing the following questions: Did clerics act differently in comparison to other diplomats in the period? What did their personal preconceptions as confessors and ministers add to their role as diplomats, and could these roles interfere with one another? How did lay diplomats address questions of, and conflicts over, religion, especially in differing confessional settings? Can we see a change in these following the religious settlements of the late sixteenth and early seventeenth centuries?

The essays collected here confront these questions by bringing together established and young researchers in diplomatic history, most of whom are connected by the Premodern Diplomats Network (PDN), and for the most part the chapters are based on papers presented at the Splendid Encounters conferences.

Confessional Diplomacy in Early Modern Europe is separated into three parts. The first part is concerned with papal diplomacy, focusing on the relations and diplomatic aims of this decidedly confessional power. Moving on from the confessional ruler or state, the second part is concerned with clerics as diplomats. The chapters analyse to what extent a background as priest, chaplain, or otherwise spiritual professional changed an actor's approach to diplomacy. The third part looks at religion, confessional strife, and places of worship as matters of international relations.

In Part I, Dorota Gregorowicz will illustrate the confessional politics of papal diplomats in the Polish–Lithuanian Commonwealth during the periods of interregna in the sixteenth and seventeenth centuries. Based on the diplomatic dispatches of the apostolic nuncios and their instructions, she will demonstrate the evolution of the confessional aims of the papacy in Poland–Lithuania and explain its origins.

Béla Vilmos Mihalik moves us to the anti-Ottoman Holy League organised by Innocent XI (1676–1689) and how it played a decisive role in the expulsion of the Ottoman Empire from Central Europe, especially from the Kingdom of Hungary. His chapter examines the way the papal and the imperial diplomatic networks interacted in this complex situation: how the victories over the Ottomans influenced decisions in Rome and how the Ottoman Empire tried to hinder financial support, and finally how confessional concerns appear in the argument.

The mission of Fr Bonaventure de Burgo, by Cristina Bravo Luzano, examines the priest's function as interlocutor of the pope and representative of Irish Catholic interests, which reveal the prominent role he played in the defence of Catholicism in eighteenth-century Ireland. Owing to his profuse correspondence with various exiled bishops, he was well informed about religious conditions in his homeland. His privileged position at the papal court also gave him the opportunity to mediate with the pope, Clement XI. The new pope took advantage of the political tensions prevailing in Ireland to emphasise the papacy's peacemaking role and, at the same time, to promote the Catholic faith in territories where the Reformation had been successful.

Part II opens with a chapter in which Katharina Beiergrößlein introduces the diplomatic missions of the runaway heretic Friar Robert Barnes to the Schmalkaldic League and Denmark, in which he sought support for Henry VIII's 'Great Matter': the annulment of his marriage with Catherine of Aragon. She discusses how Robert Barnes qualified in ways that outweighed the specific shortcoming of being regarded as a heretic, exploring how contemporary writings on diplomacy dealt with heresy.

Ernesto Oyarbide Magaña focuses on a usually disregarded figure at the Spanish embassy who nonetheless played an important role in Anglo-Spanish relations: the embassy's confessor, Friar Diego de la Fuente, and his role as chargé d'affaires, *ad interim*, during the Spanish ambassador Diego Sarmiento d'Acuna's leave of absence to Spain from 1618 to 1620. By using Friar Diego's letters, still held in Madrid's Royal Library, Magaña will narrate this Dominican friar's dealings with James VI & I and many others, including the Archbishop of Canterbury.

The role of confessor-ambassador in Habsburg politics is discussed by Rubén González Cuerva in his chapter on the Capuchin Diego de Quiroga in his role as confessor to the future Empress, Maria Anna of Austria. In 1630, he travelled from Madrid to Vienna with Maria Anna, remaining with her until her death in 1649. Quiroga's spiritual prestige and political talent enabled him to develop a double role as theologian and diplomat: while Spanish ambassadors came and went, Quiroga represented a stable and reliable agent with privileged access to the imperial entourage. This analysis will be reinforced by diplomatic sources from Spain, Austria, and Italy in order to consider which were the benefits and limits of this type of agency, and which confessional implications had this double role to develop an orthodox Catholic policy in the House of Austria.

In Part III, Roberta Anderson examines the problems attached to being a Catholic ambassador at the Protestant English court during the reign of James VI & I (1603–1625). In the aftermath of the Reformation, rulers almost invariably chose men of their own religion to represent them and their states abroad. This presented problems whenever the embassy was to a state practising a different religion. With no church in which to practise their faith, ambassadors provided for their own spiritual needs and those of their entourage by establishing chapels inside their residences and appointing a chaplain to conduct services there. This rested on the notion, which was becoming recognised by all of Europe's rulers, that the embassy was transformed into foreign soil by the presence of the ambassador, and so was inviolate, and that the host government did not merely have no right to intervene, but was actually obliged to protect the ambassador and his staff. This chapter will examine the embassy chapel question, the ambassador's support for his English co-religionists and the Catholic cause in England, and the ways in which Catholic ambassadors to Protestant England did this, both within and without the Court of James VI & I.

As a fully Lutheran confessional state, the entrusting of sensitive diplomatic duties to Calvinist diplomats, ambassadors, clergymen, and spies might seem anomalous. After all, it remains a commonly held belief that it was against the law to be anything other than a Lutheran to live and work in Sweden during the reigns of Sigismund Vasa (r. 1592–1599), Karl IX (r. 1604–1611), or Gustav II Adolf (r. 1611–1632). Steve Murdoch, in his chapter, examines the curious case of a 'special dispensation' being given for the Calvinist Sir James Spens to be allowed to serve as an ambassador for Lutheran Sweden, and for this dispensation to continue to allow him to be elevated into the Swedish House of Nobility.

Even after the centuries marked by the so-called wars of religion, religious factors played a role in international relations, writes Charlotte Backerra in her examination of religion and diplomacy in London and Vienna in the period 1700–1745. This chapter will illustrate the differences in the daily lives of diplomats in foreign countries, especially for those posted in territories with a religious majority not their own, taking examples from the relations between the courts of London and Vienna in the early eighteenth century. Chapels, clerics and services will be analysed as part of a diplomat's daily life. In a second part, the actions of two imperial diplomats and of a British envoy will serve as case studies for the practical implications of confessional diplomacy in the 1730s and 1740s.

The study by Martin Bakeš and Jiří Kubeš has two main parts. First, it sums up the latest research focused on the chapels of the Emperor's envoys in Lutheran Saxony and the Scandinavian kingdoms during the reign of Leopold I. This will indicate not only the spatial possibilities and material furnishings of the embassy chapels, but the number of clashes between the foreign element and local clergy, municipal authorities, or king's and elector's servants. The second part focuses on the particular Catholic embassy chaplains and their activities. Most of them were known to have been members of the Austrian and Bohemian provinces of the Society of Jesus. Thus, this chapter will summarise and compare some typical strategies that were used by Catholic chaplains during their illegal activities. It will also introduce the network of contacts among several chosen imperial diplomats' chaplains and the local Catholic community alongside postal connections with Czech and Austrian patrons.

The final chapter, by Gábor Kármán, examines the legitimation strategies of the political endeavours of Prince Ferenc Rákóczi II, the leader of the Hungarian uprising in the 1700s. In his communication with European courts, he emphasised political rather than religious grievances. One of his most important addressees, Charles XII of Sweden, was keen to see himself as an important promoter of his Protestant co-religionists, repeatedly reminding the Emperor, Leopold I, to respect the rights of Hungarian Protestants, while at the same time offering no military or financial help to the Hungarian prince. Thus, through the discussion of Rákóczi's various legitimation strategies and Charles XII's responses, this chapter illustrates the surviving legacy of the common Protestant cause as a factor determining foreign policy decisions until the early eighteenth century.

The concluding remarks will first address the role of clerics as diplomats and their distinct view of diplomacy and diplomatic behaviour. Second, it will place papal diplomacy in the context of the diplomatic relations of other powers in the early modern period. Furthermore, the case studies for diplomats at courts with a different confessional majority will be compared over time and place to help come to a better understanding of the vital role of religion for early modern diplomacy even after the so-called 'age of confessionalisation' and into the eighteenth century.

Notes

1 Heinz Schilling, *Konfessionalisierung und Staatsinteressen: Internationale Beziehungen 1559–1660* (Paderborn: Ferdinand Schöningh, 2007).
2 Matthew Anderson, *The Rise of Modern Diplomacy, 1450–1919* (London: Longman, 1993).
3 See, for example, Jan Hennings, *Russia and Courtly Europe: Ritual and the Culture of Diplomacy, 1648–1725* (Cambridge: Cambridge University Press, 2016); Harriet Rudolph, 'The Ottoman Empire and the Institutionalization of European Diplomacy, 1500–1700,' in *Islam and International Law: Engaging Self-Centrism from a Plurality of Perspectives*, ed. Marie Luisa Frick and Andreas Th. Müller (Leiden and Boston: Nijhoff, 2013), 161–83; Erica Heinsen-Roach, *Consuls and Captives: Dutch-North African Diplomacy in the Early Modern Mediterranean* (Woodbridge and Suffolk, UK: Boydell & Brewer, 2019); Sabina Brevaglieri, 'Japan in Rom: Wissensräume der Keichô-Gesandtschaft zwischen Diplomatie und Mission (1615–1617),' in *Diplomatische Wissenskulturen der Frühen Neuzeit: Erfahrungsräume und Orte der Wissensproduktion*, ed. Guido Braun (Berlin and Boston: De Gruyter, 2018), 235–64.
4 Christine Isom-Verhaaren, *Allies with the Infidel: The Ottoman and French Alliance in the Sixteenth Century* (London: I. B. Tauris, 2011); Maartije van Gelder and Krstić Tijana, 'Introduction: Cross-Confessional Diplomacy and Diplomatic Intermediaries in the Early Modern Mediterranean,' in *Journal of Early Modern History* 19/2–3 (2015), 93–105, https://doi.org/10.1163/15700658-12342452.
5 David Scott Gehring, *Anglo-German Relations and the Protestant Cause: Elizabethan Foreign Policy and Pan-Protestantism* (London: Pickering & Chatto, 2013).
6 John Watkins, 'Toward a New Diplomatic History of Medieval and Early Modern Europe,' in *Journal of Medieval and Early Modern Studies* 38/1 (2008), 1–14, https://doi.org/10.1215/10829636-2007-016; Hillard von Thiessen, 'Abschlusskommentar: Geschichte der Außenbeziehungen/Neue Diplomatiegeschichte,' in *Konstruktionen Europas in der Frühen Neuzeit: Geographische und historische Imaginationen*, ed. Susan Richter et al. (Heidelberg: Heidelberg University Publishing, 2017), 315–23. For a general overview, see Lucien Bély, *Les Relations internationales en Europe XVIIe–XVIIIe siècles* (Paris: Presses Universitaires de France, 2007); Heidrun Kugeler et al., 'Einführung: Internationale Beziehungen in der Frühen Neuzeit. Ansätze und Perspektiven,' in *Internationale Beziehungen in der Frühen Neuzeit: Ansätze und Perspektiven*, ed. Heidrun Kugeler et al. (Münster: Lit Verlag, 2006), 9–35. Examples of studies following the principles of the new diplomatic history are Toby Osborne, *Dynasty and Diplomacy in the Court of Savoy: Political Culture and the Thirty Years' War* (Cambridge: Cambridge University Press, 2002); Hillard von Thiessen, *Diplomatie und Patronage: Die spanisch-römischen Beziehungen 1605–1621 in akteurszentrierter Perspektive* (Epfendorf/Neckar: bibliotheca academica Verlag, 2010).
7 There is a growing literature that examines, at least in part, the importance of religion within diplomatic relations. Besides those already mentioned, see, for example, Daniel H. Nexon, *The Struggle for Power in Early Modern Europe:*

Religious Conflict, Dynastic Empires, and International Change (Princeton: Princeton University Press, 2009); Christoph Kampmann et al. (eds.), *L'art de la paix: Kongresswesen und Friedensstiftung im Zeitalter des Westfälischen Friedens* (Münster: Aschendorff, 2011); Daniel Riches, *Protestant Cosmopolitanism and Diplomatic Culture: Brandenburg-Swedish Relations in the Seventeenth Century* (Leiden: Brill, 2013); Benjamin de Carvalho, 'The Confessional State in International Politics: Tudor England, Religion, and the Eclipse of Dynasticism,' in *Diplomacy & Statecraft* 25/3 (2014), 407–31; Diego Pirillo, 'Venetian Merchants as Diplomatic Agents: Family Networks and Cross-Confessional Diplomacy in Early Modern Europe,' in *Early Modern Diplomacy, Theatre and Soft-Power: The Making of Peace*, ed. Nathalie Rivère de Carles (London: Palgrave, 2016), 183–203.

Bibliography

Literature

Anderson, Matthew. *The Rise of Modern Diplomacy, 1450–1919*. London: Longman, 1993.

Bély, Lucien. *Les Relations internationales en Europe XVIIe–XVIIIe siècles*. Paris: Presses Universitaires de France, 2007.

Brevaglieri, Sabina. 'Japan in Rom: Wissensräume der Keichô-Gesandtschaft zwischen Diplomatie und Mission (1615–1617).' *Diplomatische Wissenskulturen der Frühen Neuzeit: Erfahrungsräume und Orte der Wissensproduktion*, edited by Guido Braun, 235–64. Berlin and Boston: De Gruyter, 2018.

Carvalho, Benjamin de. 'The Confessional State in International Politics: Tudor England, Religion, and the Eclipse of Dynasticism.' *Diplomacy & Statecraft* 25/3 (2014): 407–31.

Gehring, David Scott. *Anglo-German Relations and the Protestant Cause: Elizabethan Foreign Policy and Pan-Protestantism*. London: Pickering & Chatto, 2013.

Heinsen-Roach, Erica. *Consuls and Captives: Dutch-North African Diplomacy in the Early Modern Mediterranean*. Woodbridge and Suffolk, UK: Boydell & Brewer, 2019.

Hennings, Jan. *Russia and Courtly Europe: Ritual and the Culture of Diplomacy, 1648–1725*. Cambridge: Cambridge University Press, 2016.

Isom-Verhaaren, Christine. *Allies with the Infidel: The Ottoman and French Alliance in the Sixteenth Century*. London: I. B. Tauris, 2011.

Kampmann, Christoph et al. (eds.). *L'art de la paix: Kongresswesen und Friedensstiftung im Zeitalter des Westfälischen Friedens*. Münster: Aschendorff, 2011.

Kugeler, Heidrun et al. 'Einführung: Internationale Beziehungen in der Frühen Neuzeit. Ansätze und Perspektiven.' *Internationale Beziehungen in der Frühen Neuzeit: Ansätze und Perspektiven*, edited by Heidrun Kugeler et al., 9–35. Münster: Lit Verlag, 2006.

Nexon, Daniel H. *The Struggle for Power in Early Modern Europe: Religious Conflict, Dynastic Empires, and International Change*. Princeton: Princeton University Press, 2009.

Osborne, Toby. *Dynasty and Diplomacy in the Court of Savoy: Political Culture and the Thirty Years' War*. Cambridge: Cambridge University Press, 2002.

Pirillo, Diego. 'Venetian Merchants as Diplomatic Agents: Family Networks and Cross-Confessional Diplomacy in Early Modern Europe.' *Early Modern Diplomacy, Theatre and Soft-Power: The Making of Peace*, edited by Nathalie Rivère de Carles, 183–203. London: Palgrave, 2016.

Riches, Daniel. *Protestant Cosmopolitanism and Diplomatic Culture: Brandenburg-Swedish Relations in the Seventeenth Century*. Leiden: Brill, 2013.

Rudolph, Harriet. 'The Ottoman Empire and the Institutionalization of European Diplomacy, 1500–1700.' *Islam and International Law: Engaging Self-Centrism from a Plurality of Perspectives*, edited by Marie Luisa Frick and Andreas Th. Müller, 161–83. Leiden and Boston: Nijhoff, 2013.

Schilling, Heinz. *Konfessionalisierung und Staatsinteressen: Internationale Beziehungen 1559–1660*. Paderborn: Ferdinand Schöningh, 2007.

van Gelder, Maartije and Tijana, Krstić. 'Introduction: Cross-Confessional Diplomacy and Diplomatic Intermediaries in the Early Modern Mediterranean.' *Journal of Early Modern History* 19/2–3 (2015): 93–105. https://doi.org/10.1163/15700658-12342452.

Thiessen, Hillard von. *Diplomatie und Patronage: Die spanisch-römischen Beziehungen 1605–1621 in akteurszentrierter Perspektive*. Epfendorf/Neckar: bibliotheca academica Verlag, 2010.

Thiessen, Hillard von. 'Abschlusskommentar: Geschichte der Außenbeziehungen/Neue Diplomatiegeschichte.' *Konstruktionen Europas in der Frühen Neuzeit: Geographische und historische Imaginationen*, edited by Susan Richter et al., 315–23. Heidelberg: Heidelberg University Publishing, 2017.

Watkins, John. 'Toward a New Diplomatic History of Medieval and Early Modern Europe.' *Journal of Medieval and Early Modern Studies* 38/1 (2008): 1–14. https://doi.org/10.1215/10829636-2007-016.

Part I
Papal diplomacy

.

2 The Polish–Lithuanian interregna and papal diplomacy[1]

Dorota Gregorowicz

Papal diplomacy could be defined as an art of negotiation according to the assumptions of both canonical and international law. It shapes relations between states and the Catholic Church in order to enable their peaceful and effective cooperation.[2] The role of papal diplomacy for European politics in the sixteenth century, and in some aspects also in the seventeenth century, confirms Heinz Schilling's statement on the ubiquity of the process of confessionalisation of the Old Continent, the post-medieval remnant of *Res Publica Christiana*.[3] Discussing the Holy See's 'international' position in the early modern era, one cannot forget its dual nature, suspended between its religious and secular dimension. For this reason, papal politics and the diplomatic activity of the Holy See in this period have to be examined from the point of view both of secular interest and the protection of Catholicism.

The leading question of the paper is the problem of the Polish–Lithuanian interregna and subsequent royal elections as faced by the Holy See and its diplomatic service. The time frame of the analysis constitutes the second half of the sixteenth century and the seventeenth century. In the period taken into examination, there were seven vacancies of the Polish–Lithuanian throne: after the death of Sigismund II Augustus (1572–1573), after the escape of Henry de Valois (1574–1576), after the deaths of Stephen Bàthory (1587), Sigismund III Vasa (1632), and Władysław IV Vasa (1648), after the abdication of John II Casimir Vasa (1668–1669), and after the death of Michael Korybut Wiśniowiecki (1673–1674). The interregnum after the death of John III Sobieski (1696–1697) is intentionally excluded from the study as, considering the political position both of Poland–Lithuania and of the Holy See, it related more to the Enlightenment century.

The intensification of papal diplomatic activity in Central and Eastern Europe that had taken place since the mid-sixteenth century was the response of the Holy See towards the progressive spread of the Reformation's ideas in these territories.[4] Not without reason, Cardinal Stanisław Hozjusz described the Polish–Lithuanian Commonwealth in terms of *asylum hereticorum*.[5] During the Council of Trent, in the circles of the Roman Curia, there was a growing interest towards the religious and political situation in this part of Europe. It reached its peak during Gregory XIII's pontificate (1572–1585), as his horizons included not only the war with the Ottoman Empire, but also the success of the Counter-Reformation on the vast territories of the Polish–Lithuanian state.[6] At that time, the Commonwealth occupied a special place in the political vision of the Holy See, due to its geopolitical position and role in the hopes of the evangelisation of North-Eastern Europe, with particular reference to the Baltic area: Muscovy and Sweden. As the interregna constituted particularly delicate moments for both political and socio-religious relations in Poland–Lithuania, the Holy See could not do otherwise than intervene by means of its diplomacy and through possible impacts on the local episcopate, in order to defend its political and confessional interests regarding the area in question. The attitude of the Holy See towards the interregna and royal elections in the Polish–Lithuanian Commonwealth raised quite a lot of historiographical attention, already since the nineteenth century.[7] Nevertheless, the confessional factors of papal politics did not gather much interest from historians.[8]

The primary sources used for the following analysis originate mainly from Archivio Segreto Vaticano, from the *Segreteria di Stato, Polonia* section. Moreover, some important information was drawn from the *Teki Rzymskie* section stored in the Scientific Library of the Polish Academy of Sciences and the Polish Academy of Arts in Cracow. Several documents included into the analysis derive from the collections of Archivio Graziani. As well as manuscripts, some important editions of documents were used.[9] The sources exploited are primarily constituted by the correspondence of the diplomatic service of the Holy See and political diaries.

The first part of the article regards the political and religious context of the creation of the Apostolic Nunciature in Poland, as well as the royal elections' early modern political practice. It also concerns the papal reactions on the Polish–Lithuanian throne's vacancy and the main political and religious interests of the Holy See to be realised on the occasion of the election. The following chapters refer to papal politics' priority regarding the election of a Catholic prince for the Polish–Lithuanian throne, as well as to the question of the Warsaw Confederation[10] and other confessional concessions for religious dissenters during the interregna. Subsequently, the problems of the Eastern Churches, as well as their relationship with Rome on the occasion of elections, are studied. Then the papal attitude towards the Muscovite, Swedish, and other Protestant aspirations to the Polish–Lithuanian throne are analysed.

The royal elections and the Polish–Lithuanian Apostolic Nunciature

In order to gain control over the dynamic progresses of the Reformation in such a strategic area as Poland–Lithuania, the pope decided to establish a permanent Apostolic Nunciature at the Jagiellonian court. However, the Bishop of Verona, Luigi Lippomano, the newly appointed nuncio in

Poland, was unable to come in time for the sejm (the parliamentary assembly of the Polish–Lithuanian nobility) of 1555 and to oppose himself to the new constitutions regarding the confessional freedom of nobles. Once arrived in the place of his mission, Lippomano commented that the religious situation in Poland 'could not be worse than it is.'[11] In fact, the Polish–Lithuanian Commonwealth was a state in which the reformative ideas obtained considerable success. It became a refuge for Protestants from all over Europe. Besides, numerous Orthodox Christians, Jews, and Tatars had inhabited its territories for centuries. This complex confessional situation reflected the political one. The so-called 'noble democracy' was based on the ideas of equality and tolerance within the noble social stratum.

The free election of the monarch was one of the particularly distinctive elements of the Polish–Lithuanian libertine political system. Such political practice first appeared after the extinction of the Piast dynasty with the Angevin succession's failure (1370–1386) and with the elevation of Władysław II Jagiełło to the throne (1386). A dubious legitimacy of the new Lithuanian dynasty imposed the succession mechanism based on the free noble volition (represented in the Late Middle Ages only by the members of the Royal Council, then, with the beginning of the early modern period, by the whole noble *universum*), not on the right of inheritance. Such practice became further stabilised and juridically circumscribed with the death of the last Jagiellonian, Sigismund II Augustus, and with the election of Henry de Valois in 1573.

After the king's death, the Archbishop of Gniezno, Jakub Uchański, Primate of the Kingdom, invoked the so-called Convocation Sejm. During this assembly, the nobility had to decide the way, date, and place of the future election.[12] The election sejms were then chaired by the primate. Noblemen participated in it *viritim*, meaning all together. In order to elect a new sovereign, the method of acclamation was practised, even if a unanimous approval of the nobility was officially required. The newly elected monarch was informed about being chosen, after which the primate handed over the election decree to the king or his ambassadors. It took place during the final ceremony in Warsaw's Collegiate Church of St John. At that point, the oath of *pacta conventa* used to follow.[13] Before the coronation, the king was obliged to warrant all the traditional laws of the Kingdom. They were gathered in a composite document, called *Articuli Henriciani*, which concerned all the ancient liberties of the nobility, the traditional prerogatives of the sejm, the specific rights of the Grand Duchy of Lithuania, and the rule of *non praestanda oboedientia* towards the king in case of his not considering the noble privileges. It also contained the principles of religious tolerance, included in the Warsaw Confederation from 1573.[14]

Each time, the Roman Curia, after receiving the news of the beginning of an interregnum in the Polish–Lithuanian Commonwealth, verified immediately how the throne being vacant could influence both political and religious interests of the Holy See in Central and Eastern Europe. A special consistory on this issue used to follow. The popes also carried out individual consultations with cardinals and Curial experts, in order to determine the tactics towards the new election of the Polish–Lithuanian sovereign.

The benefits that the Holy See tried to pursue in the Polish–Lithuanian state during the interregna and the subsequent elections were both political and confessional. The main political interests can be identified with the papal hopes that the new sovereign would be willing to take part in the more (sixteenth-century) or less (seventeenth-century) imaginary offensive of Christian Europe against the Ottoman Empire, thought and organised under the papal leadership. However, in a territory particularly complex from a confessional point of view, in which the Reformation had achieved a remarkable success, the main concern should be attributed to religious considerations; regarding religion, it was possible to lose or gain the most during the interregna. The absence of sovereign power, which in normal conditions guaranteed the Catholicity of the state (as it was the Polish–Lithuanian monarch who applied the religious policy line in the Commonwealth), meant an increased risk for the local Catholic Church.[15] The papacy wanted to keep the Commonwealth in the Catholic bastion of the European monarchies, generating pressure for the election of a Catholic monarch, loyal to the Holy See and possibly uncompromising towards other confessions.

The priority of Catholicism

For the Holy See, the main qualities of the candidate for the Polish–Lithuanian throne were his Catholicity (or the prospective possibilities of conversion), position on ecclesiastical matters, religious intransigence, political independence, military experience, relations with the Ottoman court, and readiness to adhere to the Holy League. His confession, of course, always constituted an absolute priority.

In particular, the culminating moments of interregna, reflecting the papal desire of choosing a Catholic monarch, were the public audiences of papal diplomats during the election sejms. In 1573, Cardinal Legate Giovanni Francesco Commendone emphasised the need to not only choose a Catholic king, but also to avoid serious danger to the Polish–Lithuanian Catholic Church as embodied in the Warsaw Confederation.[16] He underlined the role played by the Commonwealth for the European Christendom. According to the Legate, a peaceful coexistence of different confessions within the same State was unthinkable. Instead, Commendone warned that a false religious peace could cause the eruption of new internal conflicts.[17] In 1587, the nuncio, Annibale Di Capua, appealed for the preservation of the inner peace of the Kingdom and for the harmonious election of a Catholic monarch. Officially, the nuncio did not support any candidate in particular, but suggested that Catholicism should be mother's milk to the new sovereign.[18] It was the clear stand of Di Capua: sympathising with the Habsburgs against the Swedish candidature, questioning the religiosity of Prince Sigismund Vasa, whose mother, Catherine Jagiellon, was Catholic, while his father, John III Vasa, originated from the Lutheran dynasty of Vasas. During the interregnum of 1632, the nuncio, Honorato Visconti, tried to convince the nobles of the need for defending the Catholic faith, praising the religious zeal of Władysław Vasa in a public audience. It was clearly rhetoric, as it was known that the religious life of Władysław had previously raised Visconti's doubts.[19] Nuncio Giovanni de Torres, who had his public audience during the election sejm of 1648, called again for the preservation of inner peace and for the election of a Catholic prince, suggesting the pretenders from the Polish line of the Vasa dynasty.[20] During the election of 1669, papal representative Galeazzo Marescotti strongly recommended the election of a Catholic monarch, placing himself in opposition to Muscovite aspirations.[21] Furthermore, Francesco Buonvisi, in his public audience in 1674, persuaded the nobility to elect a Catholic monarch, offering in return papal subsidies for the war with the Ottoman Empire.[22]

The papacy tried several times to influence Polish–Lithuanian elites, in order to obtain the introduction of a rule obligating the nobility to choose a Catholic monarch during future elections. It took place during the sejms of 1588 and 1589, when the Roman Curia exerted pressure in this matter on the primate, Stanisław Karnkowski. Also, on that occasion, Cardinal Secretary of State, Alessandro Peretti de Montalto, threatened the signatories of the Warsaw Confederation with excommunication and loss of ecclesiastical benefits.[23] Nonetheless, at that moment, papal diplomatic efforts did not succeed. Years later, according to papal claims, as recorded in the diploma of the abdication of John II Casimir Vasa (1668), the king should have promised that the new monarch would be Catholic.[24] However, such a royal declaration could not become law in the noble republic. Despite this, during the election sejm of 1669, the nuncio, Galeazzo Marescotti, submitted a formal draft of a new constitution, which would require every new king and queen of the Commonwealth to be Catholic. By then, it eventually became law.[25] Marescotti also urged the Marshal of the Kingdom, Jan Sobieski, to take care that Catholic interests guided the decisions during the forthcoming election, recalling the necessity to choose a Catholic monarch, 'as the holy and inviolable Laws of the Kingdom state, and as the Polish nobility always supported with their own blood.'[26]

In 1673, with the beginning of the interregnum after the death of Michael Korybut Wiśniowiecki, the problem of the new ruler's confession seemed not to worry the Holy See too much any more. Papal certainty about the election of a Catholic king came by that time from both tradition and the existing law of the Commonwealth. In the seventeenth century, the progressive recatholicisation of the Polish nobility and the conversion of Orthodox elites to Catholicism helped in creating the new noble Catholic mentality.[27] Moreover, in 1673, no noble support was expected for the Muscovite, Prussian, and Orange candidates, due to the lack of any prospect for their conversion, by then a necessary condition of election.[28] Nuncio Francesco Buonvisi could observe the electoral battle with calm, as his instructions in this matter required him only to assure the election of a Catholic monarch – not difficult in the Commonwealth, which at that time was barely tolerant towards religious dissenters.

The Warsaw Confederation and other confessional concessions for dissenters

The problem of concessions for religious dissenters remained important during the interregna of the sixteenth and seventeenth centuries. During the sixteenth century, the most significant issue became the Warsaw Confederation and its inclusion into the royal oath of each newly elected monarch. In fact, the resolution on religious tolerance became part of a special document stipulated in order to maintain the internal security of the Polish–Lithuanian Commonwealth during interregna and elections.

During the first interregnum, Papal Legate Giovanni Francesco Commendone tried to stay away from political intrigues, in consideration of the neutral *imagine* of *padre comune*. He instead concentrated his activity on the religious aspects of the imminent election, primarily on the question of the Warsaw Confederation and its inclusion into the royal oath. On the eve of the election, the Legate accentuated the fact that the main tasks of his Polish–Lithuanian mission were the opposition to the Warsaw Confederation's religious resolutions and the election of a Catholic monarch, and not affecting the political choice of the nobility.[29] Commendone explained that from a jurisdiction point of view, the Confederation could not become law, as it was refused by the entire episcopate (except by the Bishop of Cracow, Franciszek Krasiński).[30] The Legate underlined that the agreement was supposed to be a temporary solution, even though he was still worried that the act was supported by most of the Catholic nobility, and that without such a guarantee of religious tolerance Protestants would never agree on the election of a Catholic monarch, conscious of the former French events of the St Bartholomew's Day massacre.[31]

In the same way as his predecessors during the first interregnum, Nuncio Vincenzo Lauro appealed to remove the Warsaw Confederation from the royal oath in 1576, proposing to replace it only with a brief remark regarding religious toleration: *quod rex pacem intra dissidentes de religione et tuebitur manutenebit*. As Lauro explained, 'this could be always interpreted by the king that motto *pacem* did not mean to spread heresy in the kingdom, but not to cause a civil war from religious diversity.'[32]

During the Convocation Sejm of 1587, a special commission was appointed, in order to discuss religious matters, primarily the Warsaw Confederation. The debate lasted from 3rd to 9th March, 1587, with the positive effect of including the Confederation into the official conclusions of the assembly. It is interesting to note that Nuncio Girolamo Bovio showed himself ready to accept the commission's resolutions temporarily, in order to protect the internal security of the Commonwealth during the interregnum period. He feared, however, that the Confederation would not only extend confessional freedom, but also undermine ecclesiastical jurisdiction in Poland–Lithuania.[33] After the inauguration of the election sejm of 1587, the new nuncio, Annibale Di Capua, organised a meeting of the Polish–Lithuanian episcopate, during which he appealed for the election of a Catholic sovereign and for universal involvement against the Warsaw Confederation. Accordingly, Pope Sixtus V also issued a breve dated 18th April, 1587.[34]

During the seventeenth century, the problem of concessions for the confessional minorities remained important, even if the inclusion of the Warsaw Confederation into the royal oath became common practice. In fact, in 1632, Władysław Vasa included in his electoral promises the resolutions regarding the religious peace. At that time, it did not cause many protestations. Nevertheless, the primate Jan Wężyk habitually opposed it, but it seemed to be rather a symbolic act.[35] Wężyk repeated his remonstration during the coronation of Władysław.[36] As Nuncio Honorato Visconti reported to the Roman Curia, Władysław had no other choice and 'he could not refuse to swear the same formula as his three Predecessors, Henry, Stephen, and Sigismund the Third, regarding the maintenance of peace between religious dissidents.'[37] However, further protests against the Warsaw Confederation occurred during the seventeenth century, for example in 1674, when Nuncio Francesco Buonvisi was obliged to oppose it by his Roman instructions.[38]

Even if, in the seventeenth century, the papal diplomats had to tolerate the traditional inclusion of the Warsaw Confederation into the royal oath, they made every effort not to permit any other confessional concessions on the occasion of an interregnum. During the election sejm of 1648, Nuncio Giovanni De Torres remained in close contact with the Bishop of Cracow, Piotr Gembicki, in order to prevent any new laws being introduced that were advocated by heretics. The papal diplomat could be satisfied, as no compromise was found in the Protestants' favour at that time.[39] Moreover, after the election of John Casimir Vasa, De Torres instructed the newly elected monarch to support only deserving prelates for the vacant ecclesiastical offices, and exclusively Catholics for the senatorial dignities, in order not to strengthen the Protestant party.[40] Furthermore, in 1668, Cardinal Secretary of State Giacomo Rospigliosi argued that the situation before the crowning of Sigismund III Vasa should not be repeated (at that time, Protestant nobles held many offices of state).[41]

The problem of the Eastern Churches

During the interregnum of 1632, after the death of the ultra-Catholic Sigismund III Vasa, confessional issues played a particularly important role. Throughout the Convocation Sejm, which started on 22nd June, 1632, Protestants and Orthodox Christians postulated together the further regulation of the religious situation in the Commonwealth. Nuncio Visconti wrote to Cardinal Secretary of State Barberini:

> The main conflicts consist on the pretensions of heretics and schismat-ics, who would like to secure their interests during this convocation. Otherwise, they threaten and declare that they will never participate in the election. Especially the matter of schismatics proves to become every day more difficult and dangerous.[42]

There was a special Catholic commission convoked, debating on the Protestants' issues, while the Orthodox Church's situation should have been discussed by Władysław Vasa with the representatives of nobility and with senators.[43] The prince was also expected to solve the conflict between the Ruthenian Catholic Church (Ruthenian Uniate Church) and traditional Orthodox hierarchy.[44] The Ruthenian Bishop of Lutsk, Jeremiasz Poczapowski, informed Pope Urban VIII about the danger for the Uniate Church's position in the interregnum period.[45] Władysław's involvement in the issue of the Eastern confessions delighted Nuncio Visconti and also restored his hopes of the prince's religious zeal.[46]

During the election sejm of 1632, the confessional problems further played an important role. The commission to examine the relationship with the Eastern Churches was again assembled.[47] In Visconti's opinion, the confessional problems occupied a more important place in the discussion than the election of a new monarch, as Władysław Vasa was the only serious candidate to the throne.[48] The members of the Ruthenian Catholic Church and their protectors, in concert with Nuncio Visconti, hoped that the Holy See would defend the position of their confession in the Commonwealth. Even before the conclusion of the election sejm, they beseeched the pope not to allow Władysław Vasa to support the Orthodox Christians' revindications. The papal reaction was immediate. On 27th December, 1632, the Congregation de Propaganda Fide published a statement instructing the nuncio to counter the approval of the Sedation Points (Polish *Punkty uspokojenia*, a document that was supposed to lead to the religious consent between Catholic and Orthodox Churches, at the expense of the Ruthenian Catholic Church). In a letter from 1st January, 1633, Urban VIII personally urged the newly elected monarch to take care of the Uniates.[49]

The Muscovite aspirations for the Polish–Lithuanian throne

Mainly for confessional reasons, but also in order to form a common military front against the Ottoman Empire, the Holy See traditionally supported all the unification projects between the Polish–Lithuanian Commonwealth and Muscovy.[50] According to Janusz Smolucha, the papal hopes of establishing an ecclesiastical union with Muscovy originated mainly from the lack of knowledge of the political and cultural reality of Central and Eastern Europe in Rome. The tsars soon learned to use the Holy See's hopes to pursue their own political interests, yet without any real intentions of establishing a religious union with the Church of Rome.[51] This trend gained particular importance during the Polish–Lithuanian interregna of the second half of the sixteenth century. The Holy See carefully monitored every possible Muscovite candidacy to the throne of Cracow, even though they did not support any Russian candidate, and in any case showed distrust of them.

After the death of Sigismund II Augustus in 1572, the Muscovite aspirations in Poland–Lithuania were not treated seriously by the Roman Curia, especially because Ivan IV the Terrible had never officially submitted his candidacy. Nevertheless, since the papal aims for the election were clear (election of a Catholic sovereign who would potentially undertake the fight with the Ottoman Empire), Gregory XIII was willing to accept the tsar or one of his sons on the throne of Cracow, but only if they would convert to Catholicism. In the case of success of the Muscovite candidacy, Cardinal Legate Giovanni Francesco Commendone would have been sent to Moscow for an official visit of congratulations.[52]

In the second interregnum (1574–1575), after the escape of Henry de Valois, the Muscovite candidacy obtained considerable support in the nobility, especially among the Lithuanians, thanks to its linguistic and cultural proximity.[53] The brief French reign made the nobility realise how many problems could be caused by a lack of understanding. As before, the candidacy of a Muscovite prince aroused the interest of the Holy See, but again on the condition of his converting to Catholicism and of the Orthodox hierarchy recognising the primacy of the pope.[54]

In the third interregnum (1587), a candidate from Muscovy was supported by the primate Stanisław Karnkowski, who promoted Eastern politics regarding the extension of Polish–Lithuanian political impact and the expansion of Catholicism in this direction. He even asked the nuncio, Annibale Di Capua, if he was in possession of the faculties necessary in order to empower the tsarevich's conversion, and possibly, in the case of his election, to admit him to the Catholic Church.[55]

In the seventeenth century, Roman officials felt more anxieties and fears than hopes regarding any Muscovite aspirations. Even so, in 1668, the Holy See assessed the possibility of the election of a Muscovite candidate: Tsar Alexey Mikhailovich, and later one of his sons, Fyodor or Alexey, were considered. Nuncio Galeazzo Marescotti was rather distrustful towards any one of them. Cardinal Secretary of State Rospigliosi shared the nuncio's doubts about the sincerity of Muscovite intentions regarding conversion; on the other hand, however, the vision of a future union remained encouraging.[56]

Initially, the papal diplomat did not know how to behave towards possible Muscovite aspirations and asked for further instructions on the matter.[57] Cardinal Rospigliosi ordered Marescotti to remain vigilant towards any news regarding Eastern candidates. Despite the uncertainties of the Holy See, the reunion of Catholic and Orthodox Churches still had to be attractive.[58] Rospigliosi wrote:

> If Muscovite would seriously consider a union with the Catholic Church and if together with his sons he would convert to the real faith, we could have a reasonable motif to support the election of one of his sons as King of Poland.[59]

The nuncio asked, in particular, how to act in regard to the Muscovite ambassadors.[60] In his response, the Cardinal Secretary of State instructed Marescotti to limit any contacts with them. The papal diplomat in Poland–Lithuania was allowed to negotiate a possible confessional union, but not a single conversion of the tsarevich or facilities for Catholics living in the Grand Duchy of Moscow.[61]

According to Marescotti's opinion, if the tsarevich really meant to convert, he would have done so in advance of the election. For the nuncio, the fundamental aspect of any conversion was its sincerity. The Muscovite candidate should therefore have cooperated with the Holy See, obtained the blessing of Clement IX, and acted according to papal advice and directives.[62] Such a conversion, which as a result would constitute the union of the Orthodox and Roman Churches, would require years rather than months prior to the election. For this reason, Marescotti insisted that before the election sejm, the bishops should request the official exclusion of the Muscovite candidate. The Bishop of Cracow, Andrzej Trzebicki, took charge of presenting such an appeal during the Convocation Sejm. Moreover, after the nuncio's petitions in the Senate, Marescotti decided that he would wish to have some written assurances, so he formulated a proposal for a special oath to this purpose.[63] The nuncio also desired to send a universal letter concerning this matter, addressed to all *sejmiki*, but he was advised not to interfere so strongly in the internal affairs of the Commonwealth.[64] Nevertheless, he decided to prepare a written pronouncement on this subject: *Rationes militantes contra Moschum.*[65] However, most decided not to sign the declaration, which led to Marescotti being accused of interfering in state affairs.[66] Some of the nobles even called for his expulsion from Poland–Lithuania. Nevertheless, there were also voices in defence of the nuncio, which permitted him to stay in the Commonwealth for the time of the election.[67]

In Rome, it was soon realised that the danger of the tsarevich being elected had been exaggerated by the primate Mikołaj Prażmowski, in order to realise his own political interests connected with the activity of the Francophile party.[68] In March 1669, Italian merchants trading with Moscow were assured that neither the tsar nor the patriarch had any intention to allow the tsarevich's conversion, in order to permit him to become the Polish–Lithuanian monarch.[69] In spite of this, in spring 1669, just before the inauguration of the election sejm, the nuncio was still being urged not to allow the election of the Muscovite candidate. In Rome, they even feared a military intervention on his behalf.[70] Finally, by May 1669, the Holy See was no longer afraid of the tsarevich's election, because of the lack of any political steps made by the tsar.[71] Nevertheless, Marescotti still took the opportunity to protest the Muscovite candidacy during the election sejm. The tsar, however, did not actually submit his name as a candidate for the Polish–Lithuanian crown.[72]

In 1673, despite new voices regarding a Muscovite candidacy having emerged, Nuncio Francesco Buonvisi did not consider it to be a real danger any more.[73] The possibility of a Muscovite candidate was always treated with respect both by the Holy See and its diplomats. Even though anxious and distrustful towards the election of the tsar or a tsarevich, the papacy still dreamed of the conversion of Muscovy and a common offensive against the Tatars and the Ottoman Empire.[74] The hopes for the Catholicisation of Eastern Europe by electing the tsarevich to the Polish–Lithuanian throne were very fervent during the sixteenth century, but throughout the following century they slowly evolved into a fear towards the expansion of Orthodox Christianity.

The Swedish candidacies to the Polish–Lithuanian throne

As in the case of Muscovite aspirations, the Holy See wanted to use the rivalry for the Polish–Lithuanian throne for a conversion of the Kingdom of Sweden. In the 1580s, a Jesuit, Antonio Possevino, worked intensively for this purpose. In Rome, the Scandinavian monarchy joined with the Polish–Lithuanian Commonwealth in a personal union – a Baltic Empire was imagined, to provide a solid political and confessional basis against Protestant Denmark and England.[75]

The Swedish candidacy had been noted by the Holy See during the first interregnum (1572–1573), when the envoys of John III Vasa, Paulo Ferrato, and Pontus de la Gardie went to Rome in order to establish good relations between the Swedish court and the papacy. Antonio Maria Graziani reported that the Polish–Lithuanian nobility would gladly welcome the Swedish Prince Sigismund Vasa (at that time only 6 years old) on the Cracovian throne, as a descendent, in the female line, from the Jagellonians. The young age of the prince would have facilitated his education according to Polish customs and would allow for the manipulation of his future government. However, throughout the interregnum following the death of Sigismund II Augustus, the Swedish aspirations to the Polish–Lithuanian throne did not obtain any great support from the Holy See. The papal diplomats, resident in Poland, Cardinal Legate Giovanni Francesco Commendone and apostolic nuncio Vincenzo Dal Portico, treated the Vasa candidacy with great distrust, avoiding direct contact with the Protestant ambassadors of the Swedish monarch.[76]

The Vasas' aspirations to the Polish–Lithuanian crown were reborn after Henry de Valois' escape in 1574. At that time, John III Vasa organised a significant diplomatic action focused on gaining the support of the Catholic Church. Preparing himself for the eventuality of a new election in the Commonwealth, the Swedish monarch decided once more to send his envoy, Peter Rosinus, to Rome looking for Gregory XIII's support. Similar diplomatic action, conducted by Andreas Lorichs, was taken towards the apostolic nuncios, Vincenzo Lauro in Poland–Lithuania and Giovanni Dolfin at the imperial court. The main task of Lorichs was to ensure the papal diplomats about the future conversion of the Swedish king. The diplomatic activity was accompanied and supported by the correspondence of Catherine Jagiellon, the Catholic Queen of Sweden. However, the results of this diplomacy did not come up to expectations: on the one hand, Gregory XIII willingly received the efforts of the Swedish royal couple; on the other, he avoided granting them his real support in Poland–Lithuania. The prevailing opinion in Rome was, in fact, a disbelief in any possible conversion by John III Vasa and towards the sincerity of his intentions.[77]

During the third interregnum in 1587, despite the attractiveness of the Swedish candidacy, deriving from papal hope for the conversion of Scandinavia, it was once again destined to fail, as it invoked too much distrust of the Holy See.[78] Although the candidate, Prince Sigismund Vasa, was a proven Catholic, the excessive tolerance of a sovereign who had grown up in a Protestant environment was feared.[79] Furthermore, there was no certainty that the young Vasa would accept the Polish–Lithuanian crown, and there was also the question of his father, John III's, position. For these reasons, the Holy See preferred to support the Habsburg candidate. Nevertheless, after the coronation of Sigismund Vasa on 27th December, 1587, the papacy showed satisfied.

In the seventeenth century, the Swedish aspirations to the Polish–Lithuanian throne vanished, and with them papal interest. With the loss of the Swedish crown by Sigismund III Vasa in 1599, there were no more hopes for the reconversion of Scandinavia. Only in 1632, the information about the Swedish aspirations in Poland–Lithuania were passed on to Rome by the nuncio at the imperial court, Ciriaco Rocci. At that time, the papacy feared the possibility of a candidacy by Gustav II Adolf, who enjoyed military triumphs in the Thirty Years' War, even if the probabilities of his success in the election were very small.[80]

Protestant aspirations

Over the entirety of the sixteenth and seventeenth centuries, the Holy See was strongly ambivalent towards any Protestant candidacies for the Polish–Lithuanian throne, even if they were accompanied by promises of conversion to Catholicism. More importantly in terms of the papacy, the diplomats' activities focused especially against any Prussian candidate.[81] In 1648, during the interregnum after the death of Władysław IV Vasa, Frederick William, Elector of Brandenburg, appeared as a protector of Polish–Lithuanian Protestants, but his aspirations to the throne were not taken seriously, neither among the nobility nor in Rome.[82] After the abdication of John Casimir Vasa in 1669, the nuncio, Galeazzo Marescotti, requested instructions regarding any possible Brandenburg aspirations to the throne of Cracow, based on the promise of conversion of one of the elector's sons.[83] In response, Cardinal Secretary of State Rospigliosi ordered the nuncio to strongly oppose any Prussian candidacies. In case of the election of one of the Hohenzollerns, Marescotti should act in order to obtain from the newly elected monarch a promise to not give any state offices or *beneficia* to non-Catholics.[84] The nuncio should also be attentive to possible Danish aspirations to the Polish–Lithuanian throne.[85] There were also some rumours about the candidacy of William of Orange in 1669, accompanied again by the promises of his conversion.[86] Marescotti was supposed to protest decisively against all Protestant candidates, as the Holy See was no longer interested in any possible conversion in order to achieve political advantages.[87]

In 1673, the danger of Ottoman aggression, together with a difficult economic situation in the Commonwealth, increased the chances for any candidate able to offer financial and military support for Poland–Lithuania. For this reason, the son of the Elector of Brandenburg, Charles Emil Hohenzollern, became an attractive candidate for the crown.[88] He could certainly count on the Polish–Lithuanian Protestants' support. Moreover, on 9th December, 1673, Charles Emil obtained support from two important Catholics: the Bishop of Chelm, Andrzej Olszowski, and the Bishop of Cracow, Andrzej Trzebicki, beforehand both opponents of a Prussian candidacy.[89] In exchange, the bishops demanded subsidies for the war with the Ottoman Empire, a military alliance with Prussia, and the return of the cities of Drahim, Bytów, and Lębork to the Commonwealth, as well as the Prussian king renouncing any claims to Elbląg.[90] Nevertheless, Polish church officials did not require the prince's conversion; Charles Emil was only supposed to participate passively in important public religious celebrations.[91] However, the postulate of conversion quickly reappeared, in accordance with the Catholic nobility's expectations.[92] In fact, Charles Emil's conversion was first promised in 1674. Nuncio Buonvisi was subsequently supposed to observe the Brandenburg aspirations and the sincerity of such promises made by the Prussian ambassadors.[93] In the meantime, the papal diplomat ran an anti-Prussian campaign among the Polish–Lithuanian episcopate.[94] In his opinion, the Hohenzollerns clearly temporised the issue of conversion, which proved the insincerity of their promises.[95]

Similarly, in 1674, there were also rumours of the conversion of the King of Denmark, Christian V, which apparently had already taken place, in order to obtain the right to compete for the Polish–Lithuanian crown.[96] On the one hand, this aroused disbelief in Rome, but on the other hand there was the hope for further conversions within the Danish dynasty.[97]

Conclusion

Confessional factors were crucial for the policy of the Holy See towards the elections of the Polish–Lithuanian kings. It may be moot, but they probably overtook the political aspects, especially during the Counter-Reformation period. From the papal point of view, a new monarch in Poland–Lithuania should have been a real Catholic warrior, ready to undertake a struggle with the Protestant and Orthodox neighbours of the Commonwealth, as well as with the Ottomans. The priority was the election of a Catholic prince and to preserve the Polish–Lithuanian state under the Holy See's influence, maintaining it as a bastion of Catholicism in Central and Eastern Europe.

Throughout the sixteenth century, the missionary activity of the Holy See and the desire to convert the states of Northern and Eastern Europe caused great papal interest in the non-Catholic candidates for the Polish–Lithuanian crown. The problems of conversion of Protestant and Orthodox candidates resonate over the whole period analysed in this chapter. The apostolic nuncios were generally sceptical towards any projects for conversion to Catholicism, calculated for meeting the requirements necessary to compete for the Polish–Lithuanian throne.[98] On one hand, the Holy See denied the sense of conversion for political purposes, but on the other hand considered it as a way of extending its influence. Although only in 1697, with the election of Augustus II the Strong, can we see a change of confession entirely intended for the acquisition of the Polish–Lithuanian crown.

The other aspects of papal confessional policy and Rome's diplomatic activities during the interregna and elections in the Polish–Lithuanian Commonwealth were the fight against the Reformation, the control of Counter-Reformation progresses, and the battle against the local tendencies to support religious tolerance, which reached their apogee in the Warsaw Confederation of 1573. These elements of papal diplomacy were particularly important throughout the sixteenth century, while in the seventeenth century they were gradually marginalised. During the reign of Sigismund III Vasa, the Counter-Reformation enjoyed its final triumph in Poland–Lithuania. The position of Catholicism was stabilised, while the idea of religious expansion slightly lost its importance. Yet in the seventeenth-century interregna, new confessional problems emerged, regarding, in particular, the coexistence of the Eastern Churches and the Orthodox and Ruthenian Catholics.

Notes

1 The paper was created as a result of research carried out under the Sonatina 2 project entitled *The Holy See and the Crisis of Sovereignty of John Casimir Vasa and Michael Korybut Wiśniowiecki's Election (1660–1669)* [Polish: *Stolica Apostolska wobec kryzysu władzy królewskiej Jana Kazimierza Wazy oraz elekcji Michała Korybuta Wiśniowieckiego (1660–1669)*], project no. 2018/28/ C/HS3/00176, financed by the National Science Centre, Poland (Narodowe Centrum Nauki).

2 Igino Cardinale, *Le Saint-Siège et la diplomatie: aperçu historique, juridique et pratique de la diplomatie pontificale* (Paris: Desclée, 1962), 13.

3 Heinz Schilling, *Konfesjonalizacja: Kościół i państwo w Europie doby przednowoczesnej* (Poznań: Wydawnictwo Poznańskie, 2010), 81, 137, 457.

4 Ludwig von Pastor, *Storia dei papi dalla fine del Medio Evo compilata con sussidio dell'Archivio segreto pontificio e di molti altri Archivi. Vol. 9: Storia dei papi nel periodo della Riforma e restaurazione cattolica. Gregorio XIII (1572–1585)* (Roma: Desclée, 1925), 48; Mark F. Feldkamp, *La diplomazia pontificia: Da Silvestro I a Giovanni Paolo II: un profilo* (Milano: Jaca Book, 1998), 73; Silvano Giordano, 'Uomini e apparati della politica internazionale del papato,' in *Papato e politica internazionale nella prima età moderna*, ed. Maria A. Visceglia (Roma: Viella, 2013), 132.

5 Jan W. Woś, *Fonti per la storia della nunziatura polacca di Annibale di Capua (1586–1591)* (Trento: Università degli Studi di Trento, 1992), 15; Wojciech Tygielski, *Włosi w Polsce XVI–XVII wieku: Utracona szansa na modernizację* (Warszawa: Więzi, 2005), 145–47.

6 Mario Caravale and Alberto Caracciolo, *Lo Stato Pontificio da Martino V a Pio IX* (Torino: UTET, 1978), 336.

7 Cf. Wincenty Zakrzewski, *Po ucieczce Henryka: dzieje bezkrólewia 1574–1575* (Kraków: Akademia Umiejętności, 1878); Henry Biaudet, *Les nonciatures apostoliques permanentes jusqu'en 1648* (Helsinki: Suomalainen Tiedeakatemia, 1910); id., *Sixte-Quint et la candidature du Sigismond de Suède au trône de Pologne en 1587: d'après des documents inédits des archives secrètes du Saint-Siège* (Helsinki: Suomalainen Tiedeakatemia, 1910); Czesław Nanke, *Z dziejów polityki Kuryi rzymskiej wobec Polski (1587–1589)* (Lwów: Towarzystwo Naukowe, 1921); Włodzimierz Kaczorowski, 'Stanowisko Stolicy Apostolskiej wobec elekcji królewicza Władysława,' *Odrodzenie i Reformacja w Polsce* 39 (1984); Wojciech Tygielski, *Z Rzymu do Rzeczypospolitej: Studia z dziejów nuncjatury apostolskiej w Polsce, XVI i XVII w.* (Warszawa: Wydawnictwa Fundacji 'Historia pro Futuro,' 1992); Almut Bues, 'Polityka papieska wobec pierwszego bezkrólewia w Polsce,' *Odrodzenie i Reformacja w Polsce* 41 (1997); id., 'Die päpstliche Politik gegenüber Polen-Litauen zur Zeit der ersten Interregna,' in *Kurie und Politik: Stand und Perspektiven der Nuntiaturberichtsforschung*, ed. Alexander Koller (Tübingen: Niemeyer, 1998); Jan W. Woś, *Santa Sede e Corona Polacca nella corrispondenza di Annibale di Capua (1586–1591)* (Trento: Università degli Studi di Trento, 2004); Ewa Dubas-Urwanowicz, 'Między troską o losy Kościoła w Rzeczypospolitej a sympatią do Habsburgów. Hannibal z Kapui w Rzeczypospolitej w latach 1588–1591,' in *Od Kijowa do Rzymu: Z dziejów stosunków Rzeczypospolitej ze Stolicą Apostolską i Ukrainą*,

ed. Mariusz R. Drozdowski, Wojciech Walczak, and Katarzyna Wiszowata-Walczak (Białystok: Instytut Badań nad Dziedzictwem Kulturowym Europy, 2012); id., 'Działalność polityczna Hannibala z Kapui w bezkrólewiu po śmierci Stefana Batorego,' in *Nuncjatura Apostolska w Rzeczypospolitej*, ed. Teresa Chynczewska-Hennel and Wiszowata-Walczak (Białystok: IHiNP UWB, 2012); Ryszard Skowron, 'Nuncjusz i ambasador: Korespondencja Annibala z Capui z San Clemente (1586–1591),' in *Od Kijowa do Rzymu*, ed. Mariusz R. Drozdowski, Wojciech Walczak, and Katarzyna Wiszowata-Walczak (Białystok: Instytut Badań nad Dziedzictwem Kulturowym Europy, 2012); Henryk Litwin, *Chwała Północy: Rzeczpospolita w europejskiej polityce Stolicy Apostolskiej w pierwszej połowie XVII wieku. (1599–1648)* (Lublin: Katolicki Uniwersytet Lubelski, 2013); Paweł Duda, 'Nuncjatura apostolska w Warszawie i w Wiedniu wobec elekcji Władysława IV – przyczynek do badań nad czwartym interregnum,' in *Wokół wolnych elekcji: O znaczeniu idei wyboru – między prawami a obowiązkami w państwie polsko-litewskim XVI–XVIII wieku*, ed. Mariusz Markiewicz, Dariusz Rolnik, and Filip Wolański (Katowice: Wydawnictwo Uniwersytetu Śląskiego, 2016); Dorota Gregorowicz, 'W cieniu legata Commendonego: Vincenzo Dal Portico jako dyplomata papieski wobec pierwszej elekcji,' in *Dyplomacja papieska wobec Rzeczypospolitej*, ed. Walczak and Wiszowata-Walczak (Białystok: Instytut Badań nad Dziedzictwem Kulturowym Europy, 2016); id., 'Dylematy papieskiej dyplomacji: Stanowisko polityczne Stolicy Apostolskiej a działalność nuncjusza Annibale Di Capua wobec elekcji 1587 roku,' in *Wokół wolnych elekcji*; id., 'The Role of Papal Diplomats in the Interregnum's Parliamentary Practice of the Polish-Lithuanian Commonwealth (16th–17th Centuries),' *Dimensioni e problemi della ricerca storica* 29/1 (2016).

8 Cf. Charles Keenan, 'Polish Religious Toleration and Its Opponents: The Catholic Church and the Warsaw Confederation' in *Polish Culture in the Renaissance: Studies in the Arts and Political Thought*, ed. Daniele Facca and Valentina Lepri (Firenze: Firenze University Press, 2013), 37–51.

9 Cf. the edited sources in this chapter's bibliography.

10 'Confederatio Generalis Varsoviensis,' in *Volumina Constitutionum*, vol. 2, 1, ed. Stanisław Grodziski, Irena Dwornicka, and Wacław Uruszczak (Warszawa: Wydawnictwo Sejmowe, 2005), 306–7. The Warsaw Confederation was a document issued on 28 January 1573 during the Convocation Sejm. It was supposed to guarantee the inner peace of the Commonwealth throughout the interregnum and election. Within it, a special addendum guaranteed religious tolerance for the nobility (*pax inter dissidentes in religione*), juridically affirming the de facto existing religious peace. Cf. Kazimierz Lepszy, 'Walka sejmowa o konfederację warszawską w roku 1587,' *Odrodzenie i Reformacja w Polsce* 4 (1959), 113–37; Stanisław Płaza, 'Nowe spojrzenie na konfederację warszawską z 1573 roku,' *Czasopismo prawno-historyczne* 21/2 (1969), 193–200; Antoine Jobert, *De Luther à Mohila: la Pologne dans la crise de la chrétienté: 1517–1648* (Paris: Institut d'études slaves, 1974), 169–70; Gottfried Schramm, 'Ein Meilenstein der Glaubensfreiheit: Der Stand der Forschung über Ursprung und Schicksal der Warschauer Konföderation von 1573,' *Zeitschrift für Ostforschung* 24 (1975), 711–36; Stanisław Grzybowski, 'The Warsaw Confederation of 1573 and Other Acts of Religious Tolerance in Europe,' *Acta Poloniae Historica* 40 (1979), 75–96; Janusz Tazbir, *Konfederacja warszawska 1573 roku, wielka karta polskiej tolerancji* (Warszawa: PAX, 1980); id., *Tradycje tolerancji religijnej w Polsce* (Warszawa: Książka i Wiedza, 1980), 50–54; id., *Państwo bez stosów i inne szkice* (Kraków: Universitas, 2000), 88–95; Maciej Serwański, 'La Confédération de Varsovie (1573),' in *Conflitti e compromessi nell'Europa di centro fra XVI e XX secolo. Atti del 2 Colloquio Internazionale*

(Viterbo, 26–27 Maggio 2000), ed. Gaetano Platania (Viterbo: Sette città, 2001); Keenan, 'Polish Religious Toleration.'

11 Luigi Lippomano to Carlo Carafa, Warsaw, 23rd January, 1556, in *Acta Nuntiaturae Polonae. Vol. 3. Aloisius Lippomano (1555–1557)*, ed. Henryk D. Wojtyska (Rome: Institutum Historicum Polonicum, 1992), 127.

12 Władysław Konopczyński, 'Konwokacje,' in *Studia historyczne ku czci Stanisława Kutrzeby*, vol. 1 (Kraków: Nakł. Komitetu, 1938), 247.

13 The *pacta conventa* document was an agreement between the king and the Polish–Lithuanian nobility, in which the new monarch used to announce his promises and political programme.

14 Henryk Rutkowski, 'Wolna elekcja – zasady i praktyka wybierania królów polskich,' in *Elekcje królów Polski w Warszawie na Woli 1575–1764: upamiętnienie pola elekcyjnego w 400-lecie stołeczności Warszawy*, ed. Marek Tarczyński (Warszawa: Rytm, 1997), 39–40, 51–54; Jan Dzięgielewski, 'Wolna elekcja viritim – najgłośniejsze z dokonań okresu bezkrólewia po śmierci ostatniego Jagiellona,' in *Rok 1573: Dokonania przodków sprzed 440 lat*, ed. Krzysztof Koehler Dzięgielewski and Dorota Muszytowska (Warszawa: UKSW, 2014), 174.

15 Lepszy, 'Walka sejmowa,' 115. Cf. Tygielski, *Z Rzymu do Rzeczpospolitej*, 130.

16 Tolomeo Gallio to Giovanni Francesco Commendone, Roma, 16th May, 1573, Archivio Segreto Vaticano, Segreteria di Stato [hereafter cited as ASV, Segr. di Stato], Polonia 172, 96. Cf. Antonio M. Graziani, *La vie du Cardinal Commendon* (Lyon: Du Puis, 1702), 246; Bues, 'Polityka papieska wobec pierwszego bezkrólewia w Polsce,' 136.

17 Cf. Reinhold Heidenstein, *Dzieje Polski od śmierci Zygmunta do r. 1594 ksiąg XII*, vol. 1 (Petersburg: B. M. Wolff, 1857), 59–60; Hector De La Ferrier, 'L'élection du duc d'Anjou au trône de Pologne,' *Revue des questiones historiques* 44 (1888), 496; Pierre De Cenival, 'La politique du Saint-Siège et l'élection de Pologne (1572–1573),' *Mélanges d'archéologie et d'histoire* 36 (1916–1917), 168–69; Biaudet, *Le Saint-Siège et la Suede durant la seconde moitié du XVI siècle: études politiques* (Paris: Plon-Nourrit, 1907), 325; Von Pastor, *Storia dei papi*, vol. 9, 674; Keenan, 'Polish Religious Toleration,' 40; id., 'The Limits of Diplomatic Ritual: The Polish Embassy of Giovanni Francesco Commendone (-1572–1573) and Criticism of Papal Legates in Early Modern Europe,' *Royal Studies Journal* 3 (2016), 99; Gregorowicz, 'The Role of Papal Diplomats,' 128–29.

18 'Discorso di Annibale di Capua al Senato polacco lituano, 1587,' in *Fonti per la storia*, 78: 'Ab ineunte infantia atque ab ipsis incunabulis cum materno lacte sacrosancte catholicae religionis doctrinam penitus imbiberit.'

19 Kaczorowski, 'Stanowisko Stolicy Apostolskiej,' 164–65; Władysław Czapliński, *Władysław IV i jego czasy* (Kraków: Universitas, 2008), 94; Zofia Sułowska, 'Działalność nuncjusza Viscontiego w Polsce (1630–1635),' *Roczniki Humanistyczne* 9/2 (1960), 40–41; Kaczorowski, *Sejmy konwokacyjny i elekcyjny w okresie bezkrólewia 1632 r.* (Opole: Instytut Śląski w Opolu, 1986), 290–91.

20 Francis Gordon, *Elekcyja Władysława Ivgo*, ed. Wincenty F. Kuczyński (London: Grono Historyczne Polskie, 1854), 8; De Torres's election speech, 31st October, 1648, in *Vetera monumenta Poloniae et Lithuaniae gentiumque finitimarum historiam illustrantia: maximam partem nondum edita ex tabularis Vaticanis deprompta collecta ac serie chronologica disposita. Vol. 3, A Sixto PP. V usque ad Innocentium PP. XII. 1585–1695*, ed. Augustin Theiner

(Romae: Typis Vaticanis, 1863), 454; Janusz Stanisław Dąbrowski, *Diariusz Sejmu Elekcyjnego 1648 roku* (Kraków: Historia Iagiellonica, 2013), 118–20.

21 Mieczysława Chmielewska, *Sejm elekcyjny Michała Korybuta Wiśniowieckiego 1669 roku* (Warszawa: Wydawnictwo Sejmowe, 2006), 203–4; Adam Przyboś, *Michał Korybut Wiśniowiecki 1640–1673* (Kraków: Wydawnictwo Literackie, 2007), 47.

22 Von Pastor, *Storia dei papi dalla fine del Medio Evo compilata con sussidio dell'Archivio segreto pontificio e di molti altri Archivi. Vol. 14: Storia dei papi nel periodo dell'Assolutismo dall'elezione di Innocenzo X sino alla morte di Innocenzo XII (1644–1700). Parte I: Innocenzo X, Alessandro VII, Clemente IX, Clemente X* (Roma: Desclée, 1963), 650–51.

23 Lepszy, 'Walka sejmowa,' 124–25.

24 Galeazzo Marescotti to Giacomo Rospigliosi, Warsaw, 29th August, 1668, ASV, Segr. di Stato, Polonia 81, 332r; Rospigliosi to Marescotti, Rome, 22nd September, 1668, ASV, Segr. di Stato, Polonia 182, 84r.

25 Rospigliosi to Marescotti, Rome, 6th July, 1669, ASV, Segr. di Stato, Polonia 182, 112.

26 Marescotti to Jan Sobieski, Warsaw, 22nd June, 1668, ASV, Segr. di Stato, Polonia 81, 177r.

27 Ibid., 24.

28 Francesco Buonvisi to Paluzzo Paluzzi-Altieri, Warsaw, 13th December, 1673, in *Francesco Buonvisi, Nunziatura a Varsavia*, vol. 2, ed. Furio Diaz and Nicola Carranza (Roma: Istituto storico italiano per l'età moderna e contemporanea, 1965), 414.

29 Commendone to Gallio, Sulejów, 18th March, 1573, ASV, Segr. di Stato, Polonia 3, 100. Cf. Keenan, 'The Limits of Diplomatic Ritual,' 100.

30 All the Polish–Lithuanian bishops were members of the Senate of the Commonwealth.

31 Commendone to Gallio, Sulejów, 31st January, 1573, ASV, Segr. di Stato, Polonia 3, 63–64.

32 Vincenzo Lauro to Gallio, Warszawa 18 II 1576, in *Vincent Laureo, évêque de Mondovì, nonce apostolique en Pologne, 1574–1578*, ed. Teodor Wierzbowski (Varsovie: J. Berger, 1887), 352.

33 Lepszy, 'Walka sejmowa,' 116–18; Anna Pieńkowska, *Zjazdy i sejmy z okresu bezkrólewia po śmierci Stefana Batorego* (Pułtusk: Akademia Humanistyczna im. Aleksandra Gieysztora, 2010), 115, 189.

34 Alessandro Montalto to Annibale Di Capua, Roma, 11th July, 1587, ASV, Segr. di Stato, Polonia 23, 150.

35 Honorato Visconti to Francesco Barberini, Warsaw, 19th November, 1632, Biblioteka Naukowa Polskiej Akademii Umiejętności i Polskiej Akademii Nauk w Krakowie, Teka Rzymska [hereafter cited as BNPAUiPAN, TR] 64, 49. Cf. Henryk Wisner, *Władysław IV Waza* (Wrocław: Ossolineum, 2009), 61.

36 Wisner, *Władysław IV*, 63–64.

37 Visconti to Barberini, Warsaw, 19th November, 1632, BNPAUiPAN, TR 64, 49.

38 Paluzzi-Altieri to Buonvisi, Rome, 6th October, 1674, in *Francesco Buonvisi*, vol. 2, 211.

39 Giovanni De Torres to Giovanni Giacomo Panzirolo, Warsaw, 14th November, 1648, ASV, Segr. di Stato, Polonia 56, 360; id., BNPAUiPAN, TR 74, 155–57.

40 De Torres to Panzirolo, Warsaw, 28th November, 1648, ASV, Segr. di Stato, Polonia 56, 379; id., BNPAUiPAN, TR 74, 173–75.

41 Rospigliosi to Marescotti, Rome, 18th August, 1668, ASV, Segr. di Stato, Polonia 82, 46r; id., ASV, Segr. di Stato, Nunz. Diverse 151, 162–63.
42 Visconti to Barberini, Warsaw, 30th June, 1632, BNPAUiPAN, TR 64, 8.
43 In the Polish–Lithuanian context, senators were lifetime members of the Upper House of the Commonwealth's sejm. The various senatorial offices in Poland–Lithuania, after the Union of Lublin in 1569, were in total 140, and they were characterised by an established order of seniority.
44 Wisner, *Władysław IV*, 60. The Union of Brest was the 1595–1596 decision of the Ruthenian Catholic Church to break relations with the Orthodox Church, recognising the authority of the pope. Cf. Edward Likowski, *Unia brzeska (1596)* (Warszawa: Gebethner & Wolf, 1907); *Unia brzeska: Geneza, dzieje i konsekwencje w kulturze narodów słowiańskich*, ed. Ryszard Łużny, Franciszek Ziejka, and Andrzej Kępiński (Kraków: Universitas, 1994).
45 Jeremiasz Poczapowski to Urban VIII, Warsaw, 3rd November, 1632, in *Monumenta Ucraine Historica*, vol. 9–10: supplementum (1075–1623), ed. Andrej Septyckyj (Roma: Università Cattolica Ucraina, 1971), 149–59.
46 Kaczorowski, 'Stanowisko Stolicy Apostolskiej,' 161–62.
47 Ibid., 163–64.
48 Visconti to Barberini, Warsaw, 29th October, 1632, BNPAUiPAN, TR 64, 37.
49 Dzięgielewski, *O tolerancję dla zdominowanych: polityka wyznaniowa Rzeczypospolitej w latach panowania Władysława IV* (Warszawa: PWN, 1986), 61.
50 Wojtyska, *Papiestwo – Polska 1548–1563* (Lublin: Katolicki Uniwersytet Lubelski, 1977), 34; Feldkamp, *La diplomazia pontificia*, 49–50; Janusz Smołucha, *Papiestwo a Polska w latach 1484–1526: Kontakty na tle zagrożenia tureckiego* (Kraków: Towarzystwo Naukowe 'Societas Vistulana,' 1999), 207.
51 Smołucha, *Papiestwo a Polska*, 24–25.
52 Antonio Maria Graziani to Gallio, Vienna, 28th July, 1572, in *Uchańsciana, czyli zbiór dokumentów wyjaśniających życie i działalność Jakóba Uchańskiego, arcybiskupa gnieźnieńskiego, legata urodzonego, Królestwa Polskiego prymasa i pierwszego księcia, vol. 4, Poselstwa papieskie w Polsce, 1560–1581. Różne dokumenty z lat 1534–1592*, ed. Wierzbowski (Warszawa: J. Berger, 1892), 25; Commendone to Gallio, Sulejów, 12th September, 1572, ASV, Segr. di Stato, Polonia 2, 127; Gallio to Commendone, Rome [May 1573], ASV, Segr. di Stato, Polonia 172, 92; Gallio to Commendone, Rome [May 1573], ASV, Segr. di Stato, Polonia 172, 97. Cf. Wincenty Zakrzewski, *Stosunki Stolicy Apostolskiej z Iwanem Groźnym, Carem i W. Księciem Moskiewskim* (Kraków: L. Paszkowski, 1872), 72.
53 Henry of Valois (19th September, 1551–2nd August, 1589), son of Henry II of France and of Caterina de' Medici, was elected King of Poland on 11th May, 1573. After few months of government, Henry was reached by the news about the death of his royal brother Charles IX of France. As a consequence, in Poland, talks began about the convocation of a sejm, which would decide whether to authorise the temporary return of the king to his fatherland, in order to ensure the crown of France for himself. Henry had no time to lose and feared the difficulties the nobility could put in front of him regarding the departure. For this reason, he decided to escape secretly. The getaway took place during the night between 18th and 19th June, 1574. The king remained in France, where he reigned from 1574 to 1589, under the name of Henry III. Cf. Maciej Serwański, *Henryk III Walezy w Polsce: Stosunki polsko-francuskie w latach 1566–1576* (Kraków: Wydawnictwo Literackie, 1976), 126–28; Francesca De Caprio, 'Un Re "fugge", viva il Re: Il caso di Enrico di Valois sovrano di Polonia e l'avvento al trono del transilvano Stefan Batory,' in *Da Est ad Ovest da Ovest ad Est, viaggiatori per le strade del mondo*, ed. Platania (Viterbo: Sette città, 2006), 20–33; Jerzy Besala, *Stefan Batory* (Poznań: Zysk, 2010), 81.

54   Cf. Lauro to Henry de Valois, Skierniewice, 6th March, 1575, in *Acta Nuntiaturae Polonae. Vol. 9/2. Vincentius Lauro (1572–1578)*, ed. Mirosław Korolko and Lucjan Olech (Romae: Institutum Historicum Polonicum, 1999), 184; id., 189–93; Giovanni Dolfin to Gallio, Vienna, 11th July, 1574, in *Nuntiaturberichte aus Deutschland. Nebst ergänzenden Aktenstücken. Dritte Abteilung. Vol. 7: Nuntiatur Giovanni Delfinos 1573–1574*, ed. Bues (Tübingen: Niemeyer, 1990), 552; Lauro to Gallio, Warsaw, 10th October, 1575, in *Vincent Laureo*, ed. Wierzbowski, 257; Wierzbowski, *Uchańsciana, czyli zbiór dokumentów wyjaśniających życie i działalność Jakóba Uchańskiego, arcybiskupa gnieźnieńskiego, legata urodzonego, Królestwa Polskiego prymasa i pierwszego księcia, vol. 5, Jakób Uchański, arcybiskup gnieźnieński, (1502–1581): monografia historyczna* (Warszawa: J. Berger, 1892), 572; Boris Floria, 'Rosyjska kandydatura na tron polski u schyłku XVI wieku,' *Odrodzenie i Reformacja w Polsce* 16 (1971), 87–88, 91.
55   Cf. Di Capua to Montalto, Warsaw, 24th April, 1587, Archivio Graziani, ms. 59, fasc. L90–111, nr. 95; Ewa Dubas-Urwanowicz, 'Geneza układu politycznego podczas obrad konwokacji w trzecim interregnum,' *Barok: historia, literatura, sztuka* 18/1 (2011), 204.
56   Rospigliosi to Marescotti, Rome, 4th August, 1668, ASV, Segr. di Stato, Polonia 82, 40–41r.
57   Marescotti to Rospigliosi, Warsaw, 27th June, 1668, ASV, Segr. di Stato, Polonia 82, 286.
58   Cf. Rospigliosi to Marescotti, Rome, 28th July, 1668, ASV, Segr. di Stato, Polonia 82, 34v–35; id. ASV, Segr. di Stato, Nunz. Diverse 151, 154–55; Rospigliosi to Marescotti, Rome, 22nd September, 1668, ASV, Segr. di Stato, Nunz. Diverse 151, 171; id., ASV, Segr. di Stato, Polonia 82, 54–56r.
59   Rospigliosi to Marescotti, Rome, 28th July, 1668, ASV, Segr. di Stato, Polonia 82, 34v–35; id., ASV, Segr. di Stato, Nunz. Diverse 151, 154–55.
60   Marescotti to Rospigliosi, Warsaw, 16th September, 1668, ASV, Segr. di Stato, Polonia 82, 356; id., ASV, Segr. di Stato, Nunz. Diverse 151, 96–97r; BNPA-NiPAU, TR 85, 46–47.
61   Rospigliosi to Marescotti, Rome, 6th October, 1668, ASV, Segr. di Stato, Polonia 82, 61r; id., ASV, Segr. di Stato, Nunz. Diverse 151, 177–78.
62   Marescotti to Rospigliosi, Warsaw, 7th July, 1668, ASV, Segr. di Stato, Polonia 81, 190.
63   Marescotti to Rospigliosi, Warsaw, 12th December, 1668, ASV, Segr. di Stato, Polonia 81, 539. Cf. Marescotti to Rospigliosi, Warsaw, 12th December, 1668, ASV, Segr. di Stato, Polonia 81, 539v.
64   Marescotti to Rospigliosi, Warsaw, 28th November, 1668, ASV, Segr. di Stato, Polonia 81, 512–13.
65   'Ego in fragtus iuro Deo omnipotenti, Beatissime Virgini Deiparae, quod in proxima novi Regis electione non eligam in Regem Poloniae nec Magnum Duce Moschovia, nec alique ex ipsius filijs, nec ullum ex Principus hereticis, et omnes petitores tanquam incapaces, et inhabiles ad regimen sceptri eius et Regni, tam Catholici, quam politice loquendo, nec non proposse meo, ac per meos subditos, ad herontes, consanguineos amicos, et familiares impediam, ne ullus exceptis inducatur in possessione eiusdem sceptri, et curabo, quod coeteri omnes Domini electores in eandem descendant sententiam. Sic me Deus adiuvet, et Sanctissima ipsius Passio. Dati Varsaviae hac die [...]' Cf. Marescotti to Rospigliosi, Warsaw, 5th December, 1668, ASV, Segr. di Stato, Polonia 81, 521r; id., ASV, Segr. di Stato, Polonia 81, 523r.
66   Marescotti to Rospigliosi, Warsaw, 5th December, 1668, ASV, Segr. di Stato, Polonia 81, 523r.

67 Marescotti to Rospigliosi, Warsaw, 12th December, 1668, ASV, Segr. di Stato, Polonia 81, 540r.
68 Rospigliosi to Marescotti, Rome, 29th December, 1668, ASV, Segr. di Stato, Polonia 82, 82v–83r; Rospigliosi to Marescotti, Rome, 12th January, 1669, ASV, Segr. di Stato, Polonia 82, 88; id., ASV, Segr. di Stato, Nunz. Diverse 151, 313.
69 Marescotti to Rospigliosi, Warsaw, 27th March, 1669, ASV, Segr. di Stato, Polonia 82, 608r; id., ASV, Segr. di Stato, Nunz. Diverse 151, 237v–39 (dated 3rd April, 1669).
70 Rospigliosi to Marescotti, Rome, 13th April, 1669, ASV, Segr. di Stato, Polonia 82, 103; id., ASV, Segr. di Stato, Nunz. Diverse 151, 328; Rospigliosi to Marescotti, Rome, 27th April, 1669, ASV, Segr. di Stato, Polonia 82, 105v–6r; id., ASV, Segr. di Stato, Nunz. Diverse 151, 331.
71 Rospigliosi to Marescotti, Rome, 4th May, 1669, ASV, Segr. di Stato, Polonia 82, 106; id., ASV, Segr. di Stato, Nunz. Diverse 151, 331v–32r; Rospigliosi to Marescotti, Rome, 11th May, 1669, ASV, Segr. di Stato, Polonia 82, 106v; id., ASV, Segr. di Stato, Nunz. Diverse 151, 332; Rospigliosi to Marescotti, Rome, 18th May, 1669, ASV, Segr. di Stato, Polonia 82, 107r; id., ASV, Segr. di Stato, Nunz. Diverse 151, 333r.
72 Przyboś, *Michał Korybut Wiśniowiecki*, 36–37.
73 Buonvisi to Paluzzi-Altieri, Warsaw, 17th January, 1674, ASV, Segr. di Stato, Polonia 90, 37v; Buonvisi to Paluzzi-Altieri, Warsaw, 25th April, 1674, ASV, Segr. di Stato, Polonia 90, 208.
74 Cf. Floria, 'Rosyjska kandydatura,' 90; Karol Olejnik, *Stefan Batory* (Warszawa: Rytm, 2013), 58.
75 Tygielski, *Z Rzymu do Rzeczypospolitej*, 31–34.
76 Cf. Graziani to Gallio, Vienna, 28th July, 1572, in *Uchańsciana*, vol. 4, 25; Commendone to Gallio, Warsaw, 3rd May, 1573, ibid., 84–85; Tadeusz Glemma, 'Zapiski nuncjusza polskiego Wincentego Dal Portico z roku 1568,' *Collectanea Theologica* 17 (1936), 282; Ryszard Skowron, 'El espacio del encuentro de los confines de Europa. España y Polonia en el reinado de Felipe II,' in *Felipe II (1527–1598): Europa y la monarquía católica: Congreso Internacional 'Felipe II (1598–1998), Europa dividida, la monarquía católica de Felipe II* (Universidad Autónoma de Madrid, 20–23 abril 1998), vol. 1, 2, ed. José Martìnez Millán (Madrid: Parteluz, 1998), 886; id., 'El Mar Báltico en la estrategia española de guerra en los Países Bajos, 1568–1648,' in *El mar los siglos modernos*, vol. 2, ed. Manuel Reyes García Hurtado, Domingo L. Gonzáles Lopo, and Enrique Martínez Rodríguez (Santiago de Compostela: Dirección Xeral de Turismo, 2009), 346.
77 Cf. Gallio to Lauro, Rome, 6th November, 1574, in *Acta Nuntiaturae Polonae. Vol. 9/2*, ed. Korolko and Olech, 40; Lauro to Gallio, Skierniewice, 7th January, 1575, ibid., 119; Ludwik Bazylow, 'Starania Stefana Batorego o koronę polską,' *Nauka i Sztuka* VII (1948), 78.
78 Von Pastor, *Storia dei papi dalla fine del Medio Evo compilata con sussidio dell'Archivio segreto pontificio e di molti altri Archivi. Vol. 10: Storia dei papi nel periodo della Riforma e restaurazione cattolica: Sisto V, Urbano VII, Gregorio XIV e Innocenzo IX: (1585–1591)* (Roma: Desclée, 1955), 400; Kazimierz Lepszy, *Walka stronnictw w pierwszych latach panowania Zygmunta III* (Kraków: Gebethner & Wolff, 1929), 66, n. 2.
79 Pieńkowska, *Zjazdy i sejmy*, 281.
80 Ciriaco Rocci to Barberini, Vienna, 13th December, 1631, in *Nuntiaturberichte aus Deutschland. Nebst ergänzenden Aktenstücken. Vierte Abteilung. Vol. 5,*

Nuntiatur des Ciriaco Rocci: Außerordentliche Nuntiatur des Girolamo Grimaldi (1631–1633), ed. Rotraud Becker (Tübingen: de Gruyter, 2013), 110.
81 Graziani to Gallio, Vienna, 28th July, 1572, in *Uchańsciana*, vol. 4, 25.
82 Barbara Szymczak, 'Działalność dyplomacji brandenburskiej w okresie bezkrólewia w Rzeczypospolitej w 1648 r.,' *Przegląd Historyczny* 89/1 (1998), 30.
83 Rospigliosi to Marescotti, Rome, 10th October, 1668, ASV, Segr. di Stato, Polonia 82, 308r; id., ASV, Segr. di Stato, Nunz. Diverse 151, 104r; BNPANi-PAU, TR 85, 57.
84 Rospigliosi to Marescotti, Rome, 24th November, 1668, ASV, Segr. di Stato, Polonia 82, 66; id., ASV, Segr. di Stato, Nunz. Diverse 151, 182.
85 Rospigliosi to Marescotti, Rome, 24th November, 1668, ASV, Segr. di Stato, Polonia 82, 69; id., ASV, Segr. di Stato, Nunz. Diverse 151, 185.
86 Marescotti to Rospigliosi, Warsaw, 13th February, 1669, ASV, Segr. di Stato, Polonia 82, 568v.
87 Rospigliosi to Marescotti, Rome, 16th March, 1669, ASV, Segr. di Stato, Polonia 82, 98v–99; id., ASV, Segr. di Stato, Nunz. Diverse 151, 322–23.
88 Andrzej Kamieński, *Polska a Brandenburgia-Prusy w drugiej połowie XVII wieku* (Poznań: Wydawnictwo Poznańskie, 2002), 89.
89 The events of interregna often connected the interests of the nobility of different confessions. In 1669, it was no surprise that the Bishop of Chelm, Andrzej Olszowski, and Calvinist Bogusław Radziwiłł were in the same political party. Cf. Chmielewska, *Sejm elekcyjny*, 172.
90 Lębork and Bytów constituted a Polish fief in the years 1525–1657. After the death of Bogusław XIV, it was formally incorporated into the Pomeranian Voivodeship, but still had a large autonomy. In 1657, according to the treaties of Welawa and Bydgoszcz, this land was transferred to Brandenburg. As for Drahim, the incomes from its eldership were pledged to Elector Frederick Wilhelm during the Swedish Deluge, in return for his military help. Having not received the money, the elector conquered Drahim militarily (1668). According to the Welawa and Bydgoszcz arrangements, Frederick Wilhelm also obtained permission to conquest Elbląg, but the Polish–Lithuanian Commonwealth still had the right to ransom the city for the amount of 200,000 thalers. Cf. Jacek Wijaczka, 'Sukces czy klęska?: traktat welawsko-bydgoski z 1657 roku,' *Zapiski Historyczne: kwartalnik poświecony historii Pomorza* 72/4 (2007), 7–21; Dariusz Makiłła, 'Zniesienie Hołdu pruskiego: uwolnienie Prus Książęcych z podległości lennej wobec Rzeczypospolitej w latach 1657–1658,' *Miscellanea Historico-Archivistica* 23 (2016), 139–51.
91 Kamieński, *Polska a Brandenburgia-Prusy*, 93.
92 Ibid., 99–100; Otto Forst de Battaglia, *Jan III Sobieski król Polski* (Warszawa: Państwowy Instytut Wydawniczy, 1983), 66.
93 Buonvisi to Paluzzi-Altieri, Warsaw, 17th January, 1674, in *Francesco Buonvisi*, vol. 1, 431–32.
94 Von Pastor, *Storia dei papi*, vol. 14, 651; Kamieński, *Polska a Brandenburgia-Prusy*, 100.
95 Buonvisi to Paluzzi-Altieri, Warsaw, 14th February, 1674, in *Francesco Buonvisi*, vol. 1, 444.
96 Ibid.
97 Buonvisi to Paluzzi-Altieri, Warsaw, 14th March, 1674, in *Francesco Buonvisi*, vol. 1, 464–65; Buonvisi to Paluzzi-Altieri, Warsaw, 9th April, 1674, ibid., 502–3.
98 Buonvisi to Paluzzi-Altieri, Warsaw, 10th January, 1674, ASV, Segr. di Stato, Polonia 91, 259v–60r.

Bibliography

Archival sources

Archivio Graziani, Manuscript nr 59.
Archivio Segreto Vaticano Segreteria di Stato, Polonia 2, 3, 56, 81, 90, 91, 172, 182; Segreteria di Stato, Nunziature Diverse 151.
Biblioteka Naukowa PAU i PAN w Krakowie, Teki Rzymskie 24, 64, 74.

Edited sources

Acta Nuntiaturae Polonae. Vol. 3. Aloisius Lippomano (1555–1557). Edited by Henryk D. Wojtyska. Rome: Institutum Historicum Polonicum, 1992.
Acta Nuntiaturae Polonae. Vol. 9/2. Vincentius Lauro (1572–1578). Edited by Mirosław Korolko and Lucjan Olech. Romae: Institutum Historicum Polonicum, 1999.
Dąbrowski, Janusz Stanisław. *Diariusz Sejmu Elekcyjnego 1648 roku.* Kraków: Historia Iagiellonica, 2013.
Francesco Buonvisi, Nunziatura a Varsavia, vol. 1. Edited by Furio Diaz and Nicola Carranza. Roma: Istituto storico italiano per l'età moderna e contemporanea, 1963.
Francesco Buonvisi, Nunziatura a Varsavia, vol. 2. Edited by Furio Diaz and Nicola Carranza. Roma: Istituto storico italiano per l'età moderna e contemporanea, 1965.
Gordon, Francis. *Elekcyja Władysława IVgo.* Edited by Wincenty F. Kuczyński. London: Grono Historyczne Polskie, 1854.
Graziani, Antonio M. *La vie du Cardinal Commendon.* Lyon: Du Puis, 1702.
Heidenstein, Reinhold. *Dzieje Polski od śmierci Zygmunta do r. 1594 ksiąg XII*, vol. 1. Petersburg: B. M. Wolff, 1857.
Monumenta Ucraine Historica, vol. 9–10: supplementum (1075–1623). Edited by Andrej Septyckyj. Roma: Università Cattolica Ucraina, 1971.
Nuntiaturberichte aus Deutschland. Nebst ergänzenden Aktenstücken. Dritte Abteilung. Vol. 7: Nuntiatur Giovanni Delfinos 1573–1574. Edited by Almut Bues. Tübingen: Niemeyer, 1990.
Nuntiaturberichte aus Deutschland. Nebst ergänzenden Aktenstücken. Vierte Abteilung. Vol. 5: Nuntiatur des Ciriaco Rocci. Außerordentliche Nuntiatur des Girolamo Grimaldi (1631–1633). Edited by Rotraud Becker. Tübingen: de Gruyter, 2013.
Vetera monumenta Poloniae et Lithuaniae gentiumque finitimarum historiam illustrantia: maximam partem nondum edita ex tabularis Vaticanis deprompta collecta ac serie chronologica disposita. Vol. 3: A Sixto PP. V usque ad Innocentium PP. XII. 1585–1695. Edited by Augustin Theiner. Romae: Typis Vaticanis, 1863.
Vincent Laureo, évêque de Mondovì, nonce apostolique en Pologne, 1574–1578. Edited by Tedor Wierzbowski. Varsovie: J. Berger, 1887.
Volumina Constitutionum, vol. 2, 1. Edited by Stanisław Grodziski, Irena Dwornicka, and Wacław Uruszczak. Warszawa: Wydawnictwo Sejmowe, 2005.
Wierzbowski, Teodor. *Uchańsciana, czyli zbiór dokumentów wyjaśniających życie i działalność Jakóba Uchańskiego, arcybiskupa gnieźnieńskiego, legata*

urodzonego, Królestwa Polskiego prymasa i pierwszego księcia. Vol. 4: Poselstwa papieskie w Polsce, 1560–1581. Różne dokumenty z lat 1534–1592. Warszawa: J. Berger, 1892.

Woś, Jan W. *Fonti per la storia della nunziatura polacca di Annibale di Capua (1586–1591).* Trento: Università degli Studi di Trento, 1992.

Literature

Bazylow, Ludwik. 'Starania Stefana Batorego o koronę polską.' *Nauka i Sztuka* 7 (1948): 70–120.

Besala, Jerzy. *Stefan Batory.* Poznań: Zysk, 2010.

Biaudet, Henry. *Le Saint-Siège et la Suede durant la seconde moitié du XVI siècle: études politiques.* Paris: Plon-Nourrit, 1907.

Biaudet, Henry. *Les nonciatures apostoliques permanentes jusqu'en 1648.* Helsinki: Suomalainen Tiedeakatemia, 1910.

Biaudet, Henry. *Sixte-Quint et la candidature du Sigismond de Suède au trône de Pologne en 1587: d'après des documents inédits des archives secrètes du Saint-Siège.* Helsinki: Suomalainen Tiedeakatemia, 1910.

Bues, Almut. 'Die päpstliche Politik gegenüber Polen-Litauen zur Zeit der ersten Interregna.' In *Kurie und Politik: Stand und Perspektiven der Nuntiaturberichts-forschung*, edited by Alexander Koller, 116–36. Tübingen: Niemeyer, 1998.

Bues, Almut. 'Polityka papieska wobec pierwszego bezkrólewia w Polsce.' *Odrodzenie i Reformacja w Polsce* 41 (1997): 131–39.

Caravale, Mario, and Alberto Caracciolo. *Lo Stato Pontificio da Martino V a Pio IX.* Torino: UTET, 1978.

Cardinale, Igino. *Le Saint-Siège et la diplomatie: aperçu historique, juridique et pratique de la diplomatie pontificale.* Paris: Desclée, 1962.

Chmielewska, Mieczysława. *Sejm elekcyjny Michała Korybuta Wiśniowieckiego 1669 roku.* Warszawa: Wydawnictwo Sejmowe, 2006.

Czapliński, Władysław. *Władysław IV i jego czasy.* Kraków: Universitas, 2008.

De Battaglia, Otto Forst. *Jan III Sobieski król Polski.* Warszawa: Państwowy Instytut Wydawniczy, 1983.

De Caprio, Francesca. 'Un Re "fugge", viva il Re: Il caso di Enrico di Valois sovrano di Polonia e l'avvento al trono del transilvano Stefan Batory.' In *Da Est ad Ovest da Ovest ad Est: viaggiatori per le strade del mondo*, edited by Gaetano Platania, 11–33. Viterbo: Sette città, 2006.

De Cenival, Pierre. 'La politique du Saint-Siège et l'élection de Pologne (1572–1573).' *Mélanges d'archéologie et d'histoire* 36 (1916–1917): 109–204.

De La Ferrier, Hector. 'L'élection du duc d'Anjou au trône de Pologne.' *Revue des questiones historiques* 44 (1888): 448–506.

Dubas-Urwanowicz, Ewa. 'Geneza układu politycznego podczas obrad konwokacji w trzecim interregnum.' *Barok: historia, literatura, sztuka* 18/1 (2011): 203–21.

Dubas-Urwanowicz, Ewa. 'Działalność polityczna Hannibala z Kapui w bezkrólewiu po śmierci Stefana Batorego.' In *Nuncjatura Apostolska w Rzeczypospolitej*, edited by Teresa Chynczewska-Hennel and Katarzyna Wiszowata-Walczak, 131–44. Białystok: IHiNP UWB, 2012.

Dubas-Urwanowicz, Ewa. 'Między troską o losy Kościoła w Rzeczypospolitej a sympatią do Habsburgów: Hannibal z Kapui w Rzeczypospolitej w latach 1588–1591.' In *Od Kijowa do Rzymu: Z dziejów stosunków Rzeczypospolitej ze*

Stolicą Apostolską i Ukrainą, edited by Mariusz R. Drozdowski, Wojciech Walczak, and Katarzyna Wiszowata-Walczak, 431–51. Białystok: Instytut Badań nad Dziedzictwem Kulturowym Europy, 2012.

Duda, Paweł. 'Nuncjatura apostolska w Warszawie i w Wiedniu wobec elekcji Władysława IV – przyczynek do badań nad czwartym interregnum.' In *Wokół wolnych elekcji: O znaczeniu idei wyboru – między prawami a obowiązkami w państwie polsko-litewskim XVI–XVIII wieku*, edited by Mariusz Markiewicz, Dariusz Rolnik, and Filip Wolański, 257–78. Katowice: Wydawnictwo Uniwersytetu Śląskiego, 2016.

Dzięgielewski, Jan. *O tolerancję dla zdominowanych: polityka wyznaniowa Rzeczypospolitej w latach panowania Władysława IV*. Warszawa: PWN, 1986.

Dzięgielewski, Jan. 'Wolna elekcja viritim – najgłośniejsze z dokonań okresu bezkrólewia po śmierci ostatniego Jagiellona.' In *Rok 1573: Dokonania przodków sprzed 440 lat*, edited by Jan Dzięgielewski, Krzysztof Koehler, and Dorota Muszytowska, 169–86. Warszawa: UKSW, 2014.

Feldkamp, Mark F. *La diplomazia pontificia: Da Silvestro I a Giovanni Paolo II: un profilo*. Milano: Jaca Book, 1998.

Floria, Boris. 'Rosyjska kandydatura na tron polski u schyłku XVI wieku.' *Odrodzenie i Reformacja w Polsce* 16 (1971): 85–95.

Giordano, Silvano. 'Uomini e apparati della politica internazionale del papato.' In *Papato e politica internazionale nella prima età moderna*, edited by Maria A. Visceglia, 131–48. Roma: Viella, 2013.

Gregorowicz, Dorota. 'Dylematy papieskiej dyplomacji: Stanowisko polityczne Stolicy Apostolskieja działalność nuncjusza Annibale Di Capua wobec elekcji 1587 roku.' In *Wokół wolnych elekcji: O znaczeniu idei wyboru – między prawami a obowiązkami w państwie polsko-litewskim XVI–XVIII wieku*, edited by Mariusz Markiewicz, Dariusz Rolnik, and Filip Wolański, 143–64. Katowice: Wydawnictwo Uniwersytetu Śląskiego, 2016.

Gregorowicz, Dorota. 'The Role of Papal Diplomats in the Interregnum's Parliamentary Practice of the Polish-Lithuanian Commonwealth (16th–17th Centuries).' *Dimensioni e problemi della ricerca storica* 29/1 (2016): 119–48.

Gregorowicz, Dorota. 'W cieniu legata Commendonego: Vincenzo Dal Portico jako dyplomata papieski wobec pierwszej elekcji.' In *Dyplomacja papieska wobec Rzeczypospolitej*, edited by Wojciech Walczak and Katarzyna Wiszowata-Walczak, 41–69. Białystok: Instytut Badań nad Dziedzictwem Kulturowym Europy, 2016.

Glemma, Tadeusz. 'Zapiski nuncjusza polskiego Wincentego Dal Portico z roku 1568.' *Collectanea Theologica* 17 (1936): 273–88.

Grzybowski, Stanisław. 'The Warsaw Confederation of 1573 and Other Acts of Religious Tolerance in Europe.' *Acta Poloniae Historica* 40 (1979): 75–96.

Jobert, Antoine. *De Luther à Mohila: la Pologne dans la crise de la chrétienté: 1517–1648*. Paris: Institut d'études slaves, 1974.

Kaczorowski, Włodzimierz. *Sejmy konwokacyjny i elekcyjny w okresie bezkrólewia 1632 r.* Opole: Instytut Śląski w Opolu, 1986.

Kaczorowski, Włodzimierz. 'Stanowisko Stolicy Apostolskiej wobec elekcji królewicza Władysława.' *Odrodzenie i Reformacja w Polsce* 29 (1984): 155–66.

Kamieński, Andrzej. *Polska a Brandenburgia-Prusy w drugiej połowie XVII wieku*. Poznań: Wydawnictwo Poznańskie, 2002.

Keenan, Charles. 'Polish Religious Toleration and Its Opponents: The Catholic Church and the Warsaw Confederation.' In *Polish Culture in the Renaissance:*

Studies in the Arts and Political Thought, edited by Danilo Facca and Valentina Lepri, 37–52. Firenze: Firenze University Press, 2013.

Keenan, Charles. 'The Limits of Diplomatic Ritual: The Polish Embassy of Giovanni Francesco Commendone (1572–1573) and Criticism of Papal Legates in Early Modern Europe.' *Royal Studies Journal* 3 (2016): 90–111.

Konopczyński, Władysław. 'Konwokacje.' In *Studia historyczne ku czci Stanisława Kutrzeby*, vol. 1, edited by Stanisław Kutrzeba, 247–61. Kraków: Nakł. Komitetu, 1938.

Lepszy, Kazimierz. 'Walka sejmowa o konfederację warszawską w roku 1587.' *Odrodzenie i Reformacja w Polsce* 4 (1959): 113–35.

Lepszy, Kazimierz. *Walka stronnictw w pierwszych latach panowania Zygmunta III.* Kraków: Gebethner & Wolff, 1929.

Likowski, Edward. *Unia brzeska (1596).* Warszawa: Gebethner & Wolf, 1907.

Litwin, Henryk. *Chwała Północy: Rzeczpospolita w europejskiej polityce Stolicy Apostolskiej w pierwszej połowie XVII wieku. (1599–1648).* Lublin: Katolicki Uniwersytet Lubelski, 2013.

Makiłła, Dariusz. 'Zniesienie Hołdu pruskiego: uwolnienie Prus Książęcych z podległości lennej wobec Rzeczypospolitej w latach 1657–1658.' *Miscellanea Historico-Archivistica* 23 (2016): 139–51.

Nanke, Czesław. *Z dziejów polityki Kuryi rzymskiej wobec Polski (1587–1589).* Lwów: Towarzystwo Naukowe, 1921.

Olejnik, Karol. *Stefan Batory.* Warszawa: Rytm, 2013.

Pastor, Ludwig von. *Storia dei papi dalla fine del Medio Evo compilata con sussidio dell'Archivio segreto pontificio e di molti altri Archivi.* Vol. 9: *Storia dei papi nel periodo della Riforma e restaurazione cattolica: Gregorio XIII (1572–1585).* Roma: Desclée, 1925.

Pastor, Ludwig von. *Storia dei papi dalla fine del Medio Evo compilata con sussidio dell'Archivio segreto pontificio e di molti altri Archivi.* Vol. 10: *Storia dei papi nel periodo della Riforma e restaurazione cattolica: Sisto V, Urbano VII, Gregorio XIV e Innocenzo IX: (1585–1591).* Roma: Desclée, 1955.

Pastor, Ludwig von. *Storia dei papi dalla fine del Medio Evo compilata con sussidio dell'Archivio segreto pontificio e di molti altri Archivi.* Vol. 14: *Storia dei papi nel periodo dell'Assolutismo dall'elezione di Innocenzo X sino alla morte di Innocenzo XII (1644–1700). Parte I: Innocenzo X, Alessandro VII, Clemente IX, Clemente X.* Roma: Desclée, 1963.

Pieńkowska, Anna. *Zjazdy i sejmy z okresu bezkrólewia po śmierci Stefana Batorego.* Pułtusk: Akademia Humanistyczna im. Aleksandra Gieysztora, 2010.

Płaza, Stanisław. 'Nowe spojrzenie na konfederację warszawską z 1573 roku.' *Czasopismo prawno-historyczne* 21/2 (1969): 193–200.

Przyboś, Adam. *Michał Korybut Wiśniowiecki 1640–1673.* Kraków: Wydawnictwo Literackie, 2007.

Rutkowski, Henryk. 'Wolna elekcja – zasady i praktyka wybierania królów polskich.' In *Elekcje królów Polski w Warszawie na Woli 1575–1764: upamiętnienie pola elekcyjnego w 400-lecie stołeczności Warszawy*, edited by Marek Tarczyński, 269–75. Warszawa: Rytm, 1997.

Schilling, Heinz. *Konfesjonalizacja: Kościół i państwo w Europie doby przednowoczesnej.* Poznań: Wydawnictwo Poznańskie, 2010.

Schramm, Gottfried. 'Ein Meilenstein der Glaubensfreiheit: Der Stand der Forschung über Ursprung und Schicksal der Warschauer Konföderation von 1573.' *Zeitschrift für Ostforschung* 24 (1975): 711–36.

Serwański, Maciej. *Henryk III Walezy w Polsce: Stosunki polsko-francuskie w latach 1566–1576*. Kraków: Wydawnictwo Literackie, 1976.

Serwański, Maciej. 'La Confédération de Varsovie (1573).' In *Conflitti e compromessi nell'Europa 'di centro' fra XVI e XX secolo. Atti del 2 Colloquio Internazionale* (Viterbo, 26–27 Maggio 2000), edited by Gaetano Platania, 13–29. Viterbo: Sette città, 2001.

Skowron, Ryszard. 'El espacio del encuentro de los confines de Europa: España y Polonia en el reinado de Felipe II.' In *Felipe II (1527–1598): Europa y la monarquía católica: Congreso Internacional Felipe II (1598–1998), Europa dividida, la monarquía católica de Felipe II (Universidad Autónoma de Madrid, 20–23 abril 1998)*, vol. 1, 2, edited by José Martínez Millán, 881–92. Madrid: Parteluz, 1998.

Skowron, Ryszard. 'El Mar Báltico en la estrategia española de guerra en los Países Bajos, 1568–1648.' In *El mar los siglos modernos*, vol. 1, edited by Manuel Reyes García Hurtado, Domingo L. Gonzáles Lopo, and Enrique Martínez Rodríguez, 978–84. Santiago de Compostela: Dirección Xeral de Turismo, 2009.

Skowron, Ryszard. 'Nuncjusz i ambasador: Korespondencja Annibala z Capui z San Clemente (1586–1591).' In *Od Kijowa do Rzymu: Z dziejów stosunków Rzeczypospolitej ze Stolicą Apostolską i Ukrainą*, edited by Mariusz R. Drozdowski, Wojciech Walczak, and Katarzyna Wiszowata-Walczak, 453–67. Białystok: Instytut Badań nad Dziedzictwem Kulturowym Europy, 2012.

Smołucha, Janusz. *Papiestwo a Polska w latach 1484–1526: Kontakty na tle zagrożenia tureckiego*. Kraków: Towarzystwo Naukowe 'Societas Vistulana,' 1999.

Sułowska, Zofia. 'Działalność nuncjusza Viscontiego w Polsce (1630–1635), *Roczniki Humanistyczne* 9/2 (1960): 31–99.

Szymczak, Barbara. 'Działalność dyplomacji brandenburskiej w okresie bezkrólewia w Rzeczypospolitej w 1648 r.' *Przegląd Historyczny* 89/1 (1998): 25–48.

Tazbir, Janusz. *Konfederacja warszawska 1573 roku, wielka karta polskiej tolerancji*. Warszawa: PAX, 1980.

Tazbir, Janusz. *Państwo bez stosów i inne szkice*. Kraków: Universitas, 2000.

Tazbir, Janusz. *Tradycje tolerancji religijnej w Polsce*. Warszawa: Książka i Wiedza, 1980.

Tygielski, Wojciech. *Włosi w Polsce XVI–XVII wieku: Utracona szansa na modernizację*. Warszawa: Więzi, 2005.

Tygielski, Wojciech. *Z Rzymu do Rzeczpospolitej: Studia z dziejów nuncjatury apostolskiej w Polsce, XVI i XVII w*. Warszawa: Wydawnictwa Fundacji 'Historia pro Futuro,' 1992.

Unia brzeska. Geneza, dzieje i konsekwencje w kulturze narodów słowiańskich. Edited by Ryszard Łużny, Franciszek Ziejka, and Andrzej Kępiński. Kraków: Universitas, 1994.

Wierzbowski, Teodor. *Uchańsciana, czyli zbiór dokumentów wyjaśniających życie i działalność Jakóba Uchańskiego, arcybiskupa gnieźnieńskiego, legata urodzonego, Królestwa Polskiego prymasa i pierwszego księcia. Vol. 5, Jakób Uchański, arcybiskup gnieźnieński, (1502–1581): monografia historyczna*. Warszawa: J. Berger, 1892.

Wijaczka, Jacek. 'Sukces czy klęska?: traktat welawsko-bydgoski z 1657 roku.' *Zapiski Historyczne: kwartalnik poświęcony historii Pomorza* 72/4 (2007): 7–21.

Wisner, Henryk. *Władysław IV Waza*. Wrocław: Ossolineum, 2009.

Wojtyska, Henryk D. *Papiestwo – Polska 1548–1563*. Lublin: Katolicki Uniwersytet Lubelski, 1977.

Woś, Jan W. *Santa Sede e Corona Polacca nella corrispondenza di Annibale di Capua (1586–1591)*. Trento: Università degli Studi di Trento, 2004.

Zakrzewski, Wincenty. *Stosunki Stolicy Apostolskiej z Iwanem Groźnym, Carem i W: Księciem Moskiewskim*. Kraków: L. Paszkowski, 1872.

Zakrzewski, Wincenty. *Po ucieczce Henryka: dzieje bezkrólewia 1574–1575*. Kraków: Akademia Umiejętności, 1878.

3 Catholics, heretics and the 'common enemy'[1]

Papal diplomacy and the Great Turkish War during the papacy of Innocent XII, 1691–1700

Béla Vilmos Mihalik

The relationship between the Holy See and the Viennese court was relatively rippling in the seventeenth century. Papal diplomacy aimed to uphold the status quo in the Holy Roman Empire at the beginning. Based on political reasoning, the Holy See supported the emperors with varying sums during the Thirty Years' War. The Peace of Westphalia in 1648 eliminated Rome from the new power system of Europe. It was changed temporarily at the end of the century when, by organising the Holy League against the Ottoman Empire, Pope Innocent XI raised the papacy again on the grand stage of European diplomacy.[2]

This chapter will examine how the cooperation between Vienna and the Holy See changed in the last decade of the Great Turkish War. It will also look at how the different sides tried to hinder papal aid to the others, and during this competition how confessional arguments appeared in the Roman theatre of diplomacy.

The Holy League

After the Siege of Vienna in 1683, the Habsburg monarchy finally decided on a great war against the Ottoman Empire. The support of the Holy See, as well as the diplomatic activity of Innocent XI, gave rise to the Holy League between the Holy Roman Empire, Poland, and Venice, and efforts against the 'common enemy' unified the confessionally divided Europe. Both Protestants and Catholics cooperated during the war, and even this fact did not hinder the Holy See's financial support of Emperor Leopold I and his allies.[3] According to Peter Rauscher, it is hardly possible to discover the exact amount of the aid given by the papacy. However, he refers to the French historian Jean Bérenger, who suggests that Innocent had granted the imperial court 2 million florins, from Italian tithes, until his death in 1689. In 1683, he sent 500,000 florins in direct aid to the emperor and another 200,000 to the Polish king, John III Sobieski. In the year of the Siege of Vienna and in 1684, the pope had also taxed the clergy of the Habsburg monarchy, which resulted in an additional annual 500,000 florins.[4]

When war erupted again between France and the Holy Roman Empire in 1688, the Habsburgs were forced to fight on two fronts. At the same time as he was still fighting against the Ottomans, Emperor Leopold I found himself on the side of the Protestant William III of England against Louis XIV. Meanwhile, the conflict between the Holy See and France, which had been sparked off by the Declaration of the Four Gallican Articles in 1682, worsened by the end of the decade, so much so that Louis ran the risk of excommunication. In response, Louis threatened the papal state with direct military action.[5]

The situation changed dramatically during the reign of Innocent XI's successor, when Alexander VIII (1689–1691) made approaches to the King of France, which troubled relations with Vienna. Although Alexander promised the emperor papal aid several times, he never fulfilled it.[6] While French diplomacy was trying to hinder papal aid to Vienna, the imperial court found itself in a competition with Poland and the exiled King James II for financial support.[7] At the beginning of the 1690s, the military circumstances deteriorated on the Eastern Front, the former conquest of the Balkans had been lost, and the Ottomans reoccupied Belgrade on 8th October, 1690. The Habsburg court needed auxiliary forces from the empire, even from the Protestant princes, even though soldiers from Brandenburg and Brunswick had already come to fight against the common enemy in the first years of the Great Turkish War.[8] After the outbreak of the Nine Years' War with France, this help became more sorely needed in both theatres of the war. The need for military aid on the Western and Eastern Fronts led to scissions between the imperial court and her allies. Spain, the Dutch Republic, and England demanded imperial support against Louis XIV and urged for peace with the Ottoman Empire. The Holy See, on the other hand, aimed at a universal peace between the European princes, the *Pax Christiana*, and wished them to fight in a concerted action against the Ottoman forces.[9]

The heretic elector

Pope Alexander VIII died on 1st February, 1691. After a long conclave, Cardinal Antonio Pignatelli was elected on 12th July and three days later he was crowned as Innocent XII. As he had been a papal nuncio to Vienna between 1668 and 1671, the imperial court expected to see an improvement in relations with the Holy See.[10] The Habsburg court decided against its former intention to recall the imperial envoy, Prince Anton Florian von Liechtenstein, from Rome; rather, they elevated him to the rank of ambassador.[11] After a vacancy of three years, a new papal nuncio, Sebastiano Antonio Tanara, was sent to Vienna.[12] This complete restoration of diplomatic relations raised the hopes of both courts.

The good news about the great Christian victory over the Ottomans in the Battle of Slankamen on 19th August, 1691, reached Rome in a hopeful atmosphere. The first news arrived at the imperial court on 24th August, and Francesco Tucci, who represented the Holy See in Vienna as the auditor of the nunciature, immediately reported the victory to the cardinal secretary, Fabrizio Spada. As Tucci wrote, a few imperial ministers had declared the outcome of the battle showed that God would like to make the pontificate of Innocent XII glorious.[13]

Irrespective of this victory, imperial diplomats in Rome informed the court that the new pope had showed his willingness to support the war against the Ottomans. Innocent XII decided to support Leopold with 100,000 florins, while at the same time he sent aid of 100,000 French livres to the exiled James II. Since the treasury of the Holy See had been almost bankrupt, the pope had to take out a loan, which he acquired from different traders at an interest rate of 4 per cent.[14] The papal aid given to James II was supported by the French faction at the Roman court: they argued that the emperor's war against the Ottomans was a purely offensive war, while James II had been exiled from Great Britain because of his intention to restore the Catholic faith there.[15]

With this decision, the pope actually pre-empted the request of the emperor: Leopold I sent his instructions to Prince Liechtenstein on 25th August, one day after the news of the victory reached Vienna. The emperor informed his ambassador that he would send Count Antonio Piccolomini as an extraordinary envoy to the pope, and one of his tasks would be to request papal aid for the war against the Ottomans.[16]

The imperial court had difficulties not only with financial issues, but also with military issues. Due to the activity of the French diplomats, some of the auxiliary armies were withdrawn from Hungary. Furthermore, Ernest August of Brunswick-Lüneburg had come to an understanding with the envoys of Louis XIV in late 1690 that he would not help the imperial forces on the Western Front. Brandenburg also withdrew their armies from Hungary. The emperor reacted by giving a solemn promise to Ernest August that he would be granted the long-awaited title of Elector of Hanover on the condition that he assisted the emperor in his campaign against the Ottomans and gave up his pact with France.[17]

The papal representative, Auditor Francesco Tucci, informed the Holy See at the beginning of 1691 that Ernest August had promised 10,000 soldiers against the Ottomans, the free exercise of Catholicism in his principalities, and the cession of the Diocese of Osnabrück to the Catholics. The auditor had the opinion that under such terms, the Protestant prince's help would be more useful than injurious to the Catholic Church.[18] The imperial court and Ernest August signed an arrangement on 22nd March, 1692. In exchange for the electorate, the Brunswick prince would send 6,000 soldiers for two years against the Ottomans, after which 2,000 soldiers against

France, and, if the Habsburg monarchy would sign a peace, he would send 6,000 men to the Western Front.[19]

The Hanoverian arrangement caused diplomatic turbulence for the imperial court. By the end of 1692, Ernest August had practically blackmailed the emperor, ordering his envoy to inform Leopold I that if he did not affect his elevation to the electorate, his armies would be withdrawn from Hungary.[20] At the same time, in protest against the Hanoverian electorate, the Danish king, who was a prince of the empire as well, and the Bishop of Münster ordered their armies to leave Hungary. They offered the emperor that they would replace the Hanoverian soldiers, if the emperor would withdraw his promise to grant Brunswick the electorate. The imperial court tried to avoid the further difficulties, and thus renewed the negotiations with three of the Protestant princes of the Holy Roman Empire: Brunswick, Brandenburg, and Saxony.[21]

On 19th December, 1692, the emperor inaugurated Ernest August, who was represented by his minister, Otto von Grote, into the electorate. On the next day, Grote sent Abbot Hecher, the Viennese resident to Hanover, to the nuncio to express the new elector's appreciation toward the Holy See and the hope that the pope would not set a bar against the new electorate. The nuncio sent his auditor, Francesco Tucci, to Abbot Hecher on a complimentary, mutual visit to emphasise that they would pray for the elector and his return to the Catholic Church.[22] The Holy See had maintained a moderate viewpoint on the Hanoverian question since 1689. Ernest August kept a direct connection with the Holy See through Cardinal Francesco Brancati di Lauria, who told Baron Peter von Goëss, nephew of Cardinal Goëss, in 1692 that the elector had promised him that he would convert to Catholicism. The cardinal's response to the baron was that the Holy See had examined the Hanoverian issue, and they had formed the opinion that the majority of the electors and the emperor would support the new electorate. Therefore, they felt it more advisable not to further intervene in the matter.[23] Even the requests and protests of the Catholic bishops and the three archbishop-electors of Mainz, Cologne, and Trier would not change the position of the Holy See.[24]

The *Pax Christiana*

The aim of papal diplomacy at the beginning of the 1690s was to reach a peace between the Christians in Europe, and to continue the war against the common enemy, the Ottoman Empire. Of course, this purpose was in the Holy See's own interest also. One of the main theatres of the Nine Years' War was in northern Italy. Although the papal state and the other ecclesiastical territories did not suffer from direct military actions, the imperial taxation and the billeting of the armies affected even the feuds of the papacy.[25]

Innocent XII had already in autumn 1691 urged in a papal brief that the three Catholic sovereigns, Charles II of Spain, Louis XIV, and Leopold I, sign a peace treaty.[26] The negotiations were begun in 1692 and continued until 1693, but without any success. The primary purpose of Louis XIV was to drive a wedge between the allies, while Spain and Leopold I wanted to reduce the borders of 1648/1659, and the Austrian Habsburg monarchy wanted to end one of her two parallel wars. Furthermore, William of Orange wanted France to recognise his rule and to respect the colonial interests of England.[27] The imperial diplomats accused the French diplomats of trying to divide not just the members of the Grand Alliance, but also those of the Holy League. Prince Liechtenstein also complained that the French ambassador, Count Rebenac, had tried to encourage both Poland and Venice to quit the league, or at least to not wage an offensive war against the Ottoman Empire.[28] He also accused the French of aiding Count Imre Thököly in his revolt against the emperor, of supporting the Ottomans against the Habsburg monarchy, and finally of themselves attacking the Holy Roman Empire.[29] The emperor did not rule out a peace with France, but he wanted a lasting peace. He explained in a directive to Prince Liechtenstein that if they had obeyed the pope's wish and ended the war, either in a universal peace treaty or in a separate one, and then the Habsburg monarchy had progressed against the Ottoman Empire successfully once more, they could not have been assured that France would not have attacked the Holy Roman Empire again.[30]

By the mid-1690s, relations between the Roman Curia and the Viennese court began to deteriorate when Innocent XII demanded the peace treaty between the Catholic sovereigns as a requirement for further papal aid against the Ottomans.[31] The new imperial ambassador, Count Georg Adam von Martinitz, explained the situation in one of his reports to the emperor in spring 1696. As he wrote, the ageing pope, influenced by malevolent councillors, had come to the conclusion that although the pontiff was the *padre commune* of Christianity, he was not liable to finance the war against the 'common enemy.' Martinitz further pointed out, with the usual arguments, that Innocent's predecessors had always supported the struggles against the Ottomans, and it would be injurious to his position if he did not continue the payments. Martinitz emphasised that the sultan and the Ottomans were mobilising vast forces against Christianity, and in this situation papal aid would be more necessary than ever. The pope, in a counterargument, affirmed that for the same reason it would be beneficial to affect peace among the Catholic nations, particularly when the Protestants had been gaining significant power in Europe. Innocent condemned with this argument the politics of the emperor, which had come to a limited arrangement with the Protestant princes of the empire under the pressure of necessity. Martinitz defended the alliance with the Protestants, because the war with France was not the emperor's choice, and the pope should not feel sorry for the help of the 'heretics,' who contributed so much against the Ottomans and defended the empire against France as well. Without the help of the Protestant princes, Martinitz explained the pope, the emperor would have had to surrender to the common enemy and to the Most Christian king.[32]

In August 1696, the imperial army began a late siege against Timisoara (Temesvár), one of the last Ottoman strongholds in Hungary, but they had to withdraw soon afterwards because of the arrival of relief Ottoman troops.[33] At an audience in early September, the pope expressed his disappointment to Count Martinitz about the unsuccessful siege. The ambassador answered that with papal aid, the siege would have started earlier, to which the pope responded that peace with France would have helped the campaign much more.[34]

The Treaty of Rijswijk, signed between 20th September and 30th October, 1697, finally ended the Nine Years' War between France and the Grand Alliance of England, Spain, the Holy Roman Empire, and the Dutch Republic.[35] With this peace, the requirements of the pope were fulfilled and the *Pax Christiana* restored. However, the backbiting continued behind a veil of diplomacy. As Martinitz reported, the French had told the pope that the emperor and Venice had begun peace negotiations with the Ottomans, and according to the imperial ambassador, the French had only wanted to hinder any new papal aid being provided to the emperor in his fight against the Ottoman Empire.[36]

Despite the peace with France and the decisive victory of 11th September, 1697, when the imperial army, led by Eugene of Savoy, annihilated the Ottoman forces at the Battle of Zenta, the Holy See was still unwilling to give any ultimate aid to the emperor.[37] The pope, furthermore, awaited the official announcement of the Treaty of Rijswijk by the imperial ambassador, but Martinitz was unable do that without an order from the emperor.[38] Finally, on 5th April, 1698, the pope decided to grant 50,000 scudi to the emperor to aid his campaign against the Ottomans.[39]

Heretic soldiers against the 'common enemy'

As noted above, at the same time that the pope was criticising the growing power of the heretics inside the Holy Roman Empire due to the parallel wars against France and the Ottomans, the imperial ambassador was praising the contribution made by the Protestant soldiers against the 'common enemy.' Brandenburg, Brunswick, and Denmark had aided the emperor against the Ottoman Empire from the very beginning of the war, although the Viennese court paid for it dearly. As we have seen, Ernest August was elevated to electorate, and, under the terms of the agreement between the imperial court and Brandenburg, the Habsburg monarchy had paid significant support and, in turn for military help, assigned Schwiebus, today's Świebodzin, as a Silesian exclave to Brandenburg.[40]

In 1695, the imperial court had no choice but to accept the help of the young Lutheran Elector of Saxony, Frederick August, who provided 6,000 men. As well as paying the elector 200,000 florins, Vienna also appointed him as the supreme commander of the Christian armies. This decision proved rather unfortunate. The Ottoman forces were on the advance: in 1695, the elector's plans to besiege Timisoara were stalled by the Ottoman army, who reoccupied the fortress of Titel, and they also defeated the Christian troops sent from Transylvania to help out Frederick August.[41] At the Battle of Lugoj (Lugos) on 21st September, several imperial officers were killed or captured, and the experienced Italian general, the commander-in-chief of the Transylvanian forces, Federico Veterani, died on the battlefield.[42] In the following year, the Elector of Saxony brought 12,000 men with the intention of occupying Timisoara, but he was unsuccessful again. Finally, in 1697, Frederick August became King of Poland on the death of John III Sobieski. His election was beneficial to Vienna in several ways: it hindered the strengthening of French influence in Poland, because the French candidate, Prince Conti from the cadet branch of the Bourbon dynasty, had lost the election.[43] It also gave Vienna the opportunity to appoint the young Eugene of Savoy as new supreme commander, and it was he who finally defeated the Ottomans in September 1697, thereby resolving the outcome of the Great Turkish War.[44] However, to be eligible for election to the throne of the Polish–Lithuanian Commonwealth, Frederick August had to convert to Catholicism. His admittance to the Church of Rome took place in the Loretto Chapel in Baden, near Vienna, on 1st June, 1697, with the assistance of the elector's cousin, Christian August of Saxony-Zeitz, Bishop of Győr.[45]

As Augustus II, the Strong, as Polish king changed his religion, the Viennese court reviewed their position vis-à-vis the Protestant soldiers. As the war with France ended, they were able to move these forces from the Western Front to fight against the Ottoman armies. Cardinal Leopold Kollonich, in a letter to Nuncio Andrea Santacroce on 3rd May, 1698, explained how he wished to control the proper distribution of papal aid. The cardinal had a conversation with the emperor too about how they could use the financial support the best. Cardinal Kollonich and the emperor pointed out that during wartime, when auxiliary armies from Denmark, Brandenburg, and Brunswick had helped the emperor, the Protestant community in Hungary had been strengthening. The local Protestant communities in Hungary now felt more self-confident, especially after the foreign Protestant troops stayed over the winter. The imperial court accused the Hungarian Protestants of abusing Catholics and disrespecting the Eucharist. The court wanted to replace the Protestant soldiers with Catholic troops from Bavaria, Salzburg, and Milan, but if they released the auxiliary Protestant armies, they would have to disburse the arrears owed to the men. Therefore, Cardinal Kollonich suggested they use papal aid to dismiss the heretic soldiers once and for all. He asked the nuncio to communicate his plan to the Holy See for approval.[46]

The nuncio wrote to the cardinal secretary, explaining that Cardinal Kollonich's plan would serve the Catholic Church in two ways. First, papal aid would help the emperor to continue the war against the 'common enemy'; and second, it would allow the court to free itself from the Protestant armies.[47] The Holy See naturally received this news with satisfaction.[48]

However, the new Catholic soldiers, who replaced the 'heretics,' did not participate in any large-scale military actions. The campaign of 1698 was uneventful, and in October 1698 peace negotiations opened between the members of the Holy League and the Ottoman Empire at Sremski Karlovci.[49] The Treaty of Karlowitz was signed on 26th January, 1699. It marked the end of Ottoman control in much of Central Europe, with their first major territorial losses after centuries of expansion, and established the Habsburg monarchy as the dominant power in Central and South-Eastern Europe.

Peace with the 'common enemy'

The emperor signed a mutual defensive and offensive alliance with Russia and Venice on 8th February, 1697, and with this they consented that none of the allies sign a separate peace treaty with the Ottoman Empire. However, the position of the imperial court changed after the end of the Nine Years' War and the victory at Zenta – the emperor also wanted to end the war with the Ottomans, and pre-emptive exploratory talks had begun with the mediation of the Dutch and English ambassadors in Constantinople. The emperor received the sultan's offer for peace in April 1698, and although Poland and Russia had wanted to continue the war, finally they too sent their representatives to the peace conference.[50]

Before opening the peace conference, the papal diplomats tried to put across the interests of the Catholic Church by compiling two memoranda which were handed to the emperor. One of these concerned the situation of the Catholics living in the Ottoman Empire, which contained nine points.[51] It urged that all Catholic prelates be allowed to continue in their seat or should be allowed to travel freely in case of disposition. The memorandum demanded that all Catholic churches should be maintained and those that had been destroyed should be rebuilt. The Holy See underlined especially the restoration of the Franciscan monastery in Chiprovtsi, Bulgaria, which had been a centre for Roman Catholics in the region until their anti-Ottoman uprising in 1688. The third point stressed that the Ottoman leaders should not allow any violent acts against the Catholic community. They urged for a new hospital and church for the German Trinitarians in the Pera and Galata quarters of Constantinople, where other nationals had their own churches. The task of these Trinitarian fathers would have been to free Christians from Ottoman slavery. Therefore, they demanded the free movement of the Trinitarian fathers in the Ottoman Empire and in the Crimean Khanate; the Church of the Holy Sepulchre should be left in the hands of the Franciscans and no pilgrims should be hindered from visiting. The next two points asked for the possibility for Christians to be buried by their own priests and for the free movement of monks to their superiors in the territories occupied by the Ottomans. Finally, the Holy See asked the sultan to keep goodwill with the Christians of his empire.

The nuncio, Andrea Santacroce, handed the memorandum to the imperial envoys sent to the peace conference and a copy to the Venetian ambassador as well. The imperial envoys and the Venetian ambassador assured the nuncio that their first point would be to secure the Catholics' situation in the Ottoman Empire. The nuncio was of the opinion that to guarantee the status of the Catholics, it would be necessary to re-establish the position of Ignatius Peter VI, the patriarch of the Syriac Catholic Church. The patriarch would have been the highest ecclesiastical representative of the Catholics in the Ottoman Empire, and he also accepted the supremacy of the pope.[52]

The peace treaty was signed by the imperial plenipotentiaries on 26th January, 1699. The thirteenth article concerned religious matters, and in general it followed the guidelines of the Holy See.[53] But it emphasised that in the future, the imperial ambassador to Constantinople would be assigned to represent religious matters to the Sublime Porte.[54] It left open the question of further guarantees regarding the status of the Roman Church in the Ottoman Empire. Nevertheless, the cardinal secretary expressed his satisfaction with the treaty, and ordered the nuncio to communicate the pope's approval to the imperial court.[55]

After signing the treaty, the Holy Roman Empire and the Ottoman Empire restored mutual diplomatic relations. The emperor sent Count Wolfgang von Oettingen-Wallerstein as his ambassador to Constantinople. Consequently, the Holy See ordered the nuncio to remind the emperor that according to the treaty, the imperial ambassador should represent the interests of Christians in the Ottoman Empire.[56] In March, Rome sent a memorandum to Andrea Santacroce to talk about the matter with Count Oettingen. This document discussed the most important issues concerning the Catholics living in the Ottoman Empire in 14 points.[57] These points would also suggest more defence for the Catholics, particularly against the hostile acts of Orthodox Christians.

Final considerations

In the centre of the Castle of Buda, there is a statue dedicated to Innocent XI. The monument was erected for the 250th anniversary of the liberation of Buda in 1936. On the reverse of the statue, a relief shows the medallion of the Holy League, which portrays the four rulers: Pope Innocent XI; Emperor Leopold I; John III Sobieski, the King of Poland; and Marcantonio Giustinian, the Doge of Venice. Large parts of the medieval Kingdom of Hungary were liberated, by the Holy League, from 150 years of Ottoman rule during the Great Turkish War. Most historical works celebrate the role of Innocent XI in this victory but forget the other Innocent, Innocent XII, although the war ended during his pontificate.

It should not be forgotten that Innocent XII also supported the war against the 'common enemy' – the Ottoman Empire. Of course, the international situation had changed since 1683, and the Holy See, as an actor in the European theatre, had to regard these changes. The outbreak of the Nine Years' War pushed Leopold I to the side of the Protestant William III. The emperor in that situation even consulted his theologians for advice as to whether he could conclude an alliance with a Protestant ruler, one who had recently expelled his Catholic father-in-law from the English throne.[58]

From the pope's point of view, the war between the Holy Roman Empire and France was tragic. As the leader of the Catholic Church, he had to guard over the peace between the Catholic sovereigns. On the other hand, as the head of the papal state, his own interest was to maintain the tranquillity between the two powers in northern Italy, near the border of his territories. It was not surprising that the refusal of the Spanish king and the emperor to accept his peace initiatives saddened Innocent XII. The mood of the day is reflected accurately in a conversation between the pope and Prince Liechtenstein, the imperial ambassador, on 2nd February, 1692. Liechtenstein accused the French of indirectly helping the Ottomans to continue the war against the Habsburg monarchy and Christianity. The pope responded that the imperial court had accepted the Protestants' help against France, but Liechtenstein denied this, arguing that the Protestants had fought only against the Ottomans.[59]

We can consider this dispute between the Roman court and the imperial court as a kind of confessional pragmatism. The Habsburg monarchy needed the military help offered by the Protestant princes of the empire, but at the same time they applied for the financial aid of the pope as well. From the Viennese viewpoint, the indirect French support for the Ottomans was a bigger fault than to accept the help of the Protestants. It was probably no coincidence that at the beginning of the 1690s, Leopold I sent the Bishop of Wiener Neustadt, Cristobal Rojas y Spinola, to negotiate with Protestant and Catholic bishops about the union between the two confessions.[60] However, at the very first chance, when Vienna had the opportunity to dismiss the Protestant auxiliary corps, the imperial court did not hesitate to take the necessary steps, and with the use of the papal aid paid off the Protestant soldiers.

As suggested above, for the papacy the war between the Catholics was more dramatic, from both a political and spiritual perspective. Therefore, the most important aim of the Holy See was to restore the *Pax Christiana*, and in that regard it was a secondary concern that France might have indirectly helped the Ottomans. The pope emphasised that the greatest advantage, and a prerequisite for a successful war against the 'common enemy,' would be the peace between the Catholic sovereigns. At this time, after a decade-long conflict had raised considerable anxiety in Vienna, the papacy finally reconciled with France.[61] The imperial court considered Innocent XII a Francophile because of the compromise between the pope and Louis XIV in ecclesiastical issues. Therefore, any further attempts by the pope to revive the peace negotiations between the Catholic powers were considered in Vienna in terms of a growing French influence at the Roman court.[62] This emerging distrust of imperial diplomacy towards the pope led to a serious breach by the end of Innocent XII's pontificate. Following a series of scandals and conflicts concerning the Roman Curia, the pope denied the imperial ambassador Count Martinitz an audience after August 1698, which forced the imperial court to recall Martinitz in early 1700.[63]

In the background, a further important question had arisen. The succession of the ailing Charles II of Spain was in dispute throughout the papacy of Innocent XII. In the mid-1690s, they became part of the first negotiations between Louis XIV and Leopold I.[64] Without a solid solution, this question became a great threat to peace after the Treaty of Rijswijk. Innocent XII died on 27th September, 1700, a month and a half before Charles II on 1st November, 1700. In the upcoming War of the Spanish Succession (1701–1714), the enemies ignored any confessional considerations, the Habsburgs allying once again with the Protestant princes and England, and in 1706 the imperial court temporarily broke diplomatic relations with the Holy See.

Notes

1 This article was supported by the János Bolyai Research Scholarship of the Hungarian Academy of Sciences.
2 Péter Tusor, *The Baroque Papacy (1600–1700)* (Viterbo: Sette Città, 2016), 39–87.
3 Vilmos Fraknói, *Papst Innocenz XI. (Benedikt Odescalchi) und Ungarns Befreiung von der Türkenherrschaft* (Freiburg im Breisgau: Herdersche Verlagshandlung, 1902).
4 Peter Rauscher, 'Defence and Expansion: Emperor Leopold I., Pope Innocent XI and Financing the Wars against the Ottoman Empire in the Late 17th Century,' in *Innocenzo XI Odescalchi: Papa, politico, committente*, ed. Richard Bösel et al. (Rome: Viella, 2014), 180–81.
5 Geoffrey Symcox, 'Louis XIV and the Outbreak of the Nine Years War,' in *Louis XIV and Europe*, ed. Ragnhild Hatton (London: Macmillan, 1976), 179–212.
6 Sigismund von Bischoffshausen, *Papst Alexander VIII. und der Wiener Hof (1689–1691)* (Stuttgart and Wien: Joseph Roth'sche Verlagshandlung, 1900), 57–63.
7 Ibid., 61, 156.
8 Michael Hochedlinger, *Austria's Wars of Emergence: War, State and Society in the Habsburg Monarchy, 1683–1797* (New York and London: Longman, 2003), 159–64. For Brunswick, see: Georg Schnath, *Geschichte Hannovers im Zeitalter der neunten Kur und der englischen Sukzession 1674–1714* (Hildesheim and Leipzig: August Lax Verlagsbuchhandlung, 1938), 348–54. Two sons of Ernest August, Duke of Brunswick-Lüneburg, Charles Philip and Frederick

August, died on the Hungarian front: Martin Wrede, 'The House of Bruns-wick-Lüneburg and the Holy Roman Empire: The Making of a Patriotic Dyn-asty, 1648–1714?,' in *The Hanoverian Succession: Dynastic Politics and Monarchical Culture*, ed. Andreas Gestrich and Michael Schaich (London and New York: Routledge, 2016), 54–56. The other son of Ernest August, the later British king, George I, participated in the Siege of Vienna in 1683 and fought in the campaign in 1684: Schnath, *Geschichte Hannovers*, 351.

9 Hochedlinger, *Austria's Wars*, 160–61, 163.
10 Donato Squicciarini, *Die Apostolischen Nuntien in Wien* (Vatican: Libreria Editrice Vaticana, 2000), 176–78.
11 Pope Alexander VIII granted cardinalate to the French Toussaint de Forbin-Janson, Bishop of Beauvais in 1690. The imperial court claimed that Forbin-Janson had a role in the Ottoman attacks and the rebellion of the Hungarian Count Imre Thököly. On the other hand, the Habsburg court denied accept-ing the nomination of Lorenzo Corsini as nuncio to Vienna. These worsened the relations between the two courts, and Emperor Leopold I wanted to call back his envoy, Prince Liechtenstein, from Rome. Bischoffshausen, *Papst Alexander VIII*, 106–7, 169–70. The letter of credentials to Prince Liechten-stein as legatus, 16th February, 1691, OeStA, HHStA, StA, Rom, Hofkorre-spondenz, 15.
12 Squicciarini, *Die Apostolischen Nuntien*, 189–90.
13 Francesco Tucci to Cardinal Fabrizio Spada, Vienna, 24th August, 1691, ASV, Segr. di Stato, Germania 218, 138r–v. The news arrived to Rome through Venice on 1st September: Cardinal Johannes von Goëss to Father Pietro Giuseppe Ederi SJ, 1st September, 1691, OeStA, HHStA, StA, Rom, Korrespondenz, 71, 10r.
14 Letter of Abbot Pompeo Scarlatti, 25th August, 1691, OeStA, HHStA, StA, Rom, Korrespondenz, 71, 32r–39v.
15 Letter of Abbot Pompeo Scarlatti, 18th August, 1691, OeStA, HHStA, StA, Rom, Korrespondenz, 71, 24r–31v.
16 Leopold I to Prince Anton Florian von Liechtenstein, Vienna, 25th August, 1691, HAL, FA, 111. The emperor repeated his request in the instruction to Prince Liechtenstein on the next week again: Vienna, 2nd September, 1691, HAL, FA, 111.
17 Schnath, *Geschichte Hannovers*, 592–95.
18 Francesco Tucci to Cardinal Pietro Ottoboni, Vienna, 7th January, 1691, ASV, Segr. di Stato, Germania 218, 8r–9v.
19 Schnath, *Geschichte Hannovers*, 605–7.
20 Ibid., 638–39.
21 Newsletter (foglio d'avvisi), Vienna, 27th December, 1692, ASV, Segr. di Stato, Germania 224, 611r–12v, 615r–16r; the secret report of Sebastiano Antonio Tanara to Cardinal Fabrizio Spada, Vienna, 6th December, 1692, ASV, Segr. di Stato, Germania 220, 76r–v.
22 The secret report of Sebastiano Antonio Tanara to Cardinal Fabrizio Spada, Vienna, 20th December, 1692, ASV, Segr. di Stato, Germania 220, 84r–v.
23 Baron Johannes Peter von Goëss to Leopold I, Rome, 12th July, 1692, KLA, Familienarchiv Goëss, C80.
24 Béla Vilmos Mihalik, 'A Szentszék és a magyar választófejedelemség gondolata a 17. század végén,' *Történelmi Szemle* 58 (2016), 393–98.
25 Béla Vilmos Mihalik, 'The Fall of an Imperial Ambassador: Count Georg Adam von Martinitz and His Recall from Rome,' *Theatrum Historiae* 19 (2016), 255–56.
26 Innocent XII to Leopold I, 1st October, 1691, OeStA, HHStA, StA, Rom, Hof-korrespondenz, 15.

27 Hochedlinger, *Austria's Wars*, 172.
28 Prince Anton Florian von Liechtenstein to Leopold I, Rome, 2nd February, 1692, OeStA, HHStA, StA, HHStA, Rom, Korrespondenz, 72, 1r–7v. The imperial diplomacy was also aware of Rebenac's other mission to the northern Italian states. France tried to build up an alliance with these states to alienate them from the emperor. Leopold I to Prince Anton Florian von Liechtenstein, Vienna, 15th December, 1691, HAL, FA, 111.
29 Prince Anton Florian von Liechtenstein to Leopold I, Rome, 24th November, 1691, OeStA, HHStA, StA, Rom, Korrespondenz, 71, 70r–85v.
30 Leopold I to Prince Anton Florian von Liechtenstein, Vienna, 15th December, 1691, HAL, FA, 111.
31 Mihalik, 'The Fall of an Imperial Ambassador.'
32 Count Georg Adam von Martinitz to Leopold I, Rome, 10th March, 1696, OeStA, HHStA, StA, Rom, Korrespondenz, 76, 42r–47v.
33 Hochedlinger, *Austria's Wars*, 164.
34 Count Georg Adam von Martinitz to Leopold I, Rome, 8th September, 1696, OeStA, HHStA, StA, Rom, Korrespondenz, 76, 39r–44v.
35 Hochedlinger, *Austria's Wars*, 173.
36 Count Georg Adam von Martinitz to Leopold I, Rome, 21st December, 1697, OeStA, HHStA, StA, Rom, Korrespondenz, 78, 98r–109v.
37 Hochedlinger, *Austria's Wars*, 165. About 25,000 Turks remained on the battlefield and Sultan Mustapha II escaped to Timisoara. After the battle, the raids of the Christian soldiers reached as far as Sarajevo.
38 Count Georg Adam von Martinitz to Leopold I, Rome, 25th January, 1698, OeStA, HHStA, StA, Rom, Korrespondenz, 78, 21r–30v.
39 Paolo Campello della Spina, 'Pontificato di Innocenzo XII: Diario del Conte Gio. Battista Campello,' *Studi e documenti di storia e diritto* 12 (1891), 385.
40 Hochedlinger, *Austria's Wars*, 159.
41 Ibid., 164.
42 Newsletter (foglio), Vienna, 1st October, 1695, ASV, Segr. di Stato, Germania 232, 892r–95r.
43 Markus Milewski, *Die polnische Königswahl von 1697* (Innsbruck, Wien and Bozen: Studienverlag, 2008), 84–98.
44 Hochedlinger, *Austria's Wars*, 164–65.
45 Narratio conversionis ad Catholicam Fidem Serenissimi Saxoniae Electoris, ASV, Segr. di Stato, Germania 234, 516r–v.
46 Cardinal Leopold Kollonich to Andrea Santacroce, Vienna, 3rd May, 1698, ASV, Segr. di Stato, Germania 235, 406r–v.
47 Andrea Santacroce to Cardinal Fabrizio Spada, Vienna, 10th May, 1698, ASV, Segr. di Stato, Germania 235, 402r–3v.
48 Cardinal Fabrizio Spada to Andrea Santacroce, Rome, 24th May, 1698, ASV, Segr. di Stato, Germania 43, 437v–38r. During the next weeks, the imperial court indeed reinforced their armies from Bavaria, Salzburg, and the Franconian Circle of the Holy Roman Empire: Newsletter (foglio d'avvisi), Vienna, 17th May, 1698, ASV, Segr. di Stato, Germania 43, 424r–v.
49 Also known as Karlóca or Karlowitz: Hochedlinger, *Austria's Wars*, 165.
50 Ernst D. Petritsch, 'Rijswijk und Karlowitz: Wechselwirkungen europäischer Friedenspolitik,' in *Der Friede von Rijswijk 1697*, ed. Heinz Duchhardt, Matthias Schnettger, and Martin Vogt (Mainz: Verlag Philipp von Zabern, 1998), 297–302.
51 Consultatio pro secura subsistentia Sacrae Romanae Catholicae Religionis Nostrae instituendae sub Imperio Ottomanico, ASV, Segr. di Stato, Germania 235, 765r, 766r–67v.

52 Andrea Santacroce to Cardinal Fabrizio Spada, Vienna, 27th September, 1698, ASV, Segr. di Stato, Germania 235, 763r–64r. The question of the Syrian patriarch was handled with high priority from the side of the Holy See: Stefano Pfifferi, 'Carlowitz, gli Asburgo e la Santa Sede nella nunziatura di Andrea Santacroce,' in *Gli archivi della Santa Sede e il mondo asburgico nella prima età moderna*, ed. Matteo Sanfilippo, Alexander Koller and Giovanni Pizzorusso (Viterbo: Sette Città, 2004), 302–3.
53 Andrea Santacroce to Cardinal Fabrizio Spada, Vienna, 14th February, 1699, ASV, Segr. di Stato, Germania 236, 93r–v.
54 László Szita and Gerhard Seewann, *A karlócai béke és Európa: Dokumentumok a karlócai béke történetéhez 1698–1699* (Pécs: MTT, 1999), 220.
55 Petritsch, 'Rijswijk und Karlowitz,' 307; Cardinal Fabrizio Spada to Andrea Santacroce, Rome, 21st February, 1699, ASV, Segr. di Stato, Germania 43, 570r.
56 Cardinal Fabrizio Spada to Andrea Santacroce, Rome, 11th April, 1699, ASV, Segr. di Stato, Germania 43, 584r–v.
57 The memorandum was attached to the letter of the cardinal secretary on 21st March, 1699, ASV, Segr. di Stato, Germania 43, 576r–77v.
58 Klaus Malettke, *Hegemonie – multipolares System – Gleichgewicht: Internationale Beziehungen 1648/1659–1713/1714* (Paderborn: Ferdinand Schöningh, 2012), 428.
59 Prince Anton Florian von Liechtenstein to Leopold I, Rome, 2nd February, 1692, OeStA, HHStA, StA, Rom, Korrespondenz, 72, 1r–7v.
60 András Forgó, *Kirchliche Einigungsversuche in Ungarn: Die Unionsverhandlungen Christophorus Rojas y Spinolas in der zweiten Hälfte des 17.* Jahrhunderts (Mainz: Philipp von Zabern, 2007).
61 Pierre Bilet S.J., 'Innocent XII et Louis XIV,' in *Riforme, religione e politica durante il pontificato di Innocenzo XII (1691–1700)*, ed. Bruno Pellegrino (Lecce: Congedo, 1994), 339–43.
62 Pfifferi, 'Carlowitz,' 298.
63 Mihalik, 'The Fall of an Imperial Ambassador,' 261–71.
64 Malettke, *Hegemonie*, 434–35.

Bibliography

Archival Sources

Archivio Segreto Vaticano (ASV), Segreteria di Stato (Segr. Di Stato), Germania.
Hausarchiv der regierenden Fürsten von Liechtenstein (HAL), Familienarchiv (FA).
Kärntnerisches Landesarchiv (KLA), Familienarchiv Goëss.
Österreichisches Staatsarchiv Vienna (OeStA), Haus-, Hof- und Staatsarchiv (HHStA), Staatenabteilungen (StA) Rom: Hofkorrespondenz; Korrespondenz.

Printed sources

Campello della Spina, Paolo. 'Pontificato di Innocenzo XII: Diario del Conte Gio. Battista Campello.' *Studi e documenti di storia e diritto* 12 (1891): 379–91.
Szita, László, and Seewann, Gerhard. *A karlócai béke és Európa: Dokumentumok a karlócai béke történetéhez 1698–1699* [*The Treaty of Karlowitz and*

Europe: Documents for the History of the Treaty of Karlowitz 1698–1699].
Pécs: MTT, 1999.

Literature

Bilet, Pierre S.J. 'Innocent XII et Louis XIV.' In *Riforme, religione e politica durante il pontificato di Innocenzo XII (1691–1700)*, edited by Bruno Pellegrino, 335–52. Lecce: Congedo, 1994.

Forgó, András. *Kirchliche Einigungsversuche in Ungarn: Die Unionsverhandlungen Christophorus Rojas y Spinolas in der zweiten Hälfte des 17. Jahrhunderts*. Mainz: Philipp von Zabern, 2007.

Fraknói, Vilmos. *Papst Innocenz XI. (Benedikt Odescalchi) und Ungarns Befreiung von der Türkenherrschaft*. Freiburg im Breisgau: Herdersche Verlagshandlung, 1902.

Hochedlinger, Michael. *Austria's Wars of Emergence: War, State and Society in the Habsburg Monarchy, 1683–1797*. New York and London: Longman, 2003.

Malettke, Klaus. *Hegemonie – multipolares System – Gleichgewicht: Internationale Beziehungen 1648/1659–1713/1714*. Paderborn: Ferdinand Schöningh, 2012.

Mihalik, Béla Vilmos. 'A Szentszék és a magyar választófejedelemség gondolata a 17. század végén.' [The Holy See and the Idea of a Hungarian Electorate at the End of the Seventeenth Century] *Történelmi Szemle* 58 (2016): 383–407.

Mihalik, Béla Vilmos. 'The Fall of an Imperial Ambassador: Count Georg Adam von Martinitz and His Recall from Rome.' *Theatrum Historiae* 19 (2016): 247–73.

Milewski, Markus. *Die polnische Königswahl von 1697*. Innsbruck, Wien and Bozen: Studienverlag, 2008.

Petritsch, Ernst D. 'Rijswijk und Karlowitz: Wechselwirkungen europäischer Friedenspolitik.' In *Der Friede von Rijswijk 1697*, edited by Heinz Duchhardt, Matthias Schnettger and Martin Vogt, 291–311. Mainz: Verlag Philipp von Zabern, 1998.

Pfifferi, Stefano. 'Carlowitz, gli Asburgo e la Santa Sede nella nunziatura di Andrea Santacroce.' In *Gli archivi della Santa Sede e il mondo asburgico nella prima età moderna*, edited by Matteo Sanfilippo, Alexander Koller and Giovanni Pizzorusso, 295–319. Viterbo: Sette Città, 2004.

Rauscher, Peter. 'Defence and Expansion: Emperor Leopold I, Pope Innocent XI and Financing the Wars against the Ottoman Empire in the Late 17th Century.' In *Innocenzo XI Odescalchi: Papa, politico, committente*, edited by Richard Bösel, Antonio Menniti Ippolito, Andrea Spiriti, Claudio Strinati and Maria Antonietta Visceglia, 167–83. Rome: Viella, 2014.

Schnath, Georg. *Geschichte Hannovers im Zeitalter der neunten Kur und der englischen Sukzession 1674–1714*. Hildesheim and Leipzig: August Lax Verlagsbuchhandlung, 1938.

Squicciarini, Donato. *Die Apostolischen Nuntien in Wien*. Vatican: Libreria Editrice Vaticana, 2000.

Symcox, Geoffrey. 'Louis XIV and the Outbreak of the Nine Years War.' In *Louis XIV and Europe*, edited by Ragnhild Hatton, 179–212. London: Macmillan, 1976.

Tusor, Péter. *The Baroque Papacy (1600–1700)*. Viterbo: Sette Città, 2016.

Bischoffshausen, Sigismund von. *Papst Alexander VIII. und der Wiener Hof (1689–1691)*. Stuttgart and Wien: Joseph Roth'sche Verlagshandlung, 1900.

Wrede, Martin. 'The House of Brunswick-Lüneburg and the Holy Roman Empire: The Making of a Patriotic Dynasty, 1648–1714?' In *The Hanoverian Succession: Dynastic Politics and Monarchical Culture*, edited by Andreas Gestrich and Michael Schaich, 43–70. London and New York: Routledge, 2016.

4 Renewing Roman diplomacy?

Irish Catholicism and the mission of Fr Bonaventure de Burgo, 1709–1711[1]

Cristina Bravo Lozano

In 1693, the Irish Franciscan Fr Bonaventure de Burgo was appointed Guardian of the College of Saint Isidore in Rome.[2] The significance of this post was not in tune with the erudition of this retired lecturer and the censor of works such as *Scrutinium doctrinarum*, written by another Franciscan, Giovanni Antonio da Palermo.[3] In addition to continuing the *Annales Minorum*, the work initiated by Luke Wadding, Fr de Burgo also played a prominent role in the defence of Catholicism in eighteenth-century Ireland. Owing to his profuse correspondence with various exiled bishops, he was well informed about religious conditions in his homeland.[4] His privileged position at the papal court also gave him the opportunity to mediate with Clement XI. The new pope took advantage of the political tensions prevailing in Europe to emphasise the papacy's peacemaking role, at the same time as promoting the Catholic faith in territories where the Reformation had been successful.

De Burgo was entrusted with submitting reports about the religious conditions in Ireland after the enactment of the Penal Laws, from 1697 onwards.[5] The new measures passed by the Irish parliament contravened the Treaty of Limerick (1691) and caused serious problems for the Catholic community. In regard to this matter, Clement XI took a resolution to safeguard Catholicism in Ireland. This political stage and a new bill in 1709 threatened to cause conditions to deteriorate even further, in an international context marked by instability and the War of the Spanish Succession. Like in 1697, the papacy's first answer was to send different briefs to certain Catholic princes. The person in charge of carrying these papal petitions was his private agent, Fr Bonaventure de Burgo. On de Burgo's journey, he discussed with important men (and women) the resolution of the *quaestio hibernica* and the coordination of a common front at the preliminary peace conference of The Hague.

This chapter focuses on papal diplomacy at the beginning of the eighteenth century through the Franciscan's journey in northern Italy and the Empire before his arrival in the United Provinces. In this context, it is also necessary to pay attention to the diplomatic negotiations carried out by the ambassadors and envoys of European Catholic princes in London in order to convince the British government to revoke or relax the latest acts that had been passed by the Irish parliament and sanctioned by Queen Anne. This analysis reveals that the Holy See hoped to introduce these complex matters into the peace negotiations to end the War of the Spanish Succession, which traditional historiography has considered eminently political in character.[6] A strategy was used to push the Irish petitions through without aggravating Protestant diplomats, in what was an openly *confessional* conflict, while a collection of Catholic *doléances* was produced to be disseminated throughout the continent.

Tolerance and persecution: the religious balance in Ireland

The Treaty of Limerick was signed on 3rd October, 1691. The treaty surrendered Limerick, the last city loyal to the deposed James II, to the king-stadholder, William III, and meant the end of the War of the Two Kings, or the Williamite War.[7] The first clause granted Catholics religious freedom, under the same conditions that had prevailed during Charles II's reign. These concessions provided Catholics with substantial advantages. The treaty initiated a new political era in Ireland: that of William III's tendency towards religious tolerance and free worship without prohibitions or obstacles.

The king's stance on tolerance, however, was not shared by Irish Protestants. A mere few months after the treaty, in 1692, the opposition crystallised in the context of the first parliament held in Ireland since the termination of the war. Measures ran contrary to the spirit of the treaty, as well as the intention of the Lord Lieutenant, Viscount Sidney, to expel the regular Catholic clergy. However, they did not prosper because of William III's decision.[8] Thus, Catholics were allowed to enjoy the privileges over the years that followed. The unease in the reformist camp meant that the concessions made by William of Orange to the 'papists' became a recurrent political issue, while the Catholics based their arguments on the clauses of the peace treaty. In 1694, the Irish civil authorities started taking measures against the practice of Catholicism, such as the closure of Franciscan chapels on the eve of St Patrick's Day.[9] Regarding the complaints, William III responded by disavowing his ministers and reiterating his commitment to the freedom of his Catholic subjects.[10] In contrast to the royal stance, and while the ratification of the Limerick capitulations was being negotiated, in 1695 the Dublin parliament resumed the debate concerning the expulsion of the friars, in the presence of the newly arrived Lord Deputy, Henry, 1st Baron Capell of Tewkesbury. Protestant rhetoric revolved around the threat posed by the friars to public peace.[11] Count Auersperg, the imperial ambassador to England, intervened and managed to stop these measures in the Privy Council.[12] Again, William III refused to bend to parliament and to endorse their punitive Penal Laws.[13]

During the negotiations that led to the end of the Nine Years' War in 1697, parliament resumed its project of expelling the friars from Ireland. The matter became one of the main diplomatic issues concerning Ireland. The political circumstances had changed. After the death of his Lord Deputy, William III agreed to revoke the first clause of the Treaty of Limerick.[14] This decision not only meant breaking his word to the Irish Catholics, but to his Habsburg allies, the Spanish king, Charles II, and the emperor, Leopold I.[15] In fact, the matter was frequently raised by Count Auersperg in his communications with the king-stadholder.

Reports from Dublin confirmed the firmness of the Protestants' position and their determination against the pope's servants. Among other measures, archbishops, bishops, and the regular clergy were to be banished before 30th April, 1698.[16] In the meantime, the facts were contraries to the good words given by the acting Secretary of State, William Blathwayt, who insisted that these measures were nothing new. During different conversations, Blathwayt offered guarantees to the imperial ambassador that the orders would not be carried out, and that the king would never endorse them. However, while the secretary was convincing Auersperg that the bill would have no effect on the regular clergy, the two Dublin Houses were sending the text to William III for his signature.[17] Under such conditions, neither diplomatic efforts were sufficient, nor the intervention of the Elector of Bavaria, general governor of the Spanish Low Countries, during William III's stay in Loo.[18] *An Act for Banishing All Papists Exercising Any Ecclesiastical Jurisdiction, and All Regulars of the Popish Clergy Out of This Kingdom* was approved five days after the signing of the Treaty of Rijswijk, on 25th September, 1697.[19]

The Catholics' main concern at this stage was how the measures would be enforced. The political conditions established by the end of the Nine Years' War were marked by a new factor: the estrangement of English–imperial relations. Count Auersperg was no longer seen as capable of mitigating the bill, let alone stopping it.[20] Thus, the strategy of Catholic ambassadors focused on abolishing the edict. Within this framework, Pope Innocent XII compelled Catholic princes to order their diplomats in London to persevere with that issue.[21] These demands seemed to have been successful, as William III introduced significant amendments to the edict shortly after its proclamation. In 1698, archbishops and bishops were made exempt from the order of banishment.[22] Despite the partial execution of the parliamentary resolution, the expulsion of friars involved a substantial diaspora to Spain and France.[23]

Furthermore, in 1698, new anti-Catholic measures were enacted in Ireland, when the Dublin parliament voted to bring in the feared Oath of Supremacy. Several friars travelled to Madrid and Vienna, seeking the mediation of the Habsburgs with the king-stadholder. However, their representatives in London and in Loo could not change the situation. The Penal Laws were a reality, and severely curtailed free worship, even if they did not directly forbid Catholic rites. The secular clergy, on the other hand, were not to be expelled from the British Isles, as the Lord Chancellor, John Methuen, pledged before Count Auersperg in a formal meeting.[24] In the opinion of William III and his favourite, Hans William Bentinck, 1st Earl of Portland, priests posed no threat to social peace, in contrast to friars who were targeted because they had disobeyed the kingdom's laws.[25]

Faced by William III's refusal to revoke the edicts, Innocent XII resorted to other mechanisms to protect the Catholics. Leaving European ambassadors with the task of keeping up diplomatic pressure, the pope circulated a brief among the Italian dioceses, prompting them to organise rogations and processions, granting plenary indulgences to participants, as well as making collections in favour of the 'persecuted' Irish. The amount collected would be added to a papal grant of 10,000 escudos and used to support the harassed Catholics.[26] This mobilisation had little political effect. During the final years of William III's reign, Ireland did not revert to the situation of religious balance established in 1691. The Treaty of Limerick remained as the shadow of a more tolerant past – it was a mere legal argument consistently ignored by the Dublin parliament.

The year 1700 witnessed the accession of Clement XI to the Holy See. While keeping an eye on the Irish question, the new pope focused on using the context created by the War of the Spanish Succession and the Great Northern War to push various confessional projects in Central Europe.[27] The Catholic counteroffensive targeted German Protestantism. Among other figures, Elector August of Saxony and the new King of Poland, as well as Duke Anton Ulrich of Brunswick-Wolfenbüttel, converted to Catholicism. Of further importance to this proselytising strategy of the *Missioni Septentrionali* was the establishment of small chapels and gathering spaces in German territories funded by Italian merchants and princes, local potentates, and Rome, through the *Congregatio de Propaganda Fide*.[28]

The Habsburg dynasty ended with the death of Charles II in 1700. The royal designation of Philip of Bourbon, Duke of Anjou and grandson of Louis XIV, as universal heir unleashed a conflict that was to have global consequences. The diplomatic relations between the European powers and Madrid were determined by the different governments' positions on the issue of succession: backing the French option or supporting the imperial candidate. Finally, William III took the side of Leopold I to defend the dynastic rights of Archduke Charles, second son of the emperor. As on previous occasions, the union of a Calvinist prince and a Catholic Habsburg was marked by pragmatism and political convenience. These alliances were to play a crucial role in the future management of the Irish question.

In March 1702, the sudden death of William III elevated his sister-in-law, Anne Stuart, to the English throne. The new queen maintained and reinforced the English alliance with the Empire and the United Provinces.

Her religious policy soon became clear: she endorsed a series of Penal Laws enacted by the Dublin parliament which aimed to prevent 'the growth of the popery.' These punitive economic measures caused dismay among Catholics, who were increasingly besieged by the restrictive legal framework. As in other times, the intervention of European ambassadors did not mitigate the impact of these measures, which made it harder for Catholics to access, buy, possess, and inherit land.[29]

In late June, an edict was passed forbidding the return of all priests and friars who had been educated on the continent, from 1st January, 1704, onwards.[30] This was followed by *An Act for registering the Popish Clergy*, enacted in March.[31] It ordered a registry of the Irish secular clergy to be initiated – including the name, address, age, parish, ordination date, and name of the ordinating prelate – as well as the payment of two £50 sureties as guarantee of their good behaviour. Unregistered priests were to be banished from the island by 20th July. The harshness of the measures did not stop there; another clause applied the 1697 Banishment Act to all unregistered clerics who were found in the country after 24th June, 1705.[32] Finally, Queen Anne offered £20 to all priests who wished to enter the service of the Church of Ireland. During the period marked by this act, 1,089 individuals were registered on the lists compiled by local magistrates, including Jesuits and several friars who, posing as priests, carried on with their pastoral mission surreptitiously.[33]

In the following years, the socio-economic pressure placed on the Catholic community increased. Various measures restricted even further the rights of Catholics to own land and carry out mercantile activities, leading to an ever-narrowing economic field.[34] As one Penal Law followed another, European ambassadors intensified their pleas to Queen Anne and her ministers. Their main argument was that these restrictive policies contravened the Treaty of Limerick.[35] Although existing measures were not revoked, this mediation at least contributed to halt the even harsher decrees being debated in the Irish parliament.[36]

In 1709, anti-Catholic legislation went one step further, and addressed the issue of the loyalty of Irish subjects to the British Crown and the queen. The Oaths of Supremacy and Allegiance were complemented by the addition of a new one – the Oath of Abjuration.[37] The parliament of Dublin had spent months working on a text by which the Irish could explicitly renounce their loyalty to James Stuart, the only male heir of the deposed James II. This public retraction was tantamount to apostatising, of abandoning a man who many believed to be the legitimate King of England, James III. By demanding this additional proof of loyalty, especially from the Irish, Queen Anne hoped to contain the growth of the Jacobite faction, and the possibility of armed action, which was looking increasingly likely based on the previous attempts of invasion.[38] This last oath placed the Catholics at a crossroads and forced them to assume an additional political obligation. The European chancelleries followed the discussions around this matter with keen interest. While the ambassadors tried to stop the oath's imposition, Rome stressed the importance of the mediation of the Catholic princes.

To Vienna: the *extraordinary* delegation of Fr Bonaventure

In April 1709, Clement XI decided to give Fr Bonaventure de Burgo credentials as his extraordinary representative. The pope's aim was to gain supporters for the Irish cause in both London and at the peace conference in The Hague, where the end of the War of the Spanish Succession was being discussed. His mission led the friar through different courts and republics in northern Italy and Central Europe. The pope's main target was Joseph I, as it was hoped that the mediation of the emperor could persuade his ally, Anne Stuart, to observe the all-but-cancelled treaties of Limerick. The papal commission reveals that the relationship between the Empire and the Holy See had improved, after the pope controversially recognised the Habsburg, Charles III, as the legitimate King of Spain in the winter of 1709; this issue had even led to an open conflict for the pontifical *legatio* in Romagna.[39]

The informal diplomatic formula adopted by the papacy dispensed with the need for direct negotiations. De Burgo had neither official title nor strict instructions. His mission was to unofficially find allies for what was regarded as a private matter of the pope. His function was to act as the personal agent of Clement XI, handling the pope's briefs in person. During his audiences, Fr Bonaventure was to explain the realities faced by Catholics in Ireland in more detail than was possible in the papal documents. The Franciscan's mission allowed the pope to raise the diplomatic profile of the Holy See and to make its presence known in the peace negotiations for the War of the Spanish Succession.

Indeed, this commission was entirely conditioned by the international context. The Bourbons' ability to resist the pressure posed by the Grand Alliance in The Hague was beginning to crumble. Louis XIV was no longer capable of keeping up with a war that threatened his borders on all sides, and he was forced to reconceive and negotiate with the allied powers. A very harsh winter had ruined the crops in France, leading to famine and popular revolts; and the maintenance of the large Bourbon armies in France and Spain was a heavy burden on the royal finances, which had already been weakened by a severe economic crisis. On the battlefields, the Habsburgs were winning, and they held a position of superiority both in Italy and Flanders, while also controlling important regions in the Iberian Peninsula and the Spanish Mediterranean islands, except for Sicily. Louis XIV realised that it was time to negotiate an armistice or lose everything. The conversations in The Hague established the conditions for a conference, the outcome of which was very uncertain, given the impossibility of accommodating everyone's demands. To begin with, Louis XIV rejected the 42 preliminary points submitted by the allied delegates: despite this disagreement, the king knew that he could not continue the fight for much longer. In order to confront the growing threat of the allied armies in the Low Countries, he withdrew all his troops from Spain and redeployed them to the French northern frontier.[40]

At this point, Fr Bonaventure left his residence in the college of Saint Isidore, in Rome, and set out on his diplomatic endeavour, dressed in his order's robes. The Curia was concerned that his age might be a problem for such a long mission; but despite Cardinal Imperiale's attempts to dissuade him, the Franciscan was determined to carry out the pope's commission and help his co-religionists.[41] With the Holy Roman Empire in sight, his first steps took him to Florence, where he arrived in late June. During his time in Tuscany, he lodged with the nuncio, Girolamo Mattei, who introduced him at the Grand Duke's palace.[42] During his audience with Cosimo III, Fr Bonaventure delivered Clement XI's brief and requested his help in Ireland.[43] Aside from committing to assist in whatever way necessary and to pass the orders to his legate, Jacopo Giraldi, in London, the Grand Duke also agreed to write to the Doge of Venice, the Franciscan's next stop, and to the Viennese court, to facilitate his task.[44]

On 18th July, Fr Bonaventure reached Venice, and was welcomed by Abbot Ottavio Gasparini, administrator of the nuncio's office. During their meeting, the papal representative presented the recommendation letters issued by the Secretary of State, Cardinal Fabrizio Paolucci. Given the importance of his mission, and in order to ensure maximum impact, the friar requested the help of Cardinal Priori and Monsignor De Monti, two highly regarded churchmen in the *Serenissima*.[45] Fr Bonaventure was officially received by the Senate on 24th July, when he handed the pontifical brief to Doge Giovanni II Cornaro. In the letter, Clement XI explained the state of the Irish Catholics, and this situation was later confirmed by the Roman agent in profuse detail. Aware of the city's religious disposition, the pope hoped to receive Venetian support for the cause, through the service of his ambassador in London, Francesco Cornaro.[46] The Franciscan envoy also submitted two memoranda, one an extended version of the other, with more details than could be conveyed in a personal interview.[47] Fortunately, one of the meetings was attended by the elected patriarch of Aquileia, Monsignor Gradenigo, who offered to intercede with the doge.[48] Gradenigo mediated with the procurator of St Mark's and other friends and relatives, who were asked to support the endeavours of the papal commissioner. During his time in the *Serenissima*, Fr Bonaventure acquired letters of recommendation for the three Venetian ambassadors in Vienna and for Sebastiano Foscarini, the plenipotentiary in The Hague.[49] Nearly a month after his arrival, his mission accomplished, the Franciscan left for Trent – one of the most prestigious ecclesiastical principalities in the Holy Roman Empire.[50]

While Fr Bonaventure's extraordinary commission was on its way, the Papacy was examining the formula proposed by the Dublin parliament for the Oath of Abjuration. In this instance, Rome declared it illicit and stated that Irish Catholics had no obligation to accept it.[51] This decision was accompanied by diplomatic manoeuvres, carried out through third parties, which aimed to stop the bill. In the meantime, the Franciscan had arrived in Innsbruck. Contrary to his expectations, during his visit to the archduke's palace he did not meet Franz Ludwig of Palatinate-Neuburg, Archbishop of Salzburg, Bishop of Trent, and Grand Master of the Teutonic Order. For this reason, he tried instead to curry favour with the city's governor, whose arrival was expected on 3rd September. The initial setback was compounded by fresh problems related to the impossibility of meeting the archbishop. Fr Bonaventure was also incapable of meeting the elector palatine, Johann Wilhelm, brother of the prelate. He managed to send them a letter enclosing the pontifical brief, an extensive memorandum with the details that he could not deliver in person, and finally a short letter begging them to order their legates in The Hague to support his cause.[52] In addition to these contacts, de Burgo was advised to also write to Eleonore-Magdalena of Palatinate-Neuburg. As empress dowager, and the mother of both Emperor Joseph I and of the Spanish king, Charles III, she had significant influence at the Viennese court, and, as mother-in-law of the reigning empress, Wilhelmine Amalia of Brunswick-Lüneburg, she could also recruit the help of the House of Hanover, which, although Protestant, might favour the pontifical cause.[53]

All the help Fr Bonaventure could muster was heartily welcomed, as the reports arriving from Ireland were far from encouraging. Religious pressure kept mounting, and parliament inched ever closer to passing their anti-Catholic edict. So far, diplomatic efforts seemed to be having little effect on this complex game, and no progress had been made despite the fact that the legislation already passed was in open violation of the 1691 treaties. The influence exercised by foreign representatives on Queen Anne was proving to be no match for her anti-Catholic ministers. In Rome, the Curia followed events with close attention, and the *Congregatio de Propaganda Fide* even considered spreading the idea that William III would not have approved of the new policies.[54] The cardinals praised the king-stadholder's religious practice, although they neglected to add that he had already broken the treaties in 1697 with the endorsement of the Banishment Act.[55] In spite of everything, the Roman legates persevered in their endeavour, and Clement XI continued pressing the Catholic princes to express, through their ambassadors, their disagreement with the queen's anti-Catholic measures.[56]

While the pontifical diplomatic campaign was in full swing, the Dublin parliament debated the legislation proposed by the Lord Lieutenant, Thomas, 1st Marquis of Wharton. After several sessions, the members of the House of Lords were not able to reach an agreement; therefore, there

was some hope that the decree would not be passed after all.[57] This became
the objective of all the foreign Catholic diplomats, who addressed constant
petitions to the Lord Treasurer, Sidney, 1st Earl Godolphin, and the
Secretaries of State, Charles Spencer, 3rd Count of Sunderland, and Lord
Boyle.[58] Count Gallas, imperial ambassador in London, played a very active
role in this matter and constantly exchanged letters with the British
ministers. First, he stressed that the 'strange persecution' that the Catholics
suffered in Ireland was at odds with the queen's known piety and the Treaty
of Limerick. In order to strengthen his arguments and justify his interest in
the matter, Count Gallas compared the situation of the Irish with that of the
Protestants in Silesia. His aim was to preserve the status quo in both
regions, and ultimately to improve the conditions of Catholics in Ireland. In
Silesia, Joseph I was trying to contain the spread of Protestantism
throughout his territories, but without attacking those who professed it
beforehand, as established in the Treaty of Altranstädt (1707).[59] On the
other hand, the imperial ambassador claimed that Irish Catholics ought to
be protected by previous agreements, but nonetheless they would be forced
to abjure their faith by the edicts.[60]

Sunderland and Boyle's answer justified their government's actions while
challenging the rhetoric of the diplomats. On the one hand, they doubted
that Gallas was well enough informed about the bill. In their opinion, the
decree was fully compatible with previous legislation and aimed to
safeguard social peace; that is, it was not true that the new policies
undermined the 1691 treaties. In fact, they claimed, the Irish Catholics
who kept their part of the deal were allowed to worship freely, as was the
case during the reign of Charles II.[61] On the other hand, the British
government did not agree that the situation in Silesia was in any way
comparable to that in Ireland, and thought that by creating this parallel
the ambassadors were doing little more than compromising Joseph I's
position.[62]

In his response, Gallas lamented his lack of success, especially since his
modus operandi had been inspired by that of the English ambassadors in
Vienna. In order to prove that his comparison between Silesia and Ireland
was a valid one, he demonstrated Queen Anne's far-from-impartial stance
on the matter. Indeed, her ministers had stressed the position of those
subjects who had stood against their natural lord, the emperor, and
resorted to foreign powers – the rebels in Silesia sought support from
Charles XII of Sweden, and the Hungarians from the Voivode of
Transylvania, George I Rákóczi – in order to put pressure on the
Habsburgs in matters concerning the sovereignty of their dominions.[63] At
the same time, Protestant pretensions revolved around the Treaty of
Altranstädt, in which Queen Anne and the States General had acted as
arbiters. The imperial ambassador, therefore, pointed out the extreme
loyalty shown by the Irish towards the English Crown; they had neither
rebelled nor entered the service of the pretender, James III, during his

Scottish incursions. Last but not least, Count Gallas reasoned that the Treaty of Limerick had been negotiated by William III, without his ally Leopold I having to step in as guarantor.[64]

It seemed, at any rate, unlikely that the demands and arguments put forward by Count Gallas would succeed in delaying the enactment of the Oath of Abjuration. In the meantime, other laws were being passed with the support of the powerful Presbyterian lobby.[65] Despite everything, all the possibilities for an agreement were explored, although it was soon made clear that the efforts of the Catholic diplomats and appeals to the 1691 treaties were in vain. The bill was eventually passed on 10th September, 1709, after which it was, not without difficulty, endorsed by the British monarchy.[66] The English government, embodied by the Queen's Council, ordered the act to be passed without modifications, and rejected all forms of external interference.[67] Among other dispositions, it was ordered that the possessions of Catholic parents, whose children converted to Protestantism, were to be confiscated; the teaching of Catholic children was forbidden; rewards were offered to those who informed on priests and other members of the Catholic hierarchy caught saying Mass or participating in any other of the Sacraments. The deadline for taking the Oath of Abjuration was established as 1st November, thereby forfeiting loyalty to the pretender, James III.[68] Given the dire prospects and the fact that little room for manoeuvre was left for the ambassadors, the only thing was to encourage moderation in the application of the decree, which came into force on 20th September.[69]

When Fr Bonaventure arrived in Vienna, in late November, he was informed of the latest events in Ireland. He was carrying letters of introduction to the dowager and reigning empresses.[70] Although the Franciscan was aware of the advantages of having such patronesses, he confessed to being ashamed of being a burden to them. However, the success of his mission, which to a large extent depended on the variety of his contacts, did not sit well with his conscience. One of his first intermediaries was the Bishop of Vienna, whose complaints about some ministers, who were Christian 'in name alone,' left him somewhat perplexed. As the Franciscan integrated himself into the life of the capital, he had the opportunity to see for himself that the bishop's complaints were not altogether unjustified, as he encountered the religious shortcomings of some of the high officials and prominent members of the court. However, the Cardinal of Saxe-Zeitz and the bishop assured de Burgo that his transactions would be successful, especially because he enjoyed the protection of the empresses.[71]

During his first audience with Joseph I, Fr Bonaventure handed him the papal brief and explained the situation in detail, expressing the desirability of entreating Queen Anne to respect the clauses of the Treaty of Limerick.[72] After the allied victory in Malplaquet, the emperor was immersed in the conquest of the Low Countries for his brother, Charles III of Spain. For this reason, and because he still erred on the side of caution in his dealings with the Holy See, Joseph I expressed but a limited interest in the Irish issue.[73] His priority was to maintain the good will of his allies in Flanders, where the Duke of Marlborough, commander of the British troops, and Prince Eugene, as the head of the imperial army, acted in close cooperation.[74]

The meagre success achieved by his diplomatic endeavours led Fr Bonaventure to send a second memorandum to the emperor. Promises and good words needed to be backed by an actual commitment to the Irish cause. In addition to pointing out the emperor's moral and political duty, he stressed Count Gallas' lack of success in the matter. The intervention of the British members of parliament had frustrated all attempts to stop the bill and had finally resulted in the queen's endorsement of it. As the Franciscan pointed out in his memorandum, the measure had led some Irish Catholics to abjure their faith and some others to hesitate, while others feared that, should they keep their faith, they would end up as beggars.

These adverse circumstances prompted the European ambassadors to persist in their demands and try to mitigate the effects of the new laws. The most direct way to achieve this was for Joseph I to write to Anne Stuart and request the revocation of the 'popery bill.' The Irish issue was a burden to the common cause of the allies, as the Catholic princes were unhappy about the harshness of the measures put forward by Dublin.[75] In fact, it was recommended that these ideas be shared with the Duke of Marlborough, so that he could help convince the queen and others of his contacts at court to bring about greater moderation in the enforcement of the measures.[76]

In addition, Fr Bonaventure also presented the emperor with a politically powerful argument within the framework of the friendship of the British and the Habsburgs: in 1689, the Stadholder of Holland, William of Orange, had assured Leopold I that he would respect the Catholic faith, especially in Ireland, before he set out to 'liberate' those realms from Jacobite domination.[77] William's commitment and the formal agreement reached with the Irish Catholics in 1691 had to be regarded as a solemn pledge, especially considering that the agreements of Limerick had the tacit support of the emperor. Furthermore, the Irish had agreed to take the Oath of Allegiance, showing remarkable devotion despite the 'Egyptian tyranny' that was being imposed upon them.[78] This loyalty also extended to both branches of the Habsburgs. In different situations, the Irish had provided valuable military services to both the Spanish kings and the emperors.

In his attempts to bring Joseph I over to his cause, Fr Bonaventure did not hesitate to use providential arguments. Presenting the emperor with an image of God as the only foundation of royal power, the Franciscan identified him as the restorer of Catholicism, in which role he would be rewarded by victory in the dynastic conflict and with a male heir for the imperial throne.[79]

On this occasion, Joseph I paid attention to Fr Bonaventure's petition. In late October, the allied forces successfully concluded the Siege of Mons, putting the Low Countries almost entirely under their control. The French troops were exhausted, and willing to consent to negotiate once more.[80] With the war nearly won, the emperor reiterated his previous instructions to Count Gallas. He explained that the pope had sent a special envoy, Fr Bonaventure, who expressed the Holy See's concern at the actions of the Dublin parliament. For this reason, Joseph I entreated his ambassador to convince Queen Anne and her ministers about the advantages of abiding by the 1691 agreements. Given the Lord Lieutenant Wharton's declared anti-Catholic plans, diplomatic action had to be fast and relentless.[81]

In December 1709, the legate *a latere* in Vienna, Cardinal Annibale Albani, passed on a new pontifical brief to Fr Bonaventure.[82] Clement XI regarded the behaviour of the Catholic powers in the dynastic dispute as just and 'holy,' for the transfer of cities and territories was having no religious consequences. During his time in Vienna, and after being received several times by Joseph I, de Burgo's petitions were passed to the *Geheime Konferenz*, the council responsible for imperial foreign policy, to be dealt with. As was the case in his previous destinations, the Irish envoy tried to find supporters to assist him. The Chancellor, Baron Sailern, lent him his full support, in the face of opposition from other court officials. Owing to his position, Sailern was probably the busiest of all imperial ministers, although the friar stressed that their meetings always lasted as long as was required to reach a positive conclusion.[83]

The outcome of these conversations fulfilled the pope's expectations. Joseph I and his ministers were convinced of the need to promptly assist the Irish Catholics. The emperor ordered his ambassador in London and his plenipotentiaries in The Hague to broach the issue in their respective arenas.[84] Count Wratislaw, Chancellor of the Kingdom of Bohemia, also expressed his support; his knowledge of the situation of Catholics in the British Isles was accurate, because he had acted as imperial diplomat in London earlier in the century, as successor of Count Auersperg, and was on good terms with the influential Duke of Marlborough. The first anti-Catholic laws had been passed in Dublin during his time in office, and he had a very firm opinion on the matter. However, Fr Bonaventure was not sure whether the participation of Wratislaw would do more harm than good.[85]

At the same time, the Franciscan harboured no doubts regarding Count Hamilton, a former Jacobite, who was confessor and intimate confidante of the emperor and a prominent member of Empress Eleonore-Magdalena's private circle. Hamilton, who was of English–Scottish descent, entreated everyone at court, especially his relatives, to help the pontifical envoy. Hamilton 'acted out of piety, natural genius and out of their common roots, as they both had connections with the main families in Ireland.'[86] It was also expected that Prince Eugene of Savoy would lend a hand; a brief addressed to him begged for his cooperation in the Low Countries, where he could use his close friendship with Marlborough and other British ministers to some effect.

His mission in Vienna accomplished, Fr Bonaventure set out for the peace conference at The Hague. On the way to the United Provinces, he stopped for some time in Prague, from where, in early 1710, he wrote to the imperial court asking for instructions. Recent reports had stressed 'the anguish of the Irish faithful.'[87] After the presentation of the Oath of Abjuration in Dublin by the Lord Lieutenant, Thomas, 1st Marquis of Wharton, some members of the gentry refused to take it. Several nobles had already been taken into custody, and others lived under threat of arrest. Most churchmen, whose deadline was on 25th March, also rejected the oath. Some members of the secular clergy, on the other hand, took it without much ado, in stark contrast to those who preferred exile or clandestine preaching in mountain areas.[88] In these circumstances, pleading to London through diplomatic means was a wasted effort, especially given the irreconcilable position that divided the British government.

While waiting for a reply from Vienna, Fr Bonaventure was not idle. He contacted Count Kolowrat and Count Martinitz, who had offered to issue letters of recommendation.[89] The latter maintained a fluid and frank correspondence with Joseph I and did not hesitate to give advice on different matters.[90] The news from Ireland was hardly more encouraging than had been the case in previous weeks. The return of Wharton with even stricter instructions demanded that imperial diplomatic pressure be stepped up a couple of notches.[91] In the meantime, de Burgo received the brief addressed to Prince Eugene, along with another six letters for the prince-electors, several German bishops, and King Augustus II of Poland, who, after an interview in Dresden, sent instructions to his ambassador in London to rally behind the cause of the Irish Catholics.[92]

The Franciscan's discreet mission succeeded in recruiting new allies. Few European powers were indifferent to the importance of the issue at stake. Nobody could say for certain what was going to happen after the deadline on 25th March. The oath was rejected by most churchmen and nobles. The appeals of foreign ambassadors were rebuked by Queen Anne, who demanded that diplomats restrict themselves to political issues, and not meddle in British religious and domestic matters. The anti-Catholic legislation, therefore, looked more irreversible than ever. As pointed out by Ambrose O'Connor, an ex-provincial of the Dominican Order, who was in London at the time, the only hope rested with the peace conference to be held in the Dutch village of Geertruidenberg. For this reason, Fr O'Connor compelled Clement XI to ask the main Catholic princes to instruct their plenipotentiaries at the congress to defend orthodoxy and fight the 'sophistries' and 'fallacies' of the Reformed doctrine supported by Great Britain and the United Provinces.[93] Fr Bonaventure did likewise, broaching the issue directly with the ministers in The Hague.[94]

Stop, wait, and then negotiate: the peace conference of Geertruidenberg and the Irish affair

It was Louis XIV's refusal to accept the preliminary conditions set out in The Hague which led to the conference in Geertruidenberg.[95] The negotiations began on 3rd January, 1710, chaired by Jean-Baptiste Colbert, Marquis de Torcy, the French foreign minister, who asked the allies whether Philip V was to receive any Mediterranean dominions – Naples, Sicily, Sardinia, or the Tuscan fortresses – in compensation, should he renounce his claim to the Spanish Crown in favour of Charles III, and leave Madrid.[96] As had been the case in 1709, fundamental disagreements soon emerged. The main issues of contention were articles 4 and 37, already mentioned in the preamble of The Hague talks.[97] In that case, despite his desperate need for peace, and aggravated by another bad winter, the Sun King refused to force his grandson to give up the Spanish Crown and abandon the court.[98]

When the negotiations concerning the great geopolitical issues ground to a halt, Rome appealed to the Catholic princes about the Irish question, who were begged to keep up diplomatic pressure.[99] From Vienna, the nuncio, Giulio Piazza, reported that Count Gallas was aware of his duty to his fellow Catholics, and would continue defending their cause, especially since the arrival of the new orders.[100] The envoy from Savoy, Count Annibale Maffei, also obeyed the pope's entreaty, especially after being instructed by his sovereign to broach the matter with the British ministers and his friend, the Lord Lieutenant.[101] However, even Maffei's diplomatic clout failed to abolish strict anti-Catholic legislation.[102] For his part, the Tuscan envoy, Jacopo Giraldi, also undertook to fulfil Clement XI's instructions, although he was sure that any attempt to convince Wharton to back away from the subject of the Oath of Abjuration was doomed to failure. The only hope was for someone else to take Wharton's position as Lord Lieutenant.[103] Indeed, there were rumours that such a change could be imminent, while some reports suggested that the enforcement of the anti-Catholic measures had lost some of their initial sting.[104]

During the peace talks and after his return to Dublin, Wharton appeared to have embraced a more moderate position. Fr O'Connor and the Bishop of Clogher, Hugh MacMahon, associated this with the mediation of the European ambassadors and the impact of a new political stance in England.[105] The general election of October/November 1710 had returned a Tory majority in the House of Commons and thus weakened the position of the Whigs. In Ireland, the appointment of a new Lord Lieutenant, James Butler, 2nd Duke of Ormond, did not become effective until October 1710. Under these conditions, the negotiations of Geertruidenberg became a turning point for the Irish question.

News of the arrival of Fr Bonaventure in the United Provinces was ill received by Abbot Domenico Passionei. The unofficial pontifical legate, first in The Hague and later in the Castle of Geertruidenberg, informed Cardinal Paolucci of his misgivings.[106] He complained of not having been consulted about whether he wanted the Franciscan there or not, and also that de Burgo was using the letters addressed by the pontifical Secretary of State to the Catholic plenipotentiaries. Although not fully informed of all the details, Passionei argued against the papal representative interacting with the plenipotentiaries, with whom he was already in close contact.[107] Based on his experience, the abbot thought that the presence of the Franciscan in the United Provinces was undesirable – he asked him to stay away from Antwerp and Brussels, which were under the control of Charles III – as was the use of his diplomatic credentials. He believed that any hasty move by the Catholic powers to influence events in Ireland could antagonise both the English and the Dutch, thereby undermining their alliance with the Empire. While the continuation of the war remained a possibility, Vienna was politically obliged to keep her alliance with Great Britain. However, Passionei's conversations with Count Sinzendorf, imperial ambassador to the States General, confirmed the need not to do anything until the negotiations had officially begun. Although de Burgo had always acted with prudence and discretion, Passionei wanted to keep a close eye on him, to make sure that the Irish matter was put on the table at the right moment. The plan was to broach the subject during the debates on the abolition of article 4 of the Treaty of Rijswick, according to which Catholicism was to be preserved in conquered territories returned to the allies by Louis XIV; that is, the religious situation should not be meddled with, apart from compensating for the damage caused by changes to the legal framework.[108] It was then, and not before, that the abbot was thinking of getting the Catholic plenipotentiaries to meet the Franciscan in The Hague. Any action taken before the negotiations had officially begun would be useless: the agent would gain nothing but empty promises and vague plans.[109] Any false move to excessively highlight the Irish question would undermine the pope's general interest and mediating position, by overexposing what was merely regarded as a private matter.

With the arrival of summer, Fr Bonaventure followed Passionei's orders and stayed well clear of The Hague, waiting for instructions in Cologne.[110] Betraying some confusion, the friar asked Cardinal Paolucci for advice on how to act in the framework of the conference. He did not know whether to head to the conference and approach the legates or to abstain from doing so. If he had to wait, he needed to know whether to hand Prince Eugene the pontifical brief, so the prince could begin the negotiations in full knowledge of its contents. Should the negotiations continue at the beginning of winter, as predicted, he needed to know whether to stay put or to return to Prague, after a short visit to Münster, where the elector bishop, Franz Arnold von Wolff-Metternich, was ready to receive him. Initially, he waited for the answers in the Franciscan convent of Düsseldorf, and later in Brussels.[111]

Passionei proceeded to probe the Catholic ministers without disclosing the presence of Fr Bonaventure or his mission. Confidentially, he discussed the contravention of the Treaty of Limerick with the envoy of Charles III, Baron Franz Adolf von Zinzerling, and with Prince Eugene, in order to evaluate different possibilities and to decide how to broach the issue during the sessions. It was crucial to present a united front and to avoid rash measures; Passionei proposed that by demonstrating that the Irish edicts were contrary to the treaties, the summoning of de Burgo from Brussels would be justified. A meeting with the Catholic legates could then be organised and Paolucci's letters distributed.[112] This action would also highlight the position of the Church in a conference to which it had not been officially invited.

In the event, these cautionary measures were not necessary: the plenipotentiaries, following the instructions of their governments, presented anything but a united front, as each tried to squeeze as much as possible out of the negotiations. Not even Louis XIV's incredible offer – an annual subsidy to the allies for fighting the Bourbon candidate to the Spanish Crown, his grandson Philip V – managed to unite the allies.[113] Furthermore, widespread mistrust and the excessive ambition of the English and the Dutch undermined negotiations. The conference seemed doomed to failure owing to the participants' lack of flexibility.[114] In the meantime, the situation improved for the Irish Catholics in autumn 1710, with the replacement of Wharton, the 'cruel persecutor,' by the Duke of Ormond, an experienced Irish Tory of a peaceful temperament.[115] Despite being a Protestant, it was hoped that he would not molest Catholics, and that he would adopt a policy inspired by the 1703 edict.[116]

Conclusions

The peace conference did not lead to any resolution favourable to the Catholic cause, as no major political changes ensued from the proceedings. The question was left for the following meeting of the peace conference. At the end of the sessions, Fr Bonaventure de Burgo admitted the failure of his mission. At that point, he did not know whether to remain in the United Provinces or to follow 'the sweet company of my friends in Bohemia.'[117] Finally, his itinerary took him through different cities in the Palatinate, Westphalia, and several territories belonging to the King of Prussia, Frederick I. He was magnificently welcomed by the Bishop and Elector of Münster, who appointed him the champion of the Irish cause – after asking the pope for permission – by sending letters to Queen Anne and Prince Eugene in defence of the Catholic Irish. Although his mission had already come to an end, the Franciscan was still enlisting supporters for his countrymen.

In the spring of 1711, the nuncio in Cologne, Giovanni Battista Bussi, gave Fr Bonaventure some money, so he could continue with his diplomatic efforts, although it was clear that they were to be as unsuccessful as the peace conference had been. The pontifical agent lingered in the Low Countries, hoping that the war would soon force the contenders to the negotiating table once again. While lodging in the convent of his order in Düsseldorf, the friar started to plan his return to Rome.[118] However, as the year drew to a close, the appointment of Charles III of Spain as emperor – as Charles VI – made him hope for the support of the new Habsburg sovereign, and thus for a better chance of success. By then, however, rumours were circulating about the imminence of a new peace conference – on this occasion in the Dutch city of Utrecht.[119]

In the new round of negotiations, however, the advocate of the Irish cause would no longer be de Burgo. The role of informally representing the Holy See fell to Domenico Passionei. Following strictly pragmatic lines, and unlike the Franciscan, the abbot was a known factor in European diplomatic circles, and he was able to use his connections among the plenipotentiaries to negotiate more efficiently. The outcome of Fr Bonaventure's mission was not officially censured, and no evidence exists that he was recalled. It is even possible that his disappearance from the diplomatic scene was caused by his death. His mission from the Holy See to the heads of Europe, framed as it was by the frustrated peace negotiations of 1710, came to the same inconclusive end as the peace negotiations themselves.

Notes

1 This study has been undertaken within the framework of the programme Tomás y Valiente (Universidad Autónoma de Madrid-Madrid Institute for Advanced Study) and the project funded by the Dirección General de Investigación del Ministerio de Economía y Competitividad 'Sociedad cortesana y redes diplomáticas: la proyección europea de la monarquía de España (1659–1725)' (HAR2015-67069-P MINECO/FEDER UE). I wish to thank David Govantes-Edwards for the translation.

2 Brendan Jennings, ed., *Louvain Papers, 1606–1827* (Dublin: Stationery Office for the Irish Manuscripts Commission, 1968), 285, fn. 1.

3 Giovanni Antonio da Palermo, *Scrutinium doctrinarum* (Rome: Rochi Bernabo, 1709).

4 Louis Jadin, ed., *Relations des Pays-Bas, de Liège et de Franche-Comté avec le Saint-Siège d'après les 'Lettere di vescovi' conservées aux Archives Vaticanes (1566–1779)* (Brussels: Institut historique belge de Rome, 1952), 273.

5 The Bishop of Elphin, Dominick Burgo, informed Clement XI about the anti-Catholic measures. At the same time, he nominated Fr Bonaventure as the best person to report the consequences of the bill. Dominick Burgo to Clement XI, Louvain, 4th December, 1700. Cf. Ibid.

6 Antonio Álvarez-Ossorio, Bernardo J. García García y Virginia León Sanz, eds., *La pérdida de Europa: La guerra de sucesión por la monarquía de España* (Madrid: Fundación Carlos de Amberes, 2007); Joaquim Albareda, *La Guerra de Sucesión de España (1700–1714)* (Barcelona: Crítica, 2010); David Martín Marcos, *El Papado y la Guerra de Sucesión española* (Madrid: Marcial Pons, 2011); Roberto Quirós Rosado, *Monarquía de Oriente: La*

corte de Carlos III y el gobierno de Italia durante la Guerra de Sucesión española (Madrid: Marcial Pons Historia, 2017).

 7 Wout Troost, *William III and the Treaty of Limerick, 1691–1697: A Study of His Irish Policy* (Unpublished PhD thesis. Leiden: University of Leiden, 1983); id., *William III, the Stadholder-King: A Political Biography* (Aldershot: Ashgate, 2005), 281–83; id., 'Ireland's Role in the Foreign Policy of William III,' in *Redefining William III: The Impact of the King-Stadholder in International Context*, ed. Esther Mijers and David Onnekink (Aldershot: Ashgate, 2007), 53–68.

 8 Troost, *William III, the Stadholder-King*, 285, 289.

 9 Memorial by the Franciscan father Bernard Gavan. S. l., n. d., September 1694, Archivo General de Simancas (hereafter AGS), Estado, leg. 3969.

10 Copy of a memorial of the Marquis of Canales to William III, London, 9th May, 1695, AGS, Estado, leg. 3970. Charles Irvan McGrath, 'Securing the Protestant Interest: The Origins and Purpose of the Penal Laws of 1695,' *Irish Historical Studies*, 30 (1996), 25–46.

11 John G. Simms, 'The Establishment of Protestant Ascendancy, 1691–1714,' in *A New History of Ireland. Vol. IV: Eighteenth-Century Ireland, 1691–1800*, ed. Theodore W. Moody and William E. Vaughan (Oxford: Oxford University Press, 2009), 16.

12 On the active diplomacy developed by Count Auersperg in London to defend the Catholic interest both in Ireland and England, see Cristina Bravo Lozano, '¿La última colaboración dinástica? La diplomacia hispano-imperial ante la política confesional de Guillermo III de Inglaterra (1696–1700),' in *Les Habsbourg en Europe: Circulations, échanges et regards croisés*, ed. Alexandra Merle and Éric Leroy du Cardonnoy (Reims: Editions et Presses Universitaires de Reims, 2018), 161–80.

13 Sean J. Connolly, 'The Penal Laws,' in *Kings in Conflict: The Revolutionary War in Ireland and Its Aftermath, 1689–1750*, ed. William A. Maguire (Belfast: The Blackstaff Press, 1990), 161; Craig Rose, *England in the 1690s: Revolution, Religion and War* (Oxford: Blackwell, 1999), 226.

14 Troost, *William III, the Stadholder-King*, 290.

15 Jonathan I. Israel, 'William III and Toleration,' in *From Persecution to Toleration: The Glorious Revolution and Religion in England*, ed. Ole P. Grell, Jonathan I. Israel and Nicholas Tyacke (Oxford: Clarendon Press Oxford, 2010), 139–42.

16 John G. Simms, 'The Bishops' Banishment Act of 1697 (9 Will. III, c. 1),' *Irish Historical Studies*, 17/66 (1970): 185–99; Cristina Bravo Lozano, *Spain and the Irish Mission, 1609–1707* (New York: Routledge, 2019).

17 Copy of the letter from William Blathwayt to Count Auersperg, Loo, 16th September, 1697, Archivio Storico di Propaganda Fide (hereafter ASPF), Scritture riferiti nei Congressi, Belgio ed Olanda, 6, 87r.

18 The Marquis of Canales to Charles II, London, 3rd December, 1697, AGS, Estado, leg. 3090; Secretary of the Pontifical State to Orazio Spada, Rome, 23rd November, 1697, Archivio Segreto Vaticano, Segreteria di Stato (hereafter ASV, Segr. di Stato). Fiandra, 148, 370v–71r.

19 William III, *An Act for Banishing All Papists Exercising Any Ecclesiastical Jurisdiction, and All Regulars of the Popish Clergy Out of This Kingdom* (Dublin: Andrew Crook, 1697). The Treaty of Rijswick ended the Nine Years' War (1689–1697) between France and the Grand Alliance.

20 Troost, *William III, the Stadholder-King*, 292.

21 Secretary of the Pontifical State to Giuseppe Archinto, Rome, 29th June, 1698, ASV, Segr. di Stato. Spagna, 358, 465r–66r.

22 Daniele Dolfin to Cardinal Fabrizio Spada, Paris, 2nd June, 1698, ASV, Segr. di Stato. Francia, 195, 682r–v.
23 On the Irish friars' arrival and the Spanish answer to this migratory movement, see Bravo Lozano, *Spain and the Irish Mission*, 189–200.
24 Andrea Santa Croce to Cardinal Fabrizio Spada, Vienna, 7th June, 1698, ASV, Segr. di Stato. Germania, 235, 457r–58v. Connolly, 'The Penal Laws,' 161; Rose, *England in the 1690s*, 226.
25 Francisco Bernardo de Quirós to Charles II, Brussels, 14th November, 1698, AGS, Estado, leg. 3971.
26 Decrees of the particular meeting of the Congregatio de Propaganda Fide, Rome, 5th May and 27th November, 1698, ASV, Fondo Carpegna, 55, 16r–19r.
27 Martín Marcos, *El Papado;* and Stefano Tabacchi, 'L'impossibile neutralità: Il Papato, Roma e lo Stato della Chiesa durante la Guerra di Successione Spagnola,' *Cheiron*, 39–40 (2004), 223–43.
28 Roberto Quirós Rosado, 'Diplomacia y misión en Europa durante la Guerra de Sucesión: los Habsburgo-Wolfenbüttel, el estado de Milán y el catolicismo septentrional,' *Cuadernos de Historia Moderna*, 41/1 (2016) 29–47.
29 Simms, 'The Establishment,' 19.
30 The Duke of Ormond and the Council of Ireland to the Earl of Nottingham, Dublin, 26th June 1703, The National Archives: Public Record Office (hereafter TNA), State Papers, 63/363, 410r.
31 Simms, 'The Establishment,' 18.
32 Tomas O Fiaich, 'The Registration of the Clergy in 1704,' *Seanchas Ard Mhacha*, 6 (1971), 46–69.
33 Sean J. Connolly, *Religion, Law, and Power: The Making of Protestant Ireland, 1660–1760* (Oxford: Clarendon Press, 2002), 66, 150, 274.
34 Simms, 'The Establishment,' 20.
35 Cardinal Fabrizio Paolucci to Abbot Santini, Rome, 17th April, 1706, ASV, Segr. di Stato. Germania, 44, 599r.
36 Francesco Cornaro to Cardinal Fabrizio Paolucci, London, 16th March, 1708, ASV, Segr. di Stato. Particolari, 101, 337r.
37 Connolly, *Religion, Law and Power*, 276.
38 John S. Gibson, *Playing the Scottish Card: The Franco-Jacobite Invasion of 1708* (Edinburgh: Edinburgh University Press, 1988).
39 Quirós Rosado, *Monarquía de Oriente.*
40 Albareda, *La Guerra de Sucesión*, 278–82.
41 Secretary of the *Congregatio de Propaganda Fide* to Cardinal Paolucci, Rome, 24th April, 1709, ASPF, Scritture riferitti nei Congressi. Lettere, 98, 256r.
42 Bonaventure de Burgo to Cardinal Sacripante, Venice, 3rd August, 1709, ASPF, Scritture riferitti nei Congressi. Irlanda, 7.
43 Copy of the brief from Clement XI to Cosimo III, Rome, n. d., April 1709, ASPF, Scritture riferiti nei Congressi. Irlanda, 7, 62r–v. *Clementis Undecimi Pontificis Maximi Epistolae, Et Brevia Selectiora* (Rome: s. i., 1729), 605–8.
44 Bonaventure de Burgo to Cardinal Sacripante, Florence, 30th June, 1709, ASPF, Scritture riferiti nei Congressi. Irlanda, 7, 69r–v. Clement XI ordered the papal nuncio in Florence, Girolamo Mattei, to thank Cosimo III for the courtesy and help given to Fr Bonaventure. Secretary of the *Congregatio de Propaganda Fide* to Girolamo Mattei, Rome, 31st August, 1709, ASPF, Scritture riferiti nei Congressi. Lettere, 98, 126v.
45 Ottavio Gasparini to Cardinal Paolucci, Venecia, 20th July, 1709, ASV, Segr. di Stato. Venezia, 158, 388r.

46 Copy of the brief from Clement XI to the Doge and Senato of Venice, Rome, n. d., April 1709, ASPF, Scritture riferiti nei Congressi. Irlanda, 7, 63r–v.

47 Bonaventure de Burgo to Cardinal Sacripante, Venice, 3rd August, 1709, ASPF, Scritture riferiti nei Congressi. Irlanda, 7, 71r–v. Alphons Bellesheim, *Geschichte der katholischen Kirche in Irland von 1690 bis 1890* (Mainz: Franz Kirchheim, 1891), vol. 3, 60.

48 Bonaventure de Burgo to Cardinal Paolucci, Venice, 20th July 1709, ASV, Segr. di Stato. Particolari, 104, 184r–v. On the same day de Burgo left for Vienna, Nuncio Gasparini admitted that his own 'shortcomings' had been compensated by the assistance and mediation of Patriarch Gradenigo. Oraccio Gasparini to Cardinal Sacripanti, Venice, 17th August, 1709, ASPF, Scritture riferiti nei Congressi. Irlanda, 7, 79r. Rome extended thanks to both Gasparini and Gradenigo. Secretary of the *Congregatio de Propaganda Fide* to Abbot Gasparini and Patriarch Gradenigo, respectively, Rome, 19th August, 1709, ASPF, Scritture riferiti nei Congressi. Lettere, 98, 124rv and 124v–25r. A month later, the Patriarch of Aquileia praised de Burgo's work in Venice and wished him success in alleviating the predicament of Irish Catholics. Patriarch Gradenigo to Cardinal Sacripante, Venice, 7th September, 1709, ASPF, Scritture riferiti nei Congressi. Irlanda, 7, 83r.

49 The letter addressed to the ambassadors was sent on 10th August. The letter compelled the diplomats to do everything in their power to prompt Joseph I to embrace the cause of the Irish Catholics. Lorenzo Tiepolo to the Doge and the Senato of Venice, Simmering, 28th September, 1709, Österreichisches Staatsarchiv Vienna, Haus-, Hof- und Staatsarchiv, Staatenabteilungen (hereafter OeStA, HHStA, StA) Italienische Staaten Venedig, Dispacci di Germania, 194, 11.

50 Bonaventure de Burgo to Cardinal Paolucci, Venecia, 17th August, 1709, ASV, Segr. di Stato. Particolari, 104, 273r.

51 Memorial of Cardinal Paolucci, Rome, 3rd August, 1709, ASPF, Scritture riferiti nei Congressi. Lettere, 98, 293v–94r; Simms, 'The Establishment,' 18.

52 Copy of the brief from Clement XI to the Grand Master of the Teutonic Order, Rome, n. d., April 1709, ASPF, Scritture riferiti nei Congressi. Irlanda, 7, 61r–v.

53 Bonaventure de Burgo to Cardinal Paolucci, Innsbruck, 1st September, 1709, ASV, Segr. di Stato. Particolari, 104, 311r–v.

54 Secretary of the *Congregatio de Propaganda Fide* to Cardinal Paolucci, Rome, 6th September, 1709, ASPF, Scritture riferiti nei Congressi. Irlanda, 7, 310v–11r.

55 Onno Klopp, *Der Fall des Hauses Stuart und die Succession des Hauses Hannover in Groß-Britannien und Irland* (Vienna: Wilhem Braumüller, 1887), vol. 13, 263.

56 Secretary of the *Congregatio de Propaganda Fide* to Girolamo Grimaldi, Rome, 6th September, 1709, ASPF, Scritture riferiti nei Congressi. Lettere 98, 311–12v.

57 Girolamo Grimaldi to Cardinal Paolucci, Brussels, 26th September, 1709, ASPF, Scritture riferiti nei Congressi. Irlanda, 7, 102r; Secretary of the *Congregatio de Propaganda Fide* to Cardinal Paolucci, Rome, 5th October, 1709, ASPF, Scritture riferiti nei Congressi. Lettere, 98, 335v.

58 Girolamo Grimaldi to Cardinal Paolucci, Brussels, 26th September, 1709, ASPF, Scritture riferiti nei Congressi. Irlanda, 7, 102r.

59 Count Wratislaw, the imperial legate to Altranstädt, played a crucial role in the agreement that put an end to the diplomatic conflict between Charles XII of Sweden and Joseph I. Adam Wandruszka, 'El mundo político en el siglo XVIII,'

in *Historia Universal*, ed. Golo Mann and Alfred Heuss (Madrid: Espasa-Calpe, 1988), vol. 7, II, 459–60. In February 1709, Baron Stralenheim attested that all the clauses that referred to the freedom of worship in Silesia had been honoured. Declaration of the Baron of Stralenheim, Breslau, 8th February, 1709. Cf. Guillaume de Lamberty, *Memóires pour servir à l'histoire du XVIII siècle* (The Hague: Henry Scheurleer, 1727), vol. 5, 386.

60 Copy of the letter from Count Gallas to the Count of Godolphin, the Count of Sunderland and Milord Boyle, London, 17th July, 1709, ASPF, Scritture riferiti nei Congressi. Irlanda, 7, 136r–137v; Klopp, *Der Fall des Hauses*, 263–64. The same analogy was raised by Rákóczi in 1711, during the Hungarian rebellion. Richard Bonney, '"God, Fatherland and Freedom": Rethinking Pluralism in Hungary in the Era of Partition and Rebellion, 1526–1711,' in *Persecution and Pluralism: Calvinists and Religious Minorities in Early Modern Europe, 1550–1700*, ed. Richard Bonney and David J.B. Trim (Bern: Peter Lang, 2006), 90.

61 Klopp, *Der Fall des Hauses*, 264–65; Elke Jarnut-Derbolav, *Die Österreichische Gesandtschaft in London (1701–1711)* (Bonn: Ludwig Röhrscheid Verlag, 1972), 268.

62 Copy of the letter of the Count of Sunderland and Milord Boyle to Count Gallas, Whitehall, 22nd July, 1709, ASPF, Scritture riferiti nei Congressi. Irlanda, 7, 137v–138v.

63 In the context of the Hungarian rebellion, Joseph I had to endure the Maritime Powers' persistent sympathy for the Protestant rebels. This position stood in sharp contrast to London's intolerant attitude towards their Irish subjects since the beginning of Anne Stuart's reign. Charles W. Ingrao, *In Quest and Crisis: Emperor Joseph I and the Habsburg Monarchy* (West Lafayette: Purdue University Press, 1979), 159.

64 Copy of the letter from Count Gallas to the Count of Sunderland and Milord Boyle, London, 17th August, 1709, ASPF, Scritture riferiti nei Congressi. Irlanda, 7, 138v–141r; Klopp, *Der Fall des Hauses*, 265–68; Jarnut-Derbolav, *Die Österreichische*, 269.

65 Girolamo Grimaldi to Cardinal Paolucci, Brussels, 7th November, 1709, ASPF, Scritture riferiti nei Congressi. Irlanda, 7, 119r.

66 Benedetto Viale, the Genoese legate in London, reported on the meetings he had attended in Windsor concerning the Irish issue, claiming that before he left for The Hague, there was some chance that the parliamentary edict would be revoked. Benedetto Viale to Cardinal Paolucci, The Hague, 11th October, 1709, ASPF, Scritture riferiti nei Congressi. Irlanda, 7, 114r–v.

67 The Marquis of Brianzone to Cardinal Paolucci, London, 27th September 1709, ASPF, Scritture riferiti nei Congressi. Irlanda, 7, 115r–116r. Cf. Patrick Francis Moran, ed., *Spicilegium Ossoriense* (Dublin: M.H. Gill & Son, 1878), 406.

68 Italian translation of the Act of the Irish parliament, Dublin, n. d., 1709, ASPF, Scritture riferiti nei Congressi. Irlanda, 7, 191r–198v.

69 Jacopo Giraldi to Cardinal Paolucci. London, 17th September 1709, in *Spicilegium Ossoriense*, 404–5. The pope was satisfied with the efforts made by the ambassadors to try to stop the harsh decree. He hoped that, at least, moderation would preside over its enforcement. Secretary of the *Congregatio de Propaganda Fide* to Cardinal Paolucci, Rome, 26th October 1709, ASPF, Scritture riferiti nei Congressi. Lettere, 98, 343r–v.

70 *Clementis Undecimi*, 605–6.

71 Bonaventure de Burgo to Cardinal Paolucci, Vienna, 28th September, 1709, ASV, Segr. di Stato. Particolari, 104, 356r–v.

72 Copy of the brief from Clement XI to Joseph I, Rome, n. d., April 1709, ASPF, Scritture riferiti nei Congressi. Irlanda, 7, 60r–v; *Clementis Undecimi*, 603–4.

73 As pointed out by David Martín Marcos, the Comacchio affair was still in the air. Martín Marcos, *El Papado*, 164.

74 Albareda, *La Guerra de Sucesión*, 284. For the figure of Prince Eugene and his role in the context of the War of the Spanish Succession, see Derek McKay, *Eugenio di Savoia: Ritratto di un condottiero, 1663–1736* (Turin: Società Editrice Internazionale, 1989).

75 It was repeatedly argued that the issue of the Irish Catholics was used in the rhetoric of the Bourbons to present the dynastic conflict as a war of religion. Klopp, *Der Fall des Hauses*, 264. This has been addressed by David González Cruz, *Guerra de religión entre príncipes católicos: El discurso del cambio dinástico en España y América (1700–1714)* (Madrid: Ministerio de Defensa, 2002) and Christian Mühling, *Die europäische Debatte über den Religionskrieg* (Göttingen: Vandenhoeck & Ruprecht, 2017).

76 Bellesheim, *Geschichte der katholischen*, 63. It is likely that the contacts at court referred to by Fr Bonaventure de Burgo included the Count of Godolphin. Frances Harris, *The General in Winter: The Marlborough-Godolphin Friendship and the Reign of Queen Anne* (Oxford: Oxford University Press, 2017).

77 Israel, 'William III and Toleration,' 139–42. Charles II received similar assurances. William of Orange to Charles II, Saint James, 25th January, 1689, Real Academia de la Historia (hereafter RAH), Salazar y Castro, 9/667, 81r–82r.

78 Bonaventure de Burgo to Joseph I, Vienna, 2nd November, 1709, ASV, Segr. di Stato. Particolari, 104, 529v–530r. Based on their alleged common origin and the services rendered, the Irish were naturalised as Spanish in 1680 – a decree endorsed by Philip V in 1701 – and thereafter regarded as 'brothers.' For the military contribution of the Irish to the War of the Spanish Succession, see Francisco Andújar Castillo, 'Familias irlandesas en el Ejército y la Corte borbónica,' in *Extranjeros en el ejército: Militares irlandeses en la sociedad española, 1580–1818*, ed. Enrique García Hernán and Óscar Recio Morales (Madrid: Ministerio de Defensa, 2007), 271–95.

79 Bonaventure de Burgo to Joseph I, Vienna, 2nd November, 1709, ASV, Segr. di Stato. Particolari, 104, 530r.

80 Albareda, *La Guerra de Sucesión*, 284.

81 Joseph I to Count Gallas, Vienna, 23rd November 1709, ASV, Segr. di Stato. Particolari, 104, 531r–v. Cf. Moran, *Spicilegium Ossoriense*, 410–11.

82 It is likely that these briefs included those addressed to Cardinal Johann Philipp von Lamberg, imperial councillor, and Charles of Lorraine, Bishop Elect of Osnabruck and Head Prior of Castile and León in the order of Saint John of Jerusalem, who were asked by the pope to help Bonaventure de Burgo in his mission. *Clementis Undecimi*, 605–6.

83 Secretary of the *Congregatio de Propaganda Fide* to Cardinal Paolucci, Rome, 21st December, 1709, ASPF, Scritture riferitti nei Congressi. Lettere, 98, 371r–v.

84 Ibid.

85 Bonaventure de Burgo to Cardinal Paolucci, Vienna, 7th December, 1709, ASV, Segr. di Stato. Particolari, 104, 532r.

86 Ibid.

87 One of the reports sent by the internuncio informed Rome that some ministers, including the Great Treasurer Godolphin, disapproved of the harshness

of the measures being implemented in Ireland. Girolamo Grimaldi to Cardinal Paolucci, Brussels, 9th January, 1710, ASPF, Scritture riferitti nei Congressi. Irlanda, 7, 209r.

88 Memorial of Fr Ambrose O'Connor, Lovain, 4th January 1710, ASPF, Scritture riferitti nei Congressi. Irlanda, 7, 210r–v. According to John G. Simms, only 33 laymen, among those who had registered following the 1704 edict, took the oath. Simms, 'The Establishment,' 18. The constant reduction in the number of clerics explains the constant demand for missionaries from the continent. Cardinal Fabrizio Paolucci to Antonio Felice Zondadari, Rome, 8th September, 1708, ASV, Archivio della Nunziatura di Madrid, 62, 2563r.

89 Bonaventure de Burgo to Cardinal Paolucci, Prague, 25th January, 1710, ASV, Segr. di Stato. Particolari, 105, 31r–32r.

90 Bonaventure de Burgo to Cardinal Paolucci, Prague, 5th February, 1710. Cf. Moran, *Spicilegium Ossoriense*, 416.

91 Bonaventure de Burgo to Cardinal Paolucci, Prague, 25th January, 1710, ASV, Segr. di Stato. Particolari, 105, 31r–32r.

92 Bonaventure de Burgo to Cardinal Paolucci, Prague, 5th February, 1710. Cf. Moran, *Spicilegium Ossoriense*, 417. For the letter of August II to Queen Anne, see Moran, *Spicilegium Ossoriense*, 413–14.

93 In his letter, the Dominican also reported the arrest of ten members of the Church in different regions of Ireland. In the provinces of Leinster, Munster, and Ulster, no clerics took the oath, while in Connaught the oath was taken by a single priest. Some nobles also yielded, but only one among the top echelons of the Irish gentry. Extract of letter of Ambrose O'Connor, London, 8th June, 1710, ASPF, Scritture riferitti nei Congressi. Irlanda, 7, 277r–v.

94 While de Burgo was on his way to The Hague, Count Franz Ludwig of Palatinate-Neuburg, coadjutor to the Archbishop of Mainz, wrote Clement XI in praise of the zeal and dedication of the pope's envoy in his mission. Count Franz Ludwig of Palatinate-Neuburg to Clement XI, Mainz, 24th July, 1710, ASPF, Scritture riferitti nei Congressi. Irlanda, 7, 302r–v. The Elector Archbishop of Trier, Johann VIII Hugo of Orsbeck, expressed himself in similar terms. The Archbishop Elector of Trier to Clement XI, Ehrenbreitstein, 30th July, 1710, ASPF, Scritture riferitti nei Congressi. Irlanda, 7, 302r–v.

95 For an historiographical review of Geertruidenberg, see Lucien Bély, *L'art de la paix en Europe: Naissance de la diplomatie moderne XVIe–XVIIIe siècles* (Paris: Presses Universitaires de France, 2007), 431–64.

96 Lucien Bély, 'Les larmes de Monsieur de Torcy: Un essai sur les perspectives de l'histoire diplomatique à propos des conférences de Gertruydenberg (Mars–Juillet 1710),' *Histoire, Économie et Société*, 2/3 (1983), 429.

97 Lucien Bély, *Les relations internationales en Europe, XVIIᵉ–XVIIIᵉ siècles* (Paris: Presses Universitaires de France, 2007), 409.

98 Robert A. Selig, 'Gertruydenberg (Geertruidenberg),' in *The Treaties of the War of the Spanish Succession: An Historical and Critical Dictionary*, ed. Linda Frey and Marsha Frey (Westport: Greenwood Press, 1995), 181–83; Albareda, *La Guerra de Sucesión*, 288.

99 Secretary of the *Congregatio de Propaganda Fide* to Cardinal Paolucci, Rome, 18th April and 10th May, 1710, ASPF, Scritture riferitti nei Congressi. Lettere, 99, 211, 254r.

100 Copy of the letter of Giulio Piazza to Cardinal Paolucci, Vienna, 31st May, 1710, ASPF, Scritture riferitti nei Congressi. Irlanda, 7, 245r.

101 Copy of the letter of Annibale Maffei to Cardinal Paolucci, London, 25th May, 1710, ASPF, Scritture riferitti nei Congressi. Irlanda, 7, 267r.

102 Copy of the letter of Annibale Maffei to Girolamo Grimaldi, London, 25th May, 1710, ASPF, Scritture riferitti nei Congressi. Irlanda, 7, 268r.
103 Copy of the letter from Jacopo Giraldi to Cardinal Paolucci, London, 23th May, 1710, ASPF, Scritture riferitti nei Congressi. Irlanda, 7, 257r.
104 Copy of the letter from Girolamo Grimaldi to Cardinal Paolucci, Brussels, 5th June, 1710, ASPF, Scritture riferitti nei Congressi. Irlanda 8, 258r.
105 Girolamo Grimaldi to Cardinal Paolucci, Brussels, 10th July, 1710, ASPF, Scritture riferitti nei Congressi. Irlanda, 7, 273r–v.
106 Martín Marcos, *El Papado*, 177.
107 Alberto Caracciolo, *Domenico Passionei, tra Roma e la Repubblica delle lettere* (Rome: Edizioni di storia e letteratura, 1968), 105, 108.
108 Martín Marcos, *El Papado*, 180.
109 Domenico Passionei to Cardinal Paolucci, The Hague, 12th June, 1710, ASV, Segr. di Stato. Nunziatura delle Paci, 47, 310r–312v; Martín Marcos, *El Papado*, 177. In a second letter, when the arrival of de Burgo was imminent, Passionei emphasised that the Franciscan should neither head for The Hague nor hand any letters to the plenipotentiaries – a move that would be 'loud, and, therefore, futile.' The best thing was to follow Passionei's lead, for he was sure of the ground on which he was treading. Domenico Passionei to Cardinal Paolucci, The Hague, 3rd July, 1710, ASV, Segr. di Stato. Nunziatura delle Paci, 47, 344r–345r.
110 In mid-June, the nuncio in Cologne, the Archbishop of Ancona, announced the arrival of Bonaventure de Burgo in transit to The Hague. Archbishop of Ancona to Cardinal Paolucci, Fulda, 12th June, 1710, ASV, Segr. di Stato. Colonia, 95, 353r–v.
111 Bonaventure de Burgo to Cardinal Paolucci, Colonia, 3rd August, 1710, ASV, Segr. di Stato. Particolari, 106, 76r–v.
112 Domenico Passionei to Cardinal Paolucci, The Hague, 10th August, 1710, ASV, Segr. di Stato. Nunziatura delle Paci, 47, 414r–416r.
113 Lucien Bély, *La Société des Princes: XVIe–XVIIIe siècles* (Paris: Fayard, 1999), 334–36.
114 Albareda, *La Guerra de Sucesión*, 288.
115 David Hayton, *Ruling Ireland, 1685–1742: Politics, Politicians and Parties* (Woodbridge: The Boydell Press, 2004), 160.
116 Domenico Passionei to Cardinal Paolucci, The Hague, 13th November, 1710, ASV, Segr. di Stato. Nunziatura delle Paci, 47, 588r–v.
117 Bonaventure de Burgo to Cardinal Paolucci, Düsseldorf, 14th September, 1710, ASV, Segr. di Stato. Particolari, 106, 150r–v.
118 Giovanni Battista Bussi to Cardinal Paolucci, Colonia, 29th March, 1711, ASPF, Scritture riferitti nei Congressi. Irlanda 7, 316r–317r.
119 Bonaventure de Burgo to Cardinal Paolucci, Colonia, 16th December, 1711, ASV, Segr. di Stato. Particolari, 108, 444r–v.

Bibliography

Archival sources

Archivo General de Simancas (AGS) Estado, legs. 3090, 3969, 3970, 3971.
Archivio Storico di Propaganda Fide (ASPF), Scritture Riferiti nei Congressi: Belgio ed Olanda, 6; Irlanda, 7; Lettere, 98, 99.

Archivio Segreto Vaticano (ASV), Archivio della Nunziatura di Madrid, 62; Fondo Carpegna, 55; Segreteria di Stato [Segr. di Stato]: Colonia, 95; Fiandra, 148; Francia, 195; Germania, 44, 235; Nunziatura delle Paci, 47; Particolari, 101, 104, 105, 106, 108; Spagna, 358; Venezia, 158.

Österreichisches Staatsarchiv Wien (OeStA), Haus-, Hof- und Staatsarchiv (HHStA), Staatenabteilungen, Italienische Staaten, Venedig, Dispacci di Germania, 194.

Real Academia de la Historia (RAH), Salazar y Castro, 9/667.

The National Archives: Public Record Office (TNA), State Papers (SP), 63/363.

Printed sources

Clementis Undecimi Pontificis Maximi Epistolae, Et Brevia Selectiora. Rome: s. i., 1729.

de Lamberty, Guillaume. *Memóires pour servir à l'histoire du XVIII siècle*, vol. 5. The Hague: Henry Scheurleer, 1727.

Jadin, Louis, ed. *Relations des Pays-Bas, de Liège et de Franche-Comté avec le Saint-Siège d'après les 'Lettere di vescovi' conservées aux Archives Vaticanes (1566–1779)*. Brussels: Institut historique belge de Rome, 1952.

Jennings, Brendan, ed. *Louvain Papers, 1606–1827*. Dublin: Stationery Office for the Irish Manuscripts Commission, 1968.

Moran, Patrick Francis, ed. *Spicilegium Ossoriense*. Dublin: M.H. Gill & Son, 1878.

Palermo, Giovanni Antonio da. *Scrutinium doctrinarum*. Rome: Rochi Bernabo, 1709.

William III. *An Act for Banishing All Papists Exercising Any Ecclesiastical Jurisdiction, and All Regulars of the Popish Clergy Out of This Kingdom*. Dublin: Andrew Crook, 1697.

Literature

Albareda, Joaquím. *La Guerra de Sucesión de España (1700–1714)*. Barcelona: Crítica, 2010.

Álvarez-Ossorio, Antonio, García García, Bernardo J., and León Sanz, Virginia, eds. *La pérdida de Europa: La guerra de sucesión por la monarquía de España*. Madrid: Fundación Carlos de Amberes, 2007.

Andújar Castillo, Francisco. 'Familias irlandesas en el Ejército y la Corte borbónica.' In *Extranjeros en el ejército: Militares irlandeses en la sociedad española, 1580–1818*, edited by Enrique García Hernán and Óscar Recio Morales, 271–95. Madrid: Ministerio de Defensa, 2007.

Bellesheim, Alphons. *Geschichte der katholischen Kirche in Irland von 1690 bis 1890*, vol. 3. Mainz: Franz Kirchheim, 1891.

Bély, Lucien. 'Les larmes de Monsieur de Torcy: Un essai sur les perspectives de l'histoire diplomatique à propos des conférences de Gertruydenberg (Mars–Juillet 1710).' *Histoire, Économie et Société*, 2/3 (1983): 431–64.

Bély, Lucien. *La société des princes: XVIe–XVIIIe siècles*. Paris: Fayard, 1999.

Bély, Lucien. *L'art de la paix en Europe: Naissance de la diplomatie moderne XVIe–XVIIIe siècles*. Paris: Presses Universitaires de France, 2007.

Bély, Lucien. *Les relations internationales en Europe, XVIIe–XVIIIe siècles*. Paris: Presses Universitaires de France, 2007.

Bonney, Richard. '"God, Fatherland and Freedom": Rethinking Pluralism in Hungary in the Era of Partition and Rebellion, 1526–1711.' In *Persecution and Pluralism: Calvinists and Religious Minorities in Early Modern Europe, 1550–1700*, edited by Richard Bonney and David J.B. Trim, 89–122. Bern: Peter Lang, 2006.

Bravo Lozano, Cristina. '¿La última colaboración dinástica? La diplomacia hispano-imperial ante la política confesional de Guillermo III de Inglaterra (1696–1700).' In *Les Habsbourg en Europe: Circulations, échanges et regards croisés*, edited by Alexandra Merle and Éric Leroy du Cardonnoy, 161–80. Reims: Editions et Presses Universitaires de Reims, 2018.

Bravo Lozano, Cristina. *Spain and the Irish Mission, 1609–1707*. New York: Routledge, 2019.

Caracciolo, Alberto. *Domenico Passionei, tra Roma e la Repubblica delle lettere*. Rome: Edizioni di storia e letteratura, 1968.

Connolly, Sean J. 'The Penal Laws.' In *Kings in Conflict: The Revolutionary War in Ireland and its Aftermath, 1689–1750*, edited by William A. Maguire, 157–72. Belfast: The Blackstaff Press, 1990.

Connolly, Sean J. *Religion, Law, and Power: The Making of Protestant Ireland, 1660–1760*. Oxford: Clarendon Press, 2002.

Gibson, John S. *Playing the Scottish Card: The Franco-Jacobite Invasion of 1708*. Edinburgh: Edinburgh University Press, 1988.

González Cruz, David. *Guerra de religión entre príncipes católicos: El discurso del cambio dinástico en España y América (1700–1714)*. Madrid: Ministerio de Defensa, 2002.

Harris, Frances. *The General in Winter: The Marlborough-Godolphin Friendship and the Reign of Queen Anne*. Oxford: Oxford University Press, 2017.

Hayton, David. *Ruling Ireland, 1685–1742: Politics, Politicians and Parties*. Woodbridge: The Boydell Press, 2004.

Ingrao, Charles W. *In Quest and Crisis: Emperor Joseph I and the Habsburg Monarchy*. West Lafayette: Purdue University Press, 1979.

Israel, Jonathan I. 'William III and Toleration.' In *From Persecution to Toleration: The Glorious Revolution and Religion in England*, edited by Ole P. Grell, Jonathan I. Israel and Nicholas Tyacke, 129–71. Oxford: Clarendon Press Oxford, 2010.

Jarnut-Derbolav, Elke. *Die Österreichische Gesandtschaft in London (1701–1711)*. Bonn: Ludwig Röhrscheid Verlag, 1972.

Klopp, Onno. *Der Fall des Hauses Stuart und die Succession des Hauses Hannover in Groß-Britannien und Irland*, vol. 13. Vienna: Wilhem Braumüller, 1887.

Martín Marcos, David. *El Papado y la Guerra de Sucesión española*. Madrid: Marcial Pons, 2011.

McGrath, Charles Irvan. 'Securing the Protestant Interest: The Origins and Purpose of the Penal Laws of 1695.' *Irish Historical Studies*, 30 (1996): 25–46.

McKay, Derek. *Eugenio di Savoia: Ritratto di un condottiero, 1663–1736*. Turin: Società Editrice Internazionale, 1989.

Mühling, Christian. *Die europäische Debatte über den Religionskrieg*. Göttingen: Vandenhoeck & Ruprecht, 2017.

O Fiaich, Tomas. 'The Registration of the Clergy in 1704.' *Seanchas Ard Mhacha*, 6 (1971): 46–69.

Quirós Rosado, Roberto. 'Diplomacia y misión en Europa durante la Guerra de Sucesión: los Habsburgo-Wolfenbüttel, el estado de Milán y el catolicismo septentrional.' *Cuadernos de Historia Moderna*, 41/1 (2016): 29–47.

Quirós Rosado, Roberto. *Monarquía de Oriente: La corte de Carlos III y el gobierno de Italia durante la Guerra de Sucesión española*. Madrid: Marcial Pons Historia, 2017.

Rose, Craig. *England in the 1690s: Revolution, Religion and War*. Oxford: Blackwell, 1999.

Selig, Robert A. 'Gertruydenberg (Geertruidenberg).' In *The Treaties of the War of the Spanish Succession: An Historical and Critical Dictionary*, edited by Linda Frey and Marsha Frey, 181–83. Westport: Greenwood Press, 1995.

Simms, John G. 'The Bishops' Banishment Act of 1697 (9 Will. III, c. 1).' *Irish Historical Studies*, 17/66 (1970): 185–99.

Simms, John G. 'The Establishment of Protestant Ascendancy, 1691–1714.' In *A New History of Ireland. Vol. IV: Eighteenth-Century Ireland, 1691–1800*, edited by Theodore W. Moody and William E. Vaughan, 1–30. Oxford: Oxford University Press, 2009.

Tabacchi, Stefano. '"L'impossibile neutralità: Il Papato.' Roma e lo Stato della Chiesa durante la Guerra di Successione Spagnola.' *Cheiron*, 39–40 (2004): 223–43.

Troost, Wout. *William III and the Treaty of Limerick, 1691–1697: A Study of His Irish Policy*. Unpublished PhD thesis. Leiden: University of Leiden, 1983.

Troost, Wout. *William III, the Stadholder-King: A Political Biography*. Aldershot: Ashgate, 2005.

Troost, Wout. 'Ireland's Role in the Foreign Policy of William III.' In *Redefining William III: The Impact of the King-Stadholder in International Context*, edited by Esther Mijers and David Onnekink, 53–68. Aldershot: Ashgate, 2007.

Wandruszka, Adam. 'El mundo político en el siglo XVIII.' In *Historia Universal*, vol. 7, II, edited by Golo Mann and Alfred Heuss, 457–547. Madrid: Espasa-Calpe, 1988.

Part II
Clerics as diplomats

5 'Not fit nor convenient [to] be sent on embassy in the king's business'

The diplomatic missions of the runaway Friar Robert Barnes to the Schmalkaldic League and Denmark

Katharina Beiergrößlein

Introduction

Although he had been condemned as a heretic and had fled the country in 1528, Dr Robert Barnes (*c*.1495–1540), the former prior of the Cambridge Augustinians, acted during the 1530s several times as a diplomatic representative for Henry VIII of England, who was then desperately looking for new allies. In defiance of contemporary diplomatic theory, which excluded condemned heretics from any involvement in matters connected to diplomacy, Barnes was sent on several missions to Elector John Frederik of Saxony, the League of Schmalkalden, and King Christian III of Denmark. In the following, Barnes' diplomatic missions and the way contemporary writings on diplomacy dealt with the heresy topic are examined. Finally, it will be analysed how Robert Barnes qualified for these missions and what made him still seem 'fit [or] convenient [to] be sent on embassy in the king's business.'

Robert Barnes' exile on the continent

Around the turn of 1528, the authorities in Northampton allegedly searched the waters and banks of the River Nene for seven days. Their intention was to find the body of Friar Barnes – at least according to the account of the life of Dr Robert Barnes, former prior of the Cambridge Augustinians, which John Foxe included in his famous and widely read *Acts and Monuments*, commonly referred to as the *Book of Martyrs*. Having just escaped from prison, Barnes had left a letter saying that he had gone to drown himself.[1] Another letter advised the mayor of the town 'to search for him in [the] water, because he had a letter wrytten in parchment about hys necke, closed in waxe, for my Lorde Cardinall [i.e. Thomas Wolsey] which would teach all men to beware by him.' As Foxe goes on to say, Barnes had feigned his death, and while his body was being searched for 'hee was conueyed to London in a pore mans apparell, & so taried not there but toke shipping & went by long Seas to Antwarpe.'[2]

It is no longer possible to determine how many details of this strange story are true.[3] It is clear, however, that after being imprisoned for approximately three years, first at the Fleet in London, then at Augustinian houses in London and Northampton, Robert Barnes thought it best to flee his home country and seek refuge on the continent.[4]

The answer as to why he took so drastic a move lies in the reasons for Friar Barnes' imprisonment. On Christmas Eve, 1525, he was preaching not at the chapel attached to his friary, but at St Edward's Church.[5] As Barnes relates in his *Supplication unto Henry VIII*, which he published in his defence six years later, he had done so 'at request of the paryshe.'[6] Perhaps he had been invited as a guest preacher by the parish as sermons by members of religious orders were generally thought to be more popular in style.[7] Following this sermon, however, Barnes was accused of heresy and his monastic and academic career ended abruptly. As neither the text of the sermon nor the case files have survived, it is only possible to work out indirectly what might have caused the charge. According to Foxe's account of Barnes' life, as well as Barnes' *Supplication unto Henry VIII*, in which he published the 'articles that were layed against me,' the sermon was based on Martin Luther's exegesis of Paul's Epistle to the Philippians (Phil 4:4–7) and was first and foremost a widespread criticism of the English clergy.[8] It thus took on a topic particularly common among the mendicant orders. Perhaps even more of a problem arose when it came to theological matters, such as omitting the prayers for the dead and for the Virgin Mary. Although 'perhaps not technically heretical, what he had said was enough to warrant his arrest. Moreover, it seems not to have been an isolated incident. Hostile witnesses were present at the sermon, apparently expecting trouble.'[9] Their presence suggests that Barnes and his teaching had for some time been a thorn in the side of some members of the university, who seized the opportunity 'to get him' now that he was preaching not within the walls of his friary, but within reach of episcopal, and thus university, jurisdiction.[10]

After having been questioned by the vice chancellor of the university and his refusal to sign a recantation prepared for him, Barnes was handed over to Cardinal Thomas Wolsey in London. There, he was obliged to renounce some of his religious beliefs and to do penance in a public ceremony. Instead of being allowed to return afterwards to Cambridge, he was first imprisoned at the Fleet, then later at the house of the Augustinian friars at London, where he nevertheless enjoyed a considerable amount of liberty. He was allowed to receive visitors, 'even suspicious ones,' such as two Lollards from Essex, who asked his help not only in acquiring a copy of William Tyndale's translation of the New Testament, but also in converting their parish priest.[11] Perhaps he was even permitted to carry on teaching. In any case, he managed to become part of a network of people trading with books that were categorised as heretical, which resulted in the loss of all the freedoms that had been granted him. Consequently, he was transferred to Northampton in 1528. This, he feared, was supposed to be his final destination, and hence he decided to break out of prison and to try to reach the relative safety of the continent. The probability is that he was helped by Hansa merchants, who had also been involved in the distribution of suspect books.[12]

Once on the continent, he first made his way to the northern German Hansa cities of Lübeck and Hamburg. Later, he went to Wittenberg in Saxony, where he immersed himself in theological studies, and towards the end of 1530 his first work, the *Sentenciae ex doctoribus collectae*, was printed at Joseph Klug's printing house.[13] This was a collection of 19 statements and corresponding quotations from the Bible, canon law, and patristic writings on different religious topics such as justification, the veneration of saints, the marriage of priests, and the Eucharist. The *Sentenciae* were published under the pseudonym of Antonius Anglus, which Barnes had adopted following his successful flight. While at Wittenberg, he also became acquainted with Johannes Bugenhagen, in whose house he stayed for some time, and most notably with Martin Luther and his wife, Katharina von Bora, as well as with Philipp Melanchthon. He subsequently became integrated into their intellectual network of Protestant theologians.[14]

Diplomatic missions to Saxony, the League of Schmalkalden, and Denmark[15]

In the summer of 1531, Robert Barnes found himself in Saxony again, although this time not as an exiled English theologian seeking refuge, but – *mirabile dictu* – as an agent of the King of England. It was a most delicate mission. He was sent to seek support from the Saxon Protestant theologians, particularly Martin Luther, for Henry VIII's 'Great Matter,' the annulment of his marriage with Katherine of Aragon. To this end, he was probably sought out by one of Thomas Cromwell's agents on the continent, very likely Stephen Vaughan, and commissioned to ask Luther to write an expert opinion on the question of the divorce. Barnes was only partially successful as Luther's verdict was not the one Henry had wished for: Luther was opposed to the divorce on the grounds that it would be more sinful to divorce the Queen, and thus stigmatise her and bastardise Princess Mary, than being married to his brother's widow.[16] Nonetheless, as this mission offered the possibility for Barnes to return home to England – at least temporarily, on the basis of safe conduct – he went. His main reason was to seize the opportunity to rebut the charges of heresy.[17]

During the following decade until his death in 1540, Barnes was permanently involved in diplomatic efforts to bring England into an alliance with the League of Schmalkalden. In detail, the first was a mission to the Elector of Saxony, John Frederic, in 1535/1536, which resulted in a visit of several minor Schmalkaldic delegates to England in 1538. In

1539, Barnes was eventually sent on an embassy to Christian III of Denmark. Although the Danish king was not a full member of the League of Schmalkalden, he had formed individual alliances with almost every single member of the League, and he coordinated his negotiations with Henry VIII in consultation with the heads of the League, John Frederic of Saxony and Philipp of Hesse.[18]

Robert Barnes stayed in Saxony for almost a year from August 1535 until May 1536, and his task was to prevent Philipp Melanchthon from travelling to France. Melanchthon had been invited by King Francis I for a religious conference with the theologians of the University of Paris. As soon as Barnes had managed to impede Melanchthon's travelling to France, he was commissioned to convince him to visit Henry VIII instead. Apart from his business with Melanchthon, Barnes was instructed to prepare for a major English embassy to Saxony that was expected to set out shortly. Although Edward Fox, Bishop of Hereford, was considered the chief negotiator of this embassy, which finally reached the electorate in November 1535, Barnes participated in almost all discussions with John Frederick of Saxony, the Wittenberg theologians, and the Saxon chancellor, Gregor Brück, concerning whether Henry VIII might be allowed to join the League.

Later, when the English hopes for an admission to the League began to perish, and the English king still feared an invasion by Emperor Charles V and Pope Paul III, he sought an amity with the Danish king, Christian III. As already noted above, Christian himself was allied with almost all the Schmalkaldeners. Hence, in spring 1539, Henry VIII's 'faithful and dear servant' Robert Barnes was sent to Odense to meet the Danish king.[19] As with the Saxon embassy, the English envoy once more had no authority to negotiate, let alone conclude an agreement. Instead, his major task was to convince Christian III to dispatch an embassy to England, where an alliance 'against all papists' would be concluded.[20]

Contemporary diplomatic treatises on the qualities of ambassadors

But how was it possible that a known heretic served for almost a decade as a diplomatic envoy for the English king, albeit with only limited competences? After all, according to contemporary diplomatic understanding, condemned heretics were to be excluded from any involvement in matters connected to diplomacy.

Although sixteenth-century diplomacy was far from obtaining the level of organisation and regulation of later centuries, this does not mean that there were no rules at all.[21] It rather appears that a certain set of commonly acknowledged norms, even though not codified ones, existed. These regulated 'the recognition and status of diplomatic principles, the behaviour and immunities of diplomatic agents, and the negotiations, validity and observance of diplomatic agreements.'[22] Furthermore, since the fifteenth century, more and more scholars were dealing with different aspects of international relations, and thus a growing number of treatises on the theory of diplomatic business emerged.[23]

Generally, those texts written before 1550 can be divided into two groups. On the one hand, there are treatises following the traditions of scholasticism, usually using the genre of *quaestiones*. In these texts, mainly legal issues belonging to one particular subject area are treated by piling up references from different sources: 'In fact they are collections of extracts from canon and civil law as well as corresponding comments.'[24] Thereby, the authors prepared information on complex topics in a short and easily accessible manner, which was understood all over Christendom, but usually without adding something new or innovative.[25] As a rule, this group of texts is limited to the offices of nuncios and papal ambassadors.[26] Among those also dealing with ambassadors without ecclesiastical backgrounds are, for example, Johannes Bertachinus (*Ambasiator*, 1481), Martinus Garatus Laudensis (*Tractatus de Legatis maxime Principum*, 1530), and Gundisalvus de Villadiego (*Tractatus de Legato*, 1549).[27]

On the other hand, there were writers who had abandoned the methods of scholasticism as well as the strong emphasis on legal questions. Rather, they were focusing on practical matters, such as how to choose an ambassador, or which qualities he should possess. Usually, they were sketching 'a sort of manual for the good ambassador,' often including long chapters discussing the characteristics – vices as well as virtues – an ambassador was expected not to have, or demanded to possess.[28] By and by, these 'lists became canonical and include, with some variants, probity, fidelity, prudence, strength, constancy, continence or temperance, moderation and liberality.'[29] Quite often the authors were 'humanists benefiting themselves from certain experiences in the field of diplomatic business.'[30] Due to this, some of the treatises, such as Ermolao Barbaro's *De officio legati* (1489), contain 'strong autobiographical leanings as well as aspects of self-justification,' or the rules and assignments given are modelled on the experiences and behaviour of a specific person, personally known to the author.[31] For example, Étienne Dolet, secretary to the French ambassador, Jean de Langeac, on a mission to Venice in 1528/1529, based his little treatise *De officio Legati* (1541) on his protector de Langeac, whom 'he considered as an example of the perfect ambassador.'[32] Apart from the treatises of Ermolao Barbaro and Étienne Dolet, two of the most important theoretical considerations on the ambassadorial business from the early stages of European diplomacy belong to this second group – Bernard du Rosier's *Ambaxiator Brevilogus* (1436) and Konrad Braun's *De Legationibus* (1548).[33] The *Ambaxiator Brevilogus*, published in 1546 by the Archbishop of Toulouse, Bernhard du Rosier, can be regarded as the first textbook on diplomatic practice written in Western Europe. *De Legationibus* was published more than a century later by Franz Behem at Mainz in 1548.[34] As early as the 1530s, when the German lawyer Konrad Braun had been *gelehrter Rat*, or scholarly councillor, of the Prince-Bishop of Würzburg, Konrad von Thüngen, as well as assessor for the Franconian Imperial Circle at the Imperial Chamber Court, he 'had as an academic been working on international relations.'[35] The result of this occupation was his *De Legationibus*, five books discussing the use of ambassadors, diplomatic missions, instructions, characteristics and qualities of diplomats, their legal status, recipients of envoys, and so on. Nevertheless, Braun's work was not only a 'historically profound treatise on the tradition of diplomacy'; he was also dealing with the effects and consequences that heresy and schism caused for international relations.[36]

Among other aspects of the diplomatic business, such as the privileges and immunities ambassadors enjoyed or the way a diplomatic mission should ideally be conducted, both authors are very much concerned with the ambassador's character and the qualities and qualifications he should possess.[37] When it came to virtues and mental abilities, it seems that both had some kind of 'superhero' in mind, combining enormously high moral and intellectual qualities; one can scarcely imagine someone meeting all those requirements. They were thus taking up a contemporary model, according to which envoys were 'consistently portrayed as the embodiment of the humanist ideal.'[38] According to du Rosier and Braun, it was not enough for an ambassador to be learned, skilled, eloquent, and prudent; additionally, he should be temperate, discreet, honest, just, sober, pious, liberal, patient, generous, magnanimous, calm, brave, and so on. This also applies to the texts of Barbaro and Dolet, although in a less detailed and explicit manner.[39]

Konrad Braun, however, went even further than that and included a chapter listing 'all the people who for various reasons are not fitted to fill the position of an ambassador,' and thus were to be excluded from all administrative offices and duties.[40] Here, he explicitly named heretics, and, besides the deaf and the blind, the pagans, Saracens, Jews, church thieves, ravishers of sacred virgins, and schismatics – the 'outsiders and natural enemies' of the Latin West.[41] In his opinion, heretics sent on diplomatic missions were 'bluff packages,' false envoys – *legati m[en]daces* – who could not be trusted. Bernhard du Rosier and Ermolao Barbaro do not explicitly name heretics, but their texts too imply that an ambassador must live and act in accordance with the Roman faith.[42] In Étienne Dolet's *De officio legati*, nothing points in that direction, the reason for this most likely being Dolet's own religious beliefs. The year after Dolet's treatise had been published, he was condemned for heresy – apparently because of his attacks on the ecclesiastical authorities. He was executed in 1546.[43]

By now, one might argue that during the sixteenth century discussions *de legatis et legationibus*, on their organisation, realisation, and legal status, as well as on the qualities and qualifications of the envoys, were merely academic ones, something only a few scholars and former diplomatic envoys bothered about. The discussion admittedly was above all an academic and at times even artificial one, as du Rosier and Braun's idea of the ideal ambassador suggest. Although the treatises were actually widely recognised, read, and discussed, it is not clear how many of the rules were in fact considered, or how great their impact was on everyday diplomacy.[44]

Nonetheless, diplomatic missions, the sending and receiving of envoys, did not happen in a theoretical vacuum. Instead, it would seem that diplomatic business was set on a degree of common ground, which was accepted on the continent as well as in England, one of them apparently being that 'heretics must not be legates.'[45] After all, one of Henry VIII's councillors, the Bishop of Winchester, Stephen Gardiner, had his reservations and railed at Barnes' assignment as a diplomatic envoy because of his being a condemned heretic. He reportedly said about his former Cambridge colleague and acquaintance 'that it was not fit nor convenient that Friar Barnes, being a man defamed of heresy and therefore had done penance, should be sent on embassy in the king's business.'[46] Stephen Gardiner was not the only one who had objections to Robert Barnes being sent abroad in Henry VIII's name: a few years earlier, when Barnes brought back Martin Luther's opinion on the king's 'Great Matter,' Thomas More, then Lord Chancellor, ignored the safe conduct and aimed to arrest him because of the earlier charges of heresy laid against him.[47]

Overall, it can be assumed that the diplomatic involvement of Robert Barnes was quite unusual, as it did not comply with diplomatic traditions and customs and caused irritation to his contemporaries, and doubtlessly there had been others among Henry VIII's diplomatic personnel who had been eligible for this particular task.[48] So why choose Barnes?

Reasons for choosing Barnes as an envoy[49]

It seems likely that Robert Barnes qualified in ways that outweighed the specific shortcomings of being regarded as heretical. First and foremost, we need to think about to whom Barnes was sent. After all it was of vital importance for the success of the diplomatic mission that the envoy sent was acceptable to the recipient.[50] Barnes was sent neither to the *reyes católicos*, the Catholic monarchs of Spain, nor to the *roi trés chrétien*, the Most Christian King of France, but to the Protestant German princes, joined together in the League of Schmalkalden for the purposes of defending their faith, along with the King of Denmark. From their perspective, Barnes' views, his liking for Martin Luther's theological thoughts and ideas, were by no means regarded as being heretical; rather, they were considered as both reasonable and desirable. Given the situation of English foreign politics during the 1530s, it seems possible that the assignment of a known, Protestant, heretic could prove entirely beneficial: English foreign policy was very much shaped by the consequences of the marital problems of the royal couple and the breaking away from Rome.

In short, England was worried about isolation and feared that Charles V would act in favour of his aunt, Katherine of Aragon, that the divorce would be condemned by a common council, and that Pope Paul III would initiate an invasion to end the English schism. Therefore, England was desperately in need of new allies. Preferably, these prospective allies were first of all opposed to papally summoned councils of the Church. Second, these allies would agree with Henry's idiosyncratic way of solving his marriage problems. And finally, they should either be able to distract some of Emperor Charles' soldiers and sailors from an attack on England, or 'cause trouble for [him] in his German back yard.'[51] Thus, from the perspective of Henry VIII and his chief minister, Thomas Cromwell, an alliance with the League of Schmalkalden seemed an obvious path to follow. However, to become part of a Protestant defence alliance, it was essential to give – at least to some extent – the impression of being Protestant, or at any rate to seem Protestant-friendly, and there was probably no better way to express one's Protestant inclinations – although they might be only pretended ones – than by sending an envoy known for his Protestant views. It is likely that naming Barnes in his credentials as 'our dear and faithful chaplain,' when sent to John Frederic of Saxony for the first time, was designed to strengthen this impression.[52] In fact, this seems to be the only reference to Barnes as a member of the Royal Chapel: there is neither a letter of appointment nor any corresponding note in the account books; however, as late as 1538, in the context of a commission on Anabaptists from Flanders in which Barnes took part, he is once again termed as a royal chaplain.[53] Hence, Robert Barnes was the ideal candidate to send to the Schmalkaldic League on behalf of Henry VIII, and to stress his master's desire to become a member. Besides regarding the king's 'Great Matter,' Barnes had already proven his allegiance to the king and his ability to serve him – a quality that should not be underestimated, even though a return to England nonetheless bore some risks for him: 'What rulers wanted most in their ambassadors, however, was loyalty and dedication to the cause they represented.'[54]

What is more, Barnes' friendship with the Wittenberg theologians, the way they valued and trusted him, made him especially suitable to the role of messenger, ambassador, and discussant within the Anglo-Schmalkaldic framework. During his exile on the continent, which he had mainly spent at Hamburg and Wittenberg, Barnes became part of a network that included Saxon councillors and Protestant theologians. Thus, he gained direct and indirect access to the Elector of Saxony who again was one of the leading lights of the League of Schmalkalden. In 1531, when Henry VIII sought the opinions of Luther and Melanchthon concerning his plans for a divorce, Thomas Cromwell was the first to realise that, given England's diplomatic isolation at the time, Barnes' connections with the German Lutherans could be used profitably. Like his predecessor Cardinal Thomas Wolsey, who had begun to 'break with the [earlier] formalism and pedantry' concerning the diplomatic business, Thomas Cromwell showed a pragmatic as well as a self-interested approach.[55] Finally, Barnes qualified for diplomatic missions into Germany since, following his exile on the continent, he could speak German and was quite familiar with the political and cultural conditions of the host country.[56]

Conclusion

Concerning sixteenth-century diplomacy, there are overall plenty of indications showing that theory or norms, on the one hand, and practice, on the other, did not necessarily match. That does not mean that diplomatic theory was regarded as being irrelevant and that nobody cared about. It rather shows that there was not yet a uniform practice and that many problems were solved in a down-to-earth fashion.[57] One of these problems that early modern diplomacy had to cope with was who to send, and to whom? Who was best suited for building mutual trust? The Reformation, and its resulting divisions of the *res publica Christiana* into several religious camps, caused new difficulties in this field:

> Although the consciousness of the European community of States of this epoch was based, as before, on the common Christian faith, its character had now changed. [...] The unity of faith had been destroyed by the Reformation, which led to deep and bitter confessional dissension, extending into the field of politics and determining political disputes up to the middle of the seventeenth century.[58]

As the example of Robert Barnes shows, apparent deficiencies could become insignificant or could even be turned to advantage when deemed appropriate. This was especially so when it came to the crucial task of confidence-building in a divided world.

It becomes obvious that Barnes only qualified for this particular set of circumstances, that is, as an envoy to German-speaking Protestants – and *not* for being an English diplomatic representative in general if only we consider the tragic end to his life and career. The moment Henry VIII had had enough of negotiating with German towns and princes in 1540 and decided to divorce his fourth wife, Anne of Cleves, Barnes lost his usefulness as an envoy. He fell along with his patron and protector, Thomas Cromwell. On 30th July, 1540 – two days after Cromwell had been beheaded – Barnes the heretic was burnt at the stake.[59]

Notes

1 John Foxe, 'The History of Robert Barnes Thomas Garard, and Wylliam Hierome Deuines,' in *The Acts and Monuments*, vol. 3, ed. John Foxe (London: John Day, 1563), 656–69 [John Foxe, *The Unabridged Acts and Monuments*

Online or *TAMO* (1563 edition) (HRI Online Publications, Sheffield, 2011), accessed 24th September, 2017, www.johnfoxe.org]. For John Foxe and his *Acts and Monuments*, see John N. King, *Foxe's Book of Martyrs and Early Modern Print Culture* (Cambridge: Cambridge University Press, 2006).

2 Foxe, *Acts and Monuments*, vol. 3 (1563), 659.
3 On the questionsloh of the sources Foxe's accounts are based on, as well as their reliability, see King, *Foxe's Book*, 8:

> [...] Foxean martyrologies derive to a very considerable degree from manu-scripts written by martyrs as they awaited execution or by copyists, to which the compiler added extracts concerning the prosecution of alleged heretics from documents including the episcopal registers that receive men-tion on the title page. [...] Foxe's goal is to preserve the speeches and deeds of 'true' martyrs in form of documents that memorialize the faithful suffer-ing of new-style saints.

See also ibid., 21–25. Furthermore, see also Peter Collinson, 'Truth and Legend: The Veracity of John Foxe's Book of Martyrs,' in *Clio's Mirror: Historiography in Britain and the Netherlands*, ed. Alastair C. Duke and Coenraad A. Tamse (Zut-phen: De Walburg, 1985), 34–35:

> For his original readers, Foxe established his credentials not only or even principally as an accurate narrative historian but as a kind of registrar of original documents, the 'monuments' of his title. [...] There are mistakes of both person and place, mistakes of dating in plenty, faults of transcription and in proof-reading. But the only elements of pure invention (and not pri-marily Foxe's own invention) occur in the recounting of sundry extraordin-ary 'providences' and other acts of divine judgment visited upon those responsible for the death of the martyrs.

4 Katharina Beiergrößlein, *Robert Barnes, England und der Schmalkaldische Bund* (Gütersloh: Verlagshaus, 2011), 35–37.
5 St Edward King and Martyr is located on Peas Hill, Cambridge.
6 Robert Barnes, *A Supplication unto Henry VIII* (London: John Bydell, 1534), H_{1b}. There are two editions of the *Supplication unto Henry VIII*, consider-ably varying with regard to the content. The first edition was most likely pub-lished in 1531 at Symon Cock's in Antwerp, and the second edition in 1534 at John Bydell's in London. For the different editions of the *Supplication unto Henry VIII*, as well as a merged version published posthumously at London at Hugh Singleton's, see also Beiergrößlein, *Robert Barnes*, 184–92.
7 Beiergrößlein, *Robert Barnes*, 30.
8 Barnes, *Supplication* (1534), F_{1a}.
9 Alec Ryrie, '"A Saynt in the Deuyls Name": Heroes and Villains in the Martyr-dom of Robert Barnes,' in *Martyrs and Martyrdom in England c. 1400–1700*, ed. Thomas S. Freemann and Thomas F. Mayer (Woodbridge: The Bydell Press, 2007), 145. See also Beiergrößlein, *Robert Barnes*, 30–33.
10 Richard Rex, 'The Early Impact of Reformation Theology at Cambridge Uni-versity, 1521–1547,' *Reformation and Renaissance Review* 2 (1999), 59.
11 Christopher Haigh, *English Reformations: Religion, Politics and Society under the Tudors* (Oxford: Clarendon Press, 1993), 60.
12 Beiergrößlein, *Robert Barnes*, 35–37.
13 For Barnes' *Sentenciae ex doctoribus collectae*, see Beiergrößlein, *Robert Barnes*, 173–83.

14 Beiergrößlein, *Robert Barnes*, 40–41.
15 For Barnes' diplomatic missions, see, if not otherwise stated, Beiergrößlein, *Robert Barnes*, 43–156. See also Rory McEntegart, *Henry VIII, the League of Schmalkalden, and the Reformation* (Woodbridge: The Boydell Press, 2002); Friedrich Prüser, *England und die Schmalkaldener 1535–1540* (Leipzig: Heinsius, 1929; RP New York and London: Johnson, 1971).
16 For Luther's verdict on the divorce, see *D. Martin Luthers Werke, Kritische Gesamtausgabe. Briefwechsel*, vol. 6 (Weimar: Hermann Böhlaus Nachfolger, 1935; RP Graz: Akademische Druck- und Verlagsanstalt, 1969), Nr. 1861.
17 Barnes, *Supplication* (1534), H$_{4a}$.
18 Christian III had relations to everyone apart from Duke Philipp of Brunswick and Duke Henry of Saxony. See also Gabriele Haug-Moritz, *Der Schmalkaldische Bund 1530–1541/42: Eine Studie zu den genossenschaftlichen Strukturelementen der politischen Ordnung des Heiligen Römischen Reiches Deutscher Nation* (Leinfelden-Echterdingen: DRW Verlag, 2002), 131.
19 '[...] fidel[is] at[que] dilect[us] familiar[is].' RA Copenhagen, TKUA, England, A II. 8, Nr. 19b.
20 '[...] contra [omnes] papistas.' RA Copenhagen, TKUA, England, A II. 8, Nr. 19c.
21 De Lamar Jensen, 'Diplomacy,' in *Europe 1450 to 1789. Encyclopedia of the Early Modern World*, vol. 2, ed. Jonathan Dewald (New York: Thomas Gale, 2004), 148; Ernest Nys, *Les origins de la diplomatie et le droit d'ambassade jusque'à Grotius* (Brussels: Librairie Européene C. Muquardt, 1884), 23.
22 Garret Mattingly, *Renaissance Diplomacy* (Boston: Houghton Mifflin, 1955; RP New York: Dover Publications, 1988), 18.
23 Walter Höflechner, 'Anmerkungen zum Diplomatie- und Gesandtschaftswesen am Ende des 15. Jahrhunderts,' *Mitteilungen des österreichischen Staatsarchivs* 32 (1979), 20. See also Betty Behrens, 'Treatises on the Ambassador Written in the Fifteenth and Early Sixteenth Centuries,' *English Historical Review* 51 (1936), 616–27.
24 'Ce sont en fait des collections d'extraits des droits canon et civil ainsi que de leurs commentateurs.' Étienne Dolet, *De officio legati, De immunitate legatorum, De legationibus Ioannis Langiachi Episcopi Lemovicensis*, trans. David Amherdt (Geneva: Droz, 2010), 12. See also Behrens, 'Treatises,' 617.
25 Ingrid Baumgärtner, *Martinus Garatus Laudensis: Ein italienischer Rechtsgelehrter des 15. Jahrhunderts* (Köln/Wien: Böhlau Verlag, 1986), 104–5: 'Die Bedeutung der Traktate [liegt darin], daß sie das Standardwissen ihrer Zeit relativ kurz und übersichtlich zusammenfassen, [...].' See also Mattingly, *Renaissance Diplomacy*, 92: '[...], Martino Garrati da Lodi and Giovanni Bertachino could compile their collections of maxims about diplomatic law without mentioning any innovation or setting down a phrase which would not be as immediately intelligible on one side of the Alps as on the other.'
26 For examples, see Nys, *Les origins de la diplomatie*, 38. See also Vladimir E. Hrabar (ed.), *De Legatis et Legationibus Tractatus Varii* (Dorpat: Mattieseniano, 1905), 79–86: Nicolaus Boerius (*Tractatus de Potestate Legati a latere*, [1501?]), Johannes Brunellus (*Tractatus de dignitate et potestate Legati*, 1519), Petrus Andreas Gambarus (*Tractatus de officio atque auctoritate legati de latere*, [before 1528]).
27 Hrabar, *De Legatis*, 45–52, 53–64; Baumgärtner, *Martinus Garatus Laudensis*, 20–57, 185–189, 345; Nys, *Les origins de la diplomatie*, 36–37, 37–38.
28 The years in brackets usually indicate the date of publication of the first printed edition of the text. Handwritten versions usually appeared much earlier. Samuel Anderson, *The Rise of Modern Diplomacy 1450–1919* (London and New York: Longman, 1993), 26–27.

29 '[L]eur liste deviant bientôt canonique et comprend, á quelques variants près, la probité, la fidélité, la prudence, la force, la constance, la continence ou la temperance, la moderation et la libéralité.' Dante Fedele, *Naissance de la diplomatie modern (XIIIe–XVIIe siècles): L'ambassador au croisement du droit, de l'éthique et de la politique* (Baden-Baden: Nomos Verlagsgesellschaft, 2017), 694.

30 'Ce sont des humanistes bénéficiant euxmêmes d'une certaine experience du métier d'ambassaeur.' Dolet, *De officio legati*, 12.

31 Hrabar, *De Legatis*, 65–70. See also Bruno Figliuolo, *Il diplomatico e il trattatista: Ermolao Barbaro ambasciatore della Serenissima e il De officio legati* (Naples: Guida, 1999); Mattingly, *Renaissance Diplomacy*, 94–96, 99–102, 188–89; [...] dal forte carattere autobiografico e autogiustivicativo.' Figliuolo, *Il diplomatico*, 77.

32 Hrabar, *De Legatis*, 85–88; Dolet, *De officio legati*, 42–87 [Latin text and French translation]. For Dolet, see also Nys, *Les origins de la diplomatie*, 38–39; Mattingly, *Renaissance Diplomacy*, 182–85; 'Celui [Jean de Langeac] que Dolet considérait comme un exemple du parfait ambassadeur [...].' Dolet, *De officio legati*, 10.

33 Anuschka Tischer, 'Diplomatie,' in *Enzyklopädie der Neuzeit*, vol. 2, ed. Friedrich Jäger (Stuttgart: Metzler, 2005), 1033; Hrabar, *De Legatis*, 1–28. See also Mattingly, *Renaissance Diplomacy*, 25–26, 30–40; Konrad Braun, *D. Conradi Brvni ivreconsvlti opera tria, nvnc primvm aedita. De Legationibvs Libri Qvinqve: [...], De Caeremoniis Libri Sex: [...], De Imaginbvs Liber Vnus: [...]* (Mainz: Franz Behem, 1548). See also Hrabar, *De Legatis*, 89–93; Behrens, 'Treatises,' 618–19.

34 Barbara Maria Rößner-Richarz, *Konrad Braun (ca. 1495–1563) – ein katholischer Jurist, Politiker, Kontroverstheologe und Kirchenreformer im konfessionellen Zeitalter* (Münster: Aschendorff, 1991), 176–82, 347–48.

35 'Schon seit den 1530er Jahren beschäftigte er [i.e. Konrad Braun] sich wissenschaftlich mit internationalen Beziehungen.' Rößner-Richarz, *Konrad Braun*, 230.

36 'Es ist vielmehr eine historisch fundierte Abhandlung über die Tradition des Gesandtenwesens.' Rößner-Richarz, *Konrad Braun*, 230; 'Auch in Konrad Brauns Denken war die mittelalterliche Einheitsidee von Kirche, Kaiser und Reich noch lebendig. [...] Deshalb setzte er sich immer wieder mit Gegebenheiten und Folgen für das Gesandtschaftswesen auseinander, die durch Häresie und Schisma aufträten [...] Er spürte wohl den Verlust der Universalvorstellung, zog aber keine ausdrücklichen Forderungen daraus. Deshalb blieb sein Werk weitgehend ein historisches Kompendium. Doch kam auch in den analytischen Schwerpunkten und Perspektiven ein Problembewusstsein zum Vorschein, das auf die Entwicklung konfessionellen Denkens hinweist.' Rößner-Richarz, *Konrad Braun*, 229–32.

37 Braun, *De Legationibus*, Lib. IV; Hrabar, *De Legatis*, 26: Bernhard du Rosier, Cap. XXVI De privilegis ambaxiatorum; See Braun, *De Legationibus*, Lib. II, Cap. IX De iustitia Legatorum; Hrabar, *De Legatis*, 5: du Rosier, Cap. II De qualitate et moribus ambacxiatorum [*sic*]. See also Behrens, 'Treatises,' 624–25.

38 'Welch große Bedeutung man der Rolle des Gesandten beimaß, zeigt sich darin, daß er in dieser Literatur [i.e. die Traktatliteratur zum Gesandtschaftswesen] durchwegs als Verkörperung des humanistischen Idealmenschen dargestellt wird.' Höflechner, 'Diplomatie,' 20. See also Fedele, *Naissance de la diplomatie*, 688–701.

39 See Figliuolo, *Il diplomatico*, 83; Dolet, *De officio legati*, 18–25, 51–65.

40 Behrens, 'Treatises,' 624.
41 Behrens, 'Treatises,' 624. Also: '[...] a Legationibus remouemus impios, haereticos, & schismaticos, & omnes qui Dei nomen & doctrinam blasphemant. Qui enim in Deum inique sunt, quomodo hominibus quae sunt iusta praestabunt.' [Margins: Matth, 6; Coloss. 3; Haeretici n[on] debent esse Legati], Braun, De Legationibus, Lib. II, Cap. IX, 58; Mattingly, Renaissance Diplomacy, 17.
42 Braun, De Legationibus, Lib. II, Cap. IX, 59; Hrabar, De Legatis, 5: Du Rosier, Cap. II De qualitate et moribus ambacxiatorum [sic!]: 'Qualem et quibus moribus pollentem ambaxiatorem esse debere ostendit ratio magistraque rerum efficax experiencia manifestat: [...], non supersticiosum, [...], iustum et pium [...].' See also: 'Si deve operare secondo i dettami della religiosità.' Figliuolo, Il diplomatico, 83.
43 Dolet, De officio legati, 9.
44 Baumgärtner, Martinus Garatus Laudensis, 18, 58; Behrens, 'Treatises,' 616; Tischer, 'Diplomatie,' 1033.
45 'Haeretici n[on] debent esse Legati.' Braun, De Legationibus, Lib. II, Cap. IX, 58.
46 Quoted from Glyn Redworth, In Defence of the Church Catholic. The Life of Stephen Gardiner (Oxford: Blackwell, 1990), 102. The rumour was spread by an agent of Thomas Cromwell. The agent again had heard it from Gardiner's archivist. See also James Arthur Muller, Stephen Gardiner and the Tudor Reaction (London: Society for Promoting Christian Knowledge, 1926), 82.
47 Beiergrößlein, Robert Barnes, 49–50.
48 For Henry VIII's diplomatic personnel, see Gary M. Bell, A Handlist of British Diplomatic Representatives 1509–1688 (Woodbridge: Boydell & Brewer Ltd, 1990).
49 For this, see, if not otherwise stated, Beiergrößlein, Robert Barnes, 65–68, 129–33, 167.
50 'La première qualité, assez générique, qu'un ambassadeur doit posséder, afin de ne pas compromettre sa mission dès le début, est d'être agréable au princes auquel il est destine; C'est la condition essentielle pour qu'il soit écouté avec bienveillance.' Fedele, Naissance de la diplomatie, 635. See also Jensen, 'Diplomacy,' 148.
51 Haigh, English Reformations, 125.
52 '[D]ilectum ad fidelem Cappelanum nostrum.' ThHStAW, Ernestinisches Gesamtarchiv, Reg. H 105, 2r.
53 Beiergrößlein, Robert Barnes, 73, n. 164.
54 Jensen, 'Diplomacy,' 148. See also Arnd Reitemeier, 'Das Gesandtschaftswesen im spätmittelalterlichen England,' in Aus der Frühzeit europäischer Diplomatie: Zum geistlichen und weltlichen Gesandtschaftswesen vom 12. bis zum 15. Jahrhundert, ed. Claudia Zey and Claudia Märtl (Zürich: Chronos Verlag, 2008), 253; Anderson, Rise, 11: 'So, more fundamentally, did the natural tendency of governments to employ the same man, once he had proved his ability and readiness to serve, in a series of different embassies.'
55 'Wolsey et Perrenot surtout rompent avec le formalisme et le pédantisme de leur prédécesseurs.' Nys, Les origins des la diplomatie, 30.
56 See also Jensen, 'Diplomacy,' 148. On the qualifications of English envoys and the way they were chosen, see Reitemeier, 'Gesandtschaftswesen,' 239–46.
57 'Theorie und Praxis der nzl. D[iplomatie] klafften mitunter auseinander. Viele Probleme wurden pragmatisch gelöst, so dass man eine konsequente einheitliche Praxis zunächst oft nicht erkennt.' Tischer, 'Diplomatie,' 1034. See also Jensen, 'Diplomacy,' 147.

58 Wilhelm G. Grewe, *The Epochs of International Law* (Berlin and New York: Walter de Gruyter, 2000), 141. See also Tischer, 'Diplomatie,' 1030; Jensen, 'Diplomacy,' 148.
59 For this, see Beiergrößlein, *Robert Barnes*, 157–65.

Bibliography

Archival sources

RA Copenhagen, TKUA, England, A II. 8, Nr. 19b-c.
Thüringisches Hauptstaatsarchiv Weimar (ThHStAW), Ernestinisches Gesamtarchiv, Reg. H 105.

Printed sources

Barnes, Robert. *A Supplication unto Henry VIII*. London: John Bydell, 1534.
Braun, Konrad. *D. Conradi Brvni ivreconsvlti opera tria, nvnc primvm aedita. De Legationibvs Libri Qvinqve: [...], De Caeremoniis Libri Sex: [...], De Imagnibvs Liber Vnus: [...]*. Mainz: Franz Behem, 1548.
Dolet, Étienne. *De officio legati, De immunitate legatorum, De legationibus Ioannis Langiachi Episcopi Lemovicensis*. Translated by David Amherdt. Geneva: Droz, 2010.
Foxe, John. 'The History of Robert Barnes Thomas Garard, and Wylliam Hierome Deuins.' In *The Acts and Monuments*, vol. 3, edited by John Foxe, 656–69. London: John Day, 1563.
Foxe, John. *The Unabridged Acts and Monuments Online* or *TAMO* (1563 edition) (HRI Online Publications, Sheffield, 2011). Available from: www.johnfoxe.org. Accessed 24th September, 2017.
Hrabar, Vladimir E., ed. *De Legatis et Legationibus Tractatus Varii*. Dorpat: Mattieseniano, 1905.
D. Martin Luthers Werke, Kritische Gesamtausgabe. Briefwechsel, vol. 6. Weimar: Hermann Böhlaus Nachfolger, 1935; RP Graz: Akademische Druck- und Verlagsanstalt, 1969.

Literature

Anderson, Matthew S. *The Rise of Modern Diplomacy 1450–1919*. London and New York: Longman, 1993.
Baumgärtner, Ingrid. *Martinus Garatus Laudensis: Ein italienischer Rechtsgelehrter des 15. Jahrhunderts*. Köln and Wien: Böhlau Verlag, 1986.
Behrens, Betty. 'Treatises on the Ambassador Written in the Fifteenth and Early Sixteenth Centuries.' *English Historical Review* 51 (1936): 616–27.
Beiergrößlein, Katharina. *Robert Barnes, England und der Schmalkaldische Bund*. Gütersloh: Verlagshaus, 2011.
Bell, Gary M. *A Handlist of British Diplomatic Representatives 1509–1688*. Woodbridge: Boydell & Brewer Ltd, 1990.
Collinson, Peter. 'Truth and Legend: the Veracity of John Foxe's Book of Martyrs.' In *Clio's Mirror: Historiography in Britain and the Netherlands*, edited by Alastair C. Duke and Coenraad A. Tamse, 31–54. Zutphen: De Walburg, 1985.

De Lamar, Jensen. 'Diplomacy.' In *Europe 1450 to 1789: Encyclopaedia of the Early Modern World*, vol. 2, edited by Jonathan Dewald, 147–52. New York: Thomas Gale, 2004.

Fedele, Dante. *Naissance de la diplomatie modern (XIIIe–XVIIe siècles): L'ambassador au croisement du droit, de l'éthique et de la politique*. Baden-Baden: Nomos Verlagsgesellschaft, 2017.

Figliuolo, Bruno. *Il diplomatico e il trattatista: Ermolao Barbaro ambasciatore della Serenissima e il De officio legati*. Naples: Guida, 1999.

Grewe, Wilhelm G. *The Epochs of International Law*. Berlin and New York: Walter de Gruyter, 2000.

Haigh, Christopher. *English Reformations: Religion, Politics and Society under the Tudors*. Oxford: Clarendon Press, 1993.

Haug-Moritz, Gabriele. *Der Schmalkaldische Bund 1530–1541/42: Eine Studie zu den genossenschaftlichen Strukturelementen der politischen Ordnung des Heiligen Römischen Reiches Deutscher Nation*. Leinfelden-Echterdingen: DRW Verlag, 2002.

Höflechner, Walter. 'Anmerkungen zum Diplomatie- und Gesandtschaftswesen am Ende des 15. Jahrhunderts.' *Mitteilungen des österreichischen Staatsarchivs* 32 (1979): 1–23.

King, John N. *Foxe's Book of Martyrs and Early Modern Print Culture*. Cambridge: Cambridge University Press, 2006.

Mattingly, Garret. *Renaissance Diplomacy*. Boston: Houghton Mifflin, 1955. RP New York: Dover Publications, 1988.

McEntegart, Rory. *Henry VIII, the League of Schmalkalden, and the Reformation*. Woodbridge: The Boydell Press, 2002.

Muller, James Arthur. *Stephen Gardiner and the Tudor Reaction*. London: Society for Promoting Christian Knowledge, 1926.

Nys, Ernest. *Les origins de la diplomatie et le droit d'ambassade jusque'à Grotius*. Brussels: Librairie Européene C. Muquardt, 1884.

Prüser, Friedrich. *England und die Schmalkaldener 1535–1540*. Leipzig: Heinsius, 1929. RP New York and London: Johnson, 1971.

Redworth, Glyn. *In Defence of the Church Catholic: The Life of Stephen Gardiner*. Oxford: Blackwell, 1990.

Reitemeier, Arnd. 'Das Gesandtschaftswesen im spätmittelalterlichen England.' In *Aus der Frühzeit europäischer Diplomatie: Zum geistlichen und weltlichen Gesandtschaftswesen vom 12. bis zum 15. Jahrhundert*, edited by Claudia Zey and Claudia Märtl, 231–53. Zürich: Chronos Verlag, 2008.

Rex, Richard. 'The Early Impact of Reformation Theology at Cambridge University, 1521–1547.' *Reformation and Renaissance Review* 2 (1999): 38–71.

Rößner-Richarz, Barbara Maria. *Konrad Braun (ca. 1495-1563) – ein katholischer Jurist, Politiker, Kontroverstheologe und Kirchenreformer im konfessionellen Zeitalter*. Münster: Aschendorff, 1991.

Ryrie, Alec. '"A saynt in the deuyls name": Heroes and Villains in the Martyrdom of Robert Barnes.' In *Martyrs and Martyrdom in England c. 1400–1700*, edited by Thomas S. Freemann and Thomas F. Mayer, 144–65. Woodbridge: The Boydell Press, 2007.

Tischer, Anuschka. 'Diplomatie.' In *Enzyklopädie der Neuzeit*, vol. 2, edited by Friedrich Jäger, 1028–42. Stuttgart: Metzler, 2005.

6 A most venerable provisional envoy

Friar Diego de la Fuente's diplomatic missions to Jacobean London, 1618–1620 and 1624[1]

Ernesto Oyarbide Magaña

On 19th October, 1618 (os), the English courtier Sir Abraham Williams wrote a letter to his friend, Sir William Trumbull, who had been sent to Brussels by King James as his ambassador:

> Whom have you sente us hether for a Spanishe Agent? A Dominican frere? One that hath ben an officer heretofore in the Spannishe Inquisition? And one that hath ben long a confessor to the late [Spanish] ambassador here?[2]

In this letter, Trumbull playfully informed his friend about the return to London of friar Diego de la Fuente, the Spanish embassy's chaplain. This Dominican friar had recently crossed the Channel with the Spanish ambassador on their way to Spain. Thus, at the moment this letter was penned, the friar was geographically closer to a Brussels-based Trumbull. However, while in France, De la Fuente was ordered by Philip III to return to England and from there report to Madrid about any event until his master's return. As a result, during the Spanish ambassador's absence, friar Diego de la Fuente became an important Spanish agent at the English court. Through an analysis of his correspondence, this chapter will explore some episodes of De la Fuente's diplomatic mission to Jacobean London between the years 1618 and 1620. It will do so with the purpose of showing how the friar endeavoured to emulate his master's diplomatic strategies so as to more successfully transact with English courtiers. In addition, this chapter will also comment on De la Fuente's diplomatic mission to London in 1624. During that time, the Dominican friar endeavoured to restore much deteriorated Anglo-Spanish relations, which were greatly affected by the failure of the Spanish Match in 1623.

The first Count of Gondomar and the Spanish embassy (1612–1622)

In 1612, Diego Sarmiento de Acuña, later the first Count of Gondomar, was appointed Spanish ambassador to the court of King James VI & I in

London.[3] For the following ten years, Gondomar played an essential role in the protection of English Catholics and the prevention of piracy in the Americas. He also succeeded in initially keeping England neutral during the first stages of the Thirty Years' War (1618–1648), mainly through the promise of a marriage between the Prince of Wales and the Spanish *Infanta*, which came to be known as the Spanish Match. Gondomar is credited, too, with being one of the most notable Spanish ambassadors to hold a post in Europe during the reign of Philip III (1598–1621).[4] During the past decades, Gondomar's diplomacy has been amply studied by scholars.[5] Nevertheless, this chapter aims to address a lesser-known field in the history of embassies. Indeed, over the past years, some studies have endeavoured to recognise the important role played by embassy personnel in day-to-day diplomatic business. For instance, Loomie revealed how the Spanish ambassador often relied on his secretaries of languages in order to transact with English courtiers. These secretaries were the English-speaking Francis Fowler, Henry Taylor, and Richard Berry.[6] In addition, thanks to a recent study by Ruiz, we now have more information about other individuals who lived at the Spanish embassy.[7] Sure enough, many of the administrative tasks were carried out by Spanish-born secretaries, such as Julián Sánchez de Ulloa, Tomás Ramírez, and Agustín Pérez. On a similar note, the steward Maese Pedro and Gondomar's wife, Doña Constanza, played a part in the embassy's upkeep.[8] Still, the embassy also had a confessor. As this chapter will show, during Gondomar's tenure, the confessor not only tended to the spiritual needs of the Spanish delegation; he also played an important diplomatic role. During this time, the post was mostly held by the Dominican friar Diego de la Fuente, who became one of the Spanish ambassador's closest confidants. Eventually, he also got involved in his master's trade. Certainly, while in London, the Dominican priest earned King James' affection. Through his relationship with the English king, De la Fuente managed to attain great political sway at the Court of St James's.

The life and deeds of Diego de la Fuente

When it comes to providing a biographical account for Diego de la Fuente, one is at a loss on where to find strong historical evidence. The Spanish *Diccionario Biográfico Español* has no specific entry for this priest. Little is known about him before he entered the service of Gondomar. According to an enthusiastically hagiographic 1940 volume on the history of the Dominicans living at the *Colegio de San Gregorio* in Valladolid, De la Fuente was born in Torrecilla de Sobresalenco, a small village within the diocese of Calahorra, although no birth date is provided. Still, the available records suggest that he entered the Dominican *Colegio de San Gregorio* in October 1601, and it seems he was regularly based there until it was decided that he should be sent to England.[9]

At the beginning of the seventeenth century, England's strongly Protestant stance led Spanish authorities to give great importance to the embassy's confessor in London. Accordingly, when Gondomar was appointed to the post in 1612, the count received many offers to fill this position. The Spanish ambassador eventually chose De la Fuente.[10] Friar Diego arrived with Gondomar at Portsmouth in August 1613. He was in charge of administering the Sacraments and celebrating Mass at the embassy for all the Spanish household and the English Catholics who decided to attend. De la Fuente was also the one to give extreme unction to the self-appointed Spanish missionary Luisa de Carvajal. This noblewoman arrived in England in 1605 with the ambitious intention of converting all of London through her proselytising. Nonetheless, she eventually fell ill and died in 1614.[11] The Dominican friar also officiated her funeral at the embassy's chapel. The Mass was attended by the ambassadors of France, Flanders, and Savoy.

Thanks to the correspondence held and the Gondomar library, there are many records about the confessor's endeavours during the 1610s and 1620s. Remarkably, the count's library holds a collection of letters that were once produced by the Dominican friar himself. These dispatches were penned between 1618 and 1620, a period during which the Dominican became the de facto main Spanish agent in London.[12] Certainly, for many years, the confessor tended to the religious needs of all those who came to the Spanish embassy, following Gondomar's wish to enhance it as the principal centre of Catholic worship in the city.[13] Nevertheless, De la Fuente also helped his master with other tasks.

As it is, the Spanish ambassador relied on the procurement of local English documents for developing his intelligence. Many of these sources were eventually preserved in the Gondomar library, which became an important tool for the Spaniard's diplomacy.[14] This detail can be observed, for instance, in the ambassador's efforts to censure anti-Spanish or anti-Catholic activity in London. As part of this strategy, the count often acquired books with Protestant doctrines produced in England. These tracts were usually sent to religious authorities in Catholic Europe for their examination. In a similar spirit, Gondomar also monitored publications with contents that were deemed detrimental to the interests of Spain. In fact, almost immediately after his arrival to London, the Spanish ambassador wrote to Pope Paul V requesting permission to read forbidden books for him, his secretaries and his confessor.[15] In May 1614, permission was granted.[16] The Dominican therefore assisted the count with this kind of intellectual monitoring. With the passing of time, probably through the bond created by spiritual direction, Gondomar and De la Fuente came to share a deep friendship. As a result, the count might have received most of his religious guidance from the friar. The confessor, in turn, appears to have obtained diplomatic training from the ambassador, who often trusted him to convey important messages. Indeed, a clear sign of the count's trust in the Spanish Dominican can be observed in a letter personally carried by De la Fuente to Philip III during the last months of 1616. In that missive, one can read the following statements from Gondomar:

> My most truthful Lord: Having in mind that Your Majesty (whom God protect) asked me in your letter from 9th last July to send from here [London] a person of my trust. Someone who understands the businesses and affairs concerning this kingdom [England] and who is also in your royal service, so that he, arriving at your court, can give you a detailed account of everything, I have decided to send the reverend father friar Diego de la Fuente, my confessor. This is due to the great satisfaction and confidence I have in his prudence, fidelity, and discretion.[17]

The conveying of this message by De la Fuente in person to Philip III was important for the Spanish ambassador. For many years, Gondomar had suspected that his diplomatic dispatches were being intercepted by English officials.[18] In this respect, the missive sent to the Spanish Council of State in late 1616 required the utmost secrecy. Indeed, this letter contained a plan for an invasion of England, should the need arise. This report was written around the same time that Sir Walter Raleigh was gathering support in England for a campaign in the Americas.[19] Thus, in this document, Gondomar advised his king to maintain peace, but at the same time he suggested that Spanish authorities should be prepared for the possibility of a war. Regardless of the many political comments one could draw from such a message to Madrid, this chapter wants to highlight Gondomar's trust in his confessor for delivering such an important dispatch.[20]

First diplomatic mission (1618–1620)

De la Fuente's political commissions did not end there. In 1618, the Spanish ambassador was granted leave to return to Spain in August so that he could recover from bad health. Originally, Diego de la Fuente set out to return with the count. Nevertheless, while in France, he received a letter from Madrid ordering him to go back to London and from there report on everything until his master's return. This turn of events was completely unexpected for the Dominican. In a letter dated 1st September, 1618, one can read his expressions of surprise and his prompt determination to comply with the king's commission, with God's assistance: 'I very humbly kiss Your Majesty's feet for such a particular honour and kindness; and for the confidence Your Majesty has decided to bequeath in my zeal to serve'.[21]

In this way, an unknown Dominican friar became interim Spanish envoy to the majority-Protestant Court of St James's. Surprisingly, when providing a narrative of Anglo-Spanish relations during the late 1610s, most historians usually fast-forward from mid-1618 to March 1620, the time when Gondomar returned to England. As a notable exception, Roberta Anderson mentions that during this interim moment the embassy was put in the charge of the Spanish secretary, Julián Sánchez de Ulloa, with support from De la Fuente.[22] However, when reading contemporary documents, one can see that during this period the Spanish priest held more sway with English courtiers. This can be appreciated in a letter that Sánchez de Ulloa sent to Spain on 28th October, 1618. In this document, the embassy's secretary acknowledged De la Fuente's appointment as an agent, but also requested Spanish authorities for specific instructions about his duties within this new scenario.[23] As it transpired, Sánchez de Ulloa continued assisting De la Fuente with administrative tasks at the embassy.

The reactions of the English court further support the idea about De la Fuente's higher regard as a Spanish envoy, given the way he was amicably entertained by many English courtiers. The Dominican arrived back in London on 30th September, 1618.[24] The day after, he sent a letter requesting a royal audience to the Marquess of Buckingham at that time, George Villiers, who was King James' main administrator. He was promptly granted a meeting with English authorities while James stayed in a house in Andover.[25] The friar first transacted with the king's favourite. They amicably conversed for a while before De la Fuente was taken to see the king, who remarked that his Most Catholic Majesty could not have sent him a person more pleasing to him, other than the Count of Gondomar.[26] During that meeting, the king and De la Fuente conferred in Latin for almost an hour. Many topics where discussed. Some were of substance, such as the crisis in the Palatinate region and the Spanish Match. But the conversation soon turned to a more frivolous tone, as De la Fuente jokingly commented on the fact that the King of Spain was sending a priest to play the part of 'pimp' between the Prince of Wales and the Spanish *Infanta*. The Spanish word used by the priest in the report about this episode is *tercero*.[27] During the period, it was unmistakably associated with *La Celestina*.[28] As Glyn Redworth has remarked, this book, a tale of pimps and lovers, was regularly brought up in discussions about the Spanish Match.[29] By using this Spanish reference, De la Fuente was following Gondomar's strategy of mixing political deliberations with anecdotes and jokes.[30] Indeed, 'Old Aesop Gondomar,' as Ben Jonson calls him in his *Speech according to Horace*, was well known for constantly inserting stories and learned accounts amid his political exchanges with relevant English personages. In this respect, in a letter dated 18th January, 1619, we can see the priest asking Gondomar for new tales to keep James and other English courtiers entertained:

> I cannot finish without prompting your excellency to assist me *per modum sufragii*, with three or four hundred tons of tales; and that

these come well-seasoned from Spain, so that they reach me with a good flavour. I ask this because I am being very much favoured by this king, who loves to hear tales and I wished to have some more.[31]

King James was no stranger to this strategy of mixing political facts with puns, as evinced by his reply to the priest on their first audience. After hearing the *tercero* reference by De la Fuente, James jokingly retorted that it was a marvel to see how his Most Catholic Majesty had decided to send a humble friar to the court of an 'heretical king.' This was followed by additional cheerful comments. De la Fuente was invited later that day to eat with Buckingham, and was regularly sent drinks, food, and gifts from the king's table.[32] Two days later, the confessor was also welcomed by Queen Anne, who promptly remarked that he should learn French so that they could communicate without an interpreter.[33] De la Fuente later visited the queen quite regularly, and during her last days of illness tried to prepare her for death as a Catholic through the acceptance of the last Sacraments, though he was unsuccessful.[34] Despite this, he still procured an invitation to be at the queen's funeral in April 1619.[35]

Even though the relating of these personal encounters might appear anecdotal at first sight, they nonetheless had their diplomatic importance. In their introduction to *Practices of Diplomacy in the Early Modern World*, Hennings and Sowerby acknowledge the importance of diplomatic history's pivotal moments. However, in this study the highlight is put on a series of 'sociocultural practices' that might not be deemed political nowadays, but nonetheless helped to shape political relationships and foreign policy during the early modern period. After all, not every person involved in diplomatic business was a diplomat. On the same note, the main concern of a premodern ambassador was not always diplomatic negotiation.[36] When looking at this period, the term 'diplomacy' can serve as a somewhat inadequate label to define a series of exchanges that were multifaceted and difficult to define within just one category. This was the case with practices such as the act of giving gifts, the providing of entertainment to envoys, and their inclusion within ceremonial displays, such as those that touched on diplomatic precedence. Still, it is no less true that all these practices were important forms of communication between states. Certainly, as Sowerby and Hennings have asserted, any diplomatic encounter can become politically relevant when the evidence reveals the ways in which relations between different polities were conducted. From this perspective, what becomes important are the actions, conduct, and overall the practices of diplomatic agents and the responses these triggered – or intended – rather than the influence they eventually exerted 'upon the big turns and trends in the history of international relations.'[37] It is in this context that the narration of De la Fuente's first receiving at the English court can become politically pertinent, and a similar thing can be said about subsequent encounters with English courtiers.

Certainly, during the friar's initial stay in Andover, many of James' ministers visited him, chiefly among whom was Francis Bacon, at that time Lord High Chancellor of England. In their scholarly works, Loomie and Tobío have already discussed Gondomar's cordial friendship with the English essayist.[38] Out of respect for the count, Bacon treated the friar with great cordiality during the ambassador's absence. This can be observed in a letter dated 29th August, 1619:

> The great Chancellor of England keeps honouring me and granting me favours; and he has now done something very special, given that I was outside of London in a country house he has in 'San Albano', which they call here San Abons [St Albans], 20 miles from the city; and knowing that I had just returned from the springs, he [Bacon] sent me his secretary to ask me to go for some days to his home; and we all known the prominence and *noli me tangere* of the great Chancellor of England, who usually does not grant these favours to ordinary people; and I would faint from receiving such extraordinary gesture if I did not know that with this he [Bacon] is saying: *'non tibi sed Comiti de Gondomar'*.[39]

Bacon's attentive treatment is just one example among other forms of deference. During his time as provisional envoy, De la Fuente corresponded directly with James, his favourite, Buckingham, the English diplomats John Digby and Francis Cottington, and with Thomas Howard, Earl of Arundel, an important member of the Privy Council. These are just some courtiers among others.[40] A further example of the favour shown by English courtiers can be found in a letter written by De la Fuente to the count in March 1619. In this dispatch, he informs his master about the election of James Hay, Viscount Doncaster, as English ambassador to the German states. This event took place during the outbreak of the Palatinate crisis, one of Gondomar's most exasperating hindrances to a Spanish Match. James Hay was known for his tactful diplomatic demeanour and, even though a convinced Protestant, he usually managed to amicably negotiate with Catholic agents, as acknowledged by De la Fuente, who indicated that the election of Hay was a favourable turn for Spain. He goes on to add a note about a friendly visit from this English courtier to the Spanish embassy. On that day, the viscount became interested in a portrait of Gondomar that was in the friar's room:

> And while the Viscount visited me this past Friday, he stopped for a while to contemplate your Excellency's portrait that I have in my room, saying that it greatly resembled the original and that he was very tempted to steal it from me [...]. So, I hope you will excuse me for sending the portrait to his home, as I did.[41]

As these documents show, the Dominican friar profited from the relationships already established by his master during his first embassy, and he usually acknowledged this in his correspondence. He regularly claimed that Gondomar's efforts in winning English friends for the Spanish cause had proven fruitful and extremely useful during his absence. What is more, the Dominican's correspondence also reveals that he adopted specific documentary practices for his diplomatic transactions. In this respect, the friar seems to have imitated Gondomar as well. Indeed, in a letter dated 21st December, 1618, friar Diego explained to the count that he had sent him copies of important 'papers' – probably letters – and keeping the originals.[42] In this missive, De la Fuente jested with his master by saying that the count had managed to pass the administrative affliction of copying documents to him, and that he was amassing an unruly amount of 'papers' as a result. In the process, he also sheds some light on the use of personal libraries for the conducting of diplomacy. Indeed, while Gondomar was away, the friar created his own compendia of documents. As a result, in this letter he jokingly brought a comparison between Gondomar's library, which was ultimately preserved in a house adjacent to the church of Saint Benedict in Valladolid, and his personal collection of documents, which he playfully put under the auspices of the monastery, where he professed:

> If the library of Saint Benedict the Old [Gondomar's library], *Plus quam Vaticana*, ever wants to put a lawsuit ['*pleyto*'] to these paper morsels [I send you], I suppose I would have to surrender, unless I can use the strength of the *Casa de San Gregorio* [his own collection of documents].[43]

In the case of friar Diego and many other early modern individuals, correspondence formed part of their libraries. Thus, letters shared a common space with books, maps, printed images, pamphlets, and other documentary sources.[44] These documents were often used by diplomatic agents to produce regular reports for authorities back home.[45] Sure enough, from London, De la Fuente informed Spain about English responses to the Spanish Match negotiations. He also reported about the current state of English Catholics, who during that period were experiencing a brief respite from persecution.[46] De la Fuente also kept the Spanish Council of State informed about the trial of Sir Walter Raleigh, who was ultimately held responsible for the raid of Spanish settlements during his campaign in the Americas.[47] Following his master's habit of sending long and detailed letters to Spain, De la Fuente recorded happenings in London: gossip, news about court events, and information about the doings of what he called the *malintencionados*: those negatively disposed towards Spain.[48] This group was regularly very outspoken about their discontent over Spanish interference. Indeed, while in England, De la Fuente was very much disliked for his continuous protesting to the English authorities whenever something offensive against Spain or Catholicism was printed or put to stage. In October 1619, for example, he discussed with King James about the removal of some papers printed in Holland that depicted Frederick, the Elector Palatine, as King of Bohemia. This was done in detriment of the Holy Roman Emperor, who was deemed by Spanish authorities to be the rightful ruler of that region.[49] The friar also managed to supress a print that depicted a beaten pope at the king's feet.[50] In addition, he was successful in removing from the stage a play called *The Whore of Babylon*, which abused the Pope and attacked the Spanish alliance. This can be observed in a report sent to Spain:

> I have been brave these days, given that I have [put] in jail five or six men who have been found guilty for [publishing] a print that came out these days against His Holiness; and I have managed to suspend with great effect the representation in here [London] of a Play they call *The Whore of Babylon*, [which] is full of a thousand blasphemies and lies against the Pope and Spain.[51]

Unsurprisingly, some English courtiers noticed how De la Fuente's actions damaged their political and religious interests. In one of his letters, the English news-gatherer John Chamberlain complained to Sir Dudley Carleton, English ambassador to the United Provinces, about De la Fuente's unhindered access to King James.[52] However, the priest was far from attempting to overthrow Protestantism or the English status quo. His letters show that he was aware that the road to Catholic toleration required a careful balance of confessional policies. Certainly, De la Fuente met on many occasions with English Catholics, and he usually did urge them to keep the peace so that English authorities would not resort to persecution again:

> The Catholics enjoy more peace at present than in previous times; and the King [James] is being true to what he promised the Count [of Gondomar]; I desire, and make sure, that they [the Catholics] use it in a way that is not taken as an opportunity to return to the old rigours; and I try to convince their heads [leaders] of this so that they convey it to the rest.[53]

Another clear sign of the priest's understanding of the delicate state of Catholicism in England can be seen in many letters written in December 1618. In some dispatches, he regretted the fact that many English Catholic priests, who had been recently freed and sent away during the previous summer as a favour to Gondomar, were nonetheless coming back to England and causing indignation among Protestant groups.[54] However, not all the friar's dealings had to do with confessional affairs. During the late months of 1619, he had to appease James over popular discontent when it came to England's passivity in the Palatinate crisis. From London, De la Fuente informed how the *malintencionados* whispered all around the streets that the king had abandoned his daughter, Elizabeth Stuart, and his son-in-law, Frederick V, to satisfy Spanish interests.[55]

When considering al these episodes, one wonders how this humble Dominican friar managed to move so aptly within these complicated political scenarios. In this respect, his letters reveal to us that in all these situations, he tried to emulate Gondomar's diplomatic strategies. In one of his dispatches to the count, De la Fuente even resorted to a playful shift of roles. After relating events from London, he sought the Spanish ambassador's approval by assigning him the task of confessor in all things related to diplomacy:

> It greatly pains me to have tired your excellency with such a long letter. But such was the pleasure of writing it that it is also true I could not easily stop my hand. I wanted to do a General Confession and tell your excellency all my sins; and before receiving the absolution, I just wish to reassure you that I am your servant now more than ever.[56]

Diego de la Fuente endeavoured to maintain an amicable relationship between England and Spain during Gondomar's leave of absence from 1618 to 1620. His imitation of the count's diplomatic tactics allowed him to become an effective diplomatic proxy for the Spanish ambassador. This can be observed in a letter penned by the count himself. Once he returned to London for his second embassy, Gondomar praised the friar while commenting on the current state of the Spanish Match negotiations:

> Because undoubtedly [negotiations] would have been broken already if they had not been preserved by the prudence and skill of the '[Padre] Maestro' friar Diego de la Fuente. Great is the reputation he has here among the king and everybody else, when it comes to his [good] character and trustworthiness.[57]

Second diplomatic mission (1624)

As the historian John Elliott once claimed, Gondomar became one of the greatest European specialists in English affairs of the early seventeenth century.[58] In a similar spirit, one could argue that De la Fuente learned from his master and became a remarkable Spanish authority on English matters. This can be appreciated in subsequent diplomatic appointments. In 1621, he was sent to Rome to defend the convenience of obtaining papal dispensation for an Anglo-Spanish marriage. More importantly, in 1624, he was dispatched back to London to try to restore the much deteriorated diplomatic relations between both countries. Certainly, in May 1622, Gondomar was replaced by Carlos Coloma at the Spanish embassy.

Even though he still kept the title of ordinary ambassador, the arrival of a new Spanish envoy to England meant, at least in practice, that Gondomar would no longer be the main interlocutor with English authorities once he left for Spain.[59] However, the unexpected appearance of the Prince of Wales in Madrid on March 1623 would again put him in the first line of diplomatic negotiations. In previous studies, Redworth and Samson have greatly increased our understanding of the events that followed from Charles' impromptu appearance in Spain in a last bid to request the *Infanta*'s hand. Gondomar played an important role as Anglo-Spanish liaison during the prince's visit. However, after the initial festivities, negotiations gradually reached an impasse as a result of mutual misinterpretations and misunderstandings. In the end, the Prince of Wales left Spain without a Spanish bride.[60] As a result, after more than eight tiring years of negotiations, the Spanish Match finally reached a deadlock and both nations were again close to renewing hostilities. Indeed, following Charles' return to England in October 1623, anti-Spanish sentiment reached a high point in London.[61] Consequently, English streets were filled with derisory pamphlets.[62]

Between June 1623 and September 1624, just as hopes for a Spanish Match were at their highest, the number of Spanish agents in London increased. However, as the prospects for a marriage declined, diplomatic estrangement ensued, along with a reduction of agents.[63] Certainly, during the first months of 1624, the Spanish embassy had not only one, but two, ambassadors: Carlos Coloma and Juan de Mendoza, Marquis of Hinojosa. Nevertheless, this did not lead to more political leverage, as these two men were not on the best of terms with King James and his Privy Council.[64] For months, the Spanish Council of State intended to send Gondomar on a third embassy to the Court of St James's, but his poor health did not allow it.[65] It was then decided that De la Fuente should head back to England. Unfortunately, he was ambushed while travelling through France and most of his dispatches where stolen.[66] Notwithstanding this setback, after his arrival in London in early April 1624, De la Fuente obtained an audience with the king in less than a week.[67] On that occasion, the friar was not only amicably received by the English monarch, but also managed to convince the king to distrust the intentions of the recently made Duke of Buckingham, George Villiers, who had become one of Spain's most passionate enemies following his trip to Madrid with the Prince of Wales.[68] Sure enough, in the spring of 1624, De la Fuente informed a very old and sick King James about the many rumours of a plan devised by the anti-Spanish faction, which was now championed by Buckingham. According to these rumours, this group aimed to gradually retire James from power and hand over the reins of government to his son.[69] The intelligence was obtained by the Spanish embassy's agents with the help of Francis Cottington, who at the time worked as secretary to Prince Charles.[70]

It would go beyond the scope of this chapter to fully discuss the many backstage details behind this political manoeuvre. For the moment, suffice to say that James believed De la Fuente, demonstrating that he trusted the Spanish priest to the point of making him doubt the intentions of his favourite.[71] In the end, however, Buckingham managed to regain the king's good graces with the support of Prince Charles, who regarded this campaign as a personal attack. Facing the decision of having to choose between De la Fuente and the Spanish ambassadors, on the one hand, and his own son, on the other, James chose the latter in May 1624.[72] After these events, Anglo-Spanish relations gradually reached their lowest point since the days of Queen Elizabeth. Only King James' reluctance to declare war on Spain postponed the hostilities. This would, however, soon change following his death in March 1625, but by that point the Spanish ambassadors and Diego de la Fuente had already left London.

Regardless of this inglorious finale to Anglo-Spanish relations during this time, it cannot be denied that friar Diego de la Fuente became an influential Spanish agent at the Jacobean court. Further proof of this can be found in the fact that when preparing to leave for Spain in late summer 1624, the Dominican received a message from King James through the Secretary of State, Sir Edward Conway. In a somewhat ambiguous strategy, the monarch conveyed to him that his present displeasure was of a personal nature, that is, against the current Spanish ambassadors only. As a result, De la Fuente should tell the King of Spain that his brother in England would be glad to keep the peace and receive any other new ambassador.[73] In a moment of great political tension, James chose the Spanish friar, rather than other Spanish agents, for this message of appeasement.

Friar Diego's last years

As it is, much less is known about Diego de la Fuente after he returned to Spain in 1624. It seems that he abandoned the diplomatic scene and became a Provincial of the Dominican Order. He continued to be based in the *Colegio de San Gregorio* in Valladolid until his death in 1630.[74] This chapter has used a small number of De la Fuente's letters, which are still held at the Royal Library in Madrid, to provide a very brief narrative of the ambassadorial role played by the Spanish embassy's confessor at the English court, and it has done so with the purpose of better revealing how these usually disregarded secondary members of the Spanish embassy often helped in the shaping of European politics. Indeed, the study of these minor agents provides a more nuanced understanding of the complex nature of premodern Anglo-Spanish relations. In the case of this humble Dominican friar who eventually became a Spanish agent, the documentary evidence also reveals that religious differences and social rank could sometimes take a secondary role in premodern political circles, which often favoured personal affinities. This can be observed through King James' cordial relationship with De la Fuente. Furthermore, from the point of view of confessional diplomacy, the letters penned by De la Fuente also provide us with the candid testimony of a well-meaning friar who intended to keep Protestant England and Catholic Spain at peace. Moreover, his dispatches, usually so profuse in detail, offer an exceptional insight into the inner life and workings of an early modern embassy. All in all, the extant records show that this Dominican friar managed to earn a place among the list of diplomatic agents that were deployed in Europe by imperial Spain, a power that was to gradually lose its political predominance over the following decades of the seventeenth century.[75]

Notes

1 This chapter was written with the support of the I + D + i Research Project 'Poder y representaciones culturales en la época moderna: agentes diplomáticos como mediadores culturales de la Edad Moderna (siglos XVI-XVIII)' funded by the Spanish Ministry of Science and Innovation (MICINN) (Reference: HAR2016-78304-C2-2-P).

2 *Report on the Manuscripts of the Marquess of Downshire*, ed. E. K. Purnell, Geraint Dyfnallt Owen, and Sonia P. Anderson, 6 vols (London: Historical Manuscripts Commission, 1924), 6, letter 1163.

3 Even though he was appointed Spanish ambassador in 1612, Sarmiento arrived in London in 1613. He was given the title of first Count of Gondomar by Philip III in 1617. However, for the sake of clarity, and because that is how he came to be known, this chapter will refer to him as 'Gondomar', regardless of the year. Unless otherwise stated, for all documents cited, this article will use the new style of dating according to the Gregorian calendar. For manuscripts from Madrid's Real Biblioteca, the abbreviation 'RB' will be used.

4 Garrett Mattingly, *Renaissance Diplomacy* (Baltimore: Penguin Books, 1955), 222. See also, Miguel Ochoa Brun, *Historia de la Diplomacia Española* (Madrid: Ministerio de Asuntos Exteriores, 1990–2006), vol. 7, 84.

5 See, for instance, José García Oro, *Don Diego Sarmiento de Acuña, Conde de Gondomar* (Santiago de Compostela: Xunta de Galicia, 1997); Fernando Bartolomé Benito, *Don Diego Sarmiento de Acuña, Conde de Gondomar: El Maquiavelo Español* (Gijón: Trea, 2005); Glyn Redworth, 'Diego Sarmiento de Acuña (1567–1626)', *ODNB*; Carmen Manso Porto, 'Diego Sarmiento de Acuña, Conde de Gondomar', *DBE-RAH*; Francisco Sánchez Cantón, *Don Diego Sarmiento de Acuña, Conde de Gondomar* (Madrid: Real Academia de la Historia, 1935); Luis Tobío, *Gondomar y los Católicos Ingleses* (A Coruña: Ediciós do Castro, 1987); Luis Tobío, *Gondomar y su triunfo sobre Raleigh* (Santiago de Compostela: Bibliófilos Gallegos, 1974).

6 See Albert Loomie, 'Richard Berry: Gondomar's English Catholic Adviser', *British Catholic History*, 11, 1 (1971), 47–57; id., 'Francis Fowler II, English Secretary of the Spanish Embassy, 1609–1619', *British Catholic History*, 12, 1 (1973), 70–78; id., 'Canon Henry Taylor, Spanish Habsburg Diplomat', *British Catholic History*, 17, 2 (1984), 223–37.

7 For more information about the Spanish embassy's personnel, see Óscar Ruiz Fernández, 'Las Relaciones Hispano-Inglesas Entre 1603–1625.' (Universidad of Valladolid [Unpublished doctoral dissertation], 2012), pp. 11–19, accessed 30 October 2019, http://uvadoc.uva.es:80/handle/10324/951.

8 The 'ambassadorial' role played by Gondomar's wife in London is still a pending task. For a preliminary study, see Nuria Bezos del Amor, 'Los Consejos de Una Esposa a Su Marido El Embajador de Inglaterra: Doña Constanza de Acuña (1619),' in *IV Congreso Virtual Sobre Historia de Las Mujeres*, 2012, https://dialnet.unirioja.es/servlet/articulo?codigo=4715039.

9 Gonzalo de Arriaga and Manuel María Hoyos, *Historia del Colegio de San Gregorio de Valladolid* (Valladolid: Cuesta, 1940), vol. 3, 33–48.

10 Count of Benavente to Gondomar, 20th March 1613, RB II/2158, doc. 109.

11 Tobío, *Gondomar y los Católicos Ingleses*, 56.

12 This chapter will base many of its assertions on the letters held in the Gondomar library under the Reference RB II/551.

13 From very early after his arrival, the count wrote to his king stating that he was greatly edified by the devotion of the English Catholics attending his chapel. Supposedly, four Masses where celebrated every day. Tobío, *Gondomar y los Católicos Ingleses*, 54–59.

14 See Ernesto Oyarbide Magaña, 'Embodying the Portrait of the Perfect Ambassador: The First Count of Gondomar and the Role of Print Culture and Cultural Literacy in Anglo-Spanish Relations during the Jacobean Period,' in *Embajadores Culturales: Transferencias y Lealtades de La Diplomacia Española de La Edad Moderna*, ed. by Diana Carrió-Invernizzi and José Miguel Escribano Páez (Madrid: Universidad Nacional de Educación a Distancia, 2016), 157–85; Jeremy Lawrance, '"Une Bibliothèque Fort Complète Pour Un Grand Seigneur": Gondomar's Manuscripts and the Renaissance Idea of the Library,' *Bulletin of Spanish Studies*, 81, 7–8 (2004), 1071–90.

15 See letter dated on 30th August 1613, RB II/2341, doc. 18.

16 Gondomar to Cardinal Milino, 15th May, 1614, RB/2168, 173v–76r. For more information regarding Gondomar's dealings with forbidden books, see Carmen Manso Porto, *Don Diego Sarmiento de Acuña (1567–1626): erudito, mecenas y bibliófilo* (Santiago de Compostela, 1996), 321–29.

17 'Señor mio muy verdadero: Por cuanto su Majestad (que Dios Guarde) se sirvió de mandarme, en su carta de 9 de Julio último, que le enviase de aquí persona de mi confianza y enterada en los negocios y cosas tocantes a este reino y a su real servicio, que se puedan ofrecer, para que en llegando a esa corte pueda hacer particular relación de todo, dejé para ello al P. Fr. Diego de la Fuente, mi confesor, por la gran satisfacción y seguridad que tengo de su prudencia, fidelidad y secreto.' See Gondomar's letter to Philip III, in *Biblioteca Nacional*, MSS. 18430 (2), ff. 9–26.

18 For a contemporary account in which Gondomar expresses his suspicions about a Spanish informer, see Gondomar to the Duke of Lerma, 5th October, 1613, in Duque de Alba et al., 'Correspondencia oficial de Don Diego Sarmiento de Acuña, Conde de Gondomar', *Documentos inéditos para la Historia de España* (Madrid, 1936–1945), vol. 3, 131–35.

19 Walter Raleigh eventually reached the Americas and was deemed responsible for a raid to Spanish settlements. He was later executed in London in 1619, at the behest of Spanish authorities. See Tobío, *Gondomar y Raleigh: Españoles e Ingleses en América durante el siglo XVII*, ed. by Ciriaco Pérez Bustamante (Santiago de Compostela: Paredes, 1928).

20 For more information on the relationship between the Spanish ambassador and Raleigh, see Tobío, *Gondomar y su triunfo sobre Raleigh*.

21 'De vuestra Majestad cuyos pies beso muy humildemente por tan singular honra y miramiento; y por la confianza que vuestra Majestad muestra tener de mi buen zelo.' See de la Fuente to Philip III, 1st October, 1618, RB II/551, 1r.

22 Roberta Anderson, 'Diplomatic Representatives from the Hapsburg Monarchy to Court of James VI and I', in *The Spanish Match: Prince Charles's Journey to Madrid*, 1623, ed. Alexander Samson (London: Ashgate, 2006), 218–20.

23 Sánchez de Ulloa to Philip III, Archivo General de Simancas, Estado LEG 2598, doc. 102.

24 De la Fuente to Philip III, 12 October, 1618, RB II/551, 2r.

25 James VI & I rarely stayed in London. It appears he sometimes took residence in a house in Andover. John Nichols, *The Progresses, Processions, and Magnificent Festivities of King James the First*, 4 vols (Nichols, 1828), 2, 668; 4, 613 and 886.

26 De la Fuente to Philip III, 12th October, 1618, RB II/551, 2v.

27 De la Fuente to Philip III, 12th October, 1618, RB II/551, 3r.

28 *La Celestina* is a work entirely in dialogue published in 1499 by Fernando de Rojas. The book tells the story of the bachelor Calisto who uses the old procuress Celestina to start an affair with the unmarried girl Melibea. During the period, this work enjoyed enormous popularity among European readers. Still today, the term 'Celestina' is synonymous in Spanish with those of a sexual procurator or a matchmaker.

29 Glyn Redworth, *The Prince and the Infanta: The Cultural Politics of the Spanish Match* (New Haven, Yale University Press, 2003), 98.

30 For more information, see 'Fray Diego de la Fuente y don Diego Sarmiento, lectores del Quijote,' in *Avisos de la Real Biblioteca*, accessed 4th August, 2020, https://avisos.realbiblioteca.es/index.php/Avisos/article/view/562.

31 'No puedo dexar de suplicar a V. S. me socorra per modum sufragii con unas treçientas o quatro çientas toneladas de quentos, y que estos traygan desde allá la sal para que tengan buena saçón, que como me veo tan favoreçido de el rey que se humana a oyrme los quentos, querría tener algunos.' De la Fuente to Gondomar, 18th January, 1619, RB II/551, 73r.

32 De la Fuente to Philip III, 12th October, 1618, RB II/551, 3r–v.

33 De la Fuente to Philip III, 12th October, 1618, RB II/551, 4v.

34 The English Carmelite, Simon Stock, was a protégé of Gondomar. Under the auspices of the Spanish embassy, Stock managed to establish an amicable relationship with Anne. He left an account of her final days: 'I have had several interviews with Queen Anne, in which I explained to her the foundations of our faith, but she always put off her conversion, and finally died outside the true Church, although at heart a Catholic.' Georg Zimmermann, *Carmel in England: A History of the English Mission of the Discalced Carmelites, 1615 to 1849* (London, 1899), 30.

35 John Chamberlain to Dudley Carleton, 17th April, 1619, in *The Letters of John Chamberlain* (Philadelphia: The American Philosophical Society, 1939), vol. 2, 229–31.

36 Tracey Sowerby and Jan Hennings (eds.), *Practices of Diplomacy in the Early Modern World, c.1410–1800* (London: Routledge, 2017), 2.

37 Ibid., 3.

38 See Albert Loomie, 'Bacon and Gondomar: an unknown link in 1618', *Renaissance Quarterly*, 21, 1 (1968), 1–10; Luis Tobío, 'A amistade de Bacon e Gondomar', *Grial*, 18, 68 (1980), 210–15.

39 '[E]l Canciller de Inglaterra va continuándome en honrarme y favorecerme, y lo que ahora particularmente ha hecho; pues estando fuera de Londres en una casa de campo que tiene en S. Albano, que aquí llaman San Abons [St Albans], 20 millas de esta ciudad, en sabiendo que yo había vuelto de la fuente, me envió a visitar con su secretario y a pedirme fuese algunos días a su casa; que quíen sabe cuán grande es la deidad y el noli me tangere del Gran

Canciller de Inglaterra no le puede parecer este favor de los ordinarios, y a mi me pudiera desvanecer si, en lo que tiene de extraordinario y grande, no conociera que ello mismo está diciendo: 'non tibi sed Comiti de Gondomar.' See de la Fuente to Gondomar, 29th August, 1619, RB II/551, 180r.

40 Online listing of the friar's letters in RB II/511, accessed 15th August, 2020, https://fotos.patrimonionacional.es/biblioteca/ibis/pmi/II_00551/index.html

41 'Haciéndome el Vizconde [una visita] el Biernes pasado se detubo un buen rato a mirar el retrato que tenía de VS en mi aposento diciendo que se parecia mucho al original y que tenía tentación de urtármele [...] con que perdonará VS el haversele yo luego embiado a su casa como yo hiçe.' See de la Fuente to Gondomar, 10th March, 1619, RB II/551, 99v–103r.

42 See De la Fuente to Gondomar, 21st December, 1618, RB II/551, 55v–59v.

43 'si la librería de San Benito el Viejo, plus quam Vaticana, me pusiere pleito a estos fragmentillos, entiendo que me rendiré no obstante que me pudiera haçer fuerte con la casa de San Gregorio.' See De la Fuente to Gondomar, 21st December 1618, RB II/551, 56r.

44 See Alexandra Walsham, 'The Social History of the Archive: Record-Keeping in Early Modern Europe,' *Past & Present*, 230, 11 (2016), 9–48; Arndt Brendecke, '"Arca, Archivillo, Archivo": The Keeping, Use and Status of Historical Documents about the Spanish Conquista,' *Archival Science*, 10, 3 (2010), 267–83.

45 See Elizabeth Williamson, '"Fishing after News" and the Ars Apodemica: The Intelligencing Role of the Educational Traveller in the Late Sixteenth Century,' in *News Networks in Early Modern Europe*, ed. by Joad Raymond and Noah Moxham (Leiden: Brill, 2016), 542–62; Charles Carter, *The Secret Diplomacy of the Habsburgs* (New York: Columbia University Press, 1964), 65–76.

46 See, for example, de la Fuente to Philip III, 17th January, 1619, RB II/551, 66r–67r. See also de la Fuente to Gondomar, 6th December, 1619, RB II/551, 213r–14v.

47 See de la Fuente to Ferdinand von Boischot, 9th November, 1618, RB II/551, 32r–33v. See also de la Fuente to Philip III, 10th November, 1618, RB II/551, 33v–34v.

48 See, for example, de la Fuente to Hernando de Girón, 31st December, 1619, RB II/551, 244r.

49 See Geoffrey Parker, *The Thirty Years' War* (London: Routledge, 1997).

50 De la Fuente to Philip III, 29th October, 1619, RB II/551, 202r–3r.

51 'He sido valiente estos días, pues tengo en la cárçel çinco o seys hombres que se han allado culpados en una estanpa que salió aquí estos días contra su Santidad, y he hecho suspender con efecto el representarse aquí una Comedia que llaman la Ramera de Babilonia, llena de mil blasfemias contra el Papa y contra España.' De la Fuente to Gondomar, 1st November, 1619 RB II/551, 208v.

52 John Chamberlain to Dudley Carleton, 2nd October, 1619, in *The Letters of John Chamberlain* (Philadelphia: The American Philosophical Society, 1939), vol. 2, 264–66.

53 'Los católicos gozan al presente de mayor paz que en otros tiempos, y el Rey va cumpliendo q prometió al Conde [de Gondomar], yo desseo y procuro q ellos [los católicos] usen desto de manera q no se tome ocasión para bolver al rigor antiguo, y assi lo voy persuadiendo a las cavezas para que lo aconsejen a los demas.' See de la Fuente to Philip III, 12th October, 1618, RB II/551, 5r.

54 De la Fuente to Philip III, 21st December, 1618, RB II/551, 52v–55v.

55 De la Fuente to Juan de Ciriza, 25th October, 1619, RB II/551, 204v–5v.

56 'Arto me pesa de haver cansado a V.S. con carta tan Larga pero cierto es q como la he escrito con tanto gusto no me he podido ir a la mano. He querido hacer Confession General y decir todos mis pecados a V.S. y assegurole antes que me asuelba [sic] q soy mas su siervo, su criado y todo suyo oy mas q nunca.' See de la Fuente to Gondomar, 12th October, 1618, RB II/551, 17r.

57 '[P]or que sin duda estuviera ya roto si no lo uviera conservado con gran prudencia y maña el [Padre] Maestro fray Diego de la Fuente, que es grande la reputación que tienen aquí el Rey y todos de su persona y Verdad.' See Gondomar to Philip III, 2nd April, 1620, in Duque de Alba et al. 'Correspondencia oficial de Don Diego Sarmiento de Acuña, Conde de Gondomar', *Documentos inéditos para la Historia de España* (Madrid, 1936–1945), vol. 2, 297.

58 For more information, see John H. Elliott and José F. de la Peña, *Memoriales y Cartas del Conde-Duque de Olivares* (Madrid: Alfaguara, 1978), vol. 1, 103–15.

59 See Roberta Anderson, 'Foreign Diplomatic Representatives to the Court of James VI and I' (Bath Spa University [Unpublished doctoral dissertation], 2001), 209–22.

60 See Glyn Redworth, *The Prince and the Infanta: The Cultural Politics of the Spanish Match* (New Haven: Yale University Press, 2003); Alexander Samson, 'Introduction,' in *The Spanish Match: Prince Charles's Journey to Madrid, 1623*, ed. by Alexander Samson (Aldershot: Ashgate, 2006).

61 See Thomas Cogswell, *The Blessed Revolution: English Politics and the Coming of War, 1621–1624* (Cambridge: Cambridge University Press, 1989), 6–50.

62 For more context on the type of anti-Spanish literature produced during this period, see Trudy Darby, 'The Black Knight's Festival Book? Thomas Middleton's "A Game at Chess",' in *The Spanish Match: Prince Charles's Journey to Madrid, 1623*, ed. Alexander Samson (London: Ashgate, 2006), 173–87.

63 After Gondomar's departure in 1622, the Spanish embassy was headed by Carlos Coloma (May 1622 to September 1624); the Marquis of Hinojosa, Juan de Mendoza y Velasco (June 1623 to October 1624); Diego Hurtado de Mendoza (October to December 1623); and Diego de Messía (October to December 1623). Between Coloma's departure, on September 1624, and England's attack on Cadiz in 1625, the embassy was run by Jacques Bruneau, a diplomatic agent that did not have the rank of ambassador. For more information on Anglo-Spanish relations between 1623 and 1625, see Óscar Ruiz Fernández, 'Las relaciones hispano-inglesas entre 1603 y 1625: Diplomacia, comercio y guerra naval' (unpublished doctoral thesis) (PhD diss., Universidad de Valladolid, 2012), 86–87, accessed 13th August, 2018, http://uvadoc.uva.es/handle/10324/951.

64 Óscar Ruiz Fernández, 'Las relaciones hispano-inglesas entre 1603 y 1625: Diplomacia, comercio y guerra naval' (unpublished doctoral dissertation) (PhD diss., Universidad de Valladolid, 2012), 89–106, accessed 13th August, 2018, http://uvadoc.uva.es/handle/10324/951.

65 See Mark Hutchings, 'The Spectre of Gondomar in the Wake of A Game at Chess,' *The Seventeenth Century*, 27, 4 (2012), 435–53.

66 De la Fuente to Philip IV, 31st March, 1624, RB II/2172, doc. 85.

67 De la Fuente to Philip IV, 9th April, 1624, RB II/2172, doc. 91.

68 Glyn Redworth, *The Prince and the Infanta: The Cultural Politics of the Spanish Match* (New Haven: Yale University Press, 2003), 134–40.

69 De la Fuente to Philip IV, 14th April, 1624, RB II/2172, doc. 104.

70 Fernández, 'Las relaciones hispano-inglesas, 107.

71 Letters from Hinojosa, Coloma and friar Diego in RB II/2172, docs. 115–17.

72 Fernández, 'Las relaciones hispano-inglesas, 109.
73 Carlos Coloma to the Cardinal of la Cueva, 5th July, 1624, Archivo de la Casa de Alba, 233, 24.
74 Diego de la Fuente died in Vitoria on 15th August, 1630, while visiting a Dominican Monastery in the region. Gonzalo de Arriaga and Manuel María Hoyos, *Historia del Colegio de San Gregorio de Valladolid* (Valladolid: Cuesta, 1940), vol. 3, 48
75 See John Elliott, *Imperial Spain, 1469–1716* (London: Penguin, 2002).

Bibliography

Archival sources

Archivo de la Casa de Alba, Madrid, Manuscript letter in reference 233, 24.
Archivo General de Simancas, manuscript letter in reference Estado LEG 2598, doc. 102.
Biblioteca Nacional, Madrid, Manuscript letter in reference MSS. 18430 (2).
Real Biblioteca (RB), Madrid, Manuscript letters in references II/551, II/2158, II/2172, II/2341.

Printed sources

Chamberlain, John. *The Letters of John Chamberlain*, vol. 2. Philadelphia: The American Philosophical Society, 1939, vols 2 and 3.
de Alba, Duque et al. 'Correspondencia oficial de Don Diego Sarmiento de Acuña, Conde de Gondomar', *Documentos inéditos para la Historia de España* (Madrid, 1936–1945), vol. 3.
Nichols, John, ed., *The Progresses, Processions, and Magnificent Festivities of King James the First* (Nichols, 1828), vols. 2 and 4.
Pérez Bustamante, Ciriaco. *Españoles e Ingleses en América durante el siglo XVII*, ed. (Santiago de Compostela: Paredes, 1928).
Purnell, F.K. et al., eds., *Report on the Manuscripts of the Marquess of Downshire*. London: Historical Manuscripts Commission, 1924, vol. 6.

Literature

Anderson, Roberta. 'Diplomatic Representatives from the Hapsburg Monarchy to the Court of James VI and I,' in *The Spanish Match: Prince Charles's Journey to Madrid, 1623*, ed. by Alexander Samson. Aldershot: Ashgate, 2006.
Bartolomé Benito, Fernando. *Don Diego Sarmiento de Acuña, Conde de Gondomar: El Maquiavelo Español*. Gijón: Trea, 2005.
Bezos, Nuria. 'Los consejos de una esposa a su marido el embajador de Inglaterra: Doña Constanza de Acuña (1619),' in *IV Congreso Virtual sobre Historia de las Mujeres*. Accessed 30th October, 2019. www.revistacodice.es/publi_virtuales/iv_congreso_mujeres/comunicaciones/NURIABEZOS.pdf.
Brendecke, Arndt. '"Arca, Archivillo, Archivo": The Keeping, Use and Status of Historical Documents about the Spanish Conquista,' *Archival Science* 10, 3 (2010), 267–83.

Carter, Charles. *The Secret Diplomacy of the Habsburgs, 1598–1625*. New York: Columbia University Press, 1964.

Cogswell, Thomas. *The Blessed Revolution: English Politics and the Coming of War, 1621–1624*. Cambridge: Cambridge University Press, 1989.

Darby, Trudy. 'The Black Knight's Festival Book? Thomas Middleton's "A Game at Chess",' in *The Spanish Match: Prince Charles's Journey to Madrid, 1623*, ed. by Alexander Samson. Aldershot: Ashgate, 2006.

De Arriaga, Gonzalo and Manuel María Hoyos. *Historia del Colegio de San Gregorio de Valladolid*, vol. 3. Valladolid: Cuesta, 1940.

Elliott, John. *Imperial Spain, 1469–1716*. London: Penguin, 2002.

Elliott, John and José F. de la Peña. *Memoriales y Cartas del Conde-Duque de Olivares*, vol. 1. Madrid: Alfaguara, 1978.

García Oro, José. *Don Diego Sarmiento de Acuña, Conde de Gondomar*. Santiago de Compostela: Xunta de Galicia, 1997.

Gardiner, Samuel Rawson. *History of England from the Accession of James I to the outbreak of the Civil War: 1603–1642*, vol. 2. London: Longman, 1883–1884.

Hutchings, Mark. 'The Spectre of Gondomar in the Wake of A Game at Chess,' *The Seventeenth Century* 27, 4 (2012), 435–53.

Lawrance, Jeremy. '"Une Bibliothèque Fort Complète Pour Un Grand Seigneur": Gondomar's Manuscripts and the Renaissance Idea of the Library,' *Bulletin of Spanish Studies* 81, 7–8 (2004): 1071–90.

Loomie, Albert. 'Bacon and Gondomar: An Unknown Link in 1618,' *Renaissance Quarterly* 21, 1 (1968): 1–10.

Loomie, Albert. 'Richard Berry: Gondomar's English Catholic Adviser,' *British Catholic History* 11, 1 (1971): 47–57.

Loomie, Albert. 'Francis Fowler II, English Secretary of the Spanish Embassy, 1609–1619,' *British Catholic History* 12, 1 (1973): 70–78.

Loomie, Albert. 'Canon Henry Taylor, Spanish Habsburg Diplomat,' *British Catholic History* 17, 2 (1984): 223–37.

Manso Porto, Carmen. *Don Diego Sarmiento de Acuña (1567–1626): erudito, mecenas y bibliófilo*. Santiago de Compostela: Xunta de Galicia, 1996.

Manso Porto, Carmen. 'Diego Sarmiento de Acuña, Conde de Gondomar,' *Diccionario Bibliográfico Español – Real Academia de la Historia*. Accessed 30 October 2019. http://dbe.rah.es/biografias/14582/diego-sarmiento-de-acuna.

Mattingly, Garret. *Renaissance Diplomacy*. Baltimore: Penguin Books, 1955.

Michael, Ian and A. Ahijado. 'La Casa del Sol: la biblioteca del conde de Gondomar en 1619-23 y su dispersión en 1806,' in *El Libro Antiguo Español: El libro en Palacio y otros estudios bibliográficos*, vol. 3, ed. by Pedro Mª Catedra, Mª Luisa and López Vidriero. Salamanca: Cátedra, 1996, pp. 185–200.

Ochoa Brun, Miguel. *Historia de la Diplomacia Española*, vol. 7. Madrid: Ministerio de Asuntos Exteriores, 1990–2006.

Oyarbide Magaña, Ernesto. 'Embodying the Portrait of the Perfect Ambassador: The First Count of Gondomar and the Role of Print Culture and Cultural Literacy in Anglo-Spanish Relations during the Jacobean Period,' in *Embajadores Culturales: Transferencias y Lealtades de La Diplomacia Española de La Edad Moderna*, ed. by Diana Carrió-Invernizzi and José Miguel Escribano Páez. Madrid: Universidad Nacional de Educación a Distancia, 2016, pp. 157–85.

Parker, Geoffrey. *The Thirty Years' War*. London: Routledge, 1997.

Patrimonio Nacional. 'Fray Diego de la Fuente y don Diego Sarmiento, lectores del Quijote,' in *Avisos de la Real Biblioteca*. Accessed 30th October, 2019. http://avisos.realbiblioteca.es/?p=article&aviso=75&art=1088.

Redworth, Glyn. 'Diego Sarmiento de Acuña (1567–1626),' *Oxford Dictionary of National Bibliography*. Accessed 30th October, 2019.

Redworth, Glyn. *The Prince and the Infanta: The Cultural Politics of the Spanish Match*. New Haven: Yale University Press, 2003.

Ruiz Fernández, Óscar. 'Las relaciones hispano-inglesas entre 1603 y 1625: Diplomacia, comercio y guerra naval' PhD diss., Universidad de Valladolid, 2012. Accessed 30th October, 2019. http://uvadoc.uva.es/handle/10324/951.

Samson, Alexander, ed. *The Spanish Match: Prince Charles's Journey to Madrid, 1623*. London: Ashgate, 2006.

Sánchez Cantón, Francisco. *Don Diego Sarmiento de Acuña, conde de Gondomar 1567–1626*. Madrid: Real Academia de la Historia, 1935.

Sowerby, Tracey and Jan Hennings, eds. *Practices of Diplomacy in the Early Modern World c.1410–1800*. London: Routledge, 2017.

Tite, Colin. *Early Records of Sir Robert Cotton's Library*. London: The British Library, 2003.

Tobío, Luis. *Gondomar y su triunfo sobre Raleigh*. Santiago De Compostela: Editorial De Los Bibliófilos Gallegos, 1974.

Tobío, Luis. 'A amistade de Bacon e Gondomar,' *Grial* 18, 68 (1980): 210–15.

Tobío, Luis. *Gondomar y los Católicos Ingleses*. La Coruña: Edicios do Castro, 1987.

Walsham, Alexandra. 'The Social History of the Archive: Record-Keeping in Early Modern Europe,' *Past & Present* 230, 11 (2016): 9–48.

Williamson, Elizabeth, '"Fishing after News" and the Ars Apodemica: The Intelligencing Role of the Educational Traveller in the Late Sixteenth Century,' in *News Networks in Early Modern Europe*, ed. by Joad Raymond and Noah Moxham. Leiden: Brill, 2016, pp. 542–62.

Zimmermann, Georg. *Carmel in England: A History of the English Mission of the Discalced Carmelites, 1615 to 1849*. London: Burns and Oates, 1899.

7   The role of confessor-ambassador

The Capuchin Diego de Quiroga and Habsburg politics[1]

Rubén González Cuerva

Another grey eminence?

As the future Empress María Ana of Austria travelled from Madrid to Vienna in 1630, few members of her retinue were authorised to remain at the imperial court. Her Capuchin confessor Diego de Quiroga[2] was among them until Maria Anna's death in 1646. Apart from being a spiritual director, Quiroga became Maria Anna's spokesman for the male courtier environment. His spiritual prestige and political talent enabled him to develop a double role as theologian and diplomat: while Spanish ambassadors succeeded each other quickly, Quiroga represented a stable and reliable agent with privileged access to the imperial entourage, even acting at times as interim ambassador. Furthermore, his impeccable confessional credentials contrasted with the mischievous fame of Spanish diplomats. These were able to bribe imperial ministers, but not to convince the secluded circle of preachers and prelates with whom the pious Emperor Ferdinand II (1619–1637) consulted his key decisions. Quiroga was the only one capable to defend Spanish interests and to make them acceptable for the tormented imperial conscience.

In that sense, Quiroga was a typical figure of the confessional century (1550–1650), when several clergymen moved from contemplative to active life and began to take part in thorny contemporary diplomatic negotiations.[3] The prototypical image of these men was that of *éminence grise* ('grey eminence'), applied to another contemporary Capuchin friar, Father Joseph of Paris, the discreet advisor to Cardinal Richelieu, whose reputation of power derived from always operating secretly or unofficially.[4]

Prior to this central mission in the imperial court, Quiroga had a distinguished and atypical career: before becoming a Capuchin, Quiroga was a military man of noble origins who had served in the French Wars of Religion in the 1590s, when Father Joseph of Paris and Quiroga actually fought in opposing armies. Disillusioned by martial life, in 1598 he entered the Capuchin convent of Figueres in Girona, taking the name Diego de Quiroga. In 1609, Quiroga began his association with the Spanish court when he was summoned to Madrid to take part in the foundation of the first Castilian monastery of his order. Royal permission to expand the Capuchin reform of the

Franciscans to Castile was granted by the petition of Father Lorenzo da Brindisi (1559–1619), extraordinary papal legate and special ambassador of the Duke of Bavaria at the Spanish court. Brindisi (canonised as a saint in 1881), with his many theological attributes, earthly concerns, and charisma, represented a glowing model for Quiroga.[5]

Quiroga became a leader of the Castilian Capuchins due to his role in the foundation of the convents in Toledo (1611), El Pardo (1613), and Salamanca (1614). After that, he was elected Provincial of Valencia (1615–1618) and then of Castile (1622–1627).[6] The reputation he gained among his peers explains how Quiroga became the main interlocutor and assistant to his fellow, Father Giacinto da Casale, the second Capuchin ambassador, who arrived in Madrid in 1621, after Lorenzo da Brindisi. Like Brindisi, Casale accumulated several recommendations, from the emperor, the pope, and the Duke of Bavaria, to convince the Spanish court to support transferring the imperial electoral title from the Calvinist rebel, the Elector Palatine, to the loyal, Catholic, Duke of Bavaria, whom the Spanish authorities mistrusted, and saw as a challenge to the House of Austria in the empire.[7] In May 1622, Casale sent Quiroga to report the progress of the negotiations to the courts of Munich and Vienna. Thus, the role of Capuchin friars as reliable diplomatic agents for confessional-related issues between Central Europe and Iberia was consolidated. Moreover, Quiroga acquired first-hand experience of the functioning of the Spanish embassy in the empire and gained the confidence of Emperor Ferdinand II and the Duke of Bavaria.[8] This experience heightened Quiroga's credit when he returned to Madrid at the end of 1622, in time to be elected provincial of the Capuchins of Castile, in December of that year.

Soon after, he represented his order in the discussions on the English Match. Since 1620, the *Infanta* María Ana of Austria, sister of Philip IV, had been the candidate to marry Charles, Prince of Wales, who arrived, incognito, in Madrid in February 1623, to ask for her hand in marriage. This quixotic gesture was not enough to convince Philip IV and his favourite, the Count Duke of Olivares, to accept a match with a Protestant prince. As Spanish statecraft required that all critical decisions should be made with religion in mind, a *Junta Grande de Teólogos* was summoned. This *Junta* was a board of 54 theologians with representatives from every royal council and religious order called by King Philip IV to dictate if the marriage was beneficial for Christendom, and if so the conditions to demand. Quiroga was invited to the meetings and demonstrated his ambition, initiative, and zeal in contrast to most of his colleagues, who followed a mild and temporising position that would not disappoint Olivares. Quiroga was among the few genuine opponents to the English Match, who would only support it if the prince would convert to Catholicism. This condition for the marriage had been articulated by the papal nuncio, Massimi, to the pious entourage of the *Infanta*. The royal confessor, Antonio de Sotomayor, and Diego de Quiroga organised a meeting with Charles and Buckingham to convince them of the truth of the Catholic faith, which was unsuccessful.[9]

This confessional approach to the matrimonial question led to the failure of the English project in September 1623, but at the same time it endorsed Quiroga's skills and firmness to the Spanish court, and especially to the *Infanta* María Ana. Consequently, the negotiation of an alternative Austrian match began, an initiative preferred by a heterogeneous court group that acted as a dynastic network, including the entourage of the female members of the House of Austria, the *Infanta* María Ana herself, the Nun-*Infanta* Margarita de la Cruz, and the Infanta Isabel Clara Eugenia, governor of the Spanish Netherlands. In 1626, it was decided that the marriage of María Ana with her cousin Ferdinand, King of Hungary and heir to Emperor Ferdinand II, would be the best solution. However, the proxy wedding was delayed until 25th April, 1629, and María Ana's journey to Vienna only began in December 1629, with her arrival in March 1631.[10] A special committee of ministers, the *Junta de Casamiento*, was appointed to arrange the many issues arising from the marriage of María Ana to Ferdinand. One problem was that her confessor since childhood, Juan Venido, a discreet Franciscan, had been promoted to the Bishopric of Orense in 1626. The Spanish ministers had heated discussions on whom to appoint as a new confessor for her.[11] Quiroga's candidacy was backed by María Ana herself, although this was more due to the many overlapping roles assumed by Quiroga than to personal taste.

The 'way of conscience' in the confessors' age

What, then, were Quiroga's exceptional traits that led to his appointment? He had respectable diplomatic experience in Central Europe and a courtly background, but at the same time offered a very different profile regarding the humanist-aristocratic model of the diplomat established by influential treatises such as Castiglione's *Il Cortegiano* (1528) or Vera y Zúñiga's *El enbaxador* (1620). Quiroga also had a high Latin culture, but especially theological finesse, as well as two key elements: Capuchin charisma and a probabilist approach to spiritual counsel. As a Capuchin, Quiroga followed the path of his model Father Lorenzo da Brindisi in terms of radical poverty and mystic attitude. This near thaumaturgical prestige and living-saint image was the most efficient door-opener for European Catholic courts of the first half of the seventeenth century, when prominent clergymen and nuns of previous decades highly related to royal courts, such as Ignacio de Loyola, Teresa de Avila, Carlo Borromeo, or Francisco de Borja, had been rapidly canonised.[12] Therefore, clerical negotiators such as Quiroga offered much more than mere diplomatic mediation – a religious experience, a promise of salvation.

The second key element for Quiroga was his probabilist attitude. According to this doctrine of moral theology, in the case of the absence of certainty around difficult matters of conscience, it is legitimated to follow a probable doctrine backed by an authoritative opinion, even though the opposite opinion is more probable.[13] The new constraints of policymaking in a confessional age with no clear guidelines made it very hard to discern how to decide a pious, or at least a less sinful, course of action. Therefore, the political implications of probabilism were huge: a spiritual guide following this doctrine, as Quiroga did, could advise and legitimate the most varied, and morally lax, decisions.

In the mid-seventeenth century, the most notable proponent of the probabilist doctrine was the Spanish polymath Juan Caramuel Lobkowicz, who enjoyed Quiroga's friendship when both men stayed at the imperial court (1642–1649). Quiroga even commissioned Caramuel to draft a treatise justifying the legitimacy of the Peace of Westphalia against the fierce opposition of the Jesuits and the Holy See.[14] By his part, Caramuel held the highest regard for Quiroga and used his case in his arguments: about probabilism's need to resort to an authority to back a position, Caramuel defended that writing a book did not mean becoming an authority, because Quiroga did not leave any writings, but relied on his astonishing memory. According to Caramuel, he was 'the most subtle, learned and ingenious' philosopher he had ever met, holding very singular opinions on theological debates.[15] The Jansenists, and especially Blaise Pascal, heavily criticised these lax probabilist morals, and Quiroga served again, although in a negative sense, as an example: Quiroga's failure as spiritual guardian of the empress' household, because the spread of the lax doctrine on calumny caused uncontrolled turmoil in the Viennese court.[16] At times, Quiroga's laxist positions collided with the good reputation of the Spanish monarchy; for example, the Spanish Council of State reprimanded him in 1632 when he proposed considering a plan to assassinate King Gustav Adolf of Sweden, the greatest enemy of the House of Austria.[17]

This reprimand shows how this type of friar-politician was far from being accepted without resistance, and lay authorities attempted to limit its scope. Even the princes who demanded most eagerly to be spiritually advised quickly overruled whatever they regarded as intromissions or 'negotiations': the pious Ferdinand II, in whose court Quiroga triumphed, criticised the latter's Capuchin predecessor, Father Giacinto da Casale, for being 'a little bit ardent,' and added that 'friars should be in their cell and leave the negotiations of princes to ambassadors and ministers with authority.'[18] It was difficult to put under strict control these zealous friars who, like the Carmelite Father Ruzola, claimed Ferdinand II to hold godly legitimacy and authority.[19] The situation was ambiguous enough because these men of religion boasted that, unlike the dubious interests of secular ministers, their counsels were unbiased and pure, as the imperial confessor Lamormaini repeatedly assured Ferdinand II.[20]

Vienna, 1630

When María Ana of Austria and her confessor Diego de Quiroga finally arrived in Vienna in 1631, the Spanish ministers had targeted William

Lamormaini, the Jesuit confessor of Emperor Ferdinand II, as their main rival and the most influential imperial counsellor. Quiroga's spiritual abilities were essential to counteract the persuasive (and roughly anti-Spanish) guidance of Lamormaini. Although being a vassal of Philip IV as a native of Luxemburg, Lamormaini acted independently and was at odds with the official imperial favourite, the pro-Spanish Prince of Eggenberg. Between the rivalry of these two men, a difference in the ways of influence and international strategy arose. During the harsh conditions of the Thirty Years' War, Ferdinand II and his regime were trapped between two legitimacies and two aims, which were dictated by his position as a Catholic prince and leader of the House of Austria: he had to find a balance between confession and dynasty, between supporting the pope or the King of Spain.[21] To some extent, Quiroga arrived as a Trojan Horse (or an alternative leader) in the confessional realm.

To put it in simple terms, the Spanish embassy built up an impressive network of patronage, including most of the imperial ministers and generals. Papal diplomats, on the other hand, were unable to maintain such a complex patronage network and had to face their exclusion from decision-making circles and systems for information-gathering. Meanwhile, the irresolute Ferdinand gave a decisive role to his ministers, who were led by Eggenberg, with most of them linked to Spanish patronage.[22] As proof of their impotency, papal nuncios resorted to the only weapon at their disposal: the *via di coscienza* or 'way of conscience.' This proved to be as efficient as it was cheap. Ferdinand had been taught at the Jesuit University of Ingolstadt and assimilated a solid Catholic education.[23] His confessors, Beccanus and Lamormaini, reinforced by special legates and monks connected to the Holy See, eroded the moral scruples of the pious emperor to reverse many of the decisions advised by the largely pro-Spanish Secret Council. On those occasions, the nuncio warned Lamormaini that 'touching that issue upon conscience matters, he had to operate whatever he could with the Emperor and his ministers.'[24]

For these reasons, the Spanish ministers became highly suspicious of these 'points of conscience' because Lamormaini used these to hide crude political interests, which were contrary to the House of Austria.[25] Therefore, the appointment of a confessor for Empress María Ana required a considered decision as to the appropriate man: a prestigious theologian able to counteract Lamormaini's control of conscience and a fine statesman capable of advising or even directing the Spanish embassy in Vienna. Following the arrival of Quiroga, the Spanish authorities entered into this spiritual game of chess and were in a position to plead with Ferdinand to arrange councils of theologians, as was the Spanish custom, to advise on moral issues beyond the individual control of Lamormaini.[26]

The circles of power at the imperial court were aware of the implications of appointing a confessor for the future empress, and Ferdinand II had suggested a suitable candidate: Ambrosio de Peñalosa, a Spanish teacher of the

University of Vienna and a member of the Society of Jesus. Having experienced the dealings of Lamormaini, the Spanish ministers' mistrust of Jesuit confessors was understandable, and the appointment of Quiroga was imposed.[27]

The confessor and the embassy

Diego de Quiroga was not only close to María Ana, but also a faithful client of the royal favourite, Olivares, who introduced him to several committees of theologians and ministers between 1628 and 1630, which furthered his training as a counsellor. Olivares held a very long and intimate correspondence with Quiroga, in which Olivares' mental illness often arose.[28] Olivares provided Quiroga with secret and special instructions as he departed to Vienna with María Ana at the end of 1630, thus enhancing his status as a negotiator and showing Olivares' preclusion of ambassadors and more typical diplomats. Quiroga was instructed to implement an almost impossible balance: to accomplish a personal friendship between Philip IV and Ferdinand II, and later Ferdinand III, after years of misunderstandings, to loyally serve María Ana while maintaining his confidential relationship with Olivares, and at the same time to act as an assistant for the Spanish ambassadors, even supplanting them when ordered to. His final mission was to establish a general, perpetual, and unbreakable league, almost a confederation, between both branches of the House of Austria.[29] While Quiroga's loyalty to Empress María Ana was beyond doubt, Olivares resented the progressive loss of personal involvement with his former client.[30]

Olivares was a courtier without international experience, and his relationship with the agents of the monarchy abroad was mistrustful and intricate. At the beginning of the reign of Philip IV, Olivares shared the reins of power with his uncle, Baltasar de Zúñiga, who had been ambassador in Brussels, Paris, Prague, and Vienna. Olivares was not as competent in foreign affairs as his uncle, and after his death in October 1622, Olivares attempted to counterbalance the initiatives of ambassadors and viceroys through special agents, such as Quiroga. Between 1623 and 1628, Olivares resorted to the services of the Italian priest Matteo Renzi, a former client of Baltasar de Zúñiga, to act as his agent in Paris, Rome, and Vienna, mainly behind the backs of the Spanish ambassadors.[31]

This duality was reinforced at the imperial court, where Spanish practices dictated the presence of a powerful and solitary Spanish ambassador, who served for a long period of time and was endowed with relatively generous funding and a wide degree of autonomy. Coinciding with the collapse of imperial authority during the first phase of the Thirty Years' War, the Spanish ambassador, Íñigo Vélez de Guevara, 7th Count of Oñate (1617–1624), took an extraordinary lead, to the point of being accused of behaving more as a dictator than as an ambassador.[32] These accusations underlined both the risks of employing such powerful figures and the limitations that these

Iberian aristocrats faced in terms of patronage and alliance policy. For these reasons, after the departure of Francisco de Moncada, 3rd Marquis of Aytona, the last important ambassador, in 1629, Olivares preferred to balance ambassadors with other agents, regardless of their previous expertise. He imposed a collegiate style, in which three to six representatives simultaneously held missions at the imperial court to constitute a 'council of diplomats.' This synodal body challenged the pre-eminence of ambassadors so much that Carlo Doria, 1st Duke of Tursi, extraordinary ambassador in 1630, was eager to defend his 'authority and autonomy to negotiate and not to be present as minister or servant of the King, but his ambassador.'[33] Moreover, the war effort had serious repercussions in the Spanish embassy, as fresh money did not arrive, making it almost impossible to keep up the enormous and – also in normal circumstances – nearly unsustainable network of patronage.[34] The financial factor, combined with the disagreements among the Spanish ministers and the consequent lack of a well-defined strategy, led to an implosion of the Spanish network, evident in the signing of the humiliating Peace of Regensburg in 1630.

To avoid these setbacks, a new diplomatic structure had to be implemented by María Ana of Austria and her household. This domestic, alternative system offered more fluid and informal opportunities of contact and patronage, especially under the unassailable lead of the Queen of Hungary, later Empress, María Ana of Austria. In line with Quiroga's instructions, she also received a written and formal instruction from her brother, Philip IV. This document is quite unusual for Spanish dynastic practice, because it follows the tone and rhetoric of diplomatic and ambassadorial writings. Beyond any doubt, the instructions repeat the only line of action acceptable for María Ana, to which she devoted the rest of her life: to become an instrument of dynastic unity between the Spanish and German branches of the House of Austria, and to promote their union through thick and thin, regardless of the advice by even the most trusted of counsellors, and only limited by the conservation of the Catholic faith. To this end, she was empowered by her brother above all the Spanish diplomatic agents: 'I appoint Your Majesty my greatest ambassadress with your father-in-law and your husband.'[35]

Due to the obvious limitations imposed on María Ana because of gender and protocol, there were several candidates for the position of her broker and representative. The foremost of these was her high steward, Franz Christoph Khevenhüller, the head of her household in Vienna. Being the departing imperial ambassador in Spain, Khevenhüller had escorted her from Madrid and was thus able to provide inside knowledge of both courts. Cesare Gonzaga, 2nd Duke of Guastalla, one of the Spanish ministers in Vienna, advised María Ana to balance the roles of Khevenhüller and Quiroga as her German and Spanish counsellors to better cope with the different areas of action, while leaving the new Spanish ordinary ambassador, Lope Aux Díez de Armendáriz, 1st Marquis of Cadreita, in control.[36]

Despite his office, Khevenhüller was a politically minor character. He was busy with the management of the household and had tense relations with the many Spaniards there. Olivares had a very poor opinion of Khevenhüller, who himself realised that he could neither count on the grace of Philip IV nor was he able to take a leading role at the imperial court, where he remained rather isolated.[37] Cadreita, the new Spanish ambassador, had also escorted María Ana on the long journey to Vienna, but his political contribution was insignificant, other than being the first ambassador to be born in the Americas.[38] Cadreita was totally ignorant of diplomatic procedures and quickly made several serious and expensive mistakes, to the point that his proxy was secretly revoked and, until the arrival of another ambassador, the authority to negotiate passed to Guastalla and Quiroga as interim ambassadors. Olivares confessed to Quiroga his own ignorance of imperial diplomacy to justify the appointment of such an inadequate individual.[39]

The problems in the embassy were eased, however, due to the new collegial order of the 'ministers of Germany,' a new council that paralleled the traditional 'ministers of Italy' and 'ministers of Flanders,' and showed the complexity and intensity of the contemporary Spanish interests in the empire.[40] Quiroga was quickly integrated among these ministers and took part in several meetings arranged to decide a course of action. Philip IV openly acknowledged him as a royal representative in sensitive matters, such as the negotiations with the English ambassador for the restitution of the Palatinate or the discussion on the general league of the House of Austria.[41] This long-cherished project constituted one of the last failures of Cadreita, because he negotiated, without permission, a plan that was very far from Philip's interests. At the end of 1632, the resulting document was ignored, and new instructions were sent directly to Quiroga for the negotiations.[42] However, the true extension of his agency remained mostly hidden. Quiroga was instructed several times by Philip to use his personal initiative to prevent jealousy among the other Spanish representatives and suspicion among the imperial ministers.[43]

But these precautions were not successful, because Cadreita's replacement, Sancho de Monroy, 1st Marquis of Castañeda, resented Quiroga's influence and attempted to oppose his initiatives on several occasions.[44] However, Philip and Olivares were aware of the strategic importance of Quiroga and backed him with absolute confidence, even in his request for secret funds without detailing his goal.[45] Unlike the Spanish ambassadors, Quiroga had been able to maintain excellent relations with the imperial entourage, and at the same time he was regarded as a suitable mediator by the mistrusted Duke of Bavaria. Furthermore, Quiroga had been chosen by the imperial generalissimo, Albrecht von Wallenstein, as his only Spanish interlocutor.[46] Wallenstein had raised an impressive army, capable of defeating the Protestant forces, but at the same time he acted almost independently of the emperor, Ferdinand II, and very far from Spanish priorities. Quiroga visited Wallenstein in Bohemia in 1632 and 1633 and convinced him to accept a permanent Spanish agent, Quiroga's trusted man, Agustín Navarro Burena. Castañeda felt bypassed, but his complaints were in vain.[47]

In February 1634, some of Wallenstein's officials killed him on the veiled order of Ferdinand II, on the unsubstantiated accusation of being a traitor who was negotiating with the enemies of the emperor.[48] Quiroga's credit was not damaged, however, because he had contributed to the progressive empowerment of the future Ferdinand III, husband of María Ana of Austria. Before her arrival, Count Christoph Simon von Thun, the former tutor of Archduke Ferdinand, dominated his entourage, which was less benign towards Spanish interests than that of Ferdinand II under the Prince of Eggenberg. Papal and Tuscan diplomacy steadily appreciated the influence of Quiroga, who persuaded the archduke to press his father not to sign the Peace of Cherasco, the terms of which were so inimical to Spanish interests.[49] While Wallenstein had left the emperor with diminished forces in 1631, María Ana and Quiroga were among the most enthusiastic supporters in favour of Ferdinand III as the new commander of the imperial army, a position he obtained soon after.[50] Therefore, the assassination of Wallenstein actually broke the dynastic deadlock and, with the mediation of Quiroga and Castañeda, a definitive general league was signed in April 1634. With this agreement, the joint armies of the emperor and the King of Spain ultimately defeated the Swedish army in Nördlingen on 6th September, 1634.[51]

The Treaty of Prague was signed on 30th May, 1635, by the Habsburg Emperor Ferdinand II and the Elector John George of Saxony, who represented most of the Protestant estates of the Holy Roman Empire. This outcome was a great triumph for the Spanish, although not through the embassy in Vienna, but due to the more discreet channels of María Ana's confessor. Quiroga was invited to a committee of theologians to help absolve the conscience of the emperor, as such a treaty was considered impious. The imperial Jesuit confessor, Lamormaini, was not able, in this case, to proscribe the Secret Council's decision: Quiroga was efficient and had created a 'hidden league' with cardinals, Franz von Dietrichstein and Peter Pazmany, and fellow Capuchin friars, Valeriano Magni and Basilio d'Aire. With their support, Quiroga prevailed over Lamormaini and his confessional and providential policy.[52]

Quiroga and Ferdinand III

After the death of Ferdinand II in 1637, Quiroga and María Ana asserted Philip IV's requirements in a more discreet way. The correspondence between the Spanish king and Quiroga languished until 1643, while Olivares abandoned epistolary contact in 1639. Under Ferdinand III, the previous active interventions were less necessary. The imperial favourite, Maximilian von Trauttmansdorf, was not opposed to the dynastic entente and found less hostility from the Jesuit imperial confessor, Johannes Gans, to whom

Ferdinand III did not concede the same control over his conscience as his father had done with Lamormaini. Furthermore, the Count of Oñate, who had been the most authoritative Spanish ambassador in Vienna (1617–1624), returned as extraordinary ambassador in the years 1633 to 1637. Apart from reinforcing Castañeda's activities, and sometimes clashing with him, his presence made Quiroga's initiatives less necessary.[53] Quiroga continued to form a virtuous tandem with the empress, even if under that respectable image even María Ana was upset by his frequent visits to her ante-bedchamber for machinating with her ladies-in-waiting as she was absent from palace.[54]

From 1643 to 1644, Quiroga again had a prominent role as no Spanish ambassador resided in Vienna because the ordinary, Manuel de Moura, 2nd Marquis of Castel-Rodrigo, had been sent to the negotiations of Westphalia. Finally, Quiroga openly took the reins of the Spanish embassy under the authority of Empress María Ana.[55] Quiroga coordinated several issues: a joint military campaign for 1644, which ended without any great advances, the mission of Prince Maximilian von Dietrichstein as extraordinary Spanish ambassador to Poland, and the discussion of precedence between the ambassadors in the Congress of Münster.[56]

The thorny debate on the common position of the House of Austria in the Peace of Westphalia brought Quiroga and Empress María Ana to the forefront. The empress was even summoned to a session of the imperial Secret Council on 1st March, 1646, to state her opinion regarding the peace.[57] At the same time, Quiroga and María Ana were attempting to renew a dynastic alliance through another marriage between cousins: that of her eldest daughter, Mariana of Austria, to the Spanish Prince Baltasar Carlos. Unfortunately, María Ana died soon after, on 13th May, 1646, and Baltasar Carlos followed her a few months later, on 9th October, 1646. Despite the mourning period, new wedding plans for Mariana of Austria went ahead with Quiroga's support, and she finally married her uncle, Philip IV of Spain, on 7th October, 1649.[58]

Quiroga did not desire to return to Spain after the death of his patroness, but proposed to remain in Vienna as chaplain of the empress' chapel for the offering of the thousands of Masses established in her will. Although Ferdinand III also preferred to count on Quiroga's presence and advice, Philip IV summoned Quiroga to the Spanish court. In 1648, Archduchess Mariana started her journey to Madrid, retracing the road her mother and her household had undertaken almost 20 years before. Many of her mother's former servants escorted her, Quiroga among them, and in one action the late empress accomplished her desire to marry her daughter to Spain, at the cost of dismantling most of the Spanish presence in Vienna. Quiroga was nearly 75, but Philip IV still reserved a last honourable mission for him: to become the confessor of his eldest daughter, *Infanta* María Teresa, later Queen of France. However, Quiroga did not accomplished his last service: he arrived in Madrid very ill, and one week later he died, on 10th October, 1649.[59]

Conclusions

During the decades of general conflict around the Thirty Years' War, the different European polities and confessions were also contending for divine protection and to show which was accomplishing God's plans. For this providential understanding, actual politics posed untenable problems as a minimum communication and agreement with 'heretics' was indispensable for every Catholic actor involved, whether with England, Saxony, or the United Provinces. Where to put the limit exactly? The delicate worldly balances applied by diplomats made no sense in this realm where decision-makers required a sound and prudent theological background. In some sense, moral theology posed both impossible problems and discreet solutions through the lax approach of probabilists looking for the lesser evil. Combined with an almost charisma of sanctity, Quiroga was among the few individuals with enough authoritative resources to propose decisions: deciding is the key feature of political power, but in these times of Catholic confessionalism decisions were hidden and legitimised through boards of theologians. That was the case in the discussions on the English Match (1623), the Treaty of Prague (1635), and the Peace of Westphalia (1648) in which Quiroga took part.[60]

Furthermore, Quiroga's same resources were basic at another layer of analysis: that of the intra-dynastic relations of the House of Austria. Quiroga's combination of religious charisma, royal service, court patronage, and diplomatic authority enabled him to represent a unique vector of communication: only he had (although not simultaneously) a trusted interlocution with the pope; the Duke of Bavaria; the King of Spain, Philip IV; his favourite, Olivares; Emperor Ferdinand II; his son, Ferdinand III; the latter's wife, María Ana of Austria; and the imperial generalissimo, Wallenstein. Following a micropolitical approach, Quiroga's profile shows the preoccupation of the Spanish monarchy to appoint versatile agents, able to switch between different roles and allegiances and to communicate and agree with the many, often confronted, political actors involved.[61]

To secure his success in this field, Quiroga and his allies cultivated an image of virtue and mundane disinterest that contrasted with the arrogant image linked to Spanish diplomats. Quiroga 'is never concerned with the court and the palace except for obedience and when called upon.'[62] Therefore, Philip IV forced him, against his will, to abandon the convent quietude and to embrace state negotiations – as the king wrote – in the name of God and Christendom's advancement. In exchange, Quiroga was well integrated in the patronage networks of the Spanish king and benefited from them, and among his many recommendees his nephew Juan de Somoza obtained a military position in Flanders.[63]

Finally, in addition to the confessional and dynastic layers, national considerations also arose throughout Quiroga's career to identify his progressive services to Philip IV in terms of national allegiance to Spain. That was not the case during his first imperial mission of 1622, when Quiroga was praised as a 'Spaniard of nation, but a true Israelite at heart.'[64] It did not imply a *converso* origin, but his ability to act as a papal agent without allegiance to his king, following the trend of his compatriot Father Domingo Ruzola, an Aragonese serving successive popes without compromising with the Spanish king's interests. As Quiroga's links with the Spanish court grew tighter, he laid the suspicions for his Bavarian sympathies to rest, and in 1630 he was labelled at the imperial court as 'fully Spaniard.' The polarisation in Vienna was so intense that, even in the local Capuchin convent, the friars were defined as 'Austrians' or insulted as 'popish.' European politics had pervaded even into those microcosms, which Quiroga was supposed to control.[65]

Notes

1 This research was funded by the Spanish Ministry of Economy and Competitiveness Project HAR2015-68946-C3-2-P.
2 Quiroga (Orense), 16th August, 1574 – Madrid, 10th October, 1649.
3 Heinz Schilling, *Konfessionalisierung und Staatsinteressen: Internationale Beziehungen 1559–1660* (Paderborn: F. Schöningh, 2007), 34–41, 107–11, 394–415; Daniel H. Nexon, *The Struggle for Power in Early Modern Europe: Religious Conflict, Dynastic Empires, and International Change* (Princeton: Princeton University Press, 2009), 1–16.
4 Alexandre Dumas, *The Three Musketeers* (London: Collins, 1910), 15.
5 Rubén González Cuerva, 'La mediación entre las dos cortes de la Casa de Austria: Baltasar de Zúñiga,' in *La dinastía de los Austria: la Monarquía Católica y el Imperio*, ed. José Martínez Millán and Rubén González Cuerva (Madrid: Polifemo, 2011), 479–506.
6 Buenaventura de Carrocera, 'El Padre Diego de Quiroga, diplomático y confesor de reyes,' *Estudios Franciscanos*, 50/274 (1949), 73–76.
7 Brennan C. Pursell, *The Winter King: Frederick V of the Palatinate and the Coming of the Thirty Years' War* (Aldershot: Ashgate, 2003), 123–35.
8 Cardinal Ludovisi to Nuncio Carafa, Rome, 4th June, 1622, Biblioteca Apostolica Vaticana [BAV], Ottoboniani latini, 3218, 501; Dieter Albrecht, *Die deutsche Politik Papst Gregors XV.: Die Einwirkung der päpstlichen Diplomatie auf die Politik der Häuser Habsburg und Wittelsbach* (München: Beck, 1956), 58, 64–66.
9 Cardinal Ludovisi to Fray Diego de Quiroga, Rome, 5th September, 1622, Archivio Segreto Vaticano [ASV], Segreteria di Stato, Spagna 61, 297r; Nuncio de' Massimi to Cardinal Ludovisi, Madrid, 1st April 1623, BAV, Barberiniani Latini [Barb. lat.], 8293, 4r–4v; Albrecht, *Die deutsche Politik*, 23–24, 64–65; Henar Pizarro, 'El proyecto matrimonial entre el príncipe de Gales y la infanta María (1623): una polémica política y teológica,' preface to Fray Francisco de Jesús Jódar, *Papeles sobre el tratado de matrimonio entre el Príncipe de Gales y la infanta María de Austria (1623)* (Madrid: Ed. Carmelitanas, 2010), 35, 39, 44, 77–78.
10 Henar Pizarro, 'La elección de confesor de la infanta María de Austria en 1628,' in *La dinastía de los Austria*, vol. 2, ed. Martínez Millán and González Cuerva (Madrid: Polifemo, 2011), 759–800; Rubén González Cuerva, 'The Austrian Match: The Dynastic Alternative of the Habsburgs and European Politics,' in *Stuart Marriage Diplomacy: Dynastic Politics in their European*

Context, 1604–1630, ed. Valentina Caldari and Sara Wolfson (Woodbridge: Boydell & Brewer, 2018), 271–84.

11   Enrique Flórez, *España sagrada: Theatro geographico-historico de la iglesia de España*, vol. 17 (Madrid: Pedro Marín, 1789), 184.

12   Esther Jiménez Pablo, 'La canonización de Ignacio de Loyola (1622): lucha de intereses entre Roma, Madrid y París,' *Chronica nova*, 42 (2016), 79–102, accessed 12th November, 2018, doi:10.30827/cn.v0i42.5016.

13   The probabilist doctrine was first proposed by the Castilian Dominic Friar Bartolomé de Medina in 1577. James Franklin, *The Science of Conjecture: Evidence and Probability before Pascal* (Baltimore: Johns Hopkins University Press, 2001), 74–76.

14   Alessandro Catalano, 'Juan Caramuel Lobkowicz (1606–1682) e la riconquista delle conscienze in Bohemia,' *Römische Historische Mitteilungen*, 44 (2002), 347–48.

15   Juan Caramuel, *Theologia moralis fundamentalis*, vol. 1 (Lugduni: Anisson, 1657), 323.

16   Caramuel, *Theologia moralis fundamentalis*, 448; Blas Pascal, *Las célebres cartas provinciales de Blas Pascal sobre la moral y la política de los jesuitas* (Madrid: Colegio de sordomudos y ciegos, 1846), 245–46.

17   *Consulta* of the Council of State, Madrid, 19th February 1632, Archivo General de Simancas [AGS], Estado [E], 2333, s. fol.

18   Nuncio Carafa to Cardinal Ludovisi, Vienna, 28th August, 1621, BAV, Barb. lat., 6946, 18r–18v.

19   For the case of the Carmelite Father Ruzola, see Olivier Chaline, *La Bataille de la Montagne Blanche* (Paris: Noesis, 1999), 243–70.

20   Robert Bireley, *Religion and Politics in the Age of the Counterreformation: Emperor Ferdinand II, William Lamormaini, S.J., and the Formation of Imperial Policy* (Chapel Hill: University of North Carolina Press, 1981), 181.

21   Rubén González Cuerva and Luis Tercero Casado, 'The Imperial Court during the Thirty Years War: a Battleground for Factions?' in *Factional Struggles: Divided Elites in European Cities & Courts (1400–1750)*, ed. Mathieu Caesar (Leiden: Brill, 2017), 165–70.

22   Nuncio Carafa to Cardinal Ludovisi, Vienna, 14th and 28th August, 1621, BAV, Barb. lat., 6946, 13, 17r–18r; Nuncio Carafa to Cardinal Barberini, Prague, 24th May, 1628, BAV, Barb. lat., 6952, 49r–49v.

23   José de Pellicer, *Virtudes y vida espiritual de Ferdinando de Austria* (Zaragoza: Diego Dormer, 1640), 31–37, 57–61, 108, 133–42.

24   Nuncio Carafa to Cardinal Barberini, Prague, 1st March, 1628, BAV, Barb. lat., 6951, 49v. Apart from his Jesuit confessors, Ferdinand II was heavily impressed by the holy charisma of the Aragonese Discalced Carmelite Domingo de Jesús María Ruzola. Nuncio Carafa to Cardinal Ludovisi, Vienna, 28th August and 4th November, 1621, BAV, Barb. lat., 6946, 16, 21v.

25   *Consulta* of the Council of State, 7th September, 1631, AGS, E, 2332, n. 66.

26   *Consulta* of the Council of State, 6th May, 1631, AGS, E, 2332, n. 65, 13r–14r; Nicole Reinhardt, *Voices of Conscience: Royal Confessors and Political Counsel in Seventeenth-Century Spain and France* (Oxford: Oxford University Press, 2016).

27   Bireley, *Religion and Politics*, 160–61; Pizarro, 'La elección de confesor,' 785–89.

28   The Count-Duke of Olivares to Diego de Quiroga, Madrid, 6th March, 1630, British Library [BL], Additional Manuscripts [Add. Mss.], 24909, 162; Pizarro, 'La elección de confesor,' 792.

29   The Count-Duke of Olivares to Diego de Quiroga, Madrid, 31st December, 1629, BL, Add. Mss., 24909, 136–41v; Ronald Cueto, 'Crisis, conciencia y confesores

en la Guerra de los Treinta Años,' *Cuadernos de Investigación Histórica*, 16–17 (1995), 254–57.

30 The Count-Duke of Olivares to Diego de Quiroga, Madrid, 5th May, 1631, BL, Add. Mss., 24909, 191r–91v.

31 Rubén González Cuerva, 'Un agente discreto: Mateo Renzi y el servicio a la Casa de Austria,' *Librosdelacorte.es*, 6 (2013), 50–57.

32 *Relazione* of Francesco Erizzo and Simon Contarini (1620), in *Die Relationen der Botschafter Venedigs über Deutschland und Österreich im siebzehnten Jahrhundert*, ed. Joseph Fiedler, vol. 1 (Wien: K. K. Hof- und Staatsdruckerei, 1866), 117.

33 The Duke of Tursi to the Count-Duke of Olivares, Vienna, 27th March, 1631, AGS, E, 2332, n. 29, 1v. This tendency towards collegiate directorships is also visible in the Low Countries, where a council of six military heads led the campaign of 1630. René Vermeir, *En estado de guerra: Felipe IV y Flandes* (Córdoba: Universidad de Córdoba, 2006), 40–41.

34 Étienne Bourdeu, *Les archevêques de Mayence et la présence espagnole dans le Saint-Empire (XVIe-XVIIe siècle)* (Madrid: Casa de Velázquez, 2015), 196–207.

35 Philip IV to María Ana de Austria, Zaragoza, 13th January, 1630, in *España y Europa en el siglo XVII: Correspondencia de Saavedra Fajardo*, ed. Quintín Aldea Vaquero, t. 1 (Madrid: CSIC, 1986), 317.

36 The Duke of Guastalla to the Council of State, 21st December, 1629, AGS, E, 2331, n. 50, 30–31.

37 The Count-Duke of Olivares to Diego de Quiroga, Madrid, 27th January, 1630, BL, Add. Mss., 24909, 154; *consulta* of the Council of State, 30th August 1632, AGS, E, 2333, n. 57; Andrea Sommer-Mathis, 'María Ana de Austria: spanische Infantin – Königin von Ungarn und Böhmen – römisch-deutsche Kaiserin (1606–1646),' in *Nur die Frau des Kaisers?* ed. Bettina Braun, Katrin Keller and Matthias Schnettger (Wien: Böhlau, 2016), 151–52.

38 He was born in Peru. Fernando Negredo del Cerro, 'Un episodio español en la Guerra de los Treinta Años: la embajada del marqués de Cadreita al Sacro Imperio y el acercamiento al Elector Sajón (1629–1631),' *Hispania*, 251 (2015), 669–94, accessed 12th November, 2018, doi:10.3989/hispania.2015.020.

39 *Consulta* of the Council of State, 19th November, 1631, AGS, E, 2332, n. 5, 8r; the Count-Duke of Olivares to Diego de Quiroga, Madrid, 24th May, 1631, BL, Add. Mss., 24909, 197v–98r.

40 *Consultas* of the Council of State, 15th June and 24th December, 1630, AGS, E, 2331, n. 11 and 112.

41 The Palatinate was a state of the empire occupied by the Spanish army, whose titular was the brother-in-law of King Charles I of England. John Reeve, 'Quiroga's Paper of 1631: A Missing Link in Anglo-Spanish Diplomacy during the Thirty Years War,' *English Historical Review*, 101 (1986), 913–26, accessed 12th November, 2018, doi:10.1093/ehr/CI.CCCCI.913.

42 *Consulta* of the Council of State, Valencia, 22nd April, 1632, AGS, E, 2333, n. 51; Philip IV to Diego de Quiroga, Madrid, 24th June and 10th October, 1632, BL, Add. Mss., 24909, 18; *Correspondance de la Cour d'Espagne sur les affaires des Pays Bas au XVII siècle*, ed. Henri Lonchay, Joseph Cuvelier and Joseph Lefèvre (Brussels: Marcel Hayez, 1923), vol. 2, 648.

43 Philip IV to Diego de Quiroga, Madrid, 19th January, 1633, BL, Add. Mss., 24909, 34.

44 *Consultas* of the Council of State, 5th September and 29th October, 1633, AGS, E, 2334, n. 41 and n. 2.

45 *Consulta* of the Council of State, 4th November, 1632, AGS, E, 2333, 83.

46 Maximilian I of Bavaria to Diego de Quiroga, Regensburg, 27th May, 1632, BL, Add. Mss., 24909, 126; Dieter Albrecht, *Die auswärtige Politik Maximilians von Bayern 1618–1635* (Göttingen: Vandenhoeck & Ruprecht, 1962), 341–42.

47 Jacques Bruneau to Philip IV, Vienna, 10th March, 1632, AGS, E, 2333, n. 37; Philip IV to Diego de Quiroga, Madrid, 13th July and 15th November, 1633, BL, Add. Mss., 24909, 50, 64.

48 Mark Hengerer, *Kaiser Ferdinand III. (1608–1657): Eine Biographie* (Wien: Böhlau, 2012), 100–1.

49 Niccolò Sacchetti to Andrea Cioli, Vienna, 12th April, 1631, Archivio di Stato di Firenze [ASFi], Mediceo del Principato [MP], 4385, s. fol.; Nuncio Rocci to Cardinal Barberini, Vienna, 19th April, 1631, in *Nuntiaturberichte aus Deutschland*, ed. Rotraud Becker, vol. 4/4 (Tübingen: Max Niemeyer, 2009), 459–61; Hengerer, *Kaiser Ferdinand III.*, 91.

50 Philip IV to Diego de Quiroga, Madrid, 13th July, 1633, BL, Add. Mss., 24909, 42; *consulta* of the Council of State, 29th August, 1631, AGS, E, 2332, n. 3.

51 Victoriano Roncero, 'Visiones de la batalla: El primer blasón del Austria de Calderón y el Estebanillo González,' in *Divinas y humanas letras, doctrina y poesía en los autos sacramentales de Calderón*, ed. Ignacio Arellano (Pamplona: Universidad de Navarra, 1997), 417–33; Tibor Martí, 'Los antecedentes del viaje a Roma del cardenal Péter Pázmány en 1632,' in *La dinastía de los Austria*, ed. Martínez Millán and González Cuerva (Madrid: Polifemo, 2011), 175–205.

52 Alessandro d'Ales to Cardinal Barberini, Vienna, 20th January, 1635, in *Nuntiaturberichte aus Deutschland*, ed. Rotraud Becker, vol. 4/7 (Tübingen: Max Niemeyer, 2004), 673; Bireley, *Ferdinand II, Counter-Reformation Emperor, 1578–1637* (Cambridge: Cambridge University Press, 2014), 274.

53 Robert Bireley, *The Jesuits and the Thirty Years War: Kings, Courts, and Confessors* (Cambridge: Cambridge University Press, 2003), 210; Lothar Höbelt, *Ferdinand III.: Friedenskaiser wider Willen* (Graz: Ares, 2008), 112; Pavel Marek, *La embajada española en la corte imperial (1558–1641)* (Praga: Karolinum, 2013), 133–38.

54 María Ana de Austria to Ferdinand III, Vienna, 9th July, 1635, Österreichisches Staatsarchiv Vienna, Haus-, Hof- und Staatsarchiv (hereafter HHStA), Familienkorrespondenz A, 31, 116r–18v. I am grateful to Andrea Sommer-Mathis for this reference.

55 *Consulta* of the Council of State, 24th August, 1644, AGS, E, 2345, s. fol.; Philip IV to Diego de Quiroga, Zaragoza, 31st August, 1643, BL, Add. Mss., 24909, 82.

56 Philip IV to Diego de Quiroga, Zaragoza, 3rd April, and Fraga, 16th June, 1644, BL, Add. Mss., 24909, 85 and 93; Miguel Conde Pazos, 'La Monarquía católica y los confines orientales de la Cristiandad. Relaciones entre la Casa de Austria y los Vasa de Polonia,' (PhD diss., Universidad Autónoma de Madrid, 2016), 470–76.

57 Sommer-Mathis, 'María Ana de Austria,' 152–54.

58 Philip IV to Diego de Quiroga, Zaragoza, 13th June, 1646, BL, Add. Mss., 24909, 112; Luis Tercero Casado, 'La jornada de la reina Mariana de Austria a España: divergencias políticas y tensión protocolar en el seno de la Casa de Austria (1648–1649),' *Hispania*, 239 (2011), 641–46, accessed 12th November, 2018, doi:10.3989/hispania.2011.v71.i239.352.

59 Philip IV to Diego de Quiroga, Zaragoza, 13th June. 1646, BL, Add. Mss., 24909, 112v; Ferdinand III to Diego de Quiroga, Linz, 21st July, 1646, BL, Add. Mss., 24909, 118; Carrocera, 'El Padre Diego de Quiroga,' 97–99.

60 For the cultural approach to decision-making in early modern history, see Barbara Stollberg-Rilinger, *Cultures of Decision-Making* (London: German Historical Institute, 2016).

61 John H. Elliott, *El conde-duque de Olivares: el político en una época decadencia* (Barcelona: Crítica, 1990), 226–27; Hillard von Thiessen, *Diplomatie und Patronage: Die spanisch-römischen Beziehungen 1605–1621 in akteurszentrierter Perspektive* (Epfendorf: bibliotheca academica Verlag, 2010), 26–38.

62 Niccolò Sacchetti to Ferdinand II of Medici, Vienna, 3rd May, 1631, ASFi, MP, 4385, s. fol.

63 Philip IV to Diego de Quiroga, Madrid, 10th September, 1632, BL, Add. Mss., 24909, 24; María Ana de Austria to Cardinal-Infant Ferdinand, Vienna, 14th July, 1639, BL, Add. Mss., 24909, 114.

64 Venanzio da Lagosanto, *Apostolo e diplomatico o il p. Giacinto dei conti Natta da casale Monferrato Cappuccino* (Milano: Ghezzi, 1886), 213, 228–29.

65 The Duke of Guastalla to the Council of State, 21st December, 1629, AGS, E, 2331, n. 50, 31; Bireley, *Religion and Politics*, 186, 211; id., *Ferdinand II*, 274.

Bibliography

Archival sources

Archivio di Stato di Firenze (ASFi), Mediceo del Principato [MP]: 4385.
Archivo General de Simancas (AGS), Estado (E): 2331, 2332, 2333, 2334, 2345.
Archivio Segreto Vaticano (ASV), Segreteria di Stato, Spagna: 61.
Biblioteca Apostolica Vaticana (BAV), Barberiniani Latini (Barb. lat.): 6946, 6951, 6952, 8293; Ottoboniani latini: 3218.
British Library (BL), Additional Manuscripts (Add. Mss.): 24909.
Österreichisches Staatsarchiv Vienna, Haus-, Hof- und Staatsarchiv, Familienkorrespondenz: A, 31.

Printed sources

Aldea Vaquero, Quintín, ed. *España y Europa en el siglo XVII: Correspondencia de Saavedra Fajardo*, vol. 1. Madrid: CSIC, 1986.
Becker, Rotraud, ed. *Nuntiaturberichte aus Deutschland*, vol. 4/1–7. Tübingen: Max Niemeyer, 2004–2009.
Caramuel, Juan. *Theologia moralis fundamentalis*. Lugduni: Anisson, 1657.
Dumas, Alexandre. *The Three Musketeers*. London: Collins, 1910.
Fiedler, Joseph, ed. *Die Relationen der Botschafter Venedigs über Deutschland und Österreich im siebzehnten Jahrhundert*, vol. 1. Wien: K. K. Hof- und Staatsdruckerei, 1866.
Flórez, Enrique. *España sagrada: Theatro geographico-historico de la iglesia de España*, vol. 17. Madrid: Pedro Marín, 1789.
Lonchay, Henri, Cuvelier, Joseph and Lefèvre, Joseph, eds. *Correspondance de la Cour d'Espagne sur les affaires des Pays Bas au XVII siècle*, 6 vols. Brussels: Marcel Hayez, 1923.

Pascal, Blas. *Las célebres cartas provinciales de Blas Pascal sobre la moral y la política de los jesuitas.* Madrid: Colegio de sordomudos y ciegos, 1846.
Pellicer, José de. *Virtudes y vida espiritual de Ferdinando de Austria.* Zaragoza: Diego Dormer, 1640.

Literature

Albrecht, Dieter. *Die deutsche Politik Papst Gregors XV.: die Einwirkung der päpstlichen Diplomatie auf die Politik der Häuser Habsburg und Wittelsbach 1621–1623.* München: Beck, 1956.
Albrecht, Dieter. *Die auswärtige Politik Maximilians von Bayern 1618–1635.* Göttingen: Vandenhoeck & Ruprecht, 1962.
Bireley, Robert. *Religion and Politics in the Age of the Counterreformation: Emperor Ferdinand II, William Lamormaini, S.J., and the Formation of Imperial Policy.* Chapel Hill: University of North Carolina Press, 1981.
Bireley, Robert. *The Jesuits and the Thirty Years War: Kings, Courts, and Confessors.* Cambridge: Cambridge University Press, 2003.
Bireley, Robert. *Ferdinand II, Counter-Reformation Emperor, 1578–1637.* Cambridge: Cambridge University Press, 2014.
Bourdeu, Étienne. *Les archevêques de Mayence et la présence espagnole dans le Saint-Empire (XVIe–XVIIe siècle).* Madrid: Casa de Velázquez, 2015.
Carrocera, Buenaventura de. 'El Padre Diego de Quiroga, diplomático y confesor de reyes.' *Estudios Franciscanos*, 50/274 (1949): 71–100.
Catalano, Alessandro. 'Juan Caramuel Lobkowicz (1606–1682) e la riconquista delle conscienze in Bohemia.' *Römische Historische Mitteilungen*, 44 (2002): 339–92.
Chaline, Olivier. *La Bataille de la Montagne Blanche.* Paris: Noesis, 1999.
Conde Pazos, Miguel. 'La Monarquía católica y los confines orientales de la Cristiandad: Relaciones entre la Casa de Austria y los Vasa de Polonia.' PhD diss., Universidad Autónoma de Madrid, 2016.
Cueto, Ronald. 'Crisis, conciencia y confesores en la Guerra de los Treinta Años.' *Cuadernos de Investigación Histórica*, 16–17 (1995): 249–65.
Duindam, Jeroen. 'The Politics of Female Households: Afterthoughts.' In *The Politics of Female Households: Ladies-in-Waiting across Early Modern Europe*, edited by Nadine Akkerman and Birgit Houben, 365–70. Leiden: Brill, 2014.
Elliott, John H. *El conde-duque de Olivares: el político en una época de decadencia.* Barcelona: Crítica, 1990.
Franklin, James. *The Science of Conjecture: Evidence and Probability before Pascal.* Baltimore: Johns Hopkins University Press, 2001.
González Cuerva, Rubén. 'La mediación entre las dos cortes de la Casa de Austria: Baltasar de Zúñiga.' In *La dinastía de los Austria: la Monarquía Católica y el Imperio*, edited by José Martínez Millán and Rubén González Cuerva, 479–506. Madrid: Polifemo, 2011.
González Cuerva, Rubén. 'Un agente discreto: Mateo Renzi y el servicio a la Casa de Austria.' *Librosdelacorte.es*, 6 (2013): 50–57.
González Cuerva, Rubén. 'The Austrian Match: The Dynastic Alternative of the Habsburgs and European Politics.' In *Stuart Marriage Diplomacy: Dynastic Politics in their European Context, 1604–1630*, edited by Valentina Caldari and Sara Wolfson, 271–84. Woodbridge: Boydell & Brewer, 2018.

González Cuerva, Rubén and Tercero Casado, Luis. 'The Imperial Court during the Thirty Years War: A Battleground for Factions?' In *Factional Struggles: Divided Elites in European Cities & Courts (1400–1750)*, edited by Mathieu Caesar, 155–75. Leiden: Brill, 2017.

Hengerer, Mark. *Kaiser Ferdinand III. (1608–1657): Eine Biographie*. Wien: Böhlau, 2012.

Höbelt, Lothar. *Ferdinand III.: Friedenskaiser wider Willen*. Graz: Ares, 2008.

Jiménez Pablo, Esther. 'La canonización de Ignacio de Loyola (1622): lucha de intereses entre Roma, Madrid y París.' *Chronica nova*, 42 (2016): 79–102. Accessed 12th November, 2018, doi:10.30827/cn.v0i42.5016.

Lagosanto, Venanzio da. *Apostolo e diplomatico o il p. Giacinto dei conti Natta da casale Monferrato Cappuccino*. Milano: Ghezzi, 1886.

Marek, Pavel. *La embajada española en la corte imperial (1558–1641)*. Praga: Karolinum, 2013.

Martí, Tibor. 'Los antecedentes del viaje a Roma del cardenal Péter Pázmány en 1632.' In *La dinastía de los Austria: la Monarquía Católica y el Imperio*, edited by José Martínez Millán and Rubén González Cuerva, 175–205. Madrid: Polifemo, 2011.

Negredo del Cerro, Fernando. 'Un episodio español en la Guerra de los Treinta Años: la embajada del marqués de Cadreita al Sacro Imperio y el acercamiento al Elector Sajón (1629–1631).' *Hispania*, 251 (2015): 669–94. Accessed 12th November, 2018, doi:10.3989/hispania.2015.020.

Nexon, Daniel H. *The Struggle for Power in Early Modern Europe: Religious Conflict, Dynastic Empires, and International Change*. Princeton: Princeton University Press, 2009.

Pizarro, Henar. 'El proyecto matrimonial entre el príncipe de Gales y la infanta María (1623): una polémica política y teológica.' Preface to Fray Francisco de Jesús Jódar, *Papeles sobre el tratado de matrimonio entre el Príncipe de Gales y la infanta María de Austria (1623)*, 9–78. Madrid: Ed. Carmelitanas, 2010.

Pizarro, Henar. 'La elección de confesor de la infanta María de Austria en 1628.' In *La dinastía de los Austria: la Monarquía Católica y el Imperio*, edited by José Martínez Millán and Rubén González Cuerva, 759–800. Madrid: Polifemo, 2011.

Pursell, Brennan C. *The Winter King: Frederick V of the Palatinate and the Coming of the Thirty Years' War*. Aldershot: Ashgate, 2003.

Reeve, John. 'Quiroga's Paper of 1631: A Missing Link in Anglo-Spanish Diplomacy during the Thirty Years War.' *English Historical Review*, 101 (1986): 913–26. Accessed 12th November, 2018, doi:10.1093/ehr/CI.CCCCI.913.

Reinhardt, Nicole. *Voices of Conscience: Royal Confessors and Political Counsel in Seventeenth-century Spain and France*. Oxford: Oxford University Press, 2016.

Roncero, Victoriano. 'Visiones de la batalla: El primer blasón del Austria de Calderón y el Estebanillo González.' In *Divinas y humanas letras, doctrina y poesía en los autos sacramentales de Calderón*, edited by Ignacio Arellano, 417–33. Pamplona: Universidad de Navarra, 1997.

Schilling, Heinz. *Konfessionalisierung und Staatsinteressen: Internationale Beziehungen 1559–1660*. Paderborn: F. Schöningh, 2007.

Sommer-Mathis, Andrea. 'María Ana de Austria: spanische Infantin – Königin von Ungarn und Böhmen – römisch-deutsche Kaiserin (1606–1646).' In *Nur die Frau des Kaisers? Kaiserinnen in der Frühen Neuzeit*, edited by Bettina Braun, Katrin Keller and Matthias Schnettger, 141–56. Wien: Böhlau, 2016.

Stollberg-Rilinger, Barbara. *Cultures of Decision-Making*. London: German Historical Institute, 2016.

Tercero Casado, Luis. 'La jornada de la reina Mariana de Austria a España: divergencias políticas y tensión protocolar en el seno de la Casa de Austria (1648–1649).' *Hispania*, 239 (2011): 639–64. Accessed 12th November, 2018, doi:10.3989/hispania.2011.v71.i239.352.

Vermeir, René. *En estado de guerra: Felipe IV y Flandes*. Córdoba: Universidad de Córdoba, 2006.

Thiessen, Hillard von. *Diplomatie und Patronage: Die spanisch-römischen Beziehungen 1605–1621 in akteurszentrierter Perspektive*. Epfendorf: bibliotheca academica Verlag, 2010.

Part III

Religion as a matter of diplomacy

8 Catholic ambassadors in a Protestant court

London, 1603–1625

Roberta Anderson

This chapter takes as its specific focus the Catholic ambassadors present in London during the years 1603 to 1625. It will examine the embassy chapel question in the English context, the ambassador's support for his co-religionists and the Catholic cause in England, and the ways in which Catholic ambassadors to Protestant England did this, both within and without the Court of James VI & I.

The problems of post-Reformation diplomacy

In the aftermath of the Reformation, rulers almost invariably chose men of their own religion to represent them and their states abroad. This, of course, presented problems when that ambassador was sent to a state whose prince followed a different religion. Where there was no church in which he could practise his religion, ambassadors provided for their own spiritual needs and those of his entourage by establishing a chapel within their residence and by appointing a chaplain to conduct services therein. In an age that did not separate the home from the workplace, the embassy served as both the ambassador's home and his office.

Following the deaths of Philip II and Elizabeth I, when the Catholic and Protestant countries of Europe found it in their interest to once again resume diplomatic relations by the exchange of resident envoys, a precondition for renewed relations was the recognition by all sides of an envoy's right to practise his religion. While diplomats had enjoyed certain immunities since the Middle Ages, these most definitely did not extend to violations of the host country's fundamental laws, especially those against heresy. Even in those early years, embassy chapels were highly contested, presenting problems whenever an embassy was to a state practising a different religion. In London in 1550, for example, the English authorities had broken into the Venetian embassy and arrested the priest who they caught celebrating Mass. The emperor, Charles V, banned the English ambassador to Flanders, Sir Thomas Chamberlain, from holding Anglican services in his house in 1551, and in London the Privy Council retaliated in kind.[1] As these quarrels show, embassy chapels were operating in London and a few other cities as early as the 1550s.

Beginning with the Acts of Supremacy and Uniformity in the first year of Elizabeth's reign, legislation was passed at various times, which defined the doctrines and discipline of the newly established Church. At times of particular alarm, such as in the 1570s, after Pius V had excommunicated Elizabeth by the Bull *Regnans in Excelsis*, and in the 1580s, when foreign Catholic invasion seemed imminent, legislation against Catholics was passed that made it high treason to be reconciled to Rome, or to be ordained a priest overseas. Furthermore, the saying and hearing of Mass was punished by fines and imprisonment. Severe as the Penal Laws might seem, and rigorous as their execution could be, their enforcement depended upon the exigencies of the time and the attitude of Whitehall, which permitted Catholics periods of unofficial toleration and anxious peace.

During the reign of Elizabeth, the Bishops of Ely let their palace and chapel in Ely Place to the Spanish ambassador, and until the reign of Charles I it was occupied by the representative of the Court of Spain. During this period, the chapel was freely used by English Catholics and became a place of sanctuary for them. Catholic ambassadors were reluctantly allowed to hold Mass privately in their embassy chapels, but they could not allow English subjects to attend the services, although it is evident they did so. The government was, therefore, always suspicious of the activities of resident Catholic ambassadors, but had to proceed against them carefully so as not to offend the prince by whom they had been sent, so that even at the height of persecution, Catholic ambassadors had to be catered for.

The English Catholics and the embassy chapel

With no church in which to practise their faith, ambassadors provided for their own spiritual needs and those of their entourage by establishing chapels inside their residences and appointing a chaplain to conduct services there. By the early seventeenth century, this rested on the notion, which was becoming recognised by all of Europe's rulers, that the embassy was turned into foreign soil by the presence of the ambassador, and so was inviolate, and that the host government did not merely have no right to intervene, but was actually obliged to protect the ambassador and his staff. As John Ruggie has noted:

> Rather than contemplate heresy of a Protestant service at a Catholic court and vice versa, it proved easier to pretend that the service was not taking place in the host country at all but on the soil of the home-land of the ambassador. And so it gradually became with other dimensions of the activities and precincts of the embassy. A fictitious space, designated extraterritoriality was invented.[2]

This 'fictitious space' caused havoc when Jame's Catholic subjects tried to attend Mass at the embassies of the Catholic ambassadors. The embassy chapel question was a vexed and reoccurring one for the English government, and during the century from the 1560s through to the 1650s, the issue provoked clashes in London, some of them violent, between authorities and citizens, on the one hand, and the personnel of the Spanish, French, and Venetian embassies, on the other.

The operation of diplomacy in London during the early seventeenth century was a delicate business. Anglo-Spanish hostilities had formally ceased when:

> in the second yeare of his Majestes raigne, and in the monethe of August, came an Embassador out of Spaine to take the Kinges othe for the maintenance and continuance of the League betweene them, which was don in this manner and forme followinge, viz.:
>
> In the Chappell weare two Traverses sett up of equall state inall thincces as neare as might be.
>
> Then was there a table sett up at the halfe pace before the Communion table, neare the Kingcs Traverse, wheruppon ther laye writinges and a standishe with pen and incke.
>
> Then his Majestie cominge into the Chappell, on his righte hand went the Constable of Spayne, and on his left the Spanishe lidger Embassador, and so they went up to the Communion table together.
>
> Then his Majestic went into his Traverse where he usually sittcth, and the Constable into the other, and there they bothe remayncd till an Anthem was ended, which beganne so soone as his Majestie and the Embassador wcarc in their Traverses, till wdiich time the Organs played.
>
> Then the Kinge and the Constable cominge out of their Traverses stoode neare together uppon the halfe pace, turninge their faces the one to the other: beinge so placed, my Lord Vicounte Cranbome Principall Secretarie read the Oath, the Kinge puttinge his hande within the Embassador's in the beginninge of the Oath, and layd his handes uppon a Lattin Bible of the vulgar translacon the other part of the othe, the Bible beinge held by the Deane of the Chappell in a Coapc all the while the Oath was reade.
>
> Then after the takinge of the Oath the Kinge and Constable kissed each other, and then they went againe into their Traverses, and ther staied till an other Anthem was songe.
>
> That ended, they went out of the Chappell in the same manner that they came in, the organs playinge till they weare gone out of the Chappell.[3]

The 1604 Treaty of London thus ended nearly two decades of war between England and Spain but did not address the ongoing conflict between Catholic and Protestant. This conflict often spilled over into the ways in which Catholic ambassadors to the Court of St James tried to assist their fellow co-religionists, by haranguing the king on the subject and by opening the doors to their private chapels to his subjects.

For James, the problem became a perennial one that arose whenever the English Catholics attempted to avoid the prohibitions of the Penal Laws by attending the religious services of the various Catholic embassies. They were encouraged in this course of action by the ambassadors, most of whom maintained English chaplains on their embassy staff, especially to preach in English. When Catholic diplomats attempted to circumnavigate the Penal Laws by wrapping worship at their chapels by native Englishmen in a cloak of diplomacy, the government was faced with the problem of maintaining public policy without upsetting the delicate balance of relations with foreign princes. During the greater part of James' reign, there were always several Catholic ambassadors at court, so the problem arose because these men saw a large proportion of the population as oppressed co-religionists. By far the worst offenders in this connection were the Spanish, who felt aggrieved when James took measures to prevent his subjects attending embassy Masses. In practice, however, certain rights stopped being contested as early as the outbreak of the Thirty Years' War. This permitted the ambassador and his family, as well as their servants and embassy personnel, to worship as they pleased in private, and allowed the inclusion in their entourage of a chaplain. If compatriots of the ambassador – merchants and others in London on business, for example – attended embassy services, objections were rarely raised. Whether foreigners from other countries could do the same was a delicate issue that caused tension.

In London, the Spanish embassy caused more concern to the authorities than any other, since they were practically unable to stop the scores of Londoners attending Mass and other devotions. It became a distinct issue from the traditional right of a Catholic diplomat to provide Mass for his household and other compatriots and from the custom of Sephardic Jews to gather at the embassy for Sabbath worship when they desired; in this case, the term 'Sephardic' is used loosely to refer to the Jews of Spain, the Mediterranean, and the Middle East, and considered by English law to be Spanish Catholics.[4]

While the practice of Londoners to attend Mass secretly had developed early in the reign of Elizabeth, by the end of James' reign sizeable numbers began to frequent the Catholic embassies in London. Indirectly, it was possible to make foreign forms of worship difficult to practise in the embassies. In England, there were those who tried to deprive native-born secretaries and chaplains serving in Catholic embassies of their immunities on the grounds that they could not rescind their national responsibilities by entering the service of a foreign prince. This particular attack on ambassadors' privileges was, however, short-lived, reaching its peak in James' reign but dying out after the Restoration when religious fanaticism was on the wane. One case in particular demonstrates how customs tried to play a part in making the practice of alien religions difficult and shows, among other things, that there was a growing assumption that ambassadors' goods were exempt from customs. In England, as in Spain, customs examination was concerned not merely with the levying of duties, but also with the exclusion of religious books that might be seen as undermining the national religion. In 1612, the Spanish ambassador complained bitterly to Northampton that crates of missals destined for his chaplain had been seized by customs officials and opened. Howard, in an attempt to pacify the ambassador, said that he believed the officers had opened the crate believing it to belong to an 'ordinary person' and that an investigation would be made. Foscarini reported that, when approached about the matter, the king said that customs officers should decide these matters for themselves and referred the case to the Privy Council, where it was quietly forgotten.[5]

Attempts were made, albeit unsuccessfully, to stem this growing tide, and between 1606 and 1611, when James asked the foreign diplomats not to allow his Catholic subjects to attend their chapels or English priests to celebrate Mass there, only the Venetians complied.[6] In August 1606, a number of persons were arrested as they left the Spanish embassy after attending Mass. This was felt all the more when no action was taken against those who had attended services in the French and Venetian embassies nearby, although the authorities made it clear that others should take warning from what had happened at the Spanish embassy.[7] During Pedro de Zúñiga's first embassy, a scandal had been created not only by Mass being celebrated at the embassy chapel, but by the large procession forming in the embassy garden. In May 1610, the king had warned all ambassadors not to admit any of his subjects to the Mass, nor to allow English priests to celebrate in their chapels: 'all repaire of English subjectes to the houses of forron ambassadors to heere Mass be restrained.'[8] The Venetian ambassador concluded that 'such activity is unusual and, as a rule, some of the Ambassadors are allowed to employ English priests.'[9] Reaction to these repeated warnings was predictable: ambassadors replied that the dignity of their country would not allow the embassy doors to be closed to those who wished entry; the Spanish ignored them and the Venetian ambassador said he would do his best to prevent the English from attending his chapel. However, as the warning seemed to have little effect, the Spanish embassy was watched to see who was still attending Mass there. The Spanish ambassador predictably protested at this and was asked to appear before the Privy Council in an attempt to find a solution that did not interfere with the diplomatic privileges he enjoyed. He blustered, saying he did not know who attended his chapel, so the Privy Council threatened to send the authorities, if necessary, to arrest any Englishmen found there. So indignant did the ambassador become when informed of this proposed action that the Council realised it had gone too far and that any such action would cause a serious breach between the two nations. Nonetheless, a watch was still kept on the embassy, and on Christmas Eve, 1611, Sir George Freer and some others were assaulted by pursuivants and royal officers when leaving after Mass. Freer was arrested, while the others took refuge in the embassy, from which a group of armed men emerged and promptly freed the prisoner.

There is a letter from the Spanish ambassador, Alonso de Velasco, to the Spanish court describing the above attempt by the pursuivants to arrest English Catholics as they left the chapel of his residence near the Barbican after Mass.[10] It also reveals in some detail his method of handling the diplomatic repercussions at the English court:

> Last Christmas eve, hoping to celebrate the feast with the devotion which is customary in the Catholic Church especially in Spain, certain English gentlemen arrived with musical instruments to assist at the Matins and Midnight Mass which are sung in my chapel. A great number of people were present and more than two hundred partook of Communion.
>
> The pursuivants are always abroad keeping close watch on the houses of ambassadors to observe those who enter to hear mass, particularly on the great feasts when the Catholics come to assist· with greater devotion. During the night they blocked off the street. When some people were leaving by a secret door at two in the morning the pursuivants tried to seize one of them, the physician for my house.[11] To escape their hands he turned back to enter by the same door but the pursuivants had surrounded it in their grasping at him and my servants had to fight to clear this doorway. Then they retreated without any further disturbance.
>
> A few days later the Archbishop of Canterbury went to the king and told him that on one day there were more people in my chapel than in St. Paul's which is their principal church. He insisted strongly that the king should stop the resulting embarrassment. He advised him to fulfill his duty to maintain his dignity by effecting the proper remedies. I was informed of everything and, as I expected, I was told that the Council wanted to present a complaint to me. I decided to anticipate this by first requesting an audience with the king to set forth my own opinion of the pursuivants' violation of my liberty.
>
> In answer a day and an hour were assigned for this but there was also a request that I meet with the Council to discuss certain matters. I suspected that they would touch on this question and that it was not planned to discuss it with the king for they had arranged to have present the Archbishop and the Lord Chancellor to whom I was to present my complaint. I replied that I desired to pay my respects to the king. Finally after some assurances that they would leave and return it was decided to give me an audience where I answered the charges of the Archbishop, and the king in turn demanded that from henceforth his subjects were not to be admitted to my chapel.
>
> I said that I had only followed the custom of my predecessors without attempting any innovation, and that it was impossible that my porter could fully distinguish those who were English and those who were strangers since there are in this city so many Flemish, Italians and

French who frequent my house. Moreover those who came there must be presumed to come on particular business. However, in all ordinary affairs I offered to take care anew to satisfy him.

Then I presented my complaint condemning in every way possible the excesses of the pursuivants. To this the king replied that he would do everything he could to remedy the problem. For the present it is clear that he did so, for since then they have not appeared in my street. In spite of my promise to conceal henceforth the news about certain services in my chapel the Catholics are so consoled in them that they soon tell their Protestant relatives. It is from their slight regard for secrecy and caution that a large part of their persecutions are derived.

The Catholic ambassadors were once again summoned to appear before the Council to discuss the matter and find a solution acceptable to all parties. The Venetian ambassador continued to insist he did not admit Englishmen to his chapel, which was, of course, untrue, and the archduke's representative wrote home for advice. The Spaniard, de Velasco, noted that the archduke's ambassador, when summoned before the Council to answer a complaint against those who resorted to his chapel to hear Mass, responded that 'his master would sooner lose a million than one soul of his subjects.'[12] Meanwhile, the Spanish ambassador refused point blank to keep his chapel doors locked and the French ambassador pleaded that as the English ambassador in Paris was allowed to admit all who wished to attend his services, he should be afforded the same courtesy in London. To this, the king replied that the cases were not the same; in France, there was universal freedom of conscience, which did not happen in England. However, the problem lay not so much with the French, Venetian, or archduke's envoys, but with the Spanish, who even had a bell rung to call the faithful to Mass.[13]

Talking accomplished nothing, and in February Sir Thomas Lake wrote that the king remained determined to keep a watch on the Spanish embassy and to arrest those Englishmen found attending there. In 1612, he was once more writing in the same vein, this time after Blackman, the Jesuit confessor of the English College in Rome, was arrested at the Spanish embassy in the Barbican.[14] Two others, Blount and Pelham, escaped.[15] In September, two more priests were arrested carrying notes and memoranda showing extensive correspondence between the Jesuits and the embassy, and confirming that Philip was freely giving money for their support.[16] In 1614, Elizabeth Moore, a widow, confessed to being:

a popish recusant and that upon Sunday last ... she was at the Spanish ambassador's house about nine or ten of the clock in the morning where she stayed an hour and ... went into the chapel and said her devotions there.

Soon after, one Thomas Davies, a scrivener, was discovered walking near the Barbican carrying a 'bough of hallowed palm in his hands,' a clear sign to those in authority that he had been to an embassy service.[17]

However, as time went on, and mainly at the behest of Gondomar, some Jesuits were released from imprisonment. Both the *State Papers* and the *Records of the English Province of the Society of Jesus* document these cases. The Acts of the Privy Council note several occasions when papists were released from prison at Gondomar's request. Furthermore, according to Contarini, priests were able, on payment to their jailers of a 'trifling fee,' to go in and out of jail, 'officiating privily in one house and then another by which means they maintain themselves and make considerable profit.'[18]

In 1617, it was reported that there was now daily a:

> Resort of Multitudes of Englishe Subjects of more than a hundred at once to Masse at the French Embassad[rs] in Durham House, not only when the Embassad[r] himselfe was there, but also when he was retyred into Greenwich, leaving some servants at Durham house.[19]

On 2nd February, 1625, a letter was despatched to the Bishop of Durham about the goings-on at his property:

> His Ma[ty] hath been Informed that there is a great Liberty taken by diverse of his Subjects, which resort to the hearing of Masse at Durham House, which as it is very scandalous to the Church & of ill Example to be suffered at any time, soe is it much more now in this time of Parliam[t] and therefore wee cannot but take notice of it, and doe hereby pray & require yo[r] Lop[s] to take this into yo[r] care. And although wee would not that any disturbance or trouble be made within the House of the Embassad[r], yet such of his Mat[ies] Subjects as resort hither & shall be present at the Masse, wee wish you to apprehend, & to comitt them to prison.[20]

In the same vein, instructions were sent to the local justices of the peace, although they were also advised not to do anything that might breach the ambassador's immunity. In order to arrest illegal visitors to the chapel, constables were to be posted 'without the walls and water stairs of Durham House' the following Sunday, 26th February.[21] The English authorities might have sought to avoid a scene – not so the ambassador. He felt offended at the treatment offered to his co-religionists and arrived home early to Durham House on the Sunday 'in a private Mann[r] to make a quarrell.'[22] Shortly before Mass was to end, the authorities took up their positions, only to find the ambassador's servants emerging from the house armed with swords, 'to carry the English Papists by strong hand through the Watch.'[23] A fight broke out and injuries were sustained by each side, including the death of Sir John Bath, an Irish Catholic, who was possibly just leaving Mass.[24]

News of the brawl spread quickly, and crowds 'came in heaps to Durham House Gate with Bills & Clubs to vindicate the same' intent on entering the grounds and joining the battle. They were only dissuaded from this path by the Bishop of Durham, William James, himself, who was trying desperately to calm the situation. He demanded an audience with Desmaretz, which was granted, but the ambassador remained determined, saying:

> That he wished his ffollowers had killed the Officers, and y^t he was sorry they had not killed some of them, & that ye King his Ma^{ty} should require reason of ye King of England for y^t wch was done against the Law of Nations, And that he Expected noe Subject of England should be troubled for comeing to Masse in his house.[25]

He left the room and his servants promptly set about the officers who had escorted the bishop into the ambassador's presence. The bishop was aghast at what he saw as Desmaretz' rudeness towards him – after all, he had invited the ambassador to share his residence when he had requested lodgings closer to Whitehall than those he had been assigned at Hampton Court. The bishop had done this, despite 'crouding up himselfe and his whole ffamily (being great) into the worst and basest Roomes of ye House, leaving all ye good & large Roomes thereof, to ye Embassad^{rs} use.'[26] No action appears to have been taken against Desmaretz for allowing the local Catholics to attend Mass at his residence, his personal immunity placing him above English law.[27]

Despite orders issued against Catholics attending the embassy chapels, the ambassadors still, as late as 1625, allowed their English co-religionists access to the Sacrament. The House of Commons insisted that one of the major causes for the increase in popery was the way in which Catholics were allowed to frequently attend Mass in the embassy chapels.[28] Writing in 1621, John Chamberlain commented that Gondomar, the Spanish ambassador, had 'almost as many come to his mass,' as had attended 'the sermon at St. Andrewes over against him.'[29] Prynne, in his *Historiomatrix*, speaking of the errors of the Church of Rome, noted that 'Papifts and Iefuites transform Chrifts Paffion into a meere ridiculous Stage-play,' and directed the reader to 'witneffe the acting of Chrifts Pafsion at Elie houfe in Holborne when Gundemore lay there, on Good-Friday at night, at which there were thoufands prefent.'[30] Even the Prince of Wales' retinue was not immune from prosecution. In January 1623, two of the prince's musicians, Angelo and Drew, were dismissed from his service for assisting at Mass. However, they, like many before them, were restored at the intercession of the Spanish ambassador – in this case, Coloma.[31]

The fatal vespers

On Sunday 26th October, 1623, several hundred people flocked to a unique occasion at Hunsdon House, the home of the French ambassador, Tanneguy

Leveneur, Count of Tillières, and a recently established centre of Jesuit prayer.[32] A mixed congregation of some 300 met on the third floor of the house in Blackfriars to listen to the preaching of Robert Drury, a learned and devout Jesuit preacher. This was not a secret meeting, as was usually the case with many Catholic meetings at this time. However, the London mob knew all about the secret sermons and Masses, especially those held in the French and Spanish embassies, which had become more and more numerous since the opening of marriage negotiations with Spain.[33] As Thomas Goad tells us in the case of Hunsdon House:

> To this Garret or Gallery, (being situated ouer the Gate-house of the French Ambassadors house) there is a leading passage by a doore close to the vtter gate of the said house, but without it, open to that street: By which passage many men and women vsed to haue daily recourse to the English Priests chambers there.[34]

Hardly had Fr Drury began to preach than a rotten timber in the floor gave way under the weight of the assembly squeezed together in what was little more than a loft. Several crashed through the second floor, taking with them – to his death – Fr Whittingham, who was in his room on the lower level at the time. Over 95 people, including Fr Drury, died in the tragic accident. Fortunately for the ambassador, he was staying with the Venetian ambassador at the time of the accident. This occasion was to be remembered as the 'fatal vespers,' appearing frequently in anti-Catholic polemic.[35] The date of the accident coincided, according to the newly introduced Gregorian calendar, with 5th November. The hand of God could not fail to be detected: retribution to those who had tried to bring down the Houses of Parliament. Official tracts on the incident deployed a rhetoric of moderation, while other publications were much less sympathetic. Fletcher described the event in his furious attack on the Jesuits, *The Apollyonists*:

> So when of late that boasted Jesuite Priest
> Gath'red his flocke, and now the house gan swell,
> And every eare drew in the sugred spell
> Their house, and rising hopes, swole, busted and head-long fell.[36]

A contemporary account suggests that the survivors were treated more with malice than sympathy. The rabble 'being grown savage and barbarous ... refused to assist them with drink, aqua vitæ or any other cordials in their necessity, but rather insulted upon them with taunts and gibes.'[37] The hostile mob was reported to have attempted to stone the survivors, and it was said they even tried to 'set an injured lady afire when she was travelling in her coach as they attempted to fix a broken wheel.'[38]

The Catholic ambassadors were up in arms about the treatment of the injured and even more so about that of the dead, whom bishop George

Montaine refused burial in London churchyards, directing that 'as excommunicates they be buried on the refuse pile,' and that the clothes they wore were 'to be stripped off.'[39] The Catholics responded by blaming the puritans for the tragedy, while the Spanish diplomats pushed on with their suit for official toleration.

Extraterritoriality, immunity, and a lack of cohesion

The religious situation in England and the proposed Anglo-Spanish marriage alliance resulted in ambassadors of an extremely high calibre being sent between the two countries. This was a cause of great concern among commentators and pamphleteers, who feared any entente with Catholic Spain, so that her ambassadors were to become the most disliked of all representatives at the early Jacobean court. For example, on 16th July, 1624, John Jackson reported the desecration of Coloma's chapel, which was robbed:

> 4 or 5 dayes since, but not above x^{li} worth taken. The custodia was turned upside downe but not opened, which I think was a special providence of Our Lord, who was within the same. A silver lamp and other things taken.[40]

In April 1624, the Commons repeated their complaints, and James in his reply promised to consult with the Privy Council as to how this might best be remedied. As James noted, there were great difficulties in such dealings with the ambassadors. 'It is true,' he wrote:

> that the houses of Ambassadors are privileged places and though they can not take them [the English Catholics] out from their houses, yet the Lord Mayor and Mr. Recorder of London may take them as they come from thence and make some of them examples.[41]

In the early part of May, both Francis Nethersole and Dudley Carleton reported that the mayor and Recorder had received their instructions. This action was as doomed as any other taken to stop the ambassadors opening the doors of their chapels to the English Catholics, and it was to remain a problem until long after the king's death.

The crux of the embassy chapel problem was whether the extraterritorial nature of the ambassador's chapel safeguarded a person from prosecution under the Penal Laws, which insisted on attendance at Anglican services, penalised non-attendance, and forbade the saying and hearing of Mass. The regulation of religion in the seventeenth century was the sovereign right of the monarch, and as attending Mass at the embassies was considered a violation of the law and a failure to obey a specific command of the king, the English government had two legal alternatives – domestic law and international law – under which it could prosecute its Catholic subjects. Allowing the public use of embassy chapels was one of the most important steps taken towards the practice of modern ambassadorial immunity, since nothing an ambassador could at that time have demanded could have been more injurious to a ruler's sovereign jurisdiction, and, once accepted, other privileges followed without much difficulty. In the course of the seventeenth century, the remaining problems of ambassadorial immunity, mainly in the field of civil law, such as freedom from prosecution for debt and immunity from excise and other duties, were well on the way to being settled on a pragmatic basis. The result varied slightly from court to court, depending on reciprocity, the power wielded by the envoy's master, and the envoy's own ingenuity and strength of character.

The appearance of embassy chapels on a permanent basis resurrected other more thorny problems, however, particularly that of the immunity to be enjoyed by the ambassador's chaplain, and hence the rest of his staff, including native Englishmen. Unlike the ambassador's personal immunity, this affected large sections of the native population as victims, or creditors of the ambassador's staff, and was much resented by them. Another associated problem was the immunity of ambassadors' residences, which was disregarded whenever guards acting on behalf of the court to which the ambassador was accredited invaded the chapel to seize natives who were worshipping there. As we have seen, such invasions frequently occurred in England before the middle of the seventeenth century and caused consternation to both ambassadors and their masters. Failure to take this action, however, infuriated the native law-abiding population. Accordingly, ambassadors and host governments were forced to negotiate over the issue, and by the end of the century broad agreement had been reached throughout Europe. Nevertheless, the precise extent and nature of the immunity of diplomatic buildings remains in dispute to this day.

The Catholic ambassadors to James' court did not form a cohesive group, despite working more or less together for the English Catholics. They were constantly sniping with each other over precedence and for the favour of both James and Anna. The best example of this lack of 'joined up' thinking on the ambassadors' part was the case of Gondomar. He had few friends at court, except the Spanish 'confidantes' and Boisschot, Archduke Albert's ambassador, with whom he formed a close friendship. With the French ambassador, he remained coldly cordial, but he would have no dealings with the envoy of the States-General and he quarrelled with Foscarini, the Venetian ambassador – a quarrel that was to affect relations not only with that ambassador, but also with his two successors. Foscarini is said to have spread the rumour that Gondomar had 'poisoned a Spanish lady.'[42] Relations remained strained between the two ambassadors, in part owing to the Venetian's anti-Spanish sympathies, but also on the question of title. The propagandists played their part in keeping the Catholic ambassadors from having a united front by satirising them in plays and pamphlets, and the Protestant population's acceptance of the literature demonstrated a profound distrust of their activities.

Ambassadors and anti-Catholic literature

The acceptance of Catholic ambassadors in London was one that caused an outpouring of anti-Catholic literature. These were mainly directed towards the Spanish, but it did not mean that the French, Venetians, and representatives from the emperor escaped. The continued increase in popery, which the House attributed to the 'vigilancy of the Pope' and the printing and dispersing of 'popish seditious books and swarms of Priests and Jesuits' presently allowed into the country, was deplored.[43] The Archbishop of Canterbury, George Abbot, feared that James was labouring 'to set up the most damnable and heretical doctrine of the Church of Rome, the whore of Babylon' in England, while John Donne, himself an apostate Catholic, in *News from the Very Country*, commented on how the numbers of Jesuits to be found had increased, saying, 'Jesuits are like Apricocks, heretofore one suckled here and there in a great man's house, and cost dear: now you may have them for nothing in every cottage.'[44]

Popular opinion regarded the Spanish ambassador's activities in England, especially during Gondomar's embassies, as those of master-spies, and pamphleteers satirised Spanish diplomacy unmercifully using, for the most part, Gondomar as the butt of their wit. Thomas Middleton chose to portray him as the Black Knight, 'the fistula of Europe,' in *A Game at Chess*, in which Gondomar recounts his many disreputable activities.[45] Of course, Middleton was only repeating the views of a population that had, for years, been almost uniformly anti-Catholic and anti-Spanish. Thomas Scott, ever vigilant in pointing out the problems caused by Spain and Catholicism, published a series of pamphlets that called for a renewal of the Anglo-Dutch alliance that existed in Elizabeth's time. These included *The Belgicke Pismire* (Holland, 1622), *An Experimental Discoverie of Spanish Practises* (1623), *Digitus Dei* (Holland, 1623), *Robert Earl of Essex's Ghost* (1624), and *The Belgick Souldier* (Dordrecht, 1624). His writings advocated that Christian princes of all nations should 'resist and impeach ... the Spanish tyranny,' and at the same time he urged the king to 'beware of disuniting ... from the United States of the Netherlands' on the grounds that the States had 'increased in men, in ammunition, in shipping, and in wealth.' More importantly, and a point that should make the 'knot of unity more strong and fast,' he reminded the king that the Dutch were of the 'same true religion, which you profess.'[46]

Concluding remarks

When thinking about the attitude of the Catholic ambassadors to this question of admittance of their English co-religionists to their chapels, it must be understood that there was nothing unusual in their defence of their actions; rather, they stressed that their actions and procedures were customary for the time. In June 1610, the Spanish ambassador, for example, had stated to the

Privy Council that he 'encouraged no one to come to his house but, nonetheless, he would never bar his gates to those who wished to enter.'[47] In April 1611, in almost identical circumstances, he had told them, 'this is not an innovation over the activities of my predecessors, if some Spanish subjects are entering the chapel and some Englishmen come behind them I do not recognise them nor can I close my gates.'[48] On neither occasion did the Council take the matter further.

No less significant in this discussion is the attitude of King James himself. His fear of condemnation on the continent should he curtail the liberties of resident ambassadors is understandable. Furthermore, he was, at this time, particularly anxious to avoid placing in jeopardy his good relations with Spain, because, with the approval of Marie de Medici, the Regent of France, a Franco-Spanish marriage alliance was being negotiated that could, in James' view, all too easily isolate England.

The issue of the embassy chapels was, then, a constant thorn in James' side. Since ambassadors were the embodiment of their sovereign, they were decreed to be inviolable according to both canon and secular law. Throughout the period the doctrine of immunity for ambassadors, their residences and entourage were clearly acceptable to all nations, including England. For all that, no jurists held that the 'right of chapel' existed beyond the service of the diplomatic suite. Any abuse of this ideal was tolerated simply because of the sympathies and philosophies of individual states or from the necessity of maintaining good relations with other nations. The general practice in England, therefore, became one of non-interference, except when public pressure made it necessary, and by seizing Catholics when they left the embassy environs. To this day, the full extent of this immunity has not been agreed upon.

The same general policy was directed towards English Catholic priests employed as chaplains at the embassies. So long as they remained on embassy property, they were protected by the extraterritorial nature of the embassy. But if they attempted to leave the ambassador's residence, they became liable to arrest and expulsion from England. This in its turn presented government with another problem. Ambassadors could, on the grounds of diplomatic immunity, claim immunity for their chaplains based on their rights as a member of a diplomatic suite, and although James' government explicitly denied this right, it avoided any diplomatic incidents by means of compromises in individual cases.

Catholic ambassadors at the Court of James VI & I sought to assist their co-religionists by providing chapels in which they could worship in their embassies, and at the same time looked to ease the Penal Laws imposed upon them. They sincerely believed in what they were trying to achieve in England, and worked tirelessly on behalf of their co-religionists, seeking a lasting, peaceful arrangement between England and Rome. This in its turn caused an outpouring of anti-Catholic literature that cast Catholicism and its ambassadors as the hated and dangerous antagonist.

Notes

1 Edward R. Adair, *The Exterritoriality of Ambassadors in the Sixteenth and Seventeenth Centuries* (New York: Longmans, Green and Co, 1929), 131, 182.

2 John Gerard Ruggie, 'Territoriality and Beyond: Problematizing Modernity in International Relations.' *International Organization* 47, 1 (Winter, 1993), 165.

3 Edward Francis Rimbault, *The Old Cheque-Book, or Book of Remembrance, of the Chapel Royal, from 1561–1744* (London: Camden Society, 1872), 151–52.

4 See Daniel S. Katz, *Philo-Semitism and the Readmission of the Jews to England, 1603–1655* (Oxford: Clarendon Press, 1982), 2, 3.

5 Foscarini to the Doge, 15th October, 1612, in *Calendar of State Papers, Venetian, 1610–1613*, no. 663.

6 Adair, *The Extraterritoriality of Ambassadors*, 190.

7 Duodo to the Doge, 30th August, 1606, in *Calendar of State Papers, Venetian, 1603–1607*, 395.

8 26th May, 1610. Adair, *The Extraterritoriality of Ambassadors*, 190.

9 Correr to the Doge, 7th July, 1610, in *Calendar of State Papers, Venetian, 1610–1613*, 3–4.

10 Alonso de Velasco to Philip III, 3rd February, 1612, Archivo General, Simancas, E2589/1.

11 Sir George Freer. Several days later, he and a group of friends met the same pursuivants in the street, but once again they fought back, 'and the pursuivants were either wounded, or put to flight or forced to jump in the Thames.' In *Calendar of State Papers, Venetian, 1610–1613*, 267, 277, 287.

12 Alonso de Velasco to Philip III, 14th April, 1612, Archivo General, Simancas, E2589/24.

13 Venetian Ambassador to the Doge, 7th July, 1610, 21st April, 1611, 5th and 20th January, 10th February, 9th March, 1612, in *Calendar of State Papers, Venetian, 1610–1613*, 4, 136–38, 267, 277, 286–87, 303–4. See also 'Proceedings against Catholics for attending Mass at the Spanish Embassy on Palm Sunday, 1614,' ed. R. Stanfield and J. S. Hansom, Miscellanea VII, *Catholic Record Society Publications* 9, 122–26; Albert J. Loomie, 'The Spanish Ambassador and the Pursuivants,' *Catholic History Review* 49 (1963), 203–6.

14 I am indebted to Dr Dominic A. Bellenger, who has suggested to me that this is John Blackfan alias Blackman (1560–1641).

15 Possibly Richard Blount SJ, born 1563, and Alexander Fairclough SJ, born 1575; see *English and Welsh Priests, 1558–1800*, ed. Dominic A. Bellenger (Bath: Downside Abbey Publishing, 1984), 40, 58.

16 Foscarini to the Doge, 19th August, 1612, *Calendar of State Papers, Venetian, 1610–1613*, 412–13.

17 'Proceedings against Catholics.'

18 *Calendar of State Papers, Venetian, 1617–1619*, 414.

19 Durham House was a property rented from the See of Durham. Gaspard Dauvet, Count Desmaretz. Sir Thomas Wilson, *A True Relation of That Which Passed Betwixt the King's Officers, And the ffrench Embassaders ffollowers by Occasion of Apprehending Englishe Subjects Papists, y^t resorted daily to Masse to the Embassa^{dr} lying in Durham House. There being daily Resort of Multitudes of Englishe Subjects of more then a hundred at once to Masse at the French Embassad^{rs} in Durham House, not only when the Embassad^r himselfe was there, but also when he was retyred into Greenwich, leaving some servants at Durham house; & that in this time of the Parliam^t sitting. The Lords of the Councell, by His Maties direction, who tooke notice of the Said abuse, wrote their Letters to the Bp. of Durham and to all & every other the Justices of ye peace within the*

County of Mid, or the City or Liberties of Westminster ... in John H. Pollen, 'A Relation of a brawl between the King's officers and Servants of the French ambassador concerning the Catholics who resorted to Mass at Durham House,' *Miscellenea I, Catholic Record Society Publications* 1 (1905), 92.

20 Sir Thomas Wilson, *A True Relation*, 2.
21 Sir Thomas Wilson, *A True Relation*, 93.
22 Sir Thomas Wilson, *A True Relation*, 93.
23 Sir Thomas Wilson, *A True Relation*, 94.
24 Sir Thomas Wilson, *A True Relation*, 94.
25 Sir Thomas Wilson, *A True Relation*, 94.
26 Sir Thomas Wilson, *A True Relation*, 95.
27 Sir Thomas Wilson, *A True Relation*, 95.
28 Petition of Commons to the King, 3rd December, 1621, *Calendar of State Papers, Venetian, 1621–1623*, 187.
29 *Memoirs XII: The Letters of John Chamberlain*, ed. N.E. McClure, vol. 2, 342.
30 William Prynne, *Histrio-mastix: The Players Scourge, or, Actors Tragædie, Divided into Two Parts. Wherein it is Largely Evidenced, by Divers Arguments, by the Concurring Authorities and Resolutions of Sundry Texts of Scripture ... That Popular Stage-playes ... are Sinfull, Heathenish, Lewde, Ungodly Spectacles, and Most Pernicious Corruptions; Condemned in All Ages, as Intolerable Mischiefes to Churches, to Republickes, to the Manners, Mindes, and Soules of Men. And that the Profession of Play-poets, of Stage-players; Together with the Penning, Acting, and Frequenting of Stage-playes, are Unlawfull, Infamous and Misbeseeming Christians. All Pretences to the Contrary are here Likewise Fully Answered; and the Unlawfulnes of Acting, of Beholding Academicall Enterludes, Briefly Discussed; Besides Sundry Other Particulars Concerning Dancing, Dicing, Health-drinking, &c. of Which the Table will Informe you. By William Prynne, an vtter-barrester of Lincolnes Inne* (1633), 117.
31 Calvert to Digby, 14th January, 1623, *Calendar of Clarendon State Papers, preserved at the Bodleian Library*, 5 vols., ed. Octavius Ogle and W. H. Bliss (Oxford: Clarendon Press, 1869–1970), 219.
32 The meeting took place on the third floor of the gatehouse; on the second floor was a chamber where Mass was said, and which was occupied at this time by Fr Whittingham and Fr Percy. The ambassador used the first floor as a wardrobe and armoury.
33 In May 1622, the first Jesuit Vice-Provincial Congregation had been held in the French ambassador's house.
34 Thomas Goad, *The Dolefull Euen-Song, or a trve ... Narration of that fearefull and sudden calamity, which befell the Preacher Mr. Drvry, a Iesuite, ... by the down of all of the floore at an assembly in the Black-Friers on Sunday the 26. of Octob. last, in the after noone ...* (London, 1623).
35 See, for example, Samuel Clarke, *The Fatal Vespers: A True and Full Narrative of that Signal Judgement of God upon the Papists, by the Fall of the House in Black Friers, London, upon Their Fifth of November* (London: J. O., 1623).
36 Phineas Fletcher, *The Locusts or Apollyonists* (1627), canto 4.2.
37 Ethelred L. Taunton, *The History of the Jesuits in England, 1580–1773* (London: Methuen, 1901), 404.
38 *Spain and the Jacobean Catholics*, 2, 1613–1624, ed. Albert J. Loomie, Record Series, 68 (London: Catholic Record Society, 1978), 162.
39 *Spain and the Jacobean Catholics*, 2, 1613–1624, 162; John Gee, *The Foot out of the Snare*, 82, no 70. Some victims were buried at Ely House.
40 Archive of Archbishop of Westminster, B26/84.
41 Adair, *The Extraterritoriality of Ambassadors*, 192.

42 *Calendar State Papers, Venetian*, 1613–1615, App. no. 907, 598.
43 Joseph R. Tanner, *Constitutional Documents of the Reign of James I* (Cambridge: Cambridge University Press, 1930), 277.
44 Samuel Rawson Gardiner, *History of England from the Accession of James I to the Outbreak of the Civil War, 1603–1642* (London: Longmans, Green & Co., 1884), vol. v, 71; John Carey, *John Donne Life, Mind and Art* (London: Faber & Faber, 1990) for a discussion of Donne's apostasy and the effect this had on his writings; John Bossy, *The English Catholic Community* (London: Darton, Longman & Todd, 1975), 195.
45 Thomas Middleton, *A Game at Chesse*, ed. J. W. Harper (London: Ernest Behn Ltd, 1966), 2.2.46.
46 Thomas Scott, 'Robert Earl of Essex's Ghost.' *Harleian Miscellany* 3 (1809), 512.
47 Letter of Alonso de Velasco, 24th June, 1610, Archivo General, Simancas, E2587/86.
48 Letter of Alonso de Velasco, 27th April, 1611, Archivo General, Simancas, E2588/27, 28.

Bibliography

Archival sources

Archives of Archbishop of Westminster, B26/84.
Archivo General, Simancas E2589/1, E2589/24, E2587/86, E2588/27 and 28.

Printed sources

Calendar of State Papers Relating to English Affairs in the Archives of Venice, vol. 10, 1603–1607, edited by Horatio F. Brown. London: Her Majesty's Stationery Office, 1900.
Calendar of State Papers Relating to English Affairs in the Archives of Venice, vol. 12, 1610–1613, edited by Horatio F. Brown. London: His Majesty's Stationery Office, 1909.
Calendar of State Papers Relating to English Affairs in the Archives of Venice, vol. 14, 1615–1617, App. no. 907, edited by Allen B. Hinds. London: His Majesty's Stationery Office, 1908.
Calendar of State Papers Relating to English Affairs in the Archives of Venice, vol. 17, 1621–1623, edited by Allen B. Hinds. London: His Majesty's Stationery Office, 1911.
Calendar of the Clarendon State Papers Preserved in the Bodleian Library, edited by Octavius Ogle, et al., 5 vols. Oxford: Clarendon Press, 1869–1970.
Clarke, Samuel. *The Fatal Vespers: A True and Full Narrative of that Signal Judgement of God upon the Papists, by the Fall of the House in Black Friers, London, upon their Fifth of November*. London: J. O., 1623.
Fletcher, Phineas. *The Locusts or Apollyonists*. Cambridge: The University Press, 1627.
Gee, John. *The Foot Out of the Snare* (1624), edited by Theodorus Hendrikus Bernardus Maria Harmsen. Nijmegen: Cicero Press, 1992.

Goad, Thomas. *The Dolefvll Euen-Song, or a trve … Narration of that fearefull and sudden calamity, which befell the Preacher Mr. Drvry, a Iesuite, … by the down of all of the floore at an assembly in the Black-Friers on Sunday the 26. of Octob. last, in the after noone … London*, 1623.

McClure, Norman Egbert ed. *Memoirs XII: The Letters of John Chamberlain*. Philadelphia: American Philosophical Society, 1939.

Middleton, Thomas. *A Game at Chesse*. Edited by J. W. Harper. London: Benn, 1966.

Prynne, William *Histrio-mastix: The Players Scourge, or, Actors Tragædie, Divided into Two Parts. Wherein it is Largely Evidenced, by Divers Arguments, by the Concurring Authorities and Resolutions of Sundry Texts of Scripture … That Popular Stage-playes … are Sinfull, Heathenish, Lewde, Ungodly Spectacles, and Most Pernicious Corruptions; Condemned in All Ages, as Intolerable Mischiefes to Churches, to Republickes, to the Manners, Mindes, and Soules of Men. And that the Profession of Play-poets, of Stage-players; Together with the Penning, Acting, and Frequenting of Stage-playes, are Unlawfull, Infamous and Misbeseeming Christians. All Pretences to the Contrary are here Likewise Fully Answered; and the Unlawfulnes of Acting, of Beholding Academicall Enterludes, Briefly Discussed; Besides Sundry Other Particulars Concerning Dancing, Dicing, Health-drinking, &c. of Which the Table will Informe you. By William Prynne, an vtter-barrester of Lincolnes Inne*. London: E[dward] A[llde], Augustine Mathewes, Thomas Cotes and W[illiam] I[ones], 1633.

Stanfield, R., and J. S. Hansom, eds. 'Proceedings against Catholics for attending Mass at the Spanish Embassy on Palm Sunday, 1614.' *Miscellanea VII*. London: Catholic Record Society, 1911.

Tanner, Joseph Robson. *Constitutional Documents of the Reign of James I*. Cambridge: Cambridge University Press, 1930.

Literature

Adair, Edward R. *The Exterritoriality of Ambassadors in the Sixteenth and Seventeenth Centuries*. New York: Longmans, Green & Company, 1929.

Bellenger, Dominic A., ed. *English and Welsh Priests, 1558–1800*. Bath: Downside Abbey Publishing, 1984.

Bossy, John. *The English Catholic Community, 1570–1850*. London: Darton, Longman & Todd, 1975.

Carey, John. *John Donne Life, Mind and Art*. Oxford: Oxford University Press, 1990.

Gardiner, Samuel Rawson. *History of England from the Accession of James I to the Outbreak of the Civil War, 1603–1642*, 10 vols. London: Longmans, Green & Co., 1884.

Katz, Daniel S. *Philo-Semitism and the Readmission of the Jews to England, 1603–1655*. Oxford: Clarendon Press, 1982.

Loomie, Albert J. 'The Spanish Ambassador and the Pursuivants: A Letter to King Philip III February 3, 1612.' *Catholic History Review* 49, 2 (July, 1963): 203–9.

Loomie, Albert J., ed. *Spain and the Jacobean Catholics*, 2, 1613–1624. Record Series, 68. London: Catholic Record Society, 1978.

Pollen, J. H. 'A Relation of a Brawl between the King's Officers and Servants of the French Ambassador Concerning the Catholics Who Resorted to Mass at Durham House.' *Miscellenea I*. London: Catholic Record Society, 1905.

Rimbault, Edward Francis. *The Old Cheque-Book, or Book of Remembrance, of the Chapel Royal, from 1561–1744*. London: Camden Society, 1872.

Ruggie, John Gerard. 'Territoriality and Beyond: Problematizing Modernity in International Relations.' *International Organization* 47, 1 (Winter, 1993): 139–74.

Scott, Thomas. 'Robert Earl of Essex's Ghost, sent from Elysium to the Nobility, Gentry, and Commonalty, of England. Printed in Paradise, 1624.' *Harleian Miscellany* 3. London: Robert Dutton, 1809.

Taunton, Ethelred L. *The History of the Jesuits in England, 1580–1773*. London: Methuen & Co. 1901.

9 Scottish Calvinists and Swedish diplomacy, 1593–1632

The case of Sir James Spens of Wormiston

Steve Murdoch

Writing about a Scottish Calvinist diplomatic network at the centre of some of Lutheran Sweden's most important diplomatic endeavours in the early seventeenth century may seem a niche subject at best. After all, it remains a commonly held belief that it was against the law to be anything other than a Lutheran to live and work in Sweden in the era of Sigismund Vasa (reigned 1593–1599), Karl IX (reigned 1604–1611), or Gustav II Adolf (reigned 1611–1632). As a fully Lutheran confessional state, the entrusting of sensitive diplomatic duties to Calvinist diplomats, ambassadors, clergymen, and spies would somehow seem anomalous. It was, of course, quite normal to welcome ambassadors and political leaders of other faiths into the Swedish realm – how else could Sweden conduct any diplomatic business with non-Lutheran states otherwise? Indeed, as Daniel Riches has observed in a Swedish context, the Northern European diplomatic class 'transcended the narrow boundaries of state, dynasty and confession.'[1] It is certainly incontestable that a particular cohort of Scottish Calvinists operated at the heart of the Swedish diplomatic machine in the time period being considered. Through their diplomatic activities, they in turn were able to override any objection to the retention of their confession of faith by the Swedish Church, or any organ of government. To fully comprehend the implications of this – and their importance in Swedish diplomacy – we must first glance at the background to the Swedish Reformation.

The Swedish confessional state

From the 1520s and throughout the sixteenth century, successive Swedish monarchs from Gustav Vasa to Karl IX struggled with the problem of creating a confessional Swedish state.[2] The ultimate consequence of decades of debate and controversy led to the 'Statement of Faith' by the Uppsala Assembly on 20th March, 1593.[3] Through this declaration, Sweden adopted the Augsburg Confession of 1530 and specifically denied anyone the right to practise any form of Roman Catholicism or the quasi-Catholic rituals of Johan III.[4] When discussing this document, many scholars apply the outright rejection of all things Roman Catholic equally to any other Protestant confession of faith, whether Zwinglian, Anabaptist, or Calvinist. To do so, they rely on versions of the statement signed by Duke Karl (the future Karl IX). Problematically, this copy suffers from the later addition of punctuation and minor scribal annotation which *may* alter the document's intention.[5] The eminent Swedish Church historian Oscar Bensow followed this interpolation without question or comment and chose to add specific meanings to the text which reinforce the starkness of the declaration.[6] These remain only his understanding of what is actually written. Other scholars simply omit a final, and rather difficult, eight-word clause of the text pertaining to the other Protestant denominations, removing the possibility of alternative interpretations of the text.[7] Herman Lindqvist renders the section on other Protestants, replacing the obscure eight words with one. Not only were Calvinists and Anabaptists to be denied a place within the Lutheran Church, but to Lindqvist they now also became 'forbidden' altogether.[8] Certainly, the signatories to the Statement of Faith emphatically rejected all other forms of Protestantism within the Swedish Church, but that is not the same as banning them from within the borders of the Swedish state, as frequently avowed. Indeed, when one reads the text in its entirety (rather than cherry-picking from it), it is categorical that people of dissenting opinion will remain in the realm, as to banish them would be harmful, not least to trade. Rather, it emphasises that such believers must not assemble together for the purposes of their faith, either in their own houses or elsewhere, and nor should they speak ill of Swedish Lutheranism. To do either would incur severe punishment.[9]

Regardless of the Statement of Faith, some of these confessions had a protector in the crypto-Calvinist Duke Karl.[10] Indeed, in Sweden, confessional strife often manifested itself as a struggle between the Church and perceived royal interference in it by Karl. Therefore, much of the Church rhetoric was ensuring that his influence was kept at bay rather than targeting individual subjects for their beliefs.[11] There were, in any case, much greater threats to Swedish Lutheranism than the handful of Calvinists or Anabaptists scattered across Sweden.

In the immediate aftermath of the Uppsala Assembly, there were justifiable suspicions by many of the Swedish clergy and nobility about whether their Catholic king, Sigismund Vasa, was genuine about his promise to respect Lutheranism as the state religion of Sweden.[12] This was not helped when he arrived in Sweden for his coronation with a retinue containing numerous Catholics, including Jesuit priests. There is little need here to rehearse the tensions between the Lutheran Swedes and their Catholic king other than to note that a civil war resulted in his defeat in 1598 and Sigismund's deposition by the *Riksdag* (parliament) the following year.[13] By then, he had returned to his other realm of Poland–Lithuania (reigned 1587–1632). Sigismund III Vasa used his Polish dominions to try to regain his Swedish throne, leading to the Polish–Swedish War (1600–1629) and the establishment of a Swedish Catholic

'Émigré Chancellery' in Poland.[14] Throughout the duration of this war, Calvinists simply did not register as a meaningful threat in the Swedish psyche to the same extent as Catholics. Indeed, they would soon prove to be of immense benefit in the struggle against the Counter-Reformation.

It was in this milieu of Swedish–Polish tensions that Calvinists continued to arrive into the ever-expanding Swedish Empire. Their appearance represented a mix of pragmatic necessity by a Swedish state in a near constant state of war, but also the reflection of an ongoing dialogue between some Swedes and a number of Calvinist servants of the state, particularly among the Scottish soldiering class, but also some other notable individuals.[15] As early as 1590, Karl IX (then Duke Karl) had spent days in the company of the Calvinist monarch James VI of Scotland.[16] The two men corresponded directly and indirectly thereafter, with James providing thousands of soldiers for Karl's military campaigns almost immediately after their meeting.[17] The influx of soldiers from Scotland directly reopened inter-confessional discussion in Sweden. We need only think of the arrival of Reverend John Forbes in Uppsala as an example of how the military and theological spheres were interlinked.

Exiled from Scotland by James VI & I in 1606 for his adherence to the Presbyterian form of Calvinism, Forbes settled in the Dutch Republic. He was the brother of Captain Arthur Forbes, a soldier in the Swedish army who, while on furlough in the Dutch Republic, wrote to Karl IX about his theologian brother. Later that year, John travelled to Sweden with Arthur and Karl IX met him at Uppsala in the autumn. A theological debate between John and the Uppsala theologians was arranged.[18] Apparently, Karl's intention was to confront Swedish theologians with a well-schooled and orthodox Calvinist, to soften the theologians' views on his own confessional convictions.[19] On 16th November, the debate was held with Johannes Rudbeckius leading the Uppsala professors. Forbes proposed 68 points of discussion, and on only two of the responses from Rudbeckius he remained silent. Both sides claimed victory in the encounter.[20] John thereafter briefly returned to the Netherlands to continue his ministry. Karl IX recalled him to Sweden in 1610 to advise the king on both international affairs and counsel him on evangelical ecumenism. During this stay, he worked alongside the Swedish professor and theologian Johan Raumannus and the controversial Johannes Messenius.[21] Their brief from Karl was once again to find compromise between the Lutheran and reformed confessions long after such dialogue was supposed to have been killed off. Through such interactions, we see members of the Swedish government actively cultivating and employing a number of important Calvinists. Some positions, such as that of John Forbes, were advisory in the context of international Protestantism. Others included permanent ambassadorial appointments, most significantly Sir James Spens of Wormiston.

A Calvinist ambassador of Lutheran Sweden

The diplomatic credentials of James Spens have been thoroughly researched by a number of scholars, most notably Alexia Grosjean and Arne Jönsson, though never explicitly within a confessional framework.[22] Spens was famously a senior colonel in Sweden from 1606, eventually rising to the rank of 'General of British' troops in that country.[23] By 1610, his diplomatic duties saw him undertaking Stuart business in Sweden while also bringing the Stockholm government still more fresh troops out of Scotland. By marrying this diplomatic role with the recruitment of soldiers for Sweden's campaigns against Russia and Poland, Spens soon landed his first major diplomatic appointment. During this, he served as one of the arbiters of the Danish–Swedish Peace of Knäred in 1613 (with his stepbrother and fellow Calvinist, Sir Robert Anstruther), which sought to end the Kalmar War.[24] This treaty had been carefully choreographed by King James of Great Britain via *his* ambassadors to Denmark and Sweden to settle the intra-Scandinavian conflict.[25] In the process, both Anstruther and Spens received the appropriate diplomatic accreditation from the Scandinavian monarchs they also served. Clearly, Spens had demonstrated to the young Gustav II Adolf that he was a man who could be trusted, despite his steadfast adherence to his Calvinist confession. After all, within only four years he had brought thousands of troops into Swedish service, many covertly raised in Britain during the Kalmar War while serving as a joint Stuart–Vasa ambassador.[26] Knäred remains the best known of Spens' early diplomatic achievements, doubtless because it was a mission driven by the Stuart court and undertaken overtly. It is arguable that it was through the subsequent mission as the Vasa ambassador to London that he sealed his reputation with the Swedish government. So, what exactly did Spens do in 1614 that endeared him so much to the Swedish authorities?

In October 1613, a Muscovite embassy arrived in London bringing rich gifts of sable and fox fur for King James.[27] The Muscovites wished to both announce the succession of Tsar Mikhail and propose a full military alliance between the houses of Stuart and Romanov. They did so at a time when Sweden and Russia were at war. Fortuitously for the Swedes, James Spens arrived in London in the midst of the Muscovite embassy. Hearing that the Russians were pressing the king to try to extract both an alliance and recruit British troops into their service, Spens unilaterally intervened without diplomatic authority from Stockholm. In so doing, he both stalled the proposed troop levy for Russia and, crucially, urged King James to volunteer as arbiter in the Vasa–Romanov dispute.[28] He persuaded James that Gustav Adolf requested this arbitration, despite not being aware of the situation before hearing from Spens. Thereafter, King James dispatched Sir John Merrick to Moscow as his ambassador in June 1614 to discuss the Romanov–Stuart proposals.[29] Spens alerted the Swedish chancellor, Axel Oxenstierna (in post 1612–1654), to Merrick's mission, seriously improving the Swede's understanding of his role.[30] Over the coming year, Spens kept both the Swedes and the British informed of Merrick's progress, filtering and transmitting information between Stockholm and London. And through Spens, James congratulated Gustav II Adolf on his military success – hardly an endorsement of the Stuart monarch's neutrality.[31] Spens vowed to continue to work for the Swedish interest at the Stuart court in London.[32] Thus, when Gustav Adolf wrote to Merrick from Narva in November 1615, he did so from an informed position, having already been briefed by Spens with regard to the British king's intentions towards the warring parties.[33] Spens conveyed James' advice to the Swedes not to demand such harsh terms from the Muscovites that they would be unable to comply with them.[34] Though this particular letter from Spens arrived too late, the King of Sweden had clearly received the message through other means. Merrick himself wrote to Gustav Adolf the day after the Treaty of Stolbova had been signed. He concluded his letter with an observation that the role of James VI & I in settling the affair was to be emphasised to both the Muscovite and Swedish delegations alike.[35] Spens' previously silent role in informing King James of the Swedish position, and thus influencing the Stolbova treaty negotiations, is only now being understood. Crucially, the Swedes could see that this man had acted on his own initiative to scupper troop levies by Sweden's enemies, and extended his mission by two extra years to ensure no Stuart–Romanov military alliance was ever enacted.

The spymaster

While working overtly as a Swedish ambassador to both forge a peace with Denmark–Norway and play a crucial role in ending the Swedish–Muscovite War, Spens also had his eye on influencing the ongoing Swedish–Polish conflict. In this case, he did so through the establishment of a covert network of agents and spies across Europe with some audacious success.[36] A taster of their activities serves to explain the relationship of this ardent Calvinist to the Swedish Lutheran state. As early as 1612, Spens had reported to James in London that the pope was supposed to be sponsoring the landing of 1,200 men in Finland, supposedly backed by money from the Catholic clergy.[37] This was not too far-fetched, and over time Spens used his social capital to build a network of Scottish agents working on behalf of the Swedish state. Many of these had been embedded within Poland–Lithuania for years. One of them was Archibald Rankin. In May 1618, Rankin warned Oxenstierna of a new order of chivalry called the *Cavalieri de Jhesu* who intended to subdue Sweden with the 'Sword of Paul.' Rankin continued that 'those old dogs, the Jesuits, have come up with these young dogs, for they cannot achieve anything with the Keys of Peter.'[38] Such information warned the Swedes in advance of an apparent plan to infiltrate (and invade) Sweden, with the ultimate goal of enforcing the Counter-Reformation there. Understanding that some of the military force for the proposed invasion was to come from

Britain, Gustav Adolf sought allies there who might help foil any such levy. He therefore opened a dialogue with the Archbishop of Canterbury and readied Spens for an embassy to London.[39] Spens arrived in 1624 just as this 'Polish Plot' unfolded. Officially, he was on a mission to arbitrate on Swedish–Danish controversies, with the ultimate aim of a concerted entry of all nations into the ongoing anti-Habsburg war in the hope of a restoration of the Palatinate to Frederick V.[40] The architect behind the Polish mission was Colonel Robert Stewart, a Scot working for Sigismund III Vasa. Spens knew all about Stewart and his activities, again through the placement of his own agents at the heart of Stewart's operations.

A Scotsman, John Fairbairne, had been sent to London from Danzig by the Swedish government with instructions to infiltrate Robert Stewart's pro-Polish circle.[41] With Spens acting as his handler in London, Fairbairne quickly gained Stewart's confidence and learned the most intimate details of his plans. Stewart offered Fairbairne the position of Quartermaster General of his fledgling army, which was set to consist of 8,000 men recruited in Britain. From his vantage point as a senior staff officer in the proposed Stewart expedition, Fairbairne informed Gustav Adolf about plans to invade Älvsborg (near Gothenburg). Stewart intended to quadruple the size of his army and, with the help of disaffected members of the Swedish nobility and (undisclosed) papal backing, seize the whole of Sweden and place it under Sigismund III's control within three months.[42] However, it was too late for Stewart as the damage had been done to his plans. Spens confidently informed Gustav Adolf that Sweden had nothing to fear from Robert Stewart.[43] By the spring of 1624, King James had written in such strict conditions to Robert Stewart's warrant to levy soldiers that any troops raised by him were forbidden from landing in any of Sweden's territories.[44] Spens' spoiling mission had been a complete success. This left him free to get on with diplomacy rather than duplicity, and that involved trying to lay the groundwork for Sweden to enter the Thirty Years' War on the side of the 'Common Cause.'

Swedish diplomacy in the Thirty Years' War, 1623–1632

Attempts to lure Sweden into the conflict against the Habsburg Empire began as early as 1619. That year, Sir James Spens received instructions from King James of Great Britain to conduct embassies to both Christian IV of Denmark–Norway and Gustav II Adolf of Sweden.[45] James' concern was for the safety of his daughter, the newly crowned Queen of Bohemia, particularly after the defeat of her husband, Frederick V, and his forces at White Mountain the following year. While James had dispatched some 6,000 troops from his British and Dutch-based forces to protect his daughter, it remained his hope that a larger, pan-Protestant alliance could be built.[46]

The prospect of an 'Evangelical League' comprising both Lutheran and Calvinist powers gained traction once it became clear that a full-scale war was about to break out between the Holy Roman Empire and their various Protestant enemies in Europe. There were several potential leaders for such an alliance, including James VI & I of Great Britain, Christian IV of Denmark–Norway, or Gustav II Adolf of Sweden.[47] There followed many difficult negotiations involving James Spens and Robert Anstruther shuttling between London and the Scandinavian monarchs trying to bring them both into an alliance with King James. This process was to be sweetened by the levy of thousands of Scottish troops for service in Denmark and Sweden, the latter being raised by and under the command of Sir James Spens.[48] Both Scandinavian monarchs appeared agreeable to the concept of an alliance. Both men believed they could and should intervene in Germany. The problem lay in the jealousy and mistrust between the Scandinavian kings themselves. With the Dutch fully engaged and the British expeditionary forces in retreat throughout the early 1620s, it took until 1624 for the Scandinavians to contemplate serious joint action.

In January 1624, Spens travelled to The Hague in his capacity as both British and Swedish ambassador. His brief was to finalise the arrangements to bring the British, Scandinavians, and Dutch into closer alliance.[49] His first duty in the Dutch Republic took him to the exiled court of the King and Queen of Bohemia, where he met and delivered letters from the King and Queen of Sweden on 5th January.[50] Spens was well received, and at the meeting Elizabeth of Bohemia composed a letter to her father in support of Gustav Adolf's proposals and Spens' forthcoming mission to London under the aegis of the Swedish king.[51] Sir Robert Anstruther, acting as a dual British and Danish ambassador, also visited Frederick V at The Hague, having left London in April 1624.[52] Although it seems they did not meet in The Hague, Anstruther and Spens were explicitly instructed to stay in contact with each other. Their joint brief was to find a way to bring the Scandinavian monarchs together to restore the dignity of Frederick V, Elizabeth, and their children.[53] However, as Anstruther informed Spens, the mutual mistrust between the Scandinavian kings remained unresolved.[54] To try to get around these problems, the stepbrothers once more exchanged sensitive information to smooth the path for Swedish–Danish cooperation.[55]

When Anstruther had travelled to Copenhagen in December 1624, it was to conclude an agreement relating to further subsidies and troops for the proposed alliance.[56] This grouping was also to include George William of Brandenburg, Gustav II Adolf's brother-in-law.[57] To the chagrin of Gustav Adolf, King James accepted Christian's terms for the campaign in February 1625.[58] In doing so, he rejected the more realistic but vastly more expensive proposals of the Swedish king. To finalise these measures, a general congress of Protestant powers was scheduled to meet in The

Hague in April 1625, but James Stuart did not live to see the outcome. His heir, Charles I, hoped that despite his father's rejection of the earlier Swedish proposals, Gustav Adolf might be persuaded to join the Evangelical Alliance.[59] On 31st May, Spens was directly instructed by the Swedish court to explain that Sweden had postponed any intention of participating in the Common Cause for the time being.[60] The Treaty of The Hague was concluded on 2nd December, 1625, bringing Great Britain, the Dutch Republic, and Denmark–Norway together in alliance, but not Sweden. Instead, some of the Scottish troops that arrived in Sweden in 1624 (including Spens' own levy) on the pretext of fighting in the anti-Habsburg alliance were diverted to Livonia.[61] Spens nevertheless used his time in London to recruit another Calvinist agent into his ever-expanding covert operations network against Poland–Lithuania. This was Hugh Mowatt, who served as a Spens agent initially, but later as a fully accredited Swedish ambassador to the parliaments of Scotland and England during the 1640s.[62] It is perhaps ironic that in the period where Sweden distanced herself from her Lutheran and Calvinist allies, Spens managed to increase his network of Calvinist clergy and agents, who collectively did much to continue the international dialogue between Sweden and her neighbours.

Calvinists, clergymen, and Lutheran Sweden

From 1626, Reverend Robert Douglas, a Calvinist chaplain in James Spens' infantry regiment, apparently gave counsel to the Swedish king on a variety of matters.[63] According to Robert Wodrow, Gustav Adolf said Douglas 'might be a counselour to any Prince in Europe. For prudence and knowledge he might be Moderatour to a Generall Councill.'[64] Whether an enhanced account by Wodrow or not, Douglas' role within Spens' Calvinist clique was reinforced by the arrival of another Scottish clergyman. When Spens arrived as British ambassador at the Swedish court in Elbing in 1627, he engaged a new diplomatic secretary, the Reverend John Durie. This man served already as incumbent preacher to the Scots and English Calvinist congregation in Elbing before the Swedish takeover.[65] Once employed by Spens, Durie persuaded his new employer to pass on his petition on ecumenical peace to Gustav Adolf.[66] In consequence, the Swedish king encouraged discussions between Dr Jacob Godemann and Durie in 1628, once again in contravention of the usual narrative concerning the 1593 Statement of Faith.[67] Godemann died in 1629, but Durie maintained a correspondence with his son, Caspar. He, in turn, held several positions as a Swedish diplomat, including one to the Stuart court in 1630 where he remained in the company of James Spens and John Durie, who resided in London at the time.[68]

Spens' Calvinist crescendo

With Reverend John Durie ensconced as the second Calvinist theologian in Spens' retinue alongside Reverend Robert Douglas, Sir James sought to encourage their confessional dialogues with the Swedish king and government. Nevertheless, his primary focus remained the completion of his diplomatic instructions from London. Perhaps as a sweetener to curry favour from the Swedish king, Spens delivered the Order of the Garter to Gustav II Adolf.[69] This diplomatic courtesy out of the way, Spens could concentrate on more pressing business. Charles I had instructed him to persuade the Swedish king that an accommodation was advisable between Sweden and Poland in their ongoing war. The Stuart agenda was really quite transparent; if the Polish–Swedish War ended, there had to be a greater chance of Sweden entering the war in Germany on the side of the Evangelical League. Spens also received authority from Charles I to treat with the Magistrates of Danzig to try to ensure their neutrality in the conflict.[70] However, not long after his arrival in Elbing, Gustav Adolf wished for Spens to give up his role as ambassador for a time and secretly set about recruiting more soldiers back in Britain.[71] Scottish Calvinist troops, as Spens had consistently delivered, were clearly far more valuable to the Swedes than the vague promises they were receiving from Charles I and his London-based government.[72] Nevertheless, Spens did not give up on the notion of an alliance between the Stuart kingdoms, Sweden, and Denmark–Norway. In dialogue with Sir John Coke in London, he still believed that Christian IV's fear of Sweden's power proved to be the main obstacle to realising an alliance.[73] The Stuart wars against France and Spain were also a distraction, and Sweden seemed to have slipped down the Stuart diplomatic agenda for the moment. Indeed, by April 1628, Spens claimed he had not received any formal instructions from Britain for seven months.[74] However, the politics of the war in the Holy Roman Empire were changing at a pace that forced Sweden into direct conflict with the imperialist forces.

Under the threat of increased Habsburg power in the Baltic region, a de facto Scandinavian alliance came into being, and this involved some considerable Scottish military assets. Spens reported on the danger that an imperial harbour being established in the Baltic would pose to the Protestant powers. In consequence, Christian IV of Denmark had urgently requested the involvement of the Swedish navy to help defeat this threat.[75] Spens believed that Lübeck would be the target for a combined Swedish–Danish operation. In the end, the combined operation centred on Stralsund. Four regiments of Scottish troops (three drawn from the Danish army and one from the Swedish) directly engaged the troops of Albrecht von Wallenstein in July and August 1628, effectively breaking the Siege of Stralsund.[76] With up to 20 Swedish vessels in support, Governor Alexander Leslie thereafter concentrated on clearing the bridgehead, required to allow the landing of the main Swedish royal army under Gustav Adolf's command. These actions were being undertaken without any formal diplomatic instruction from London as Charles I was distracted by his French and Spanish conflicts. Spens could not advise Gustav Adolf as to what the British reaction to the changing political situation brought about by Swedish intervention might be. In view of this lack of contact with Whitehall, Gustav Adolf gave Spens his orders to travel to London on 16th January, 1629, to solicit the views of Charles I.[77] His purpose there caused speculation among the other British diplomats such as Sir Thomas Roe.[78] By April, Roe appeared astonished by the 'heroic designs' of Gustav Adolf and his intentions for a full-scale landing in northern Germany.[79] Spens briefed Charles on Gustav Adolf's proposition with, Spens hoped, at least 10,000 new British soldiers in support of the undertaking.[80] This main force would not materialise in the field until 1631 under the command of James, Marquis Hamilton, although by 1629 fresh levies were arriving in Sweden through Spens' intervention.[81] The Swedish invasion could not take place without an end to the Swedish–Polish War – something that Sir Thomas Roe helped to facilitate in September 1629.[82] However, while in Britain, Spens had private business to see to, and this would cement his group of Calvinist theological councillors in the Swedish Empire into an actual private congregation.

Sir James Spens had received the barony of Orreholm in 1622 and he was later matriculated into the *Riddarhus* (the Swedish House of Nobility) on 28th April, 1628. Rather than acquiesce to Lutheranism at this moment, as many would have expected, he maintained his Calvinist confession with the blessing of the Swedish government. Now a significant landholder, Spens used his time in Britain to select a suitable chaplain to instruct his fellow Calvinists in Sweden. In consequence, the Reverend Eleazer Borthwick became ordained as the minister to Orreholm in Sweden by John Abernethy, Bishop of Caithness, on 2nd September, 1629.[83] This action was without reproach from either the Swedish king or government. In case of any objections, Gustav Adolf later issued a document specifically stating that 'We forbid all of those that owe us obedience to put any obstacle or hindrance in the way of the aforesaid Jacob Spentz [*sic*] or his heirs in any shape or form now or in the future.'[84] Later events would show that this also applied to his confession of faith.

From the moment of his appointment, Borthwick was both chaplain and diplomatic informant for Spens. He also became a correspondent of John Durie and later served himself as a contracted diplomatic envoy for the Swedish government.[85] To employ an individual Calvinist such as Spens in this capacity is curious enough, but that a clergyman with Borthwick's credentials could be retained in this role is quite astounding.

Conclusion

By May 1631, James Spens received permission to travel to the Swedish court in Germany on what would prove to be his last protracted diplomatic mission.[86] Following him to Wittenberg were his military chaplain, the Reverend Robert Douglas, and his diplomatic secretary, the Reverend John Durie. Durie met Gustav Adolf in Wittenberg, leading to their famous dialogue on the reconciliation of the Protestant churches.[87] He went on to have many face-to-face meetings with Axel Oxenstierna when he held similar discussions, noting that Oxenstierna agreed to further dialogue if both sides would only use language as found in scripture or the Augsburg Confession.[88] Durie was delighted as this gave him a way to pursue his irenicist ideas using his mastery of scripture to frustrate many of the Swedish Lutheran clergy. The relationship of Durie and Oxenstierna led to the Scot acting on Oxenstierna's behalf thereafter, not only in Sweden, but also at the negotiations leading to the Heilbronn League in 1633 and elsewhere thereafter.[89] As Durie concentrated on his irenic mission, Eleazer Borthwick tended to the Calvinist congregation in Orreholm that included Spens' wife, Margaret Forratt, his sons, daughters, and the various other members of his staff. To guarantee the future security of his heirs, James Spens selected none other than Axel and Gabriel Oxenstierna as the guardians and protectors of all his children from both his marriages.[90] The extent to which Spens had broken the supposed barriers in Sweden concerning non-Lutherans becoming subjects, holding land, or even sponsoring ecclesiastical dialogue with the Swedish king and government are quite apparent.

Alexia Grosjean long ago contended that the Swedes in general seemed 'not to have taken issue with the Scots' religious adherence to Calvinism.'[91] The introduction to this chapter explained why a less myopic reading of the 1593 Statement of Faith is key to understanding why this was so. It is also certain that non-Scottish Calvinists, such as the Wallonian exile Louis de Geer, were also tolerated both in their support of fellow Calvinist exiles and despite complaints against Calvinist services being held within his properties.[92] Like Spens, de Geer employed his own reformed minister in Sweden, he too worked as a diplomat, and under his patronage a Calvinist congregation formed around him, largely composed of Dutch and Palatine exiles.[93] Nevertheless, James Spens' activities in all of the above spheres predated those of de Geer by many years. One could argue he represented something of a very successful pioneer in breaking the supposed barrier to full acceptance of himself and his faith at all levels of Swedish society. Moreover, what happened after Spens died in 1632 went much further than mere toleration or the turning of a blind eye by the Swedish state.

Sticking to his role as guardian to the Spens children, in 1633, Chancellor Axel Oxenstierna facilitated the retention of James Spens' privileges and exemptions to Colonel William Spens, his eldest son from his first marriage. This included his rights to be a member of the *Riddarhus*.[94] That the Scottish-born William received a concession to continue in his Calvinist faith and be accepted into the House of Nobility was perhaps an understandable result of his father's legacy. However, there followed a discussion in the *Riksråd* about what should be done with his younger half-brothers, Axel and Jacob. Indeed, their confession of faith came into the debate, as did the questioning of whether Calvinists or Catholics were actually allowed to be matriculated into the Swedish nobility.[95] The unequivocal answer returned in October 1635 that the young sons, even though Swedish-born, were, like their elder brother, protected by the late king's special privilege and could be matriculated into the *Riddarhus* without further hindrance.[96] While there were certainly many foreign Calvinists and Swedish crypto-Calvinists within Sweden, the Spens family practised their faith openly and with the direct support of the Swedish king, chancellor, and state council. They did so as naturalised Swedes. All this resulted directly from James Spens' extraordinary diplomatic career. He had successfully demonstrated that one could hold alternative beliefs sincerely and still prove to be a superlative servant of the Lutheran Swedish state. That other Scottish Calvinists such as Reverend John Durie, Reverend Eleazer Borthwick, and Hugh Mowatt would all be employed on diplomatic missions for Sweden by Axel Oxenstierna thereafter is surely testament to that.

Notes

1 See, for example, Daniel Riches, *Protestant Cosmopolitanism and Diplomatic Culture: Brandenburg-Swedish Relations in the Seventeenth Century* (Leiden: Brill, 2013), 2.
2 Ole Peter Grell, 'Scandinavia,' in *The Reformation World*, ed. Andrew Pettegree (London: Routledge, 2002), 271–74.
3 For this chapter, six copies of the document in Riksarkivet (hereafter RA) in Stockholm have been consulted. See 'Beslut och förening om religionen och kyrkodisciplinen (hereafter Uppsala möte), 20th March, 1593.' RA/6101 documents 14/1, 15a, 15b, 16/1, 17a and 17b. Two copies are dated 19th March (15b and 17a).
4 Anders Tidner, *Under Karl IX's Regemente: Berättelser ur svenska historien* (Stockholm: P.A. Nordstedt och Söner, 1911), 13–22.
5 20th March 1593, RA/6101/17b.
6 *Svenska kyrkans bekännelseskrifter*, ed. Oscar Bensow (Stockholm: P.A. Nordstedt och Söner, 1912), 794. I thank Bodil Roskvist for alerting me to this source.
7 Tidner's version ends with a full stop before the final clause: 'Desslikes och alldeles avsäjoms vi alle sacramenterers, zwinglianers och kalvinisters villfarelser, så ock vederdöpere ock alle andre kättere, evad nampn de helst have kunne.' The full stop here makes the section emphatic. However, it should contain the additional clause '… kunne, någon tÿdh til att inrÿme gille eller samptÿcke.' See Tidner, *Under Karl IX's Regemente*, 22. The additional words are transcribed here from RA/6101/14/1. Apart from spelling differences, it agrees with extant copies, though two copies clearly state 'gilla,' not 'gille,' which can alter the meaning. This clause may well emphatically ban these confessions outright, or plausibly give their adherents some time

('någon tÿdh') to band themselves together ('att inrÿme gille'), perhaps to consider their situation, or acquiesce to Lutheran doctrine immediately ('eller samptÿcke'). The variances in spelling and the structure of the clause make any rendering of it highly speculative. I thank Alexia Grosjean, Thomas Småberg, Anna Maria Forssberg, Ardis Dreisbach, and Ann-Marie Algemo for their discussions concerning this clause. Any errors in interpretation remain my own.

8 'Alla varianter av protestantisk oliktänkande som Zwinglis eller Calvins läror, vederdöpare "och alla andra kättare, evad namn de helst kunna hava" förbjöds.' See Herman Lindqvist, *Historien om Sverige: Gustav Vasa och hans söner och döttrar* (Stockholm: Norstedts, 1993), 411.

9 19th March, 1593, RA/6101/17a: '… licküäll efftersådana för handell och wandell sküll icke wäll kan förhindratt üarda, så är så witt samtÿckt, att the som någhon kättersk lärdom haffüa, icke skal tilstadt eller efterlåtit wara att hålle någre uppenbare samqüemmer i hüs eller annorstedes, så frampt hüar någhor ther medh befinnes, eller the som försmädhelighen taala om wår Religion, skola tilbörlighen straffadhe bliffüa.'

10 Grell, 'Scandinavia,' 274.

11 Grell, 'Scandinavia,' 274.

12 Michael Roberts, *The Early Vasas: A History of Sweden, 1523–1611* (Cambridge: Cambridge University Press, 1968), 333; Stefan Östergren, *Sigismund: En biografi över den svensk-polske monarken* (Ängelholm: Katolsk historisk förening, 2005), 72–73.

13 Östergren, *Sigismund*, 94–145.

14 Oskar Garstein, *Rome and the Counter-Reformation in Scandinavia*, 2 vols. (Leiden: Brill, 1922), I, xxx, xl, 403, and II, 264, 287–88; Axel Norberg, *Polen i Svensk Politik, 1617–1626* (Stockholm: Almqvist och Wiksell, 1974), 34; Östergren, *Sigismund*, 185, 189.

15 For the arrival of Scots from various confessions of faith into Sweden, see Steve Murdoch, *Network North: Scottish Kin, Commercial and Covert Associations in Northern Europe, 1603-1746* (Leiden: Brill, 2006), 84–124.

16 This meeting occurred when James VI opted to travel overland from Norway to Denmark with his new Danish bride and large Scottish–Danish retinue in 1590. As Calderwood observed, 'The King of Sweden [Johan III]'s brother [Duke Karl] convoyed our king and queen through a part of Sweden, accompanied with foure hundreth hors weill appoointed at the commandment of the King of Sweden, howbeit there was warre betuixt Denmark and Sweden in the meante tyme.' David Calderwood, *The History of the Kirk of Scotland*, ed. Thomas Thomson (7 vols., Edinburgh: Printed for the Wodrow Society, 1842–1849), vol. 5, 70; Alexia Grosjean, *An Unofficial Alliance: Scotland and Sweden, 1569–1654* (Leiden: Brill, 2003), 20. The most complete discussion of this episode is found in Cynthia Fry, 'Diplomacy and Deception: King James VI of Scotland's Foreign Relations with Europe, c.1584–1603' (unpublished PhD thesis, University of St Andrews, 2014), 72–73.

17 Grosjean, *An Unofficial Alliance*, 20–24.

18 *Nordisk familjebok: Konversationslexicon och realencyklopedi*, vol. 18, ed. Th. Westrin (Stockholm: Nordisk familjeboks tryckeri, 1908 edition), 829–30.

19 H. Holmquist, *Svenska Kyrkans Historia*, vol. 3, part 2 (Uppsala: Svenska Kyrkans Diakonistyrelses Bokförlag, 1933), 292–93.

20 Depending on which source you read, the phrase 'Ad hæc Forbesius nihil' (Westrin) or 'Nihil ad hoc Forbesius' (*Svenska Biografisk Lexicon*) was exclaimed at the end of the debate. The latter source agrees this statement is

a fiction unsupported in contemporary records. See Erik Wikland and Hans Gillingstam, *Svensk Biografiskt Lexikon*, 'Forbes, släkt,' accessed 7th August, 2018, https://sok.riksarkivet.se/Sbl/Presentation.aspx?id=14307; *Nordisk familjebok*, vol. 18, 829.

21 *Nordisk familjebok*, vol. 18, 829; Holmquist, *Svenska Kyrkans Historia*, vol. 3:2, 297.

22 Grosjean, *An Unofficial Alliance*, 27–78; *Rikskanslern Axel Oxenstiernas skrifter och brevväxling. Senare avdelning, trettonde bandet: Brev från James Spens och Jan Rutgers*, ed. Arne Jönsson (Stockholm: Kungliga Vitterhetsakademien, 2007), 23–274.

23 For early contact between the Swedish court and Spens, see Karl IX to James Spens, April 1606, RA, Anglica I: IV, 1.

24 Jonas Hallenberg, *Svea rikes historia under konung Gustaf Adolf den stores regering, II Bandet* (Stockholm: Johan Carlbloom, 1790), 491–94, 620–23. For more recent scholarship, see Grosjean, *An Unofficial Alliance*, 38–40; Steve Murdoch, *Britain, Denmark-Norway and the House of Stuart, 1603–1660* (East Linton: Tuckwell Press, 2003), 39–43, 58–59.

25 Instructions for James Spens, 29th April, 1612, RA, Anglica III; A copy of the contract of peace procured by the King's most Excellent Majestie of Greate Brittaine and betwixt the Kings of Denmark and Sweden, 26th January, 1613, The National Archives [hereafter TNA], SP75/5, 63, 73; Hallenberg, *Svea rikes historia*, 631–32.

26 Grosjean, *An Unofficial Alliance*, 31–38.

27 Tsar Mikhail to King James, June 1613, in Sergey Konovalov, 'Seven Russian Royal Letters (1613–23),' *Oxford Slavonic Papers* 7 (1957), 118–19, 122; Maija Jansson, Paul Buskovitch, and Nikolai Rogozhin, eds., *England and the North: The Russian Embassy of 1613–1614* (Philadelphia: American Philosophical Society, 1994), passim.

28 James Spens to Axel Oxenstierna, 10th January, 1614, RA, Anglica V, 522; James Spens to Gustav II Adolf, 10th January, 1614, RA, Anglica III, 517, 3.

29 A passe for Sir John Merrick, knight, ambassador from his Majestye unto the Emperour of Russia [...], 21st June, 1614, TNA, PC 2/27, 174; Sergey Konovalov, 'Anglo-Russian Relations, 1617–1618,' *Oxford Slavonic Papers* 1 (1950), 67, 95–99; id., 'Anglo-Russian Relations, 1620–1624,' *Oxford Slavonic Papers* 4 (1953), 74, 85–87.

30 James Spens to Axel Oxenstierna, 24th June & 25th July, 1614, RA, Anglica V, 522.

31 James Spens to Axel Oxenstierna, 1st March, 1615, RA, Anglica V, 522.

32 James Spens to Axel Oxenstierna, 26th May, 1615, RA, Anglica V, 522.

33 Receipt of the letter from Gustav II Adolf is recorded in John Merrick to Gustav II Adolf, 8th February, 1615 (29th January, 1616), RA, Anglica V, 522.

34 James Spens to Gustav II Adolf, 2nd February, 1617, RA, Anglica III, 517; James Spens to Axel Oxenstierna, 2nd February, 1617, RA, Anglica V, 522.

35 John Merrick to Gustav II Adolf, 28th February, 1616 (18th February, 1617), RA, Anglica V, 522.

36 Murdoch, *Network North*, 252–79.

37 James Spens to King James, 11th October, 1612, TNA, SP95/1.

38 Archibald Rankin to Axel Oxenstierna, 3rd May, 1618, RA, Oxenstiernska samlingen, E692.

39 Norberg, *Polen i Svensk Politik*, 194.

40 James Spens to King James, 1623 or 1624, TNA, SP95/II, 84; Grosjean, *An Unofficial Alliance*, 56–59; Murdoch, *Britain*, 58–63.

41 Gustav II Adolf to James Spens, 15th March, 1624, RA, Rigsregistraturet, vol. 147, 1624, 67.
42 John Fairbairne to Gustav II Adolf, 2nd November, 1623, RA, Anglica, 514; *Svensk agent ved Sundet: Toldkommissær og agent i Helsingør Anders Svenssons depecher til Gustav II Adolf og Axel Oxenstierna 1621–1626*, ed. Leo Tandrup (Aarhus: Universitetsforlaget i Aarhus, 1971), 376, fn.1; Norberg, *Polen i Svensk Politik*, 197–99.
43 James Spens to James VI, 1623, TNA, SP95/2, 84; James Spens to Gustav II Adolf, 24/14th January and 16th February, 1624, RA, Anglica, III, 43 and 46a; James Spens to Axel Oxenstierna, 10th March, 1624, RA, Oxenstiernska samlingen, E724; Tandrup, *Svensk agent ved Sundet*, 419, fn.12.
44 King James to James Spens, 6th July, 1624, TNA, SP95/2, 86–88.
45 King James' instructions to James Spens, 30th July, 1619, RA, Anglica V; Robert Anstruther to Christian Friis, 29th August, 1619, Rigsarkivet, Copenhagen TKUA England AII, 7.
46 Murdoch, *Britain*, 49–51.
47 Murdoch, *Britain*, 58–63.
48 For the Scottish troops, see Murdoch, *Britain*, 201–25. For the Swedish troops, see Grosjean, *An Unofficial Alliance*, 65–66.
49 Instructions to James Spens, 6th June, 1624, TNA, SP 95/2, 86–88; James Spens to Gustav II Adolf from The Hague, 17th December, 1624, RA, Anglica VIII, 54.
50 James Spens to Gustav II Adolf, 14th/24th January, 1624, RA, Anglica III.
51 Elizabeth of Bohemia to King James, 10th/20th January, 1624, in *The Correspondence of Elizabeth Stuart, Queen of Bohemia, vol. 1, 1603–1631*, ed. Nadine Akkerman (Oxford: Oxford University Press, 2015), 438–39.
52 Dudley Carlton to Elizabeth of Bohemia, 24th April, 1624, in Akkerman, *The Correspondence of Elizabeth Stuart*, vol. I, 455; Emil Marquard, *Danske Gesandter og Gesandtskabs Personale indtil 1914* (Copenhagen: Rigsarkivet, 1952), 27.
53 Instructions to James Spens, 6th June, 1624, TNA, SP 95/2, 86–88.
54 Robert Anstruther to James Spens, 1st August, 1624, RA, Anglica V.
55 Details are given in Robert Anstruther to James Spens, 1st August, 1624, RA, Anglica V; Robert Anstruther to James Spens, 13th January, 1625, RA, Anglica V.
56 An abstract of Anstruther's negotiations in Denmark, Holstein, and Germany, 1624, TNA, SP75/5, 349; Murdoch, *Britain*, 59–61.
57 Riches, *Protestant Cosmopolitanism and Diplomatic Culture*, 88–93.
58 The military proposals of the Kings of Sweden and Denmark, 1624, TNA, SP75/6, 32.
59 Johan Rusdorf to James Spens, 23rd April/4th May, 1625, RA, Anglica V.
60 Instructions to James Spens, 31st May, 1625, RA, Anglica I/IV, 36. See also Norberg, *Polen i Svensk Politik*, 234–35, 238.
61 Grosjean, *An Unofficial Alliance*, 66.
62 Murdoch, *Network North*, 268–70. Mowatt's Swedish embassy to Britain in the 1640s is written up in full in John R. Young, 'The Scottish Parliament and European Diplomacy, 1641–1647: The Palatinate, the Dutch Republic and Sweden,' in *Scotland and the Thirty Years' War, 1618–1648*, ed. Steve Murdoch (Leiden: Brill, 2001), 77–106.
63 Douglas first appears in Spens' regiment as chaplain in 1626. See Krigsarkiv, Muster Roll, 1626/4; Alexander Crawley Dow, *Ministers to the Soldiers of Scotland* (Edinburgh: Oliver & Boyd, 1962), 59–60.

64 Robert Wodrow, *Analecta: Or Materials for a History of Remarkable Providences Mostly relating to Scotch Ministers and Christians*, vol. 2 (Glasgow: The Maitland Club, 1842), 136.

65 John Durie to Samuel Hartlib, 'Narrative of his German Travels,' *c.*1632, Hartlib Papers, 60/5/1a–1b. For Durie in Sweden, see *Negotiations about Church Unity, 1628–1634: John Durie, Gustavus Adolphus, Axel Oxenstierna*, ed. Gunnar Westin (Uppsala: Almquist & Wiksells Boktryckeri, 1932); *John Durie in Sweden 1636–1638: Documents and Letters*, ed. Gunnar Westin (Uppsala: Almquist & Wiksells Boktryckeri, 1936); Murdoch, *Network North*, 280–312.

66 'The Most Humble Petition' of John Durie to Gustav II Adolf, *c.*1628, in Westin, *Negotiations about Church Unity*, 187–91.

67 Murdoch, *Network North*, 285–86.

68 Murdoch, *Network North*, 286.

69 Charles I, instructions to James Spens, June 1627, TNA, SP 95/2, 165–68; Steve Murdoch and Alexia Grosjean, *Alexander Leslie and the Scottish Generals of the Thirty Years' War, 1618–1648* (London: Pickering & Chatto, 38–39.

70 Charles I, instructions to James Spens, June, 1627, TNA, SP 95/2, 165–68.

71 James Spens to Axel Oxenstierna, 14th August, 1627, RA, Anglica V.

72 James Spens to John Coke, 30th October, 1627, TNA, SP 95/2, 197. For recruitment of Scots into the Swedish army between 1628 and 1648, see Grosjean, *An Unofficial Alliance*, 74–111.

73 James Spens to John Coke, 20th December, 1627, and 10th January, 1628, TNA, SP 95/2, 209–10 and 95/3, 1.

74 James Spens to John Coke, 6th April, 1628, TNA, SP 95/3, 9.

75 James Spens to John Coke, 4th October, 1627, TNA, SP95/2, 175–76; Michal Wanner, 'Albrecht of Wallenstein as 'General of the Oceans and the Baltic Seas' and the Northern Maritime Plan,' *Forum Navale*, 64 (2008), 8–33.

76 Murdoch and Grosjean, *Alexander Leslie*, 47–51.

77 Gustav II Adolf to James Spens, 16th January, 1629, RA, Anglica IV. The first of Spens' dispatches to the Swedish court from London can be found in James Spens to Gustav II Adolf, 15th April, 1629, RA, Anglica III.

78 Thomas Roe to Elizabeth of Bohemia, 31st March, 1629, in Akkerman, *The Correspondence of Elizabeth Stuart*, vol. I, 738–39.

79 Thomas Roe to Elizabeth of Bohemia, 1st April, 1629, in Akkerman, *The Correspondence of Elizabeth Stuart*, vol. I, 741.

80 James Spens to Gustav II Adolf, 12th July, 1629, RA, Anglica III.

81 This Hamilton army and other Scottish recruitment is discussed thoroughly in Grosjean, *An Unofficial Alliance*, 88–93.

82 Robert I. Frost, *The Northern Wars, 1558–1721* (Harlow: Longman, 2000), 103, 112–15. For Roe's role, see Michael Strachan, 'Roe, Sir Thomas (1581–1644), diplomat,' *Oxford Dictionary of National Biography*, 2011, accessed 28th August, 2018.

83 Hew Scott, *Fasti Ecclesiæ Scoticanæ. Vol. 5: Synod of Fife, and of Angus and Mearns* (Edinburgh: Oliver & Boyd,1869), 221.

84 Queen Christina's 1641 republished letter of donation by Gustav II Adolf, originally written on 11th August, 1631. The letter is quoted in full in T. Fischer, *The Scots in Sweden* (Edinburgh: Otto Schultz & Co., 1907), 236–37.

85 Sven Tunberg, *Den svenska utrikesförvaltningens historia* (Uppsala: Almqvist & Wiksell, 1935), 76–77. In July 1635, the Swedish Council contracted Borthwick for a further year, and he would thus receive 2,000 riksdaler in London. See 3rd July, 1635, in *Svenska Riksrådets Protokoll* [hereafter *SRP*] 18 vol., ed. Nils Axel Kullberg (Stockholm: P. A. Nörstedt och Söner,

1878–1959), 5, 99. News of this mission had already reached London the previous year. See Queen Christina to Marquis Hamilton, 26th October, 1634, National Records of Scotland, GD406/1/9617. Borthwick returned to Sweden in 1637 to act as an envoy for Charles I. 10th May, 1637, *SRP*, VII, 32–33; Eleazer Borthwick to James Marquis Hamilton, 3rd July, 1637, National Records of Scotland, NRAs 2177, Bundle 1404. This latter mission was, among other things, an attempt to arrange the marriage alliance of Queen Christina and Karl Ludwig of the Palatinate. His contact with Durie is discussed in John Durie to Samuel Hartlib, 'Narrative of his German Travels,' *c.*1632, Hartlib Papers, 60/5/1a–1b.

86 28th May, 1631, *SRP*, II, 97.
87 John Durie to Samuel Hartlib, 'Narrative of his German Travels,' *c.*1632, Hartlib Papers, 60/5/1a–1b.
88 John Durie to Thomas Roe, 23rd June/3rd July, 1632, in Westin, *Negotiations about Church Unity*, 206. After much discussion with Durie, Oxenstierna appeared frustrated with all dogma, Lutheran or Calvinist. See Per Sondén, *Svenska residenten Lars Nilsson Tungels efterlämnade papper* (Stockholm: Kungliga Samfundet, 1909), 137: Dagbok, 19th June, 1633, 'Om concione valedicatoria uti Heijlbrun, att Kongen hade varid reen lutherisch och hatad calvinisterne, ded hade Canzleren offenderad. Om H[un]nij book, att Canzleren hade kastad henne emot veggen och sagt sigh inted see någod bettre medell, än att man sammansamkade all de böker både lutheriske och calviniske på een hoop och förbrände dem, så att ingen book mehr öfver vore ään blotta Biblia.'
89 Murdoch, *Network North*, 290–92.
90 The Will of Sir James Spens of Wormiston (copy), 31st May, 1631, National Records of Scotland, GD334/109.
91 Grosjean, *An Unofficial Alliance*, 257.
92 Ole Peter Grell, *Brethren in Christ: A Calvinist Network in Reformation Europe* (Cambridge: Cambridge University Press, 2011), 274–78.
93 Grell, *Brethren in Christ*, 278.
94 9th October, 1633, *SRP*, III, 193; 3rd December, 1634, *SRP*, IV, 250. A cautionary note here is that the editors of the *Riksråd* series were not sure which son is meant and often conflate William and Axel Spens. See 7th October, 1634, *SRP*, IV, 229. This clearly refers to Colonel William Spens, and not the child Axel as indexed. As elder son, it must be William Spens who was being referred to in December 1634.
95 20th October, 1635, *SRP*, V, 214.
96 31st October, 1635, *SRP*, V, 257. 'Spentzens söner, så den äldre, för dedt han specialiter är privilegierat aff sahlig Konungen och de facto investierat i frijherreskapet, som den yngre, som här i Sverige född ähr, skole antagas och immatriculeras på Ridderhusett.'

Bibliography

Archival sources

Rigsarkivet, Copenhagen, TKUA England AII, 7.
Krigsarkiv, Stockholm, Muster Roll, 1626/4.

Riksarkivet, Stockholm, Anglica I: IV, III, V, Beslut och förening om religionen och kyrkodisciplinen (Uppsala möte), 19 & 20 March 1593, RA/6101/14/1, 15a, 15b, 16/1, 17a and 17b; Oxenstiernska samlingen, E692 and E724.

The National Archives, Kew (TNA), State Papers (SP), 75/5, 95/1 & 2; Privy Council (PC), 2/27.

The National Records of Scotland, Edinburgh (NRS), GD334/109, GD406/1/9617; NRAs 2177.

Printed sources

Akkerman, Nadine, ed. *The Correspondence of Elizabeth Stuart, Queen of Bohemia, vol. 1, 1603–1631*, Oxford: Oxford University Press, 2015.

Bensow, Oscar, ed. *Svenska kyrkans bekännelseskrifter*, Stockholm: P.A. Nordstedt och Söner, 1912.

Calderwood, David. *The History of the Kirk of Scotland*, edited by Thomas Thomson, 7 vols., Edinburgh: Published for the Wodrow Society, 1842–1849.

Hartlib Papers (consulted in Aberdeen University Library), 60/5/1a–1b.

Jönsson, Arne, ed. *Rikskanslern Axel Oxenstiernas skrifter och brevväxling. Senare avdelning, trettonde bandet: Brev från James Spens och Jan Rutgers*, Stockholm: Kungliga Vitterhetsakademien, 2007.

Konovalov, Sergey. 'Anglo-Russian Relations, 1617–1618.' *Oxford Slavonic Papers* 1, 1950.

Konovalov, Sergey. 'Anglo-Russian Relations, 1620–1624.' *Oxford Slavonic Papers*, 4, 1953.

Konovalov, Sergey. 'Seven Russian Royal Letters (1613–23).' *Oxford Slavonic Papers* 7, 1957.

Kullberg, Nils Axel, ed. *Svenska Riksrådets Protokoll*, 18 vols., Stockholm: P. A. Nörstedt och Söner, 1878–1959.

Sondén, Per, ed. *Svenska residenten Lars Nilsson Tungels efterlämnade papper*, Stockholm: Kungliga Samfundet, 1909.

Tandrup, Leo, ed. *Svensk agent ved Sundet: Toldkommissær og agent i Helsingør Anders Svenssons depecher til Gustav II Adolf og Axel Oxenstierna 1621–1626*, Aarhus. Universitetsforlaget i Aarhus, 1971.

Westin, Gunnar, ed. *Negotiations about Church Unity, 1628–1634: John Durie, Gusta vus Adolphus, Axel Oxenstierna*, Uppsala: Almquist & Wiksells Boktryckeri, 1932.

Westin, Gunnar, ed. *John Durie in Sweden 1636–1638: Documents and Letters*, Uppsala: Almquist & Wiksells Boktryckeri, 1936.

Literature

Dow, Alexander Crawley. *Ministers to the Soldiers of Scotland*, Edinburgh: Oliver & Boyd, 1962.

Fischer, Th. *The Scots in Sweden*, Edinburgh: Otto Schultz & Co., 1907.

Frost, Robert I. *The Northern Wars, 1558–1721*, Harlow: Longman, 2000.

Fry, Cynthia. 'Diplomacy and Deception: King James VI of Scotland's Foreign Relations with Europe, c.1584–1603.' Unpublished PhD thesis, University of St Andrews, 2014.

Garstein, Oskar. *Rome and the Counter-Reformation in Scandinavia*, 2 vols. Leiden: Brill, 1922.

Grell, Ole Peter. 'Scandinavia.' In *The Reformation World*, edited by Andrew Pettegree. London: Routledge, 2002.

Grell, Ole Peter. *Brethren in Christ: A Calvinist Network in Reformation Europe*, Cambridge: Cambridge University Press, 2011.

Grosjean, Alexia. *Unofficial Alliance: Scotland and Sweden, 1569–1654*, Leiden: Brill, 2003.

Hallenberg, Jonas. *Svea rikes historia under konung Gustaf Adolf den stores regering, II Bandet*, Stockholm: Johan Carlbloom, 1790.

Holmquist, H. *Svenska Kyrkans Historia*, vol. 3, part 2, Uppsala: Svenska Kyrkans Diakonistyrelses Bokförlag, 1933.

Jansson, Maija, Buskovitch, Paul, and Rogozhin, Nikolai, eds. *England and the North: The Russian Embassy of 1613–1614*, Philadelphia: American Philosophical Society, 1994.

Lindqvist, Herman. *Historien om Sverige: Gustav Vasa och hans söner och döttrar*, Stockholm: Norstedts, 1993.

Marquard, Emil. *Danske Gesandter og Gesandtskabs Personale indtil 1914*, Copenhagen: Rigsarkivet, 1952.

Murdoch, Steve. *Britain, Denmark-Norway and the House of Stuart, 1603–1660*, East Linton: Tuckwell Press, 2003 edition.

Murdoch, Steve. *Network North: Scottish Kin, Commercial and Covert Associations in Northern Europe, 1603–1746*, Leiden: Brill, 2006.

Murdoch, Steve and Alexia Grosjean. *Alexander Leslie and the Scottish Generals of the Thirty Years' War, 1618–1648*, London: Pickering & Chatto, 2014.

Norberg, Axel. *Polen i Svensk Politik, 1617–1626*, Stockholm: Almqvist och Wiksell, 1974.

Östergren, Stefan. *Sigismund: En biografi över den svensk-polske monarken*, Ängelholm: Katolsk historisk förening, 2005.

Riches, Daniel. *Protestant Cosmopolitanism and Diplomatic Culture: Brandenburg-Swedish Relations in the Seventeenth Century*, Leiden: Brill, 2013.

Roberts, Michael. *The Early Vasas: A History of Sweden, 1523–1611*, Cambridge: Cambridge University Press, 1968.

Scott, Hew. *Fasti Ecclesiæ Scoticanæ*. Vol. 5: *Synod of Fife, and of Angus and Mearns*, Edinburgh: Oliver & Boyd, 1869.

Strachan, Michael. 'Roe, Sir Thomas (1581–1644), diplomat.' *Oxford Dictionary of National Biography* (2011). Accessed 28th August, 2018.

Tidner, Anders. *Under Karl IX's Regemente: Berättelser ur svenska historien*, Stockholm: P.A. Nordstedt och Söner, 1911.

Tunberg, Sven. *Den svenska utrikesförvaltningens historia*, Uppsala: Almqvist & Wiksell, 1935.

Wanner, Michal. 'Albrecht of Wallenstein as 'General of the Oceans and the Baltic Seas' and the Northern Maritime Plan.' *Forum Navale* 64 (2008): 8–33.

Westrin, Th., ed. *Nordisk familjebok: Konversationslexicon och realencyklopedi*, vol. 18, Stockholm: Nordisk familjeboks tryckeri, 1908 edition.

Wikland, Erik, and Gillingstam, Hans. *Svensk Biografiskt Lexikon*, 'Forbes, släkt,' accessed 7th August, 2018, https://sok.riksarkivet.se/Sbl/Presentation.aspx?id=14307.

Wodrow, Robert. *Analecta: Or Materials for a History of Remarkable Providences Mostly relating to Scotch Ministers and Christians*, vol. II, Glasgow: The Maitland Club, 1842.

Young, John R. 'The Scottish Parliament and European Diplomacy, 1641–1647: The Palatinate, the Dutch Republic and Sweden.' In *Scotland and the Thirty Years' War, 1618–1648*, edited by Steve Murdoch, 77–106. Leiden: Brill, 2001.

10 Catholic priests and Protestant chaplains

Religion and diplomacy in London and Vienna, 1700–1745

Charlotte Backerra

Even after the centuries marked by the so-called wars of religion, religious factors played a role in international relations. In the early eighteenth century, monarchs presented themselves as representatives of their religious group. The emperors saw themselves as advocates and protectors of the Catholic faith and the Church of Rome and installed a religious practice from the seventeenth century – the 'Austrian faith' (*Pietas Austriaca*) named after their main territories.[1] For the Protestant Hanoverian kings of Great Britain, religion provided the basis of their rule, since Catholics were excluded from the British succession after the Revolution of 1688.[2] Confessional barriers were in place when an alliance was forged by marriage between princely houses. However, when talking about military or political alliances, treaties, or the balance of power, questions of religion or confession did not play a role for monarchs and their ministers.[3]

This was different in the daily life of diplomats in foreign countries, especially for those posted in territories with a religious majority not their own. These diplomats were – besides all general diplomatic work – charged with caring for the spiritual life of their household and supporting their co-religionists as a whole in such a diaspora, especially in times of need or persecution.[4] At the same time, diplomats had to be careful not to cause strife within the host country and court over religious questions and not to jeopardise the diplomatic relations for which they were responsible. These points will be illustrated in this chapter, with examples taken from the relations between the courts of London and Vienna in the 1720s, 1730s, and 1740s.

First, embassy chapels, clerics employed by envoys and ambassadors, and their religious services and other duties will be analysed as part of a diplomat's daily life. The reactions of the host countries and cities to the existence and presence of these institutions and persons will show the, sometimes difficult, situation. Second, the question of religion is placed into the context of national strife in London during the Jacobite rebellion of 1745. Third, we will focus on the 1730s and two diplomats, an imperial ambassador and a British envoy, who tried to or had to support members of their own religion, not in their city of residence, but in territories joined with or adjacent to those in which they operated. These case studies will serve as an example of the limitations the diplomats themselves placed on religious assistance.

Chapels, clergy, and religious services

Diplomats had the right to practise their religion within their homes, even if they were of a different religion to that of their host country. In these cases, it was a vital part of an ambassador's duties to care for the spiritual welfare of his diplomatic family. The diplomats' houses had chapels to use for services, as meeting places, and as a spiritual centre for their co-religionists in the city or at the court where they were stationed.[5]

In the late 1720s, the imperial envoy in London since 1728, Philipp, Count Kinsky (1700–1749), had a yearly allowance of 4,000 florins for the chapel and other 'extraordinary expenses,' which was a third of his ambassadorial allowance. After his appointment as imperial ambassador in 1732, the amount rose to 6,000 florins.[6] Expenses covered by this money were those for clothing, travel in England, and for the use of postal and banking services.[7] It is therefore not clear how much was used for the embassy chapel, priests, and religious services. In British diplomatic accounts, chapel costs were also not listed as separate expenses. They could be part of the extraordinary expenses, which at the imperial court in Vienna normally amounted to about £50 a month or £600 a year.[8] In Queen Anne's time, at the very beginning of the eighteenth century, chapel furnishings worth £350 were given to every British minister or ambassador when going abroad.[9] If this was still true decades later, these amounts would need to be added to the extraordinary expenses used for the embassy chapels. Comparing the imperial and British 'extraordinary expenses,' the sums in London and Vienna were roughly the same for envoys, but for the imperial ambassador about a third higher than for his British colleagues of lower diplomatic rank in Vienna.[10]

The costly chapels were used for the public representation of a monarchy or a monarch's successes. After an imperial victory during the War of the Polish Succession in 1734, the imperial ambassador in London, Count Kinsky, was ordered to organise an audience with George II on the subject, and before that audience 'to have … sung the Te Deum in [his] chapel'; in addition, he should publish a report of the victory in the newspapers and invite all British and foreign ministers for a celebration.[11]

An important part of the ambassadorial chapel was the clergy. Noble diplomats would have private chaplains or priests who accompanied them on their embassy. Besides taking care of the souls of the members of the diplomatic household, these men often acted as secretaries, teachers, treasurers, and so on. For British diplomats, the number of chaplains was limited according to noble rank by order of the Church of England. Private chaplains had to be registered with the Faculty Office of the

Archbishop of Canterbury. James, 1st Earl Waldegrave (1684–1741), who was the British envoy in Vienna from 1728 to 1730, would – as an earl – have been allowed to have five chaplains.[12] He sent for at least two, but more likely three, of his English chaplains to stay with him in Vienna – Anthony Thompson, Charles Bayley, and probably John Lambert.[13] Anthony Thompson (1705?–1756) was probably first employed to teach the earl's children, before becoming Waldegrave's personal secretary and chaplain.[14] When Waldegrave left Vienna in 1730, Thompson remained as legation secretary until the envoy's replacement, Sir Thomas Robinson (1695–1770), arrived.[15] Not only noblemen would have chaplains, however; gentry diplomats also had to have a chaplain for the embassy's chapel. Joshua Allen, one of Robinson's chaplains, used his services to Robinson as envoy in Vienna to recommend himself later in life when he sold his sermons, describing himself as 'late Chaplain to the Right Honourable Sir Thomas Robinson: Then His Majesty's Minister Plenipotentiary at the Court of Vienna.'[16]

When Count Kinsky went to Great Britain to represent the emperor at the Court of St James's in 1728, his whole family, including his wife, small children, a personal secretary, servants, and priests, accompanied the new envoy.[17] Because Kinsky was from an old and high-noble Bohemian family, some of his priests were from the Bohemian clergy, such as Angelikus Maria Müller (1677–1734), a Servite father.[18] The German-speaking priests were necessary for the spiritual needs of the diplomat and his family and German-speaking servants. But in London, Kinsky also employed English native speakers as priests, mainly from Ireland. One of his chaplains was Stephen Dowdall (?–1736), a native of Navan in Meath, who had studied in Lisbon and Angers in France.[19] In January 1734, Dowdall was appointed Bishop of Kildare in Ireland, but, because of anti-Catholic riots in Ireland, he remained as priest at the imperial chapel in London, perhaps to also collect money for his diocese.[20] Dowdall died there, without ever seeing Kildare, in 1736. These English-speaking priests were not needed for the immediate ambassadorial household, but for all the English, Scottish, and Irish Catholics seeking spiritual support and imperial protection by attending Mass and other services in the embassy's chapel.[21] In addition, the imperial chaplains proselytised in London and even, as an anonymous accuser wrote to the Bishop of London, 'set up a School to teach gratis.'[22]

Diplomats accredited at the Court of St James's in London were in fact not allowed to have subjects of the king as embassy chaplains. The Bishop of London, Edmund Gibson, therefore complained at the time that 'their entertaining great numbers beyond what they have occasion for, is said to be a common case – and English or Irish Priests are much more capable of making Conversions among ye English people, than foreign Priests.'[23]

The Catholic imperial embassy and its chapel were crucial to the religious life of Catholics in London. Together with the other six Catholic embassy chapels – the French, Spanish, Sardinian, Venetian, Portuguese, and Neapolitan – it served as a safe place for marriages, baptisms, and obsequies, with enough priests to take confessions and to offer regular religious services.[24] German-speaking Catholics probably also made use of the imperial chapel for their spiritual needs.[25] In reports to the Holy See, these chapels were called the 'public chapels,' which further underlines their openness and accessibility.[26] In a country with anti-Catholic laws and a political culture, at least partly, based on notions of anti-popery, this had a huge impact on the Catholic minority.

The same was true for the Protestants in Vienna, where the Dutch, Swedish, and Danish embassies were well-known centres of religious life for Protestants of the different denominations, which all were officially banned from the Habsburg territories.[27] The British envoys, the Earl of Waldegrave from 1728 to 1730 and Sir Thomas Robinson from 1730 to 1748, rented a place in the 'free house' (*Freihaus*) of the Counts of Starhemberg, one of the most prestigious families in imperial service.[28] A 'free house' was not only exempt from certain duties, but was also subject to a separate court system, and inhabitants were free to exercise their religion.[29] However, the sources tell us very little of the British chaplains' activities in Vienna at the time. It is, therefore, not clear what they did compared to the chaplains of the other Protestant embassies. It can, however, be assumed that, like their colleagues, they cared for the spiritual needs of the envoy and his household, helped the envoy with secretarial services, preached in the embassy chapel within the free house, and visited the sick of their community living in Vienna.

All these public efforts in favour of the 'wrong' religion sparked opposition. The Prince Archbishop of Vienna, Cardinal Sigismund Count Kollonitsch (1677–1751), protested against the free entry of Protestants to the Protestant embassy chapels in Vienna in 1736.[30] In his German petition to Emperor Charles VI, later published with the Latin title *Gravamina religionis Catholicae et in specie Archi-dioecesis Viennensis contra haereticos accrescentes*,[31] he wrote:

> All and one of the bunch here able to walk or crawl out of the Protes-
> tant houses fancies himself without shame and with ostensible freedom
> to go to the local prayer rooms and private religious services of the
> Protestant envoys.[32]

He also reproached the Protestant embassy chaplains, who visited the sick in the city, celebrating Communion services in their houses, and who complained about any measures taken to prevent them, the Protestant chaplains, from doing so if the house was owned by Catholics.[33] Kollonitsch was prince bishop of Vienna from 1716, and prince archbishop after 1722. He was well known for supporting the efforts of

Emperor Charles VI to recatholicise the Habsburg hereditary lands. The papacy's aim of improving priests' education and the general management of dioceses was implemented by Kollonitsch in the Diocese of Vienna with mandatory religious exercises for priests and a general visitation of the diocese in 1730. His strong anti-Protestant opinions, as cited above, accompanied these works.[34]

The Privy Council with its president, Chief Court Chancellor Philipp Ludwig Count Sinzendorff (1671–1742), discussed the matter on 13th April, 1736, with the prince archbishop present.[35] After the discussion, the Council admitted that the free entry to religious services in the houses of foreign ministers could not be forbidden to any of the 8,000 Protestants in Vienna, without fearing reprisals, because Catholics were allowed to attend Mass at foreign Protestant courts.[36] Any priest coming into contact with Protestants connected to one of the Protestant embassies should act modestly and avoid all quarrels. At the same time, it was decided that envoys should give the names of their religious relations (e.g. those attending religious service with legitimate reasons) to the authorities. In general, the Privy Council decided that it was impossible to avoid contact between Catholics and Protestants in Vienna, as demanded by the archbishop, as Vienna was a city where people from all over the world came and lived.[37] But Kollonitsch's petition was successful in gaining support for his religious policy. From the late 1730s, the Diocese of Vienna employed a special priest for converts and offered financial support to them; in addition, measures were taken to emphasise the Catholic religion of the imperial residence.[38]

The law of nations and the '45 in London

In London, measures were taken against the Catholic priests associated with embassies, especially during the Jacobite rebellion of 1745. This rebellion aimed to replace the Protestant Hanoverian monarch, George II, with the Catholic aspirant, James Edward Stuart, son of the late and deposed King James II.[39]

When the Jacobite army drew nearer to the capital in the winter of 1745, Jesuits and 'popish priests' were accused of stirring up discontent and of publishing papers in support of the Jacobites. A royal declaration was issued, first in September, commanding all Catholic priest to depart from London, Westminster, and the borough of Southwark, but because many Catholic clergy remained in these areas, the royal declaration was re-enforced on 6th/17th December, 1745,[40] implementing the laws against 'Jesuits and popish priests.'[41] It stated that 'at this time of open rebellion in favour of a popish pretender to our crown all such Jesuits and popish priests are more particularly dangerous to the peace and security of this realm.'[42] An exception was made for 'such popish priests, not being his majesty's natural born subjects, as by the law of this realm are permitted to attend foreign ministers.'[43] In London, Westminster, Southwark, and ten miles outside of the first two cities, a reward of £100 was offered for apprehending all other Catholic priests.[44] Several British Catholic priests found in the cities were arrested in the following days.[45] The Catholic foreign ministers, under the leadership of the imperial envoy Ignaz Johann Baron von Wasner (1688–1767), formally objected to this by referring to '[...] the true law of nations and the previous, long-lasting exercise of religious services of foreign Catholic ministers in their houses [...].'[46]

Wasner was the doyen of the diplomatic circles in London. He had been the diplomatic representative of the Habsburgs in London since 1736, first as imperial chargé d'affaires, then as imperial resident until the death of Emperor Charles VI. From 1743, he acted as minister plenipotentiary for Queen Maria Theresa, and in the winter of 1745 Wasner was appointed to the same office by the newly elected Emperor Francis Stephen and Empress and Queen Maria Theresa.[47]

In his first report to the emperor on the subject, Wasner noted that foreign ministers at the Court of St James's at that time had no priests of their own nationality, but only English or Irish clerics in their employ.[48] The Catholic diplomats conferred in the Venetian embassy on 8th/19th December, before they asked for meetings with the respective Secretaries of State, the Duke of Newcastle and Baron Harrington, on this day and next. The Catholic envoys and ambassadors remonstrated against the royal proclamation, because in their opinion they were allowed by the law of nations to place anyone under their protection and to have any number of clerics within their embassies. The second evening, everyone met at Baron Wasner's to discuss further actions to be taken. As the British ministers had asked for some time to speak with the king, nothing was decided.[49] But then, on the third day, the news spread around the Catholic diplomatic circle that despite the envoys' and ambassadors' objections, grenadiers and other officers had attempted to arrest two clerics employed by foreign diplomats in their apartments outside the embassies; the priests barely escaped.[50] Later that week, an English priest subject to the Portuguese embassy was arrested and transferred to Newgate Prison. Another one, named James Hamilton, was arrested by a constable in the Venetian embassy and brought before a Justice of the Peace, who pressed charges despite the priest's valid writ of protection from the Venetian ambassador.[51]

As a last resort, the Catholic diplomats drew up a protestation against the royal proclamation on 16th/27th December, 1745. One version in French was written by the imperial minister Wasner and signed by himself, Baron Haslang, the Bavarian envoy, and the Chevalier de Champigny, the envoy of the Prince Elector and Archbishop of Cologne. They sent their protest to Lord Harrington, as Secretary of State for the Northern Department.[52] Two versions in Italian were despatched to the Duke of Newcastle as Secretary of State for the Southern Department,[53] the first signed by Pietro Andrea Capello, the Venetian ambassador, the Genovese resident, Giambattista Gastaldi, and the Portuguese secretary, Caettano, and the second with the signatures of the Chevalier Giuseppe Ossorio Alarçon, the Sabaudian representative, and Vincenzo Pucci, the chargé d'affaires of the Grand Duke of Tuscany.[54] The list included all Catholic foreign ministers in London, as the Kings of France and Spain had recalled their ambassadors because of the war. The circle of Catholic diplomats therefore included representatives of powers fighting on different sides of the War of the Austrian Succession, who nevertheless worked together for one common goal.

In the protest note, the diplomats again stressed 'that the Law of Nations has been violated by the Clause of the Proclamation [...] against the Roman Catholick Ecclesiasticks [...].'[55] By the law of nations, the immunity of a foreign minister included everyone in his household. They therefore protested that by differentiating between foreigners and British natives in the employ of foreign embassies, and 'by restraining the Privileges to those who are Foreigners, [...] this Proclamation equally violates our essential Immunities, and our most valuable Prerogatives.'[56] As noted above, all of those employed British priests 'by Reason of the Custom established from Time immemorial'; enforcing the proclamation would therefore prevent the Catholic ministers from exercising their religion, 'which is allowed in all Countries [...].' Not only was the law of nations regarding the immunity and the religious freedom of diplomats seen as indispensable at the time; these rights were also preserved by an Act of Queen Anne of 1708.[57] Besides the general objections, in the two cases of arrested priests, the signatories demanded their immediate release as well as a punishment for the constable who had definitely violated the law by intruding an embassy.[58]

The memorial in French was later published together with an English translation and the answer of the Secretaries of State in French and English, which was sent to the Catholic foreign ministers on 7th/18th January, 1746.[59] The Secretaries of State confirmed the king's protection for the Catholic ministers:

> The Roman Catholic Ministers may rely upon the King's Protection for their Persons, for their Families, and for the Exercise of their Religion in their own Houses, according to the Law of Nations; and according to the Usage of all other Countries with Regard to Ministers of a different Religion from That which is establish'd in the Country where they reside.[60]

Regarding the violation of the Venetian embassy, retributions were promised after a full investigation.[61]

However, the problem remained that the high number of British Catholic priests in London had been seen as a threat to national security in the long term because of the conversions of locals to the Catholic faith, and in the current situation because there was intelligence that several of them had supported the Jacobite rebellion 'in the Heart of his [Majesty's] Dominions.'[62] The rights of maintaining embassy chapels and of religious services by domestic chaplains was not touched by the royal proclamation. The previous practice of 'an enormous Number of Priests' serving in the embassies and Mass being said 'from Morning to Night' in the chapels was, however, labelled as forbidden missionary work by the Secretaries of State. The practice was, so they answered, merely ignored at peaceful times, but did not lay the foundation for 'a natural Right.'[63] On the contrary, 'the Celebrations of Mass by National Priests' was punishable by several Acts of Parliament, and as late as in King William III's time at the end of the seventeenth century, not even Catholic ambassadors were allowed to celebrate Mass in their houses.[64] While accepting the change in the law of nations, as cited above, the king and his ministers demanded that every British subject employed as a priest in a Catholic embassy in London had to be dismissed. In future, ambassadorial households should only be served by foreign priests.[65]

The Catholic ministers replied to the secretaries' answer on 21st January/ 1st February, 1746, promising first of all to dismiss all servants guilty of treasonable crimes, but again stressing the immunities of foreign ministers protected by the laws of the land as well as the law of nations. Regarding the priests in London, they cared only about

> the few actually in their service, whose names were given in to the sec-
> retaries' office, at the beginning of the present troubles, desiring no
> extension of privilege, but only the exercise of their religion in their
> own house, of which one priest is not sufficient[66]

They insisted on the release of the imprisoned domestic priests of the Portuguese and Sardinian envoys; the latter had been arrested some time at the turn of the month. Using British priests was necessary for their spiritual needs, as there were currently no foreign priests in London, and without any, the exercise of their religion was impossible. But the foreign diplomats were waiting for their courts' answers on the topic, therefore offering an out for the future policy of the British government.[67]

In the end, the imperial envoy could not act too forcefully against the British government. The events in London happened at the time of the War of the Austrian Succession, and the emperor, Francis Stephen, and his wife, Maria Theresa, needed the help of George II. Their diplomat had to be careful to not strain the relationship too much. On the other hand, the king also relied on imperial help to secure his German territories and would not press too much for a strict execution of the declaration after the Jacobite rebellion was suppressed in 1746.

Irish Catholics and Salzburg Protestants

Similar restraints while acting on behalf of one's own co-religionists could also be seen at other times. While the situation was usually relatively good for the Catholics in London, the situation in Ireland was critical. Regularly, the Irish Catholics applied for the help of the emperor and other Catholic princes in Europe against the so-called Penal Laws, which impeded bequeathing land to Catholic heirs, favoured Protestantism in education, and restricted any political representation for the Irish Catholics; the Irish were also not chosen for the diplomatic service.[68] In this dire situation, they applied to all the Catholic powers for help; nonetheless, diplomats were, in general, only informed about the Irish situation before going to Great Britain.[69] The Irish especially asked the emperor, as protector of the Catholic Church, for his assistance.[70] In the late seventeenth and early eighteenth centuries, the emperors' protests against the treatment of Irish and Scottish Catholics by British officials and within the legal and political system of Great Britain were restrained, because the alliance against France and Louis XIV was too important to the Austrian Habsburgs during the Nine Years' War and the War of the Spanish Succession.[71] For a long time, the principal political supporter of the Irish among the European princes was therefore the French king, even after the War of the Spanish Succession, during the time of a British–French alliance in the 1720s.

Changes to European relations also affected the Irish situation, when, after a time of constant fluctuations in alliances, imperial–British relations were renewed with the Treaty of Vienna on 16th March, 1731, which formally also included the Netherlands.[72] The French court felt excluded and withdrew its support for the Irish. In that situation, Emperor Charles VI saw his chance to renew support for the suppressed believers of the 'true faith.'[73] He ordered the imperial diplomat, Count Kinsky, at the Court of St James's in London to help the Irish Catholics in any way possible, '[...] that the religion might in that place thus be preserved in the orthodox manner [...].'[74] Several Irish Catholics as well as the Primate of Ireland directly asked Count Kinsky for his aid with the government in London and in Great Britain in general.[75] The imperial envoy was, however, very reluctant to do so because in his view the Irish were too openly offensive and not discreet enough. The case was, in his opinion, 'for diplomats an all the more delicate issue, because these gentlemen [the Irish] do not act with the necessary circumspection and prudence.'[76] Any open support for them could obstruct the good relations just re-established between the courts of Vienna and London.

When talking about religious strife in Europe in the first half of the eighteenth century, the forced emigration of the Salzburg Protestants in 1731/32 is probably the most researched event.[77] Ever since the new Prince Bishop of Salzburg, Leopold Anton Baron of Firmian, wanted to recatholicise the territory, religious tensions had risen. In 1729, Firmian ordered Jesuit missionaries to preach in villages with known crypto-Protestants. The Protestants in turn openly practised their faith, which was against the regulations of the Peace of Westphalia. They asked the

Protestant princes of the empire for help to gain either the free exercise of religion or the possibility of lawful exile under the clauses of the Peace of Westphalia, with a three-year period to depart the territories with all their belongings and assets. Firmian reacted with a decree ordering the Protestants to leave within eight days or three months, respectively, if they had immovable properties, an order backed by 6,000 soldiers. While about 5,000 unpropertied servants were forced into exile in the summer and winter of 1731, pressured by Emperor Charles VI, Bishop Firmian had later to consent to more favourable terms – in accordance with the Peace of Westphalia – for the rest of the Protestants. Most craftsmen and farmers left with their families in summer 1732, keeping the rights later to their houses and properties, which could be sold from exile. While most exiled Protestants settled in eastern Prussia, a few hundred found a new home in George II's German territories, in Regensburg and Nuremberg; few emigrated to the Netherlands or to the British–American colony Georgia.[78]

Salzburg was the territory of a prince-bishop, but as a neighbouring principality to the Austrian Habsburg realms and as part of the Holy Roman Empire, anything that happened in Salzburg was also of interest to the emperor. George II was equally interested in the question, first, because as the prince-elector of Brunswick-Luneburg, he had the duty to safeguard the laws of the empire, in that case the right of exile in case of differences of religion with a territory's ruler. Second, as King of Great Britain, George II minded his representation as the leading Protestant prince, which meant helping his co-religionists, but at the same time he wanted to avoid further conflicts that might interfere with his recent treaty with the emperor. Therefore, he ordered his envoy at the imperial court in Vienna, Sir Thomas Robinson, to acquaint himself with the situation in Salzburg and to help the Protestants if needed.[79] However, on first hearing the news, Robinson was very reluctant to do anything, because he feared a strong campaign by foreign powers would be 'more likely to do the poor Protestants harm than good.'[80] When he was told to work together with the Dutch envoy to support the Protestants, he consequently did so only hesitantly.

At the same time, the monarchs, ministers, and diplomats in Vienna, London, and The Hague were discussing the concurrence of the States General of the Netherlands with the Anglo-imperial alliance between Charles VI and George II. After signing the declaration of consent in February 1732, the Dutch used very strong language to oppose the measures taken against the Salzburg emigrants, while Robinson refrained from doing the same because he feared, as he said, 'that the Emperor could demand that George II should suspend all actions taken against Catholics in Great Britain.' However, '[...] the disparity of the Governm [en]ts makes it impossible for his Ma[jes]^{ty} in particular to comply with [these demands],' as these actions (e.g. the exclusion of Catholics from public office) were based on Acts of Parliament, which the king could not change himself.[81] Therefore, the king's demand for imperial support for the Protestants could mean that '[...] the same general tranquility which the King wishes to be settled by his demand, would run an evident risk of being disturbed by His Majesty's hearkening to a like demand on the part of the Emperor.'[82]

Robinson tried instead to influence the imperial court by citing imperial laws concerning religious questions. He also suggested that any religious conflict could be dangerous if there were any new attacks by the Turks in Hungary, when the Hungarian Protestants would be too enraged to support the emperor.[83] At the same time, Charles VI, as emperor and neighbouring prince, tried to calm down the situation by first pressuring the Bishop of Salzburg to let the Protestants leave his territories according to the laws of the Holy Roman Empire, and second by pointing out, via Count Kinsky in London, that the Salzburg Protestants themselves had offended the laws by openly celebrating religious services.[84]

In the end, George II supported the man 'on the spot' and his more restrained strategy of dealing with religious problems:

> [...] as Experience shews that among zealous and bigotted Papists any instances of a publick nature have often only proved to stirr up a greater animosity & fury against ye Protestants; you who are on the Spot, will as occasion offers know best how to apply in ye most effectual manner to the Ministers, & whether private insinuations, & good Offices, without making a Noise will not be more advantagious for obtaining ye End We aim at, than open Representations, & Memorials in form; & you will act in such Cases according to your discretion, & as you shall find you are able to do most Service to ye Protestant Cause.[85]

Robinson was then, by the king's orders, free to decide himself if private and discreet talks with certain ministers or open discussions and published memorials would help to support the Protestants. He, as representative of the king, was the one who would be able to decide the rightfulness of grievances and to find possible solutions – both legal as well as political. The British monarch trusted Robinson's judgement and his commitment '[...] to procure that Relief for them, which his Majesty has so much at heart.'[86] His cautious and circumspect course of action was accepted as being for the best of the Protestant cause.

The examples of the British and Irish Catholics and the Protestants from Salzburg show the ongoing religious strife in eighteenth-century Europe. At the same time, the diplomats' caution in these matters demonstrate that the religious factors were not meant to lead to open confrontations within diplomatic relations. Neither the emperor nor the king wished for armed conflict over religion. They preferred to use negotiation, compromise, and – as Andrew Thompson recently wrote – 'smart intervention' when faced with the ongoing confessional divide in Europe.[87] The idea originated in the aftermath of the Thirty Years' War and legally constructed on the Peace of Westphalia had stabilised: religion was no longer seen as a legitimate cause of war.

Conclusion

In the eighteenth century, every envoy, resident, or ambassador was charged with the support of those of his own faith, especially in territories ruled by monarchs of another confession. To help their brothers and sisters in faith, the diplomats employed chaplains and priests to conduct religious services, educate the children connected to the embassy, and evangelise the population in their host city. Houses of official diplomatic representatives normally had a chapel for the use of the 'household' – even if this household often swelled with a large number of locals attending Sunday services. The analysis of the actions of the diplomats charged with the Catholic embassy chapels in London and the Protestant chapels in Vienna has led to the conclusion that in practice, the embassy chapels were normally accepted. The reciprocal existence of chapels with near diplomatic immunity supporting the 'wrong' confession helped to stabilise the practice, as any action by a monarch or government against an embassy chapel was restricted by the fear that the same would happen to their own chapels at other courts. The custom was only challenged in times of national unrest, when the presence of too many missionaries was feared as leading to open revolt and the priests were seen as supporters of a possible overthrow of monarchy and government.

Notes

1 The title in Latin was 'advocatus et protector ecclesiae.' Cf. Werner Goez, 'Imperator advocatus romanae ecclesiae,' in *Aus Kirche und Reich: Studien zu Theologie, Politik und Recht im Mittelalter. Festschrift für Friedrich Kempf zu seinem fünfundsiebzigsten Geburtstag und fünfzigsten Doktorjubiläum*, ed. Hubert Mordek (Sigmaringen: Thorbecke, 1983), 315–28, especially 328. Cf. Anna Coreth, *Pietas Austriaca: Österreichische Frömmigkeit im Barock* (Munich: Oldenbourg, 1982).
2 Bill of Rights 1689; renewed in the Act of Settlement, Wilhelm III., 'An Act for the further Limitation of the Crown,' in *Statutes of the Realm*. Vol. 7, 1695–1701, ed. John Raithby (London: George Eyre and Andrew Strahan, 1820), 636.
3 Cf. Charlotte Backerra, *Wien und London, 1727–1735: Internationale Beziehungen im frühen 18. Jahrhundert* (Göttingen: Vandenhoeck & Ruprecht, 2018), 318–28, 398–99. The following is partly based on the research for this book, which is the slightly rewritten, published version of my German PhD thesis.
4 Cf., in general, instructions for diplomats. The imperial instruction by Emperor Charles VI to Count Kinsky explicitly ordered him to support Catholics in Great Britain: Instructions, Neustadt, 20th June, 1728, OeStA, HHStA, StA England 66, 16v.
5 See also the chapters by Roberta Anderson and by Martin Bakeš and Jiří Kubeš in this book.

6 Account books of Ambassadors' and Envoys' Missions (Bot- und Gesandtschaften, Kontobücher) 1724–1738, OeStA, FHKA, Hs. 719, 68–69.

7 Cf. James Lord Waldegrave's Bill of Extraordinaries, Graz, 28th July, 1728, TNA, SP 80/63, 46–47; Waldegrave to Undersecretary Tilson, Graz, 11th September, 1728, TNA, SP 80/63, 125–126.

8 Dodington to Sir Robert Walpole, Whitehall, 31st December, 1739, Bodleian Library Oxford, John Johnson Mss., b. 1, Misc. *Ambassadorial Extraordinary Expense Accounts for English Ministers and Others in the Empire, Lower Saxony etc. 1712–1768.*

9 David Bayne Horn, *The British Diplomatic Service 1689–1789* (Oxford: Clarendon Press, 1961), 54.

10 For the exchange rate of pounds sterling and florins, see Olaf Simons and Matthias Böhne, *The Marteau Early 18th-Century Currency Converter: A Platform of Research in Economic History*, accessed 20th November 2018, www.pierre-marteau.com/currency/converter.html.

11 Emperor Charles VI to Count Kinsky, Vienna, 22nd November, 1734, FA Kinsky, OeStA, AVA deposit, 9 a), 18, s.f.

12 See, in general, Lambeth Palace Library, Faculty Office, V, Papers relating to Noblemen's chaplains, http://archives.lambethpalacelibrary.org.uk/CalmView/Record.aspx?src=CalmView.Catalog&id=F%2f5&pos=, accessed 30th November, 2018.

13 Thompson, Anthony, 20th December, 1729 (os), Chaplain to James, Earl Waldegrave, Lambeth Palace Library, Faculty Office, V, 1, IX, 188v; Bayley, Charles, 20th December, 1729 (os), Chaplain to James, Earl Waldegrave, Lambeth Palace Library, Faculty Office, V, 1, IX, 189; Lambert, John, 2nd September, 1726 (os), Chaplain to James, Baron Waldegrave, Lambeth Palace Library, Faculty Office, V, 1, IX, 54v.

14 Waldegrave to Tilson, Vienna, 6th November, 1728, TNA, SP 80/63, 214.

15 Waldegrave to Tilson, Vienna, 7th June, 1730, TNA, SP 80/67, 174.

16 Joshua Allen, *Twenty Six Sermons, on the Most Important Subjects of the Christian Religion; As Well Doctrinal As Practical: Preached at St. Vedast, Foster-Lane; and Long-Acre-Chapel; in 1742, 1743. by Joshua Allen, Rector of St. Bride's in Pembrokeshire; Late Chaplain to the Right Honourable Sir Thomas Robinson: Then His Majesty's Minister Plenipotentiary at the Court of Vienna* (London: W. Strahan, 1751).

17 Waldegrave to Secretary of State, the Viscount Townshend, Graz, 21st July, 1728, TNA, SP 80/63, 37.

18 Müller was appointed in 1733 and died in London in 1734. Cf. Archives of the Servite Friary in Vienna, Registrum omnium fratrum, Nr. 19, in: Veronika Čapská, 'Mendicant Friar in Contact with "Other" Religious Virtuosi: The Travel Writing of the Servite Angelikus Maria Müller (1677–1734),' in *Samotrzeć, w kompanii czy z orszakiem? Społeczne aspekty podróżowania w średniowieczu i w czasach nowożytnych*, ed. Monika Saczyńska and Ewa Wółkiewicz (Warsaw: Wydawnictwo Instytutu Archeologii i Etnologii PAN, 2012), 387–402, here 395.

19 William John Fitzpatrick, *The Life, Times, and Correspondence of the Right Rev. Dr. Doyle, Bishop of Kildare and Leighlin, vol. 2* (Dublin: James Duffy, 1861), 513.

20 Letter of Dowdall to James III, 23rd April, 1734 (os), Windsor, Stuart Papers, Vol. 169, No. 183, cited in Hugh Fenning, 'The Irish Dominican Province in the Final Decades of Persecution (1721–1745),' *Archivum Fratrum Praedicatorum* 42 (1972): 251–368, here 301–2, fn. 33; Patrick Fagan, *Catholics in*

a Protestant Country: The Papist Constituency in Eighteenth-century Dublin (Dublin: Four Courts Press, 1998), 66.

21 Cf. César de Saussure, London, 29th April, 1729 (os), in *A Foreign View of England in 1725–1729: The Letters of Monsieur César de Saussure to His Family*, ed. Georges van Muyden (London: J. Murray, 1902), 327–28.

22 Anonymus, *Memorandum of information offered to the Bishop of London against Shirley a Popish priest, and Count Kinsky's two chaplains and others for keeping public schools*, [London], 26th August, 1732, TNA, SP 36/27/ 2, 130.

23 Gibson, *Notes by Edmund Gibson concerning laws against papists*, [London], s.d., Bodleian Library, Oxford, Gibson Papers, Ms. Eng., d. 2405, 79.

24 Douglas Newton, *Catholic London* (London: Robert Hale Limited, 1950), 289.

25 Panikos Panayi, 'Germans in Eighteenth-Century Britain,' in *Germans in Britain since 1500*, ed. Panikos Panayi (London: The Hambledon Press, 1996), 29–48, here 42.

26 Report of the Missionary Richard Challoner to the Apostolic Vicar for London, Benjamin Petre, *Præsens Status Missionis Anglicanæ*, London, 1737, Westm. DA, Mss. Archiv. Westmon., A. 40, 10.

27 Johann Hieronymus Chemnitz, *Vollständige Nachrichten von dem Zustande der Evangelischen und insonderheit von ihrem Gottesdienste bey der König-lich Dänischen Gesandtschafts Capelle in der Kayserlichen Haupt und Resi-denzstadt Wien* ([?], 1761), 9. For these chapels, cf. Karl von Otto, 'Evangelischer Gottesdienst in Wien vor der Toleranzzeit,' *Jahrbuch der Gesellschaft für die Geschichte des Protestantismus in Österreich* 7 (1886), 120–31; Christian Stubbe, 'Die Dänische Gesandtschaftsgemeinde in Wien und ihre letzten Prediger,' *Schriften des Vereins für Schleswig-Holsteinische Kirchengeschichte* 9 (1932), 257–312; Ulrich Gäbler, 'Studenten in Leiden, Exulanten in Seeland, Gesandtschaftsprediger in Wien: Österreichs Protestan-ten und die Niederlande im 17. und 18. Jahrhundert,' *Jahrbuch der Gesell-schaft für die Geschichte des Protestantismus in Österreich* 98, no. 1, 4 (1982), 211–39.

28 Cf. Vienna, 21st June, 1730, *Wiener Zeitung* 49, 21st June, 1730, 6.

29 Susanne C. Pils, 'Adel, Zuzug, Adeliges Haushalten, Sozialtopographie,' in *Wien: Geschichte einer Stadt. Vol. 2: Die frühneuzeitliche Residenz (16. bis 18. Jahrhun-dert)*, ed. Karl Vocelka and Anita Traninger (Vienna: Böhlau, 2003), 242–55, here 244; Martin Scheutz, 'Legalität und unterdrückte Religionsausübung: Niederleger, Reichshofräte, Gesandte und Legationsprediger. Protestantisches Leben in der Haupt- und Residenzstadt Wien im 17. und 18. Jahrhundert,' in *Geheimprotestan-tismus und evangelische Kirchen in der Habsburgermonarchie und im Erzstift Salzburg (17./ 18. Jahrhundert)*, ed. Rudolf Leeb, Martin Scheutz, and Dietmar Weikl (Vienna: Böhlau, 2009), 209–36, here 212.

30 Constantin von Wurzbach, 'Kollonitz, Sigismund Graf von,' in *Biographisches Lexikon des Kaiserthums Oesterreich*, vol. 12, ed. Constantin von Wurzbach (Vienna: Kaiserlich-königliche Hof- und Staatsdruckerei, 1864), 363–64.

31 Sigismund Count Kollonitsch, *Gravamina religionis Catholicae et in specie Archi-dioecesis Viennensis contra haereticos accrescentes etc: ab eminentissimo cardinali et archi-episcopo viennensi Sigismundo a Collonitsch Augustissimo imperatori Carolo VI. praesentata* (Munich: Vötter, 1737).

32 Kollonitsch, *Gravamina religionis Catholicae*, 3. See also von Otto, 'Evange-lischer Gottesdienst,' 123.

33 Kollonitsch, *Gravamina religionis Catholicae*, 4.

34 Johann Weißensteiner, 'Kollonitsch (Kollonitz) Sigismund Graf von (1677–1751),' in *Die Bischöfe des Heiligen Römischen Reiches, 1648 bis 1803: Ein biographisches*

Lexikon, ed. Erwin Gatz, with Stephan M. Janker (Berlin: Duncker & Humblot, 1990), 236–39.

35 Otto, 'Evangelischer Gottesdienst,' 123.

36 Otto, 'Evangelischer Gottesdienst,' 120, 123.

37 Gerson Wolf, 'Zur Geschichte der Protestanten in Oesterreich,' *Jahrbuch der Gesellschaft für die Geschichte des Protestantismus in Österreich* 2 (1882), 70–78. For the archbishop's demands and the Privy Council's session, see 75–78; for the decision regarding embassies, see 78.

38 Salvador Miranda, *The Cardinals of the Holy Roman Church*, here (19) 2. Kollonitsch, Sigismund von (1677–1751), accessed 15th November 2018, https://webdept.fiu.edu/~mirandas/bios1727.htm#Kollonitsch.

39 For a general introduction, see Daniel Szechi, *The Jacobites: Britain and Europe, 1688–1788* (Manchester: Manchester University Press, 1994). For a concise history of the 1745 rebellion, see Christopher Duffy, *Fight for a Throne: The Jacobite '45 Reconsidered* (Solihul: Helion, 2015).

40 The dates are given in the old and new style, because while Great Britain still followed the Julian calendar, diplomats from continental Europe used the Gregorian calendar.

41 George II, 'Declaration for putting the laws in execution against Jesuits and Popish Priests,' in Francis Douglas, *The History of the Rebellion in 1745 and 1746: Extracted from the Scots Magazine: with an Appendix, Containing an Account of the Trials of the Rebels; the Pretender and His Son's Declarations, Etc.* (Aberdeen: F. Douglass and W. Murray, 1755), 81–83.

42 George II, 'Declaration,' 82.

43 George II, 'Declaration,' 82–83.

44 George II, 'Declaration,' 83.

45 Cf. Thursday, 12th December, 1745 (os), *The London Magazine, and Monthly Chronologer*, vol. 14 (London: T. Astley, 1745), 620.

46 Wasner to Emperor Francis Stephen, London, 21st December, 1745 (ns), OeStA, HHStA, StA England 88, 157–62v, here 157–57v.

47 Erwin Matsch, *Der Auswärtige Dienst von Österreich(-Ungarn) 1720–1920* (Vienna: Böhlau, 1986), 113–14.

48 Wasner, 21st December, 1745, 157v.

49 Wasner, 21st December, 1745, 157v–59.

50 Wasner, 21st December, 1745, 162–62v.

51 Wasner to Emperor Francis Stephen, London, 24th December, 1745 (ns), OeStA, HHStA, StA England 88, 163–67, here 163v. For Hamilton's letter to his master, the Venetian ambassador, see the transcription in Wasner to Emperor Francis Stephen, London, 28th December, 1745 (ns), OeStA, HHStA, StA England 88, 168–70v, 178, here 172, or the published version in *A Letter written to His Majesty's Principal Secretaries of State by the Ministers of the several Roman Catholick Princes and States residing here; Complaining of A Clause relating to Popish Priests, attending such Ministers, in His Majesty's Proclamation of the 6th of December 1745, for putting the Laws in Execution against Jesuits and Popish Priests, etc. With the answer returned thereto by His Majesty's said Principal Secretaries, and Translations of both* (London: E. Owen, 1746), 14 (French), 15 (English).

52 Wasner, 28th December, 1745, 168.

53 Wasner, 28th December, 1745, 168v.

54 *A Letter written*, 12.

55 *A Letter written*, 3. Here and in the following, only the English translation is cited.

56 *A Letter written*, 5. Differentiating between British and foreigners shows the stabilised notion of nationality in the mid-eighteenth century, which was accepted by all sides.

57 Queen Anne, *An Act for Preserving the Privileges of Ambassadors, and other Publick Ministers of Foreign Princes and States*, 7 Anne c.12, also called *Diplomatic Privileges Act*. Cf. Danby Pickering, *The Statutes at Large: From the Magna Charta, to the End of the Eleventh Parliament of Great Britain, Anno 1761*, vol. 11 (Cambridge: Joseph Bentham, 1764), 487–89.

58 *A Letter written*, 9.

59 'Answer by his majesty's Secretaries of State, Whitehall, Jan. 7, 1745–6,' in *The Gentleman's Magazine*, vol. 16 (London: Edward Cave, jun., 1746), 11–13; the print version as pamphlet. Cf. *A Letter written*.

60 *A Letter written*, 27.

61 *A Letter written*, 29.

62 *A Letter written*, 19, 21.

63 *A Letter written*, 21.

64 *A Letter written*, 25.

65 *A Letter written*, 27.

66 'Substance of the reply of the foreign Roman Catholic ministers, dated Jan. 21,' in *The Gentleman's Magazine*, vol. 16 (London: Edward Cave, jun., 1746), 109.

67 'Substance of the reply,' 109.

68 Cf. Sean J. Connolly, *Religion, Law and Power: The Making of Protestant Ireland 1660–1760* (Oxford: Clarendon Press, 1992); Karl Schweizer, 'Scotsmen and the British Diplomatic Service, 1714–1789,' *International Review of Scottish Studies* 8 (1978), 115–36, here 118.

69 Charles VI to Kinsky, Instruction, Laxenburg, 12th June, 1728, OeStA, HHStA, StA England 66, 13.

70 Bishop Ambrose O'Callaghan to Emperor Charles VI via Johann Adolf Count Metsch, deputy of the imperial vice-chancellor Schönborn, *Alla Sacra Cesarea & Cattolica Maestà di Carlo VI. Per Il Clero & Popolo Cattolico d'Irlanda*, Ferns, Ireland, 1st April, 1731, OeStA, HHStA, StA England Varia 7, 658–59.

71 Klaus Müller, *Das kaiserliche Gesandtschaftswesen im Jahrhundert nach dem Westfälischen Frieden (1648–1740)* (Bonn: Ludwig Röhrscheid Verlag, 1976), 273.

72 The Netherlands did not sign in March 1731 because of internal issues in the States General, but the Dutch were named a full partner in the treaty. For the contents and aims of this treaty and the French – and other powers' – reactions, see Backerra, *Wien und London*, 77–93.

73 Charles VI to Kinsky, Vienna, 4th August, 1731, OeStA, HHStA, StA England 68, 35.

74 Charles VI to Kinsky, in Latin, Vienna, 4th August, 1731, OeStA, HHStA, StA England 68, 35–35v.

75 Several Irish Catholics to Kinsky, Dublin, 11th December, 1731, FA Kinsky, OeStA, AVA deposit, 2 b), 57, s.f.; the Primate of Ireland to Kinsky, s.p., 20th April, 1732, FA Kinsky, OeStA, AVA deposit, 2 c), 10, s.f.

76 Kinsky to Prince Eugene as the emperor's leading minister, London, 14th September, 1731, OeStA, HHStA, Gr. Korr. 94 b, 153–153v, original in French, my own translation.

77 For the following, see Mack Walker, *The Salzburg Transaction: Expulsion and Redemption in Eighteenth-Century Germany* (Ithaca: Cornell University Press, 1992); Gabriele Emrich, *Die Emigration der Salzburger Protestanten*

1731–1732: Reichsrechtliche und konfessionspolitische Aspekte (Münster: Lit Verlag, 2002).

78 Cf. Charlotte E. Haver, *Von Salzburg nach Amerika: Mobilität und Kultur einer Gruppe religiöser Emigranten im 18. Jahrhundert* (Paderborn: Ferdinand Schöningh, 2011); Rainer Sabelleck, 'Kurhannover als Durchzugs- und Aufnahmeland für Salzburger und Berchtesgadener Emigranten: Erwartungen, Ziele und Handlungsspielräume 1732–1733,' in *Denkhorizonte und Handlungsspielräume: Historische Studien für Rudolf Vierhaus zum 70. Geburtstag*, ed. Thomas Behme and Manfred Dunger (Göttingen: Wallstein, 1992), 137–68.

79 Harrington to Robinson, Hampton Court, 10th August, 1731, TNA, SP 80/78, s.f. The elector's representative in Vienna had a similar task and presented a very restrained memorial on the topic to the emperor and his ministers. Cf. George II [as prince-elector] and Johann Wilhelm von Dieden zum Fürstenstein, *Pro Memoria So auf Befehl Sr. Königl. Groß-Brittannis. Majestät Durch Dero teutschen Ministro Hn. Joh. Wilhelm von Dieden zum Fürstenstein, Wegen deß Religions-Wesen en General-, Specialiter Aber der Saltzburgis. und Ungaris. Gravaminum Halber dem Kayserlichen Ministerio in Wien den 19. Febr. übergeben worden* (Vienna, 1732).

80 Robinson to Harrington, in cipher, Vienna, 5th September, 1731, TNA, SP 80/79, s.f.

81 Ibid.

82 Robinson to Harrington, Vienna, 25th February, 1732, TNA, SP 80/85, s.f.

83 Robinson to Harrington, in cipher, Vienna, 5th September, 1731, TNA, SP 80/79, s.f.

84 Charles VI to Kinsky, Laxenburg, 14th May, 1732, OeStA, HHStA, StA England 68, 47–50.

85 George II to Robinson, Additional Instructions, Herrenhausen, 27th July, 1732, TNA, SP 80/89, s.f.

86 Harrington to Robinson, Whitehall, 20th March, 1733, TNA, SP 80/94, s.f.

87 Andrew Thompson, 'Hanover-Britain and the Protestant Cause, 1714–1760,' in *The Hanoverian Succession: Dynastic Politics and Monarchical Culture*, edited by Andreas Gestrich, and Michael Schaich (Farnham: Ashgate, 2015), 89–106, here 106.

Bibliography

Archival sources

Bodleian Library, Oxford, Gibson Papers, Ms. Eng., d. 2405; John Johnson Mss., b. 1.
Lambeth Palace Library, Faculty Office, V, 1, IX.
Family Archive (FA) Kinsky, Österreichisches Staatsarchiv Vienna (OeStA), AVA (Allgemeines Verwaltungsarchiv), deposit, 2 b), 2 c), 9 a).
Österreichisches Staatsarchiv Vienna (OeStA), Haus-, Hof- und Staatsarchiv (HHStA), Große Korrespondenz (Gr. Korr.), 94 b; Staatenabteilung England (StA England) 66, 68, 88, Varia 7; Finanz- und Hofkammerarchiv (FHKA), Hs. 719.
The National Archives (TNA), Kew, State Papers Domestic (SP) 36; State Papers Foreign (SP) 80 (Germany/Holy Roman Empire), 63; 67; 78; 79; 85; 89; 94.
Westminster Diocese Archive (Westmin. DA), Mss. Archiv. Westmon., A. 40.

Printed sources

A *Letter written to His Majesty's Principal Secretaries of State by the Ministers of the several Roman Catholick Princes and States residing here; Complaining of A Clause relating to Popish Priests, attending such Ministers, in His Majesty's Proclamation of the 6th of December 1745, for putting the Laws in Execution against Jesuits and Popish Priests, etc. With the answer returned thereto by His Majesty's said Principal Secretaries, and Translations of both.* London: E. Owen, 1746.

Allen, Joshua. *Twenty Six Sermons, on the Most Important Subjects of the Christian Religion; As Well Doctrinal As Practical: Preached at St. Vedast, Foster-Lane; and Long-Acre-Chapel; in 1742, 1743. by Joshua Allen, Rector of St. Bride's in Pembrokeshire; Late Chaplain to the Right Honourable Sir Thomas Robinson: Then His Majesty's Minister Plenipotentiary at the Court of Vienna.* London: W. Strahan, 1751.

Chemnitz, Johann Hieronymus. *Vollständige Nachrichten von dem Zustande der Evangelischen und insonderheit von ihrem Gottesdienste bey der Königlich Dänischen Gesandtschafts Capelle in der Kayserlichen Haupt und Residenzstadt Wien.* [?], 1761.

Douglas, Francis. *The History of the Rebellion in 1745 and 1746: Extracted from the Scots Magazine: With an Appendix, Containing an Account of the Trials of the Rebels; the Pretender and His Son's Declarations, Etc.* Aberdeen: F. Douglass and W. Murray, 1755.

George II [as prince-elector] and von Dieden zum Fürstenstein, Johann Wilhelm. *Pro Memoria So auf Befehl Sr. Königl. Groß-Brittannis. Majestät Durch Dero teutschen Ministro Hn. Joh. Wilhelm von Dieden zum Fürstenstein, Wegen deß Religions-Wesen en General-, Specialiter Aber der Saltzburgis. und Ungaris. Gravaminum Halber dem Kayserlichen Ministerio in Wien den 19. Febr. übergeben worden.* Vienna, 1732.

Kollonitsch, Sigismund Count. *Gravamina religionis Catholicae et in specie Archidioecesis Viennensis contra haereticos accrescentes etc: ab eminentissimo cardinali et archi-episcopo viennensi Sigismundo a Collonitsch Augustissimo imperatori Carolo VI. praesentata.* Munich: Vötter, 1737.

Pickering, Danby. *The Statutes at Large: From the Magna Charta, to the End of the Eleventh Parliament of Great Britain, Anno 1761*, vol. 11. Cambridge: Joseph Bentham, 1764.

Raithby, John, ed. *Statutes of the Realm. Vol. 7: 1695–1701.* London: George Eyre and Andrew Strahan, 1820.

The Gentleman's Magazine, vol. 16. London: Edward Cave, jun., 1746.

The London Magazine, and Monthly Chronologer, vol. 14. London: T. Astley, 1745.

Muyden, Georges van, ed. *A Foreign View of England in 1725–1729: The Letters of Monsieur César de Saussure to His Family.* London: J. Murray, 1902.

Wiener Zeitung.

Literature

Backerra, Charlotte. *Wien und London, 1727–1735: Internationale Beziehungen im frühen 18. Jahrhundert*. Göttingen: Vandenhoeck & Ruprecht, 2018.

Čapská, Veronika. 'Mendicant Friar in Contact with "Other" Religious Virtuosi: The Travel Writing of the Servite Angelikus Maria Müller (1677–1734).' In *Samotrzeć, w kompanii czy z orszakiem? Spolezcne aspekty podro óżowania w średniowieczu i w czasach nowożytnych*, edited by Monica Saczyńska, and Ewa Woółkiewicz, 387–402. Warschau: Wydawnictwo Instytutu Archeologii i Etnologii PAN, 2012.

Connolly, Sean J. *Religion, Law and Power: The Making of Protestant Ireland 1660–1760*. Oxford: Clarendon Press, 1992.

Coreth, Anna. *Pietas Austriaca: Österreichische Frömmigkeit im Barock*. Munich: Oldenbourg, 1982.

Duffy, Christopher. *Fight for a Throne: The Jacobite '45 Reconsidered*. Solihul: Helion, 2015.

Emrich, Gabriele. *Die Emigration der Salzburger Protestanten 1731–1732: Reichsrecht-liche und konfessionspolitische Aspekte*. Münster: Lit Verlag, 2002.

Fagan, Patrick. *Catholics in a Protestant Country: The Papist Constituency in Eighteenth-century Dublin*. Dublin: Four Courts Press, 1998.

Fenning, Hugh. 'The Irish Dominican Province in the Final Decades of Persecution (1721–1745).' *Archivum Fratrum Praedicatorum* 42 (1972): 251–368.

Fitzpatrick, William John. *The Life, Times, and Correspondence of the Right Rev. Dr. Doyle, Bishop of Kildare and Leighlin*, vol. 2. Dublin: James Duffy, 1861.

Gäbler, Ulrich. 'Studenten in Leiden, Exulanten in Seeland, Gesandtschaftsprediger in Wien: Österreichs Protestanten und die Niederlande im 17. und 18. Jahrhundert.' *Jahrbuch der Gesellschaft für die Geschichte des Protestantismus in Österreich* 98, no. 1, 4 (1982): 211–39.

Goez, Werner. 'Imperator advocatus romanae ecclesiae.' In *Aus Kirche und Reich: Studien zu Theologie, Politik und Recht im Mittelalter: Festschrift für Friedrich Kempf zu seinem fünfundsiebzigsten Geburtstag und fünfzigsten Doktorjubiläum*, edited by Hubert Mordek, 315–28. Sigmaringen: Thorbecke, 1983.

Haver, Charlotte E. *Von Salzburg nach Amerika: Mobilität und Kultur einer Gruppe religiöser Emigranten im 18. Jahrhundert*. Paderborn: Ferdinand Schöningh, 2011.

Horn, David Bayne. *The British Diplomatic Service 1689–1789*. Oxford: Clarendon Press, 1961.

Matsch, Erwin. *Der Auswärtige Dienst von Österreich(-Ungarn) 1720–1920*. Vienna: Böhlau, 1986.

Miranda, Salvador. *The Cardinals of the Holy Roman Church*. Accessed 15th November, 2018. https://webdept.fiu.edu/~mirandas/bios1727.htm.

Müller, Klaus. *Das kaiserliche Gesandtschaftswesen im Jahrhundert nach dem Westfälischen Frieden (1648–1740)*. Bonn: Ludwig Röhrscheid Verlag, 1976.

Newton, Douglas. *Catholic London*. London: Robert Hale Limited, 1950.

Panayi, Panikos. 'Germans in Eighteenth-Century Britain.' In *Germans in Britain since 1500*, edited by Panikos Panayi, 29–48. London: The Hambledon Press, 1996.

Pils, Susanne C. 'Adel, Zuzug, Adeliges Haushalten, Sozialtopographie.' In *Wien: Geschichte einer Stadt. Vol. 2: Die frühneuzeitliche Residenz (16. bis 18. Jahrhundert)*, edited by Karl Vocelka and Anita Traninger, 242–55. Vienna: Böhlau, 2003.

Sabelleck, Rainer. 'Kurhannover als Durchzugs- und Aufnahmeland für Salzburger und Berchtesgadener Emigranten: Erwartungen, Ziele und Handlungsspielräume 1732–1733.' In *Denkhorizonte und Handlungsspielräume: Historische Studien für Rudolf Vierhaus zum 70. Geburtstag*, edited by Thomas Behme and Manfred Dunger, 137–68. Göttingen: Wallstein, 1992.

Scheutz, Martin. 'Legalität und unterdrückte Religionsausübung: Niederleger, Reichshofräte, Gesandte und Legationsprediger. Protestantisches Leben in der Haupt- und Residenzstadt Wien im 17. und 18. Jahrhundert.' In *Geheimprotestantismus und evangelische Kirchen in der Habsburgermonarchie und im Erzstift Salzburg (17./ 18. Jahrhundert)*, edited by Rudolf Leeb, Martin Scheutz, and Dietmar Weikl, 209–36. Vienna: Böhlau, 2009.

Schweizer, Karl. 'Scotsmen and the British Diplomatic Service, 1714–1789.' *International Review of Scottish Studies* 8 (1978): 115–36.

Simons, Olaf, and Böhne, Matthias. *The Marteau Early 18th-Century Currency Converter: A Platform of Research in Economic History*. Accessed 20th November, 2018. www.pierre-marteau.com/currency/converter.html.

Stubbe, Christian. 'Die Dänische Gesandtschaftsgemeinde in Wien und ihre letzten Prediger.' *Schriften des Vereins für Schleswig-Holsteinische Kirchengeschichte* 9 (1932): 257–312.

Szechi, Daniel. *The Jacobites: Britain and Europe, 1688–1788*. Manchester: Manchester University Press, 1994.

Thompson, Andrew. 'Hanover-Britain and the Protestant Cause, 1714–1760.' In *The Hanoverian Succession: Dynastic Politics and Monarchical Culture*, edited by Andreas Gestrich, and Michael Schaich, 89–106. Farnham: Ashgate, 2015.

Wurzbach, Constantin von. 'Kollonitz, Sigismund Graf von.' In *Biographisches Lexikon des Kaiserthums Oesterreich*, vol. 12, edited by Constantin von Wurzbach, 363–64. Vienna: Kaiserlich-königliche Hof- und Staatsdruckerei, 1864.

Otto, Karl von. 'Evangelischer Gottesdienst in Wien vor der Toleranzzeit.' *Jahrbuch der Gesellschaft für die Geschichte des Protestantismus in Österreich* 7 (1886): 120–31.

Walker, Mack. *The Salzburg Transaction: Expulsion and Redemption in Eighteenth-Century Germany*. Ithaca: Cornell University Press, 1992.

Weißensteiner, Johann. 'Kollonitsch (Kollonitz) Sigismund Graf von (1677–1751).' In *Die Bischöfe des Heiligen Römischen Reiches, 1648 bis 1803: Ein biographisches Lexikon*, edited by Erwin Gatz, with Stephan M. Janker, 236–39. Berlin: Duncker & Humblot, 1990.

Wolf, Gerson. 'Zur Geschichte der Protestanten in Oesterreich.' *Jahrbuch der Gesellschaft für die Geschichte des Protestantismus in Österreich* 2 (1882): 70–78.

11 Imperial chapels and chaplains

A comparative study of Copenhagen, Stockholm, and Dresden in the later seventeenth century[1]

Martin Bakeš and Jiří Kubeš

The activities of imperial legation chapels in early modern Protestant states constitute an often overlooked theme of Central European historiography. Although many works have recently been written on the matter of confessionalisation, so far no one has fully appreciated the influence of embassy chapels on the development of confessional minorities in capital cities (residences).[2] Fortunately, it is possible to proceed to a significant extent on the basis of recent studies focusing on the creation and development of chapels by imperial diplomats. Thanks to these works, we have at least basic information about the existence of chapels and we know which diplomats operated them when and where, as well as what problems they faced.[3]

But we find little about the activities of their chaplains. And yet the zealous activity of certain legation chaplains often undermined the attempts at confessional homogenisation of the host countries. Because of the virtually unlimited power resources of the Court of Vienna, their home government, the legation clergy developed many questionable tactics. They did not hesitate to operate at the edge of law and to break the fragile rules regulating inter-confessional coexistence. In this study, we attempt to summarise the research completed so far regarding the functioning of imperial legation chapels in the primarily Lutheran capitals of Copenhagen, Dresden, and Stockholm. We will compare the chapels' formation and development and will point out what problems they faced from the part of the host country. Taking into consideration the personalities of the legation chaplains, we will finally analyse the conflicts that the clergy caused through their activities inside and outside the embassy.

The birth of imperial embassies in the Protestant states and the selection of chaplains

The basic legal framework for the operation of these chapels was laid down by the Westphalian peace negotiations, where a graduated system of religious practice was established that differentiated between public, private, and domestic conducting of Masses. Thereafter, it was possible to legalise the chapels of foreign diplomats of a different faith, which came in the second category of *exercitium religionis privatum*. According to the Westphalian regulations, Masses could be celebrated in embassies, although these places of worship did not enjoy complete freedom. In 1765, Johann Jakob Moser concisely summarised the advantages and disadvantages of the private conduct of religion: '[...] even though I do not have a public church, I could have a chaplain come to say mass at my house.'[4] One question discussed in the second half of the seventeenth century was who could attend such a Mass. Abraham de Wicquefort asserted it was only the diplomat and his staff, but later François de Callières propagated the idea that all the subjects of the diplomat's ruler could also attend.[5] But no one said anything about whether local subjects could go to such a Mass, and in practice this became one of the most serious problems.[6]

The first permanent imperial embassies in Protestant states started to be established around the mid-seventeenth century. On principle, Emperor Ferdinand III and his son Leopold I did not send ambassadors (*Botschafter*) to Protestant rulers, but just diplomats of the second degree without formal representative character, i.e. envoys or residents (*Abgesandte, Residenten*). One of the first was Franz Paul von Lisola, who spent a long time in England as the first imperial envoy (from 1639 and after the civil war from 1666) and in Brandenburg (from 1663). Johann von Goess was sent to Denmark (from 1657), Johann Friquet to the United Dutch Provinces (from 1658), Georg von Plettenberg to Saxony (from 1665), and Hermann von Basserode went to Sweden (from 1667).[7] These men then founded the first imperial embassy chapels.[8]

The Austrian Habsburgs traditionally felt themselves to be the defenders of the oppressed Catholic minorities in these territories. For that reason, they were interested in and attempted to provide for the legation clergy, which along with the envoy was meant to ensure the basic spiritual needs of the non-tolerated Catholics. The permanent imperial embassies were created on the existing network of mission stations supported by the Sacred Congregation for the Propagation of the Faith (*Sacra Congregatio de Propaganda Fide*), from the resources of which the priesthood was largely financed.[9] In the first two decades following the Thirty Years' War, the influence of the Holy See and the emperor became separated in terms of foreign-confessional policy, expressed by the imperial court in particular in the selection of new legation chaplains and the assertion of influence over their activities.

Especially in Scandinavia, the new imperial envoys recruited legation chaplains from the ranks of Jesuit missionaries who had been operating for some time in northern German towns or the Jutland peninsula. The Jesuits were an attractive choice for many reasons. The envoy saved considerable funds for the expensive operation of the legation chapels, which were an extraordinary burden on the embassy's budget. Another advantage of hiring experienced missionaries for the position of imperial legation chaplains was their knowledge of Scandinavian matters and the Swedish or Danish language. Many missionaries, recruited primarily from the Society of Jesus, were known for their broad network of contacts, which covered the entire social spectrum of Northern Europe and often overcame otherwise serious confessional disputes. The mutual interaction also offered an important benefit to the missionaries. With the newly founded imperial embassy, the legation chaplains-missionaries gained a higher level of protection in the form of guaranteed diplomatic immunity. Any illegal activity of these significant promoters of the Catholic faith could thus continue virtually uninterrupted.[10]

However, the aforementioned practice could not last long. This first generation of imperial legation chaplains was characterised by a so-called *multiple loyalty*, and consequently there arose some serious conflicts of interest.[11] This was due to the fact that priests not only received orders from the envoy, but also via the Apostolic Nunciature from the Congregation de Propaganda Fide. The Congregation's ideas of missionary activity and the protection of the Catholic minorities differed from what the diplomatic representatives of the emperor were willing to tolerate. Later on, neither the Court of Vienna nor, more importantly, the imperial envoys wanted to allow that confessional disputes caused by the activity of the embassy clergy threatened the hard-won results of political negotiations. And for this reason, from the 1670s onwards, we see the Holy See being gradually squeezed out of its influence in the confessional foreign policy of the imperial embassies. Not even the intervention of papal nuncios in Vienna could impede this development.[12]

With the new generation of envoys, a new model for selecting legation chaplains was introduced. The chosen priests came primarily from the ranks of the Czech and Austrian clergy, and they had in common a much greater interest in teaching than in missionary work. They were often university professors or even deans with extensive scientific interests. In addition, they only had to follow the envoy and his orders. Ercole Visconti, the new nuncio in Cologne (1680–1687) and the protector of the Catholic communities in the north-west of the empire (and even in Sweden), for one, disliked the new practice. In his reports, Visconti disagreed regularly with the selection of clerics for the post of imperial legation chaplains. He pointed out their lack of experience in missionary matters, which, in his words, could threaten the existence of the small Catholic minorities in Lutheran states.[13]

Imperial chapels in Stockholm: towards the conflict of 1671

In the Kingdom of Sweden, the first imperial legation chapel was founded relatively late, in 1667 during the residency of Hermann von Basserode. Before this envoy, other representatives of the Austrian Habsburgs had visited Sweden, but none of them established or furnished a legation chapel in their home. Basserode's predecessor, Georg von Plettenberg, who had spent six months in Stockholm before the outbreak of the First Northern War, accepted the offer of the French envoy, Charles d'Avaugourt, to share a furnished chapel in Avaugour's house. The missionary for Lower Saxony and imperial legation chaplain Theodor Bothe thus celebrated regular Sunday and holiday services at the French embassy until Georg von Plettenberg was recalled. Such cooperation in matters of faith, which negated the frequent reciprocal hostility in the field of foreign policy, was not necessarily unique. There was also a similar situation in Copenhagen and in the Swedish and Danish Lutheran chapels in Vienna. For this reason, the close cooperation of the imperial legation chaplains with the clergy of allied powers, such as Spain and the Polish–Lithuanian Union, especially in the seventeenth century, comes as no surprise.[14]

The first imperial legation chapel in Sweden was founded on the central Stockholm island of Gamla stan, just a short walk from the royal palace, Tre kronor. It was a sought-after centre of the Swedish Catholic minority. In spite of the homogenising confessional policy of the local government, the representatives of this community gathered in the imperial chapel, where they participated in preaching and Masses. The celebration of certain sacraments was also connected to the institution of this legation chapel. Johann Sterck (1630–1692), the local imperial legation chaplain, regularly offered the Sacrament of the Eucharist to all secret Catholics, who did not hesitate to go to the Swedish capital, even from very distant towns such as Linköping or Norrköping. Nevertheless, like his colleague from the same order, Theodor Bothe, Sterck was not afraid to go out on the streets of Stockholm either. Dressed as a servant of the embassy, he went around to numerous Stockholm families and the houses of leading German merchants to administer the last rites, baptise children, and conduct marriages.[15]

Johann Sterck was no exception among legation chaplains in early modern Europe – his activities caused great displeasure with all the guarantors of the pure Lutheran faith. The urban elite and Swedish church representatives, in particular, regularly protested against the behaviour of this legation chaplain to the royal court and to the regency government that ruled during the reign of the underage Charles XI. A decisive turning point came in 1670 with the death of Hermann von Basserode, when the imperial embassy was deserted overnight and thus lost the right to diplomatic immunity. At that moment, the Spanish envoy, Carlos de Fernán Núñez intervened by employing most of the former imperial staff, including Johann Sterck, in his service. Regular services continued to be held in Basserode's house: every Sunday, the Spanish envoy went to the chapel established at Gamla stan. These Sunday Masses were the origins of a dispute that culminated at the beginning of 1671 with the arrest of Johann Sterck. Soldiers burst into the former imperial chapel and arrested the Jesuit chaplain, who was sentenced to death by the Stockholm city council. Fortunately, after the intervention of the Spanish envoy and the French legation secretary, Sterck was only declared *persona non grata* and directed to leave the country and go to Copenhagen, where he joined the clergy of the French embassy.[16]

In the name of the underage King of Sweden, the regency government issued a further command regulating the relationship of the host country and confessionally different legation chapels. This Swedish document essentially repeated the rules from the preceding years according to which the services were first to be conducted behind the closed doors and windows of the embassy. Second, the inhabitants of the capital were not to be disturbed by the noisy singing and preaching in Swedish that could be heard from time to time during Sunday services. And particularly, the imperial and French envoys were advised not to hire members of the Jesuit order, which by the influence of state propaganda were often associated with the recatholicisation attempts of Rome.[17]

Subsequent imperial envoys to Sweden heeded the new rescript only in part. For example, following an agreement with the Czech provincial of the Jesuit order, in 1673 Adolf Vratislav von Sternberg selected Father Emmanuel de Boy (1639–1700), the dean of the Faculty of Philosophy of the Charles-Ferdinand University in Prague, for the post of legation chaplain. Another imperial envoy, Franz Ottokar von Starhemberg, acted similarly when he requested the Jesuit Martin Gottseer (1648–1731), a newly appointed professor at Vienna University, from the Austrian provincial. The one exception in the second half of the seventeenth century was the legation chaplain of Anton Johann von Nostitz, the long-serving envoy in Sweden. Before his departure in 1685, the Count of Nostitz chose Daniel Josef Mayer (1656–1733), a priest placed near the Nostitz estates in northern Bohemia. Mayer, who towards the end of his life became Archbishop of Prague, was not a member of any religious order, and his activities were subject only to the orders of the Prague Archdiocese.[18]

Quite a different situation in Copenhagen: towards tolerance

The situation of the imperial legation chapel in Copenhagen differed in several aspects from the one in Stockholm. Primarily as a result of the specific confessional development that the Kingdom of Denmark had undergone in the first half of the seventeenth century, the Catholic legation chapels in the residence of the Oldenburg dynasty had a freer status. As in the case of the Kingdom of Sweden, a general rescript from 1613 applied that was intended to ensure state-guaranteed mono-confessionalism. However, as a result of adverse developments in foreign policy after the Thirty Years' War and the confessional tepidness of the ruler, Frederick III, the large Catholic community enjoyed such religious freedom as had no parallel in Scandinavia.[19] The ruling Lutheran elite treated the Catholic minority as a necessary evil that would always be a part of the public space.

Furthermore, in the 1650s, foreign Catholic envoys lobbied successfully at the Danish court to guarantee religious freedoms in the Danish towns of Altona and Lykstad (Glückstadt). As a result, on the periphery of the kingdom, at the heel of the Jutland peninsula, two islands of religious freedom came into being where, over the following years, Catholic mission stations operated without any restrictions.[20] The representatives of the imperial embassy in Copenhagen kept up unusually lively contacts with this Catholic community. Some Catholic envoys chose their legation chaplains from the clergy in Altona and Lykstad. Theodor Bothe, who had previously been a long-serving missionary in Lykstad, was one of those chosen to serve Georg von Plettenberg. Another significant missionary on the Jutland peninsula was a Jesuit, Heinrich Kircher, who in 1666 joined the staff of the French embassy in Copenhagen headed by Hugues de Terlon. The Jesuit missionary in Altona, Wilhelm Godefried, maintained an exceptionally large social network characterised by mutual benefits, and in 1658 he negotiated with the imperial envoy in Copenhagen, Johann von Goess, for financial support for the construction of a Catholic church.[21]

Compared with the situation in Stockholm, the Catholic minority in Copenhagen enjoyed considerable freedom. According to the estimates of certain imperial envoys and legation chaplains, there were approximately 500 Catholics on the central island of Sjælland over the course of the second half of the seventeenth century.[22] This religious community made extensive use of the Catholic chapels, which during that period had been created primarily as a part of the French, imperial, and Spanish embassies. Some legation chaplains, such as Henrik van den Linden, Sigismund Merkwart, Heinrich Kircher, and Johann Sterck, served successively at the embassies of Catholic diplomats, where they offered their services and performed the liturgy in various languages. On the initiative of the Spanish and imperial legation chapels, there was even created a register for recording burials, weddings, and baptisms of the individual members of the Danish Catholic community.[23] The unusually favourable and, to a certain extent, tolerant confessional environment, which was primarily guaranteed by the domestic policy of the ruling dynasty, led Emperor Leopold I to consider buying a house with an extensively furnished chapel within the Copenhagen city walls. In the end, the French court implemented similar plans before the Habsburgs. In 1671, represented by the ambassador, Hugues de Terlon, the French received permission to establish a permanent embassy with a spacious chapel and an adjoining graveyard.[24] Leopold I realised his former intention more than ten years later. The first long-term imperial chapel was set up in 1682 in the house situated on the most frequented street directing to the royal palace (lot Købmagergade 42).[25]

Imperial chapels in Dresden: between tolerance and conflict

In Saxony, there was a somewhat different situation. It was, on the one hand, the birthplace and stronghold of the Lutheran Reformation, where the local authorities and Dresden city council zealously guarded the orthodoxy of the inhabitants. On the other hand, the electors, Johann Georg II, Johann Georg III, and his sons, were known for their love of Italian music, theatre, and opera. They employed many Catholic foreigners, primarily of

Italian origin (artists), but also French (servants and cooks) and even Croats (guards).[26] These people were permitted by the electors to attend Catholic Masses in the chapels of the envoys in Dresden. In 1688, Johann Georg III even asked the imperial envoy to employ an Italian-speaking cleric instead of his own chaplain. The elector had a special area in that envoy's chapel assigned to his 'star' singer, Margherita Salicola, and even allowed the Catholic chaplain to come to his court and give the last rites to a Catholic servant, the popular bandmaster Carlo Pallavicini, in 1688.[27]

Documents survive concerning the operation of a chapel by imperial envoys in Dresden from the 1660s. The first diplomat to establish a chapel was evidently Georg von Plettenberg in 1665–1667. It was maintained by his successors, Heinrich Julius Baron Blum (1667–1672), Johann Philipp von Lamberg (1682–1684), Benedikt Urban von Gallenstein (1684–1685), Haro Burkhard Fridag Baron Gödens (1685–1686), Johann Markus Count von Clary-Aldringen (1686–1694), and Alois Thomas von Harrach (1694–1696). Usually when an envoy was recalled, his household and chaplain also left for home, and the house the envoy had rented was no longer an embassy. When a new imperial representative came, in most cases he established a new embassy in a different house and set up a new chapel there. In fact, every envoy brought a different chaplain, but we do not know all their names. We have information about the chaplain of Baron Blum, who in 1670 was Bernard Zeferin, but he acted incognito in Saxony, and in public used the name Karl Safir. He officially acted as the envoy's secretary, and therefore wore secular clothing in Dresden. Martin Gottseer, the Jesuit we mentioned above for the case of Sweden, held the office of chaplain with Count Lamberg. For the envoys Baron Gödens and Count Clary-Aldringen, for nearly ten years the legation chaplain was Matthäus Joseph Vitzk (1660–1713), a native of Wittichenau in Lusatia and later dean of the collegiate chapter in Bautzen, who was not a member of the Jesuit order.[28]

However, although the chapel of the imperial envoy in Dresden essentially operated continually, the city council and local diet exerted constant pressure to limit its activities just to the household of the imperial envoy or selected courtiers of the elector, although in practice the elector's crypto-Catholic subjects also went to Mass. Thus, from 1676 onwards, there were sometimes municipal patrols near the building where the imperial envoy lived, and suspected visitors were arrested. At times, the patrols acted excessively, as they did in 1683 and 1685, when they caused a diplomatic incident by arresting members of the envoy's household, although they let them go immediately, claiming they had not known who they were. Then, in 1695, the elector banned the holding of Catholic services during the imperial envoy's absence, at which time he was represented only by the legation secretary. In such a case, Mass continued to be celebrated behind closed doors, although the subjects of the Duke of Saxony were not allowed to attend. These waves of great pressure on the household of the imperial envoy were followed by times of tolerance, when once again the people secretly returned to the chapel.[29] There are records showing that during the time of Count Harrach, approximately 100 people attended the service in the legation chapel in the winter and 150–200 in the summer, which equates to about 1 per cent of the inhabitants of Dresden.[30] According to the estimates of the extraordinary imperial envoy, Count Christoph Dietmar von Schallenberg, in 1689 more than 300 Catholics were living in the *Residenzstadt* of the Dukes of Saxony, including servants of the elector himself.[31]

A qualitatively different situation occurred at the end of the seventeenth century after 1697, when the elector, Friedrich August, converted to Catholicism in connection with his election as Polish king. Although the majority of the city's inhabitants remained Lutheran, the elector set up his own Catholic chapel for his court. In general, the situation of the chapel of the imperial envoy then improved significantly, which is shown by the attention paid to it by the king's governor (*Statthalter*) of Catholic faith, Prince Anton Egon von Fürstenberg-Heiligenberg, who regularly attended it.[32]

Problematical position of confessional minorities and main reasons for conflicts

As has been indicated, the coexistence of the Catholic legation chapels with a confessionally hostile population was far from ideal. Breaking rescripts of the host governments regulating the rights and duties of the legation chapels, as it happened in many cases, provided a reason for interventions of varying intensity. For the entire seventeenth and eighteenth centuries, the confessional majority felt a direct threat from the religious minority within their midst. This fear was made all the stronger by the conversion of some leading members of the ruling dynasties. The most famous convert of the seventeenth century was, of course, Christina of Sweden, who in 1654 was baptised into the Catholic Church in the Tyrolean city of Innsbruck. Other similar cases undoubtedly include the conversion to Catholicism by the prominent brother-in-law of the Danish king, Corfitz Ulfeldt, or the aforementioned Saxon elector, who moved closer to gaining the Polish throne through this step. Sadly, all these triumphs of Catholic conversion caused considerable problems for the secret or tolerated Catholic minority in the residences of Protestant sovereigns. It also made the position of the legation chaplains significantly more difficult.[33]

Naturally, the worsening conditions for holding services in the envoys' chapels were also caused by a cooling off of mutual diplomatic relations. Certain measures placing strict restrictions on members of confessional minorities also came about during power upheavals and wars. Catholics were viewed as agents of the papacy and traitors who, through their activities, were undermining the less than solid foundations of the Kingdom of Denmark. Not even the intervention and protection of the French, Spanish, and imperial diplomats who were at the time present in the capital could stop the adverse development of the situation. In the end, even Catholic diplomats had to take steps to protect the embassy and to disallow 'undesirables' entrance to their houses. Moreover, the number of Catholics in the Kingdom of Denmark grew greatly during the war, as a result of the influx of foreign soldiers.[34] For example, this intolerable state worsened at the end of 1659, when Sjælland experienced an acute shortage of food, timber, and other basic commodities necessary for the smooth operation of a foreign embassy. In his official report written from Copenhagen, the imperial envoy, Johann von Goess, summed up the situation concerning the persecution of Catholics by the Danish government and the terrible conditions in the residence: 'The army is so large that the poor soldiers come into my house and bewail their dying of hunger.'[35]

From many aspects, the measures were similar in Vienna in 1683, when the siege by the Turkish army was expected. The general dislike on the part of the Catholic elites against the expansive activities of the embassy chapels of the Swedish, Danish, and Saxony envoys resulted in the issue of a rescript, by which all Protestants who were not members of foreign embassies were banned from participating in embassy services. The frequent complaints of the nuncio and the city council regarding primarily the religious services held in the house of the Swedish envoy, Gabriel Oxenstierna, provided the impetus for these disciplinary measures. This scion of a noble Swedish family had a large chapel set up in his rented house within the city walls. According to the testimony of several people making denunciations, around 1,000 people could fit in. The most prominent members of this Lutheran community included several representatives of the Aulic council (*Reichshofrat*) and their families. The Danish and Swedish envoys were particularly interested in these imperial courtiers, from whom they gained information and who for them represented important connections to the court.[36] Since the end of the Thirty Years' War, that practice in the Swedish embassy had been a thorn in the flesh of several leading Catholic courtiers headed by the religiously zealous Emperor Leopold I. The imperial rescript of 1683, issued primarily as a reaction to the services held at the Swedish embassy, made the already bad conditions the Lutheran community had to bear in Lower Austria even worse.[37]

As early modern diplomatic relations were to a significant extent governed by the laws of reciprocity, imperial envoys in Protestant areas could expect a similar reaction from the part of the host government. For example, the imperial envoy in Stockholm, Michael Franz von Althann, was informed in detail of the situation in Vienna, both through official reports and also from the Lord High Chancellor of Sweden, Bengt Oxenstierna, and his private correspondence network. Count von Althann was thus instructed not to give any cause for similar interventions and to stop his chaplain, ministrants, and servants from getting involved. In spite of the frequent protests of Gabriel Oxenstierna at the Viennese court, where he pointed to the same practice in the house of the imperial envoy in Stockholm, the Swedish court did not intervene to any significant extent against Althann and the legation chapel.[38]

There were several reasons for such a restrained approach, but the most fundamental appeared to be the attempts of the Kingdom of Sweden to initiate a closer cooperation with the Habsburg monarchy at the start of the 1680s. After the lost Scanian War, when, along with Louis XIV, Sweden got involved in a war with Denmark and Brandenburg, further steps were taken in the direction of a new domestic policy and regrouping of forces, where the traditionally pro-French Kingdom of Sweden turned to the side of the Habsburgs. It was the High Chancellor, Bengt Oxenstierna, who was to become the guarantor of this new direction of foreign policy and who headed the pro-imperial faction at the royal court.[39]

The Swedish ruling circles in all probability did not take steps against the imperial envoy in 1683 because of the utter difference of either confessional subculture in early modern Stockholm and Vienna. While there were approximately 300 members of the Stockholm Catholic community throughout the entire second half of the seventeenth century, in the residence of the Austrian Habsburgs there were several thousand Protestant souls. Thus, for the entire period under examination, the number of members representing the confessional minority was an important factor influencing the reciprocity of interventions against the legation chapels and chaplains.[40]

We reach similar conclusions if we study the conflicts characterising Danish–imperial relations after the Thirty Years' War. The Copenhagen Catholic community also consisted of just a few hundred members, which gave rise to a significant disproportion between the confessional minorities in both capitals. However, in contrast with their northern neighbour, the Danish kings had a powerful ace in the hole in the form of the two royal cities of Altona and Lykstad, where the right to inviolability of the local, quite large, Catholic community was guaranteed. Danish envoys in Vienna, who along with the envoys of the Swedish kings were among the most important protectors of the Lutheran community in Lower Austria, also operated on the basis of this beneficial foreign policy.[41]

We can document the extraordinarily frequent conflicts with the Viennese court using the example of the long-serving Danish envoy, Andreas Pauli von Liliencron, who came to the court of Leopold I in 1663, just as the new Imperial–Turkish War was starting. In that time, there occurred one of the many important tests of the stability of the Habsburg monarchy. Soon after his arrival, Baron von Liliencron had a spacious chapel set up at today's Neuer Markt, near the burial place of the Habsburg family. The large-scale participation in regular services held in the Danish envoy's chapel once again caused many conflicts, which we see throughout the entire 1660s. The most dramatic turn of events came in 1663, when the Danish legation's chaplain, Bartius, was actually forced to flee to nearby Pressburg (Bratislava), where there were more acceptable conditions for the celebration of Lutheran services. In addition, in this case, the young emperor, Leopold I, forbade with immediate effect services in the house of Andreas Pauli von Liliencron, provoking an angry reaction from the Danish court, which pointed out that the rights of the Catholic minorities in Altona and Lykstad were not interfered with. In the end, Leopold I was forced to rescind the strict orders, and as a result the Danish legation chaplain could return to Vienna safely.[42] The activity of the Danish legation chapel in the house of Baron von Liliecron, however, caused regular waves of displeasure, fanned primarily by the papal nuncio present in Vienna. The nuncio saw himself as an important protector of the Catholic Church in the territory of the Habsburg monarchy. As a result, there were also regular interventions against the Danish chapel with varying degrees of intensity between 1665 and 1667.[43]

The staff of the Catholic legation chapels in the capital city of the Danish Oldenburgs also managed to cause conflicts in a similar way. For example, in April 1679, the aforementioned Jesuit, Johann Sterck, had to face the displeasure of the royal authorities once again. As one of the leading representatives of the imperial embassy, Sterck had caused a serious conflict that, although it did not lead to such a dramatic course of events as the dispute with the Swedes seven years earlier, to a significant extent damaged the already fragile Danish–imperial relations at the end of the 1670s. Everything occurred in a turbulent atmosphere, when at the same time the Danish envoy in Madrid, Jörgen Reedtz, as well as his wife, son, and three daughters, converted to Catholicism to the great joy of the Spanish Habsburgs. In Copenhagen, Johann Sterck was accused by the local Lutheran clergy of offering the sacraments outside the building of the embassy. This time it did not involve the last rites being given to a dying Catholic against the will of his wife, but the baptism of two children. However, before the entire dispute could flare up with greater intensity, the legation chaplain, Sterck, escaped from the country with the aid of several Catholic envoys. As he had been forced to do seven years previously, he now moved south again, this time to Berlin, where he took up the role of legation chaplain at the newly opened embassy headed by the imperial envoy, Johann Philipp von Lamberg.[44]

From the examples outlined above, we can see that the most serious cause of conflicts between the Catholic legation chaplains and their Lutheran hosts was primarily to administer certain sacraments outside the embassy building. Moreover, administering the last rites and the baptism of newborns remained a serious and severe incident in such disputes for the entire period. The conduct of legation chaplains also gave rise to conflict between the two different confessions in Dresden. One example is a case in 1688, during the absence of the imperial envoy, Count Clary-Aldringen. Then the Catholic courtiers of the elector, Johann Georg III, managed to ensure that the envoy's chaplain, who stayed in the city, secretly visited the dying wife of the elector's French valet, Mr de la Croix, and administered the last sacraments to her. The chaplain allegedly was happy to do it because he knew that 'the patient's husband is traveling with the elector and is held in high esteem by him [the elector]'. But unfortunately, local clerics found out and complained about this behaviour to the elector, saying that the chaplain was inveigling his way into the homes of burghers and turning the heads of faithful Lutherans. The elector took heed of them and used the case to exert further pressure on the imperial diplomats. He summoned the envoy's personal secretary and informed him that the chaplain's conduct was unacceptable, that it would be investigated, and furthermore that during the envoy's absence he had no right to celebrate the Catholic Mass in the embassy at all. The elector warned that if the Masses continued, the secretary and all the envoy's domestics would be arrested because, as the envoy later wrote to Vienna, 'my house was a civil house and would be in the absence of the envoy, even if he paid for it, not be considered anything else'.[45] The tension, which lasted several weeks, gradually eased, and Emperor Leopold I then resolved the entire situation in the spring of 1689 by appointing the personal secretary of the frequently absent envoy, Clary-Aldringen, as the legation secretary, which conferred upon him the necessary diplomatic immunity.[46]

Conclusions

The first legation chapels at imperial embassies in Protestant countries of Northern and Central Europe were founded during the 1650s and 1660s, and from that time on they served as places of worship in the capitals of Copenhagen, Dresden, and Stockholm more or less continuously. Originally, the imperial envoys sought out their chaplains only from the members of the Jesuit order who had missionary experience in Northern Europe, and with the Roman Curia having a significant say in their selection. From the 1670s onwards, however, the emperor limited the influence of the papal authorities, and from then on chaplains without missionary experience were selected, some of whom did not come from the Jesuit order – for example, Mayer in Sweden and Vitzk in Saxony.

In all three of the residences in question, the chaplains attempted to operate not only in the building of the embassy, where they celebrated the regular, legally acceptable Mass for the members of the envoy's household and his guests, but also outside the embassy. Incognito, with a secular identity as cover, they walked the streets of the cities and secretly attempted to attend to the welfare of local Catholics by administering the sacraments to them, in particular baptism and the last rites. In Dresden, they occasionally did this with the permission of Elector Johann Georg III, whose court hosted a large community of Catholic artists and other courtiers. The elector's tolerance went so far that in 1688, he requested that the imperial envoy employ an Italian-speaking chaplain whom his beloved artists would understand.

In all countries, the representatives of the Lutheran Church, the city councils, and the estates put pressure on the ruler to prevent Catholic chaplains acting in public. De facto rescripts were issued restricting the chaplains' behaviour, town council patrols performed checks to see if local crypto-Catholics were attending Masses, chaplains were occasionally arrested and deported (Sterck from Sweden and later Denmark), or Catholic Masses were actually completely forbidden in embassy buildings if a sufficiently accredited imperial envoy was not present in the country (Saxony 1688, 1695). The bans, nonetheless, never lasted long, because no ruler wanted his chapel in Vienna to be affected in the same way. Furthermore, in the capitals in question in the second half of the seventeenth century, no chapel of an imperial envoy was ever attacked and ransacked by a mob, as had happened earlier, in different locations.[47]

As the eighteenth century began, the imperial legation chapels in Protestant states faced fewer and fewer restrictions and less persecution on the part of the host nations. Although there were, from time to time, the usual clashes caused by the mutual conflicts of different confessions in a narrowly defined space, their outcomes and the consensus found in each case was then of a completely different nature, primarily as a result of the gradual establishment of the principle of extraterritoriality.

Notes

1 This study originated as part of the GA ČR's standard project No. 13-12939S entitled *Bohemian and Moravian Nobility in the Habsburg Diplomatic Service (1640–1740)*.
2 The work of Martin Scheutz, who for a long time has been dealing with the Lutheran subculture in Lower Austria and its specific confessional development, is an exception. Scheutz is one of the few to notice the important status of the Danish, Swedish, and Dutch embassy chapels in forming the identity of the Viennese Protestant community. See Martin Scheutz, 'Legalität und unterdrückte Religionsausübung: Niederleger, Reichshofräte, Gesandte und Legationsprediger. Protestantisches Leben in der Haupt- und Residenzstadt Wien im 17. und 18. Jahrhundert,' in *Geheimprotestantismus und evangelische Kirchen in der Habsburgermonarchie und im Erzstift Salzburg (17./18. Jahrhundert)*, ed. Rudolf Leeb et al. (Vienna: Böhlau, 2008), 209–36. For Saxony, the research of Alexander Schunka, who drew attention to the role of the chapel of the imperial envoy in the development of the Catholic minority in Dresden and the surrounding area, is similarly valuable. See Alexander Schunka, *Gäste, die bleiben: Zuwanderer in Kursachsen und der Oberlausitz im 17. und frühen 18. Jahrhundert* (Hamburg: Lit Verlag, 2006), 180–94.
3 The basic information was summarised by Klaus Müller, *Das kaiserliche Gesandtschaftswesen im Jahrhundert nach dem Westfälischen Frieden 1648–1740* (Bonn: Röhrscheid, 1976), 152–56; Jiří Kubeš et al., *V zastoupení císaře. Česká a moravská aristokracie v habsburské diplomacii 1640–1740* [On Behalf of the Emperor. Bohemian and Moravian aristocracy in Habsburg diplomacy 1640–1740] (Prague: Nakladatelství Lidové noviny, 2018), 124–45. For The Hague, cf. Daniel Legutke, 'Die kaiserliche Gesandtschaftskapelle in Den Haag 1658–1718: Konfession und Säkularisierung in mikrohistorischer Sicht,' in *Stadt und Religion in der frühen Neuzeit: Soziale Ordnungen und ihre Repräsentationen*, ed. Vera Isaiasz et al. (Frankfurt/Main et al.: Campus, 2007), 245–74. Concerning the chapel of the imperial envoy in London in brief, cf. Jiří Hrbek, *Barokní Valdštejnové v Čechách 1640–1740* [The Baroque Waldsteins in Bohemia 1640–1740] (Prague: Nakladatelství Lidové noviny, 2013), 532–45. For more detail on Dresden, see Silke Marburg, 'Gesandte als Grenzganger: Residenzstädtische Repräsentationskultur und die Konstruktion

religiöser Exklaven unter Kurfürst Johann Georg II. von Sachsen,' in *Grenzen und Grenzüberschreitungen: Bilanz und Perspektiven der Frühneuzeitforschung*, ed. Christine Roll et al. (Cologne et al.: Böhlau, 2010), 199–213; Jiří Kubeš, 'Kaple císařských vyslanců v Drážďanech v druhé půli 17. století,' [Chapels of Imperial Envoys in Dresden in the Second Half of the 17th Century] *Folia Historica Bohemica* 30 (2015), 127–56. For Copenhagen and Stockholm, see Martin Bakeš, 'Shaping the Danish and Imperial Legation Chapels in Vienna and Copenhagen during the period after the Thirty Years' War,' *Theatrum historiae* 19 (2016), 73–94; id., 'Legační kaplani ve službách císařských vyslanců ve Stockholmu ve druhé polovině 17. století,' [Legation Chaplains in the Services of Imperial Envoys in Stockholm in the Second Half of the 17th Century] *Český časopis historický* 114 (2016), 941–67.

4 Johann Baptist Sägmüller, 'Der Begriff des exercitium religionis publicum, exercitium religionis privatum und der devotio domestica im Westfälischen Frieden,' *Theologische Quartalschrift*, 90 (1908), 225–279; Johann Jacob Moser, *Grund-Säze von dem offentlichen, privat- und Haus-Gottesdienst nebst einiger Erläuterung derselbigen aus offentlichen Staats-Handlungen* (Stuttgart: without publisher, 1765), 35: '[...] *da ich zwar keine offentliche Kirche habe, aber doch einen Prediger kan kommen lassen, der den Gottesdienst in meinem Haus verrichtet.*'

5 Abraham de Wicquefort, *L'Ambassadeur et Ses Fonction* (Den Haag: J. & D. Steucker, 1680), 880–81; François de Callières, *De la manière de négocier avec les Souverains* (Amsterdam: La Compagnie, 1716), 101.

6 Cf. Benjamin J. Kaplan, *Divided by Faith: Religious Conflict and the Practice of Toleration in Early Modern Europe* (Cambridge, MA and London: Harvard University Press, 2007), 183–90.

7 Cf. *Repertorium der diplomatischen Vertreter aller Länder seit dem Westfälischen Frieden (1648)*, vol. I, 1648–1715, ed. Ludwig Bittner, Lothar Groß (Oldenburg, Berlin: G. Stalling, 1936). For more detailed information about Lisola's missions, see Alfred Francis Pribram, *Franz Paul Freiherr von Lisola (1613–1674) und die Politik seiner Zeit* (Leipzig: Veit & comp., 1894), in particular 11–52, 293–307, 366–412.

8 The oldest known document concerning the existence of an imperial embassy chapel in a Protestant country dates from 1645: in the house of the resident Franz Paul Lisola, two English clerics were found and arrested, who had celebrated Mass in Lisola's chapel for English Catholics. Cf. William Raleigh Trimble, 'The Embassy chapel question, 1625–1660,' *The Journal of Modern History* 18 (1946), vol. 2, 97–107, esp. 102.

9 On the basis of a good knowledge of Vatican sources, the missionary activities of the clergy in the first years following the Thirty Years' War were documented by Georg Denzler, *Die Propagandakongregation in Rom und die Kirche in Deutschland im ersten Jahrzehnt nach dem Westfälischen Frieden* (Paderborn: Bonifacius-Druckerei, 1969).

10 The development of the concept of international law in regard to extraterritoriality and the guarantee of the rights of embassy chapels was, for example, covered by the works of Benjamin J. Kaplan, 'Diplomacy and Domestic Devotion: Embassy Chapels and the Toleration of Religious Dissent in Early Modern Europe,' *Journal of Early Modern History* 6 (2002), 341–61.

11 Cf. Hillard von Thiessen, 'Switching Roles in Negotiation, Levels of Diplomatic Communication between Pope Paul V Borghese (1605–1621) and the Ambassadors of Philip III,' in *Paroles de négociateurs: L'entretien dans la pratique diplomatique de la fin du Moyen âge à la fin du XIXe siècle*, ed. Stefano Andretta et al. (Rome: École française de Rome, 2010), 151–72, here 156–57.

12 The nuncios in Vienna also exerted considerable pressure on Leopold I in these matters. As guarantors of the Catholic faith, the papal representatives also monitored the activities of Protestant chapels in Vienna and regularly submitted complaints to leading Viennese courtiers. Cf., for example, Artur Levinson, 'Nuntiaturberichte vom Kaiserhofe Leopolds I. (1657 bis 1669),' *Archiv für österreichische Geschichte* 103 (1913), 547–831. On the other hand, neither the Swedish nor Danish envoys in Vienna hesitated in describing some nuncios as disturbers of confessional coexistence. These accusations are primarily found in the reports of the long-term Danish resident Andreas Pauli von Liliencron. Cf., for example, Rigsarkivet København, Tyske kancelli, Wien – diplomatisk repræsentation, Kart. 31, reports from 19 June 1666 and 10 April 1667 (all from Vienna).

13 As the protector of the Catholic community in Sweden, Visconti described the situation in his report to the representatives of the Congregation de Propaganda Fide: '*Nella Svezia bolle un gran vigore contro l'esercizio Cattolico, ne altri sacerdoti vi vengono tollerati che i familiari e i Cappellani degli Ambasciatori, ne si permette a quei del Paese, ovvero ai forastieri fatti cittadini, di frequentare le loro Cappelle. Quei sacerdoti vengono eletti dagli istessi ablegati a suo beneplacito, e sono nutriti alle loro spese, vanno e vengono con i medesimi e seguitano la corte per le Provincie del Regno e percio possano operate poco.*' Cf. Michael F. Feldkamp, 'Päpstliche Missionsbemühungen in Schweden während des 17. und 18. Jahrhunderts,' in *Ab Aquilone. Nordic Studies in Honour and Memory of Leonard E. Boyle, O.P.*, ed. Marie-Louise Rodén (Stockholm: Svenska Riksarkivet, 1999), 166.

14 See Bakeš, 'Shaping the Danish and Imperial Legation Chapels,' 73–94.

15 Joseph Stöcklein, *Allerhand so Lehr- als Geist-reiche Brief, Schrifften und Reis-Beschreibung, welche von denen Missionariis der Gesellschafft Jesu aus beyden Indien, und andern uber Meer gelegenen Ländern, seit Anno 1642 bis 1726 in Europa angelangt sind*, vol. 17 (Augspurg and Grätz: Philipp/Martin/und Johann Veith seel. Erben, 1732), 25–40.

16 We can find details of this conflict in the letters of the former imperial legation secretary, Johann Eberhard Hövel. Hövel viewed this conflict primarily as a realignment of forces driven by a pro-French party that was headed by the Swedish chancellor, Magnus de La Gardie. Cf. Johann Eberhard Hövel to Johann Walderode von Eckhausen, Stockholm, 26th February, 1671, Österreichisches Staatsarchiv Wien, Haus-, Hof- und Staatsarchiv (hereafter OeStA, HHStA), Staatenabteilungen (hereafter StA), Schweden, Diplomatische Korrespondenz, Kart. 5.

17 See Johann Schmedeman, *Kongl. stadgar, förordningar, bref och resolutioner, ifrån åhr 1528 intil 1701 ...* (Stockholm, 1706), 608. This rescript, called *Kongl[ige] Maj[estät] Declaration och Förklaring öfwer then frie Religions öfning*, is in the Saxon State Archive in Dresden. See Königlich-schwedische Deklaration wegen des den auswärtigen Königen, Fürsten und der Staaten Abgesandten und Residenten zugelassenen freien Religionsexerzitiums, Stockholm, 22nd February, 1671, Hauptstaatsarchiv Dresden, Geheimer Rat, loc. 10426/43.

18 Bakeš, 'Legační kaplani,' 949–50.

19 Many historians have studied the Catholic minority in Denmark; in their works, many frequently mentioned the crucial status of embassy chapels for the structure of this Catholic community. See, for example, Johannes Hansen, *Sankt Ansgars Kirke i hundrede Aar: Fra Kejserligt Kongeligt Østerrigsk Gesandtskabskapel til Danske Katholikkers Domkirke* (København: Skt. Ansgars Menighed, 1942), 89–102, or more recently Preben Hampton Frosell,

Diplomati og religion: Gesandterne for de katolske magter og deres kirkepolitik i Danmark c. 1622–1849 (København: C. A. Reitzel, 1990).

20 Lebrecht Dreves summarised missionary activities of Catholic clerics in the area of Lower Saxony and the Jutland peninsula in an exceptional study, especially for its compilation of facts. See Lebrecht Dreves, *Geschichte der katholischen Gemeinden zu Hamburg und Altona: Ein Beitrag zur Geschichte der nordischen Missionen* (Schaffhausen: Hurter, 1866), 76–111.

21 Reports of Johann von Goess of the years 1658–1661, OeStA, HHStA, StA, Dänemark, Diplomatische Korrespondenz, Kart. 11 and 15, here for example the report of 19th November, 1658. For more general information about the state of the Catholic community, see the report of 19th November, 1661 (all Copenhagen).

22 Feldkamp, 'Päpstliche Missionsbemühungen,' 153.

23 These registers have survived to this day in Sct. Ansgars Kirkes Arkiv, 1) Copulationsbuch 1647–1771. 2) Liber Baptizatorum Hafniae in Exercitio Catholico per Missionarios Societas Jesu. 3) Liber Defunctorum 1649–1730.

24 Peter Willemoes Becker, *Samlinger til Danmarks Historie under Kong Frederik den Tredies Regiering, II.* (Kiöbenhavn: Deichmann, 1847), 73. In his reports, the Danish envoy, Liliencron, described similar attempts of Emperor Leopold I. See the report of Andreas Pauli von Liliencron, Vienna, 9th May, 1663, Rigsarkivet København, Tyske kancelli, Wien – diplomatisk repræsentation, Kart. 30.

25 See Gesandtschaftskapellen Kopenhagen, Berlin, London etc. (1650–1778), OeStA, HHStA, Staatskanzlei, Verträge betreffende Akten, Kart. 9.

26 Schunka, *Gäste, die bleiben*, 183–84; Mary E. Frandsen, *Crossing Confessional Boundaries: The Patronage of Italian Sacred Music in Seventeenth-Century Dresden* (Oxford: Oxford University Press, 2006); Uta Deppe, *Die Festkultur am Dresdner Hofe Johann Georgs II. von Sachsen (1660–1679)* (Kiel: Verlag Ludwig, 2006); Michael Walter, 'Der Fall Salicola oder Die Sängerin als symbolisches Kapital,' *Zeitschrift für Literatur- und Theatersoziologie*, 6 (2011): 5–34.

27 Kubeš, 'Kaple císařských vyslanců,' 133, 142, 144.

28 Kubeš, 'Kaple císařských vyslanců,' 137. For more about Zeferin, see letters of Baron Blum to Prince Ferdinand of Dietrichstein, Dresden, 8th and 24th June, 1670, Moravský zemský archiv v Brně [Moravian Land Archives Brno], Rodinný archiv Ditrichštejnů [Dietrichstein Family Archive], inv. No. 716, Kart. 234, fols. 176, 178–179. For more detail about Vitzk, see Theodor Neumann, 'Chronicon venerandi capituli et collegiatae ecclesiae Budissinensis auctore Matth. Jos. Vitzk Decano nec non Administratore Ecclesiastico utramque er Lusatiam,' *Neues lausitzisches Magazin* 33 (1857), 186–231, here 186–90.

29 Kubeš, 'Kaple císařských vyslanců.'

30 Schunka, *Gäste, die bleiben*, 187.

31 Kubeš, 'Kaple císařských vyslanců', 134; Schallenberg's report to the Emperor, Teplice, 26th April, 1689, OeStA, HHStA, Reichskanzlei, Diplomatische Akten, Dresden – Berichte, Kart. 3c.

32 See Philipp Hiltebrandt, 'Die Polnische Königswahl und die Konversion August des Starken,' *Quellen und Forschungen aus italienischen Archiven und Bibliotheken* 10 (1907), 152–215; Jochen Votsche, 'Anton Egon von Fürstenberg-Heiligenberg (1656–1716),' *Sächsische Biographie*. Accessed 4th November, 2018, http://saebi.isgv.de/biografie/Anton_Egon_von_Fürstenberg-Heiligenberg_ (1656-1716). Additionally, cf. the reports of the legation secretary Johann Jahn to the Emperor, Dresden, 16th August and 6th September, 1697, OeStA, HHStA, Reichskanzlei, Diplomatische Akten, Dresden – Berichte, Kart. 4b.

33 Helge Clausen, 'Konvertiten in Dänemark im 17. und 18. Jahrhundert,' in *300 Jahre katholische Gemeinden in Mecklenburg: Geschichte und Bedeutung in*

der Nordeuropäischen Diaspora, ed. Georg Diederich (Schwerin: Heinrich-Theissing-Institut, 2009), 34–41.

34 In his travelogue for 1690, Martin Gottseer mentioned the presence of former Catholic mercenaries on the islands of Sjælland and Fyn: 'We stayed in Niburg at the coast of Fünen towards Seeland during the night, where the Swedish have been beaten by the Danish in 1659. Several Catholic soldiers, employed in Danish services, attended my mass at this place, some even went to confession and received the holy communion.' Original: '*Wir bliben zu Niburg am ufer von Fünen gegen Seeland über nacht, allwo die Schweden von den Dännemärckern im jahr 1659 aufs haupt seynd geschlagen worden. An diesem ort haben verschidene catholische soldaten, so in dänischen diensten stehen, meinem gottsdienst beygewohnt, auch theils ihre sünden gebeichtet und das göttliche abendmahl empfangen.*' Stöcklein, *Allerhand so Lehr- als Geist-reiche Brief*, 179.

35 '*Soldatesca ist so gross, dass mir die arme soldaten ins hauss khommen und klagen, dass sie* [an] *hunger sterben.*' Report of Baron von Goess, Copenhagen, 15th October, 1659, OeStA, HHStA, StA, Dänemark, Diplomatische Korrespondenz, Kart. 11.

36 The other side's viewpoint has been preserved in the reports of Gabriel Oxenstierna, the Swedish envoy. His letters also describe contacts with certain members of the Aulic council. See report by Gabriel Oxenstiern, Vienna, 24th January, 1683, Riksarkivet Stockholm, Diplomatica Germanica, Kart. 307. The *Reichshofrat* represented the supreme court for matters of individual imperial fiefdoms. In the course of the Thirty Years' War, only Catholics sat as judges, but during the Westphalian peace negotiations the Protestant estates once again ensured that non-Catholics could participate in the proceedings of the council. After the reforms of 1654, there were a total of six Protestant *Reichshofräte* (Aulic counsellors) that maintained close contacts with Protestant envoys appointed to Vienna. Cf. Oswald von Gschließer, *Der Reichshofrat: Bedeutung und Verfassung, Schicksal und Besetzung einer obersten Reichsbehörde von 1559 bis 1806* (Wien: Holzhausen, 1942).

37 The 1683 rescript represents a significant milestone in relations between the Protestant legation chapels and the Viennese government. Older Austrian historiography appreciated the importance of this document and correctly characterised it mainly as a means for disciplining registered Lutherans present at the imperial court. But without exception, older works interpret this important imperial rescript without a knowledge of Swedish, Danish, Brandenburg, and Saxony archival documents characterising the given problem from the other end. Out of the most recent works touching lightly upon the relationship of the Austrian Lutheran community and foreign embassies, Matthias Schnettger excels with 'Ist Wien eine Messe wert? Protestantische Funktionseliten am Kaiserhof im 17. und 18. Jahrhundert,' in *Grenzen und Grenzüberschreitungen: Bilanz und Perspektiven der Frühneuzeitforschung*, ed. Christine Roll et al. (Köln et al.: Böhlau, 2010), 599–633. Grete Mecenseffy, *Geschichte des Protestantismus in Österreich* (Graz – Köln: Hermann Böhlau's Nachfolger, 1956), 181–83, offers a general description of the complicated relationship of the Catholic majority to the Protestant minority in Vienna after the Thirty Years' War. The older work already mentioned probably gives the most detailed and focused account of the 1683 rescript. See G. Loesche, *Geschichte des Protestantismus im vormaligen und im neuen Österreich* (Wien: Manz, 1930), 123–25.

38 Letter of Gabriel Oxenstierna, Vienna, 10th January, 1683, OeStA Wien, HHStA, StA, Schweden, Diplomatische Korrespondenz, Varia, Kart. 6.

39 Of research literature written in English, the work of Michael Roberts remains unsurpassed, but in its syntheses it deals only with the political history of Scandinavia. See, for example, Michael Roberts, *The Swedish Imperial Experience*

1560–1718 (Cambridge: Cambridge University Press, 1979), 123–56. The latest work in Swedish is a remarkable eight-volume work that examines only the cultural history of the Kingdom of Sweden. See Nils Erik Villstrand et al., *Sveriges historia 1600–1721* (Stockholm: Norstedts, 2011).

40 In terms of numbers of participants, the Catholic Masses celebrated at the imperial embassy during the time of the envoy Althann were definitely not comparable to the services in the chapel of Gabriel Oxenstierna in Vienna. According to Althann's reports, approximately 15–20 Catholics who were not members of the embassy came together in his house for the regular Mass, so the total number of participants must have been around 50. See report of Michael Franz von Althann, Stockholm, 6th February, 1683, OeStA, HHStA, StA, Schweden, Kart. 6.

41 Swedish and Danish envoys protected the rights of Lutherans in Silesia and Hungary to a great extent. At the embassies, they did not hesitate to receive delegations complaining mainly of the attempts at recatholicisation of the ruling Habsburgs and breaches of provisions of the Treaties of Westphalia. The envoys saw the protection of Protestant minorities as their responsibility due to the fact that on the basis of the Treaty of Münster, Sweden in particular was meant to be the main guarantor for the Lutherans living in the territories of the Habsburg monarchy. In Silesia, the Vasa kingdom even undertook to build three so-called churches of peace (*Friedenskirchen*), intended to exclusively serve the local Protestant community. Out of the extensive literature, an excellent overview is provided by Robert J. W. Evans, *Vznik habsburské monarchie 1550–1700* [The Making of the Habsburg Monarchy, 1550–1700] (Praha: Argo, 2003), 148, 174.

42 Report of Andreas Pauli von Liliencron, Vienna, 31st May, 1663, Rigsarkivet København, Tyske kancelli, Wien – diplomatisk repræsentation, Kart. 30.

43 In his reports to Rome, the nuncio at the court of Emperor Leopold I, Giulio Spinola, describes the immoderate nature of the services in the Danish legation chapel. See Levinson, 'Nuntiaturberichte vom Kaiserhof,' 246, 254. We again know the reaction of the other side through the reports the Danish envoy Liliencron sent to Copenhagen. Cf., for example, reports from Vienna, 19th June, 1666, and 10th April, 1667, Rigsarkivet København, Tyske kancelli, Wien – diplomatisk repræsentation, Kart. 31.

44 After his departure from Berlin, the Jesuit Johann Sterck died in Koblenz on the Rhine in 1692. Cf. Anton Pieper, *Die Propaganda Congregation und die nordischen Missionen im siebenzehnten Jahrhundert* (Köln: J. P. Bachem, 1886), 90; Troels Kardel and Paul Maquet, eds., *Nicolaus Steno: Biography and Original Papers of a 17th Century Scientist* (Berlin – Heidelberg: Springer Verlag, 2013), 311–12.

45 See the report of Clary-Aldringen to the emperor, Teplice, 3 July, 1688, OeStA Wien, HHStA, Reichskanzlei, Diplomatische Akten, Dresden – Berichte, Kart. 3c, where he states: '[...] *der patientin mann mit Ihr dh. dem churfürsten verreißet undt bey deroselben sonderlich angesehen.*'; '[...] *so were mein hauß ein bürgerliches hauß undt würde in absentia ablegati, ob er es gleich bezahlt, vor kein anders zuhalten.*'

46 Kubeš, 'Kaple císařských vyslanců', 142–45; id., 'Jan Marek z Clary a Aldringenu jako vyslanec Leopolda I. u saského kurfiřtského dvora na konci 17. století,' [Johann Marcus von Clary-Aldringen as an Envoy of Emperor Leopold I to Saxony at the End of the 17th Century] *Český časopis historický* 113 (2015), 346–80. For more details about the differences between personal and legation secretary, see Gottfried Stieve, *Europäisches Hof-Ceremoniel* (Leipzig: Johann Friedrich Gleditschens seel. Sohn, 1723), 341–43.

47 Müller, *Das kaiserliche Gesandtschaftswesen*, 154–55.

Bibliography

Archival sources

Hauptstaatsarchiv Dresden, Geheimer Rat, loc. 10426/43.
Moravský zemský archiv v Brně [Moravian Land Archives Brno], Rodinný archiv Ditrichštejnů [Dietrichstein Family Archive], inv. No. 716, Kart. 234.
Österreichisches Staatsarchiv Wien (OeStA), Haus-, Hof- und Staatsarchiv (HHStA), Reichskanzlei, Diplomatische Akten, Dresden – Berichte, Kart. 3c, 4b; Staatskanzlei, Verträge betreffende Akten, Kart. 9; Staatenabteilungen Schweden, Diplomatische Korrespondenz, Kart. 5, 6, Varia, Kart. 6; Staatenabteilungen Dänemark, Diplomatische Korrespondenz, Kart. 11, 15.
Rigsarkivet København, Tyske kancelli, Wien – diplomatisk repræsentation, Kart. 30, 31.
Riksarkivet Stockholm, Diplomatica Germanica, Kart. 307.
Sankt Ansgars Kirkes Arkiv, Copulationsbuch (1647–1771), Liber Baptizatorum Hafniae in Exercitio Catholico per Missionarios Societas Jesu (1650-1700), Liber Defunctorum (1649–1730).

Printed sources

Callières, François de. *De la manière de négocier avec les Souverains*. Amsterdam: La Compagnie, 1716.
Moser, Johann Jacob. *Grund-Säze von dem offentlichen, privat- und Haus-Gottesdienst nebst einiger Erläuterung derselbigen aus offentlichen Staats-Handlungen*. Stuttgart: [publisher not known], 1765.
Schmedeman, Johann. *Kongl. stadgar, förordningar, bref och resolutioner, ifrån åhr 1528 intil 1701 [...]*. Stockholm: Werner, 1706.
Stieve, Gottfried. *Europäisches Hof-Ceremoniel*. Leipzig: Johann Friedrich Gleditschens seel. Sohn, 1723.
Stöcklein, Joseph. *Allerhand so Lehr- als Geist-reiche Brief, Schrifften und Reis-Beschreibung, welche von denen Missionariis der Gesellschafft Jesu aus beyden Indien, und andern uber Meer gelegenen Ländern, seit Anno 1642 bis 1726 in Europa angelangt sind, Vol. 17*. Augspurg and Grätz: Philipp/Martin/und Johann Veith seel. Erben, 1732.
Wicquefort, Abraham de. *L'Ambassadeur et Ses Fonction*. Den Haag: J. & D. Steucker, 1680.

Literature

Bakeš, Martin. 'Legační kaplani ve službách císařských vyslanců ve Stockholmu ve druhé polovině 17. Století.' [Legation Chaplains in the Services of Imperial Envoys in Stockholm in the Second Half of the 17th Century] *Český časopis historický*, 114 (2016): 941–67.
Bakeš, Martin. 'Shaping the Danish and Imperial Legation Chapels in Vienna and Copenhagen during the Period after the Thirty Years' War.' *Theatrum historiae*, 19 (2016): 73–94.
Becker, Peter Willemoes. *Samlinger til Danmarks Historie under Kong Frederik den Tredies Regiering, II*. Kiöbenhavn: Deichmann, 1847.

Bittner, Ludwig and Groß, Lothar. *Repertorium der diplomatischen Vertreter aller Länder seit dem Westfälischen Frieden (1648). Vol. I: 1648–1715*. Oldenburg, Berlin: G. Stalling, 1936.

Clausen, Helge, 'Konvertiten in Dänemark im 17. und 18. Jahrhundert.' In *300 Jahre katholische Gemeinden in Mecklenburg: Geschichte und Bedeutung in der Nordeuropäischen Diaspora*, edited by Georg Diederich, 34–41. Schwerin: Heinrich-Theissing-Institut, 2009.

Denzler, Georg. *Die Propagandakongregation in Rom und die Kirche in Deutschland im ersten Jahrzehnt nach dem Westfälischen Frieden*. Paderborn: Bonifacius-Druckerei, 1969.

Deppe, Uta. *Die Festkultur am Dresdner Hofe Johann Georgs II. von Sachsen (1660–1679)*. Kiel: Verlag Ludwig, 2006.

Die Akten des Kaiserlichen Reichshofrats. 'Materialien und Literatur.' Accessed 4th November, http://reichshofratsakten.de/.

Dreves, Lebrecht. *Geschichte der katholischen Gemeinden zu Hamburg und Altona: Ein Beitrag zur Geschichte der nordischen Missionen*. Schaffhausen: Hurter, 1866.

Evans, Robert J. W. *Vznik habsburské monarchie 1550–1700* [The Making of the Habsburg Monarchy, 1550–1700]. Praha: Argo, 2003.

Feldkamp, Michael F. 'Päpstliche Missionsbemühungen in Schweden während des 17. und 18. Jahrhunderts.' In *Ab Aquilone: Nordic Studies in Honour and Memory of Leonard E. Boyle, O.P.*, edited by Marie-Louise Rodén, 149–68, Stockholm: Svenska Riksarkivet, 1999.

Frandsen, Mary. *Crossing Confessional Boundaries: The Patronage of Italian Sacred Music in Seventeenth-Century Dresden*. Oxford: Oxford University Press, 2006.

Frosell, Preben Hampton. *Diplomati og religion: Gesandterne for de katolske magter og deres kirkepolitik i Danmark c. 1622–1849*. København: C. A. Reitzel, 1990.

Hansen, Johannes. *Sankt Ansgars Kirke i hundrede Aar: Fra Kejserligt Kongeligt Østerrigsk Gesandtskabskapel til Danske Katholikkers Domkirke*. København: Skt. Ansgars Menighed, 1942.

Hiltebrandt, Philipp. 'Die Polnische Königswahl und die Konversion August des Starken.' *Quellen und Forschungen aus italienischen Archiven und Bibliotheken*, 10 (1907): 152–215.

Hrbek, Jiří. *Barokní Valdštejnové v Čechách 1640–1740* [The Baroque Waldsteins in Bohemia 1640–1740]. Prague: Nakladatelství Lidové noviny, 2013.

Kaplan, Benjamin J. 'Diplomacy and Domestic Devotion: Embassy Chapels and the Toleration of Religious Dissent in Early Modern Europe.' *Journal of Early Modern History*, 6 (2002): 341–61.

Kaplan, Benjamin J. *Divided by Faith: Religious Conflict and the Practice of Toleration in Early Modern Europe*. Cambridge, MA and London: Harvard University Press, 2007.

Kardel, Troels, and Maquet, Paul. *Nicolaus Steno: Biography and Original Papers of a 17th Century Scientist*. Berlin and Heidelberg: Springer Verlag, 2013.

Kubeš, Jiří. 'Jan Marek z Clary a Aldringenu jako vyslanec Leopolda I. u saského kurfiřtského dvora na konci 17. století.' [Johann Marcus von Clary-Aldringen as an Envoy of Emperor Leopold I to Saxony at the End of the 17th Century] *Český časopis historický*, 113 (2015): 346–80.

Kubeš, Jiří. 'Kaple císařských vyslanců v Drážďanech v druhé půli 17. století.' [Chapels of Imperial Envoys in Dresden in the Second Half of the 17th Century] *Folia Historica Bohemica*, 30 (2015): 127–56.

Kubeš, Jiří et al. *V zastoupení císaře: Česká a moravská aristokracie v habsburské diplomacii 1640–1740* [On Behalf of the Emperor: Bohemian and Moravian aristocracy in Habsburg diplomacy 1640–1740]. Prague: Nakladatelství Lidové noviny, 2018.

Legutke, Daniel. 'Die kaiserliche Gesandtschaftskapelle in Den Haag 1658–1718: Konfession und Säkularisierung in mikrohistorischer Sicht.' In *Stadt und Religion in der frühen Neuzeit: Soziale Ordnungen und ihre Repräsentationen*, edited by Vera Isaiasz et al., 245–74. Frankfurt am Main et al.: Campus, 2007.

Levinson, Artur. 'Nuntiaturberichte vom Kaiserhofe Leopolds I. (1657 bis 1669).' *Archiv für österreichische Geschichte*, 103 (1913): 547–831.

Loesche, Gustav. *Geschichte des Protestantismus im vormaligen und im neuen Österreich*. Wien: Manz, 1930.

Marburg, Silke. 'Gesandte als Grenzganger: Residenzstädtische Repräsentationskultur und die Konstruktion religiöser Exklaven unter Kurfürst Johann Georg II. von Sachsen.' In *Grenzen und Grenzüberschreitungen: Bilanz und Perspektiven der Frühneuzeitforschung*, edited by Christine Roll et al., 199–213. Cologne et al.: Böhlau, 2010.

Mecenseffy, Grete. *Geschichte des Protestantismus in Österreich*. Graz and Köln: Hermann Böhlau's Nachfolger, 1956.

Müller, Klaus. *Das kaiserliche Gesandtschaftswesen im Jahrhundert nach dem Westfälischen Frieden 1648–1740*. Bonn: Röhrscheid, 1976.

Neumann, Theodor. 'Chronicon venerandi capituli et collegiatae ecclesiae Budissinensis auctore Matth. Jos. Vitzk Decano nec non Administratore Ecclesiastico utramque er Lusatiam.' *Neues lausitzisches Magazin*, 33 (1857): 186–231.

Pieper, Anton. *Die Propaganda Congregation und die nordischen Missionen im siebenzehnten Jahrhundert*. Köln: J. P. Bachem, 1886.

Pribram, Alfred Francis. *Franz Paul Freiherr von Lisola (1613–1674) und die Politik seiner Zeit*. Leipzig: Veit & comp., 1894.

Roberts, Michael. *The Swedish Imperial Experience 1560–1718*. Cambridge: Cambridge University Press, 1979.

Sägmüller, Johann Baptist. 'Der Begriff des exercitium religionis publicum, exercitium religionis privatum und der devotio domestica im Westfalischen Frieden.' *Theologische Quartalschrift*, 90 (1908): 225–79.

Scheutz, Martin. 'Legalität und unterdrückte Religionsausübung: Niederleger, Reichshofräte, Gesandte und Legationsprediger. Protestantisches Leben in der Haupt- und Residenzstadt Wien im 17. und 18. Jahrhundert.' In *Geheimprotestantismus und evangelische Kirchen in der Habsburgermonarchie und im Erzstift Salzburg (17./18. Jahrhundert)*, edited by Rudolf Leeb et al., 209–36. Vienna: Böhlau, 2008.

Schnettger, Matthias. 'Ist Wien eine Messe wert? Protestantische Funktionseliten am Kaiserhof im 17. und 18. Jahrhundert.' In *Grenzen und Grenzüberschreitungen: Bilanz und Perspektiven der Frühneuzeitforschung*, edited by Christine Roll et al., 599–633. Köln et al.: Böhlau, 2010.

Schunka, Alexander. *Gäste, die bleiben: Zuwanderer in Kursachsen und der Oberlausitz im 17. und frühen 18. Jahrhundert*. Hamburg: Lit Verlag, 2006.

Thiessen, Hillard von. 'Switching Roles in Negotiation: Levels of Diplomatic Communication between Pope Paul V Borghese (1605–1621) and the Ambassadors of

Philip III.' In *Paroles de négociateurs: L'entretien dans la pratique diplomatique de la fin du Moyen âge à la fin du XIXe siècle*, edited by Stefano Andretta et al., 151–72. Rome: École française de Rome, 2010.

Trimble, William Raleigh. 'The Embassy chapel question, 1625–1660.' *The Journal of Modern History*, 18, 2 (1946): 97–107.

Villstrand, Nils Erik et al., *Sveriges historia 1600–1721*. Stockholm: Norstedts, 2011.

Gschließer, Oswald von. *Der Reichshofrat: Bedeutung und Verfassung, Schicksal und Besetzung einer obersten Reichsbehörde von 1559 bis 1806*. Wien: Holzhausen, 1942.

Votsche, Jochen. 'Anton Egon von Fürstenberg-Heiligenberg (1656–1716).' *Sächische Biographie*. Accessed 4th November, 2018, http://saebi.isgv.de/biografie/Anton_Egon_von_Fürstenberg-Heiligenberg_(1656–1716).

Walter, Michael. 'Der Fall Salicola oder Die Sängerin als symbolisches Kapital.' *Zeitschrift für Literatur- und Theatersoziologie*, 6 (2011): 5–34.

12 Charles XII of Sweden and the Rákóczi uprising in Hungary

The long-lasting legacy of the Protestant cause[*]

Gábor Kármán

It is a commonplace of historiography that there is a palpable difference between the relevance of confession for early-seventeenth-century foreign policy and the role it played in the beginning of the next century. From one of the primary factors in decision-making and alliance-seeking common denomination became an auxiliary element, used for justifying political action, but in most cases not determining it.[1] Of course, this change occurred at different times in different relations. In this chapter I will present a case where the traditions of basing co-operation between two actors in the European theatre of politics upon the common confessional interests were very strong in the seventeenth century, and in the constellation of European politics in the early eighteenth century it would have been hard to replace this factor with anything else. The attempts of Ferenc (Francis) Rákóczi II, the leader of the anti-Habsburg uprising in Hungary in the first decade of the eighteenth century to raise the interests of Charles XII of Sweden for his endeavour offers a good illustration to the long-lasting legacy of politics based on common confessional interests, but at the same time clearly shows its limits

The traditions: Swedish-Hungarian co-operations in the seventeenth century

Considering the geographic distance between the two regions it may be surprising how lively the diplomatic contacts between Sweden and Hungary were in the seventeenth century. In the sixteenth century, two things happened in the medieval Kingdom of Hungary, which furthered this development. On the one hand, the country lost a third of its territory to the Ottoman Empire and as a result of a long civil war, its eastern regions formed a semi-independent state, known as the Principality of Transylvania, whose princes as a rule were elected by the local diet, but owed allegiance to the sultan as their tributaries. On the other hand, Reformation proved to be very successful in these regions: it is a generally accepted estimate that at the end of the century the ratio of Catholics was around 10% in the population of the Kingdom of Hungary (that is, the western territories), where the survival of the old faith's church structures was highest. Nevertheless, it was only in 1608 that the

Habsburg kings of Hungary could be forced to acknowledge the rights of the Lutherans and Calvinists to practice their faith and establish church organisations. The success of the Protestants was made possible by extraordinary circumstances: the exhaustion of the Habsburg Empire's military might due to the Long Ottoman War of the turn of the century, an uprising in Hungary led by István Bocskai, prince of Transylvania, and a crisis in the dynasty, the so-called Bruderzwist, in which Archduke Matthias replaced Rudolph II in several of the territories under his rule.[2]

The confirmation of the population's rights for the free choice of their confession did not bring tranquillity to Hungary's religious life. Already in the 1610s, the Protestant estates had to face the fact that their ability to implement their newly gained freedom of consciousness could at some instances be seriously hindered by the Catholic clergy that enjoyed the dynasty's support. Thus, many of the Protestants turned to the ruler from whom they could expect support: the prince of Transylvania. Joining the first phase of the Thirty Years War, Gábor (Gabriel) Bethlen entered Hungary three times with his forces against the Habsburgs, but it was actually his successor, György (George) Rákóczi I, who managed to secure further guarantees for the Protestants's rights. In the Peace of Linz in 1645, and the following legislation at the Hungarian diet of 1646–1647 the congregation was given the upper hand against the landlord in choosing which confession the local church should belong to. This principle should have theoretically had the same effect as the *Normaljahr* established in the Peace of Westphalia in the empire and brought a conservation of the country's religious composition, but in later phases of the seventeenth century, there were new developments to come, and using a conspiracy of Hungarian aristocrats as pretext, the Habsburg state administration introduced violent Catholisation measures after 1669. Although the successes of the consequent uprising forced the Habsburgs to a compromise again in 1681, this meant a step back from the legislation of the 1640s and conflicts around the Protestants' freedom to practise their faith remained a stumbling block in Hungarian politics for a long time.[3]

The princes of Transylvania played a key role in making the high tide of Protestant politics possible in the first half of the seventeenth century. The rulers of this multi-confessional principality, whose laws acknowledged four accepted religions (Lutheranism, Calvinism, Catholicism and Antitrinitarism), as well as tolerating Greek Orthodoxy, acted first on behalf of Hungary's estates, but later on became members of the European network of Protestant rulers on their own right. The diplomats of Gábor Bethlen, György Rákóczi I and his son and successor, György Rákóczi II were frequent guests at European courts and it was also these princes who established contacts with the Kingdom of Sweden.[4]

Marrying Margravine Catherine, the sister of Brandenburg's elector in 1626, Gábor Bethlen became the brother-in-law of Gustav II Adolph, king of Sweden, who pulled every string to motivate the prince to join his war against the Polish-Lithuanian Commonwealth. The rhetoric of common Protestant interests was liberally used in the argumentation of both parties; however, negotiations remained fruitless, even after the Nordic king entered the Holy Roman Empire with his troops, and the new Transylvanian prince, György Rákóczi informed him repeatedly about his interest in co-operation.[5] It was only in 1643 that the Gyulafehérvár Agreement between the prince and Swedish diplomats set the framework of the co-operation that paved the way to Rákóczi's success in the Peace of Linz. Nevertheless, this first common military endeavour did not last long: although Transylvanian troops went into war against Ferdinand III, the Swedish armies had to leave Bohemia to achieve a quick victory against Denmark; and by the time they returned to the south, the prince was already in the last phase of his peace negotiations. Uniting forces under the walls of Brünn (Brno) was soon followed by the prince's announcement that he had concluded a separate peace with the emperor.[6]

The next decade saw Swedish–Transylvanian negotiations again, but this time it was the co-operation in Polish affairs that gained the upper hand. In the second year of the First Northern War, after initial successes, the Swedish military endeavour lost its momentum and King Charles X Gustav decided to eventually accept the repeated offers of Prince György Rákóczi II and conclude an alliance against the Polish-Lithuanian Commonwealth. The Treaty of Radnót sketched a rather ambitious partition plan in December 1656, but the war effort of the prince failed next year, and brought about the fall of the Rákóczi dynasty in Transylvania.[7] After the end of the First Northern War, however, there was a hiatus in the direct contacts between Sweden and Transylvania until the grandson of György Rákóczi II started his uprising in Hungary in 1703.

It was in May 1703 that Ferenc (Francis) Rákóczi II crossed the Polish border, entered Hungary with his relatively small number of troops, and joined a peasant uprising at the Upper Tisza valley, which eventually turned out to be the beginnings of a large-scale anti-Habsburg insurrection, only ending with the compromise Peace of Szatmár in 1711. The uprising enjoyed wide support, as the new system of government introduced in Hungary after the expulsion of the Ottomans (confirmed in the Peace of Karlowitz in 1699) was a source of many grievances for various social strata. Nevertheless, Rákóczi had to be aware from the very beginning that the resources he could access in Hungary would not be enough for success against the Habsburg Empire and its overwhelmingly superior military potential. After the initial successes, when Rákóczi's army managed to gain control over significant territories in Hungary, he had to face a series of backlashes, and would have surely lost ground in a much quicker pace had the majority of the Habsburg power not been deployed at the western fronts of the War of Spanish Succession.[8]

Nevertheless, being aware of his instable position, Rákóczi dedicated considerable effort from the first moment to continue his ongoing negotiations at the French court and to receive, apart from financial and military assistance, political confirmation for that cooperation through a formal treaty. On the other hand, he also sought other possible supporters abroad, foreign rulers who could potentially assist the Hungarian cause. The only monarch who eventually signed a treaty with Ferenc Rákóczi II was Peter the Great, but the tsar only appeared on the horizon at a later stage of the insurrection in 1706. The same year, Rákóczi tried to renew the traditions of his forefathers, princes of Transylvania, to involve the Ottoman Empire in his anti-Habsburg endeavour.[9] In the first phase of the uprising, the main target for Rákóczi's diplomacy – apart from Louis XIV and his ally, Maximillian Emmanuel, Elector of Bavaria – was Charles XII, King of Sweden. The young ruler, who gained his fame exactly in these years through a series of remarkable military victories, was visited by Hungarian diplomats, who asked for his assistance, in 1704, and again in 1705; and maintaining a good relationship with Charles remained an important aim of Rákóczi's foreign policy even later on.[10]

This is all the more surprising, as the foreign policy of the Swedish king in these years was determined by war against the alliance of Denmark, Saxony(–Poland), and Russia.[11] Neither Emperor Leopold I nor his successor, Joseph I, were involved in this series of conflicts known as the Great Northern War, and thus Charles XII and Ferenc Rákóczi II lacked a common enemy – thus, the Hungarians' interest in motivating him to join their cause is a phenomenon that deserves further scrutiny.

The quest of finding common interests

Pál Ráday, the secretary of Ferenc Rákóczi II, set off from a camp near Miskolc in northern Hungary for the first time in February 1704 to visit Charles XII. After having met some Polish lords in Lemberg, later on in Warsaw, he continued his journey towards the north and found the Swedish ruler in his headquarters at Heilsberg (Lidzbark Warmiński) at the end of March. Ráday did not receive an audience for a while; he only met Chancellor Carl Piper and gave him the memorandum detailing the embassy's aims. He saw Charles XII in person for the first time in mid-April, when he also received the king's response to Ferenc Rákóczi II. The envoy then continued his journey in the direction of the Kingdom of Prussia, since, according to his instructions, he also had to visit King Frederick I.[12]

We do not have many details concerning the deliberations in the preparation phase of the mission, and Rákóczi's instructions do not give much insight into what Ráday was supposed to discuss with the Swedish king.[13] There was no mention of any military assistance; what is more, the instructions emphasised that this would be a perfect occasion to conclude a treaty with Charles XII, because the Hungarian War for Independence was not in need of either military or financial support. We are perhaps not wrong if we label this a diplomatic attempt to lull the Swedish king's worries. Although the Hungarian uprising did not meet very strong resistance in 1703, it was clear for Rákóczi that if the tides were turned in the War of the Spanish Succession, he would also need more financial and military resources; thus, he continuously petitioned for Louis XIV's help.[14] It seems, however, that he was also aware that there was very little chance to gain similar support from the Swedish king, and thus he concentrated on alternative potential diplomatic gains. According to a section of the instructions, Ráday had to raise the question whether the Hungarian estates could be included into the alliance between Sweden and Prussia; and according to another one, he was to ask the consent of Charles XII concerning a future alliance between Hungary and Poland. Ultimately, Rákóczi also requested that if the universal peace, which was going to end Louis XIV's wars, would also include Hungary, the Swedish king would accept to be its guarantor.[15]

We do not know whether it was clear to Rákóczi that the Swedish–Prussian treaty concluded on 30th July, 1703, was only a short-lived episode, of limited relevance to the quickly changing military and diplomatic scene of Europe. On receiving the news and not being informed about the details, many of his contemporaries assumed that the document was designed to revive the attempts in the 1650s that had aimed at partitioning Poland–Lithuania.[16] If we consider the preceding three years of Charles XII's reign, it is no surprise that great ambition was attributed to him: the young king left Europe astonished by winning one victory after the other against the coalition that had formed against him in 1700. He forced Frederick IV of Denmark to conclude a peace in August the same year by landing his forces, with the support of the Dutch and English fleet, in Zealand and threatening to attack the enemy's capital.[17] In late November, 1700, Charles defeated the forces of Peter the Great, besieging Narva, and then, turning south, he won a great victory against the troops of Augustus II, the Strong, King of Poland and Elector of Saxony, when crossing the River Dvina in July 1701.

Although Augustus had invaded Swedish Livonia in the previous year with only Saxon troops (that is, in his quality as elector), in one year the Rzeczpospolita also became involved in the conflict.[18] Charles XII refused to accept the peace offer of his adversaries and, upon the encouragement of some Polish and Lithuanian dignitaries, announced that the conflict could only be solved if Augustus was removed from the royal throne. Involving the Polish–Lithuanian estates meant, however, the start of a long political game between many players, in which the Swedish king could achieve only limited success, in spite of his military victories. Charles XII entered Warsaw and defeated Augustus' armies, which now also included Polish troops, at Pułtusk and at Kliszów; he then captured Thorn. Shortly after Ráday had started his journey from Hungary, on 16th February, 1704, the Polish diet at Warsaw declared Augustus deposed. Despite this, the Swedish king could only convince a part of the Polish–Lithuanian nobility to join his cause. Augustus refused to accept his deposition and solidified his alliance with Peter. At the same time, the tsar's armies restarted the Livonian campaign, and Swedish fortresses fell, one after the other.[19]

Both sides in the War of the Spanish Succession sent their diplomats to Charles XII: on the one hand, Louis XIV, who was traditionally an ally of Sweden; on the other hand, the Sea Powers. It is, nevertheless, no wonder that the young Swedish king did not feel much inclined to involve himself in yet another military conflict.[20] This was the reason why Ráday's mission failed, practically before it had taken place. Chancellor Carl Piper gave a detailed account to Rákóczi's envoy that, following the wishes of Leopold I, his monarch had just recently declared that he would not assist the rebels threatening the emperor's rule.[21] Thus, Ráday did not even mention the request to be included in the Swedish–Prussian alliance in his memorandum, only raising questions of the Hungarian–Polish alliance and the guarantee for the coming peace treaties. It was needless to bring up any further arguments for cooperation, apart from those referring to traditions and the common Protestant cause; Ráday only noted that Charles XII could gain further support from Hungary, if the alliance with the Poles actually took place.

Besides a hint to the necessity of reinstalling the political equilibrium in Europe, which surely had very little impact upon the Swedish king, Ráday's memorandum mentioned a single specific political issue: that his prince requested Charles XII's help if the Ottomans, encouraged by Vienna, would attack Rákóczi. At the time when the instructions were drafted, the leaders of the uprising were somewhat afraid of this otherwise quite unrealistic development, and as the resistance against the 'arch-foe of Christendom' was one of the justificatory strategies with the most obvious mobilising power in early modern European international society, they perhaps saw it as the only realistic chance to establish a framework for Swedish–Hungarian cooperation.[22] The only specific statement of the Swedish response that Ráday received, and which stayed on the level of generalities, must have referred to this claim, while pointing out that Charles XII did not want to miss any opportunities to serve the interests of Christianity. The rather dubious diplomatic value of the letter was further decreased by the fact that it was not signed by the king himself, but rather by his chancellor.[23] Thus, Ferenc Rákóczi II and the Hungarian estates did not even receive a clear sign that they would be treated as valid negotiating partners with the king – something that their diplomacy would have needed badly.

When the estates of Transylvania met in the assembly of 8th July, 1704, it was the above-mentioned lack of legitimacy that made the ceremonial act of electing Ferenc Rákóczi II as their prince so relevant. The prince, who had until this point used his hereditary title Prince of the Holy Roman Empire, was keen on sending news about the election to his actual and potential partners, among them the Swedish king. A new delegation that left Hungary in the late spring of 1705 hoped to receive a more serious treatment from Charles XII due to the advancement of their sender.[24]

The advisors of the prince's foreign policy also presented a more comprehensive message than in the previous year. The task of Pál Ráday, who represented Rákóczi again, was to sketch a Polish–Hungarian alliance and win Swedish support for it. According to Rákóczi's plans, with a common invasion of Silesia they would force the emperor to conclude a peace and after having broken the Saxon elector's resistance, and thus having established peace on the German front, could begin a common campaign against Peter in order to regain control over Swedish territories that had been lost in the meantime. Besides explaining these long-term strategic plans, Ráday was also supposed to suggest that some units could already at this point be exchanged: Rákóczi was willing to send light cavalry if he would receive some badly needed heavy cavalry from Charles XII.[25] The self-assured statement of the previous year, that Rákóczi's War of Independence needed neither soldiers nor money, was dropped, and although Ráday boasted of the capture of 50 castles in the memorandum he submitted to the Swedish king, it was clear that the major defeat Rákóczi's forces suffered in the Battle of Nagyszombat (Trnava) in December, 1704, and the following loss of western Hungary, left a mark upon the prince's foreign policy.[26]

This time, Ferenc Rákóczi II and his advisors also gave more thought about how to outline their requests with the necessary arguments. Still unable to explain beyond any doubts why the emperor would count as a common enemy, Ráday's memorandum nevertheless hinted that both Leopold I and Joseph I, who succeeded him, seemed to support the tsar.[27] At the same time, the plan to invade Silesia appears to have offered a solution to an important dilemma of the Swedish king. After Augustus' deposition, Charles XII managed to have the next diet elect a new Polish king in the person of Stanisław Leszczyński in July 1704. In the same year, the armies of Charles XII and his supporters won some minor victories, but also suffered some defeats, with Warsaw being reconquered by Augustus during the autumn. It was clear to anyone interested that the legitimacy of Leszczyński's rule would be uncertain as long as Augustus could not be forced to resign his Polish title.[28]

The most obvious means to achieve this was not to seek further solutions in the Polish–Lithuanian Commonwealth, which was immense and hard to control with military might, but rather to invade the elector's hereditary Saxon lands. The problem was that the Rzeczpospolita did not have common borders with Saxony, and thus the Swedish armies had to cross either Brandenburg territories (and Charles XII had just concluded another treaty of neutrality with Frederick I) or those of the emperor. Thus, when Charles XII placed his headquarters in Rawicz on the Silesian border during the winter of 1704–1705, in order to hinder further Saxon troops entering the Commonwealth's territory, this also caused a headache in Viennese circles – and in turn must have motivated Ferenc Rákóczi II to send his second embassy to the Swedish monarch.[29]

The prince's new instructions were so elaborate that they also discussed the wider implications of the planned cooperation. The document noted that if Charles XII was anxious that the Habsburgs' loss of Hungary would have brought a serious misbalance to European stability, the function of the emperor's power could be easily taken over by the military potential of the Swedish–Polish–Hungarian alliance.[30] These speculations, nonetheless, seem to have had little impact on the Swedish king, who welcomed Ráday in a benevolent manner, but promised nothing, and again had his chancellor transmit his message to the Hungarian prince.[31] Charles XII still did not want to raise the Habsburgs' suspicions that he would give assistance to rebels against the emperor. He was motivated not only by the obvious concerns not to add another enemy to the numerous group of his adversaries, but also – as Royal Secretary Olof Hermelin explained to the envoy – because of his Dutch and English contacts.[32] These powers were the emperor's supporters in the War of the Spanish Succession, and it was because of them that the Swedish king did not, as yet, enter the soil of the Holy Roman Empire – as they were guarantors of Charles XII's new peace with Frederick IV, the Swedish king could only be sure that the ambitious Danish king would not attack him again if the Sea Powers kept him at bay.[33]

Thus, Charles XII could not promise anything else than to explore at the emperor's court whether his mediation in the Hungarian conflict would be welcome, remembering that a similar offer of his had previously been refused by Leopold I.[34] The Swedish king, however, was happy to hear Rákóczi's offer that his diplomats would work at the Sublime Porte on the outbreak of a Russian–Ottoman war. Later in 1705, some letters were exchanged between the Royal Secretary, Hermelin, and Pál Ráday, strictly avoiding the involvement of persons higher in the hierarchy, but as the Hungarian mission to Constantinople was not successful, this question was taken relatively quickly from the table.[35]

In the next two years, no further attempt for direct contact was made, but this did not mean that Ferenc Rákóczi II and Charles XII had lost sight of each other. Philippe Grofey, a French agent on the Swedish king's side, not only maintained correspondence with his colleague delegated to Rákóczi, Pierre Puchot Des Alleurs, but also with the prince himself.[36] During 1706 and 1707, Charles XII carried out his plans and invaded Saxony, and Ferenc Rákóczi II explored the possibilities through Grofey, partly on the French king's initiative, as to whether another envoy of his would be received more favourably than the earlier ones.[37] This seemed reasonable since the emperor had to endure severe pressure from the part of the Swedish king in this period: he managed to practically force Joseph I, through military threats, to reinforce the Silesian Protestants' rights, secured in the Peace of Westphalia, on 1st September, 1707.[38]

Rákóczi's court, however, mainly concentrated upon another direction in its foreign policy in this period. Although Augustus resigned his royal title in 1706, the Sandomierz Confederation, consisting of those Polish magnates who enjoyed the support of Peter the Great, was not ready to acknowledge Stanisław Leszczyński as their ruler. In May 1707, the tsar's envoy, David Ivanovič Corbea, conveyed Peter's invitation to Rákóczi to take the Polish throne. After some initial hesitation, the prince decided that the most important problem of his foreign policy, his lack of legitimacy as a ruler, due to which his envoys were not seen as acceptable negotiating partners at European courts, could be solved through accepting the tsar's offer.[39] However, he wanted to avoid any conflict with Charles XII, who still supported Stanisław Leszczyński, and thus sent a memorandum via Ráday to Carl Rehnskiöld, a Swedish general, who in turn passed it on to his monarch. The document repeatedly emphasised that Ferenc Rákóczi II wanted to avoid hostile acts against the Swedish king; he took a stance against a new election and again pointed out that he was motivated in his action by the danger of cooperation between the emperor and the tsar.[40]

In his *Mémoires*, written a decade later, Ferenc Rákóczi II recalled that Charles XII's response was that 'I should take a strong stand against the tsar, because he, the king, would soon enter Poland and defeat the tsar.'[41] The very detailed memoires of the king's army chaplain draws another picture: Charles XII had his secretary, Olof Hermelin, inform the prince that he would regard anyone who took a stand against Stanisław Leszczyński and Poland his enemy.[42] Later the prince attempted again to avoid alienating Charles XII, whose quick campaign in Poland in the autumn of 1707 annihilated the plan of Rákóczi's election. His diplomats convinced a Polish magnate from Stanisław Leszczyński's party to speak in favour of the prince in front of the Swedish king, using the same arguments as the earlier memorandum.[43]

The diplomatic contacts between the King of Sweden and the Ruling Prince of Hungary, however, were not taken up again, and after the defeat of Charles XII at Poltava in 1709 this direction of foreign policy lost all relevance for Ferenc Rákóczi II as well, although he made good use of those troops who escaped from Ukraine to Hungary and served, at least temporarily, in his armies.[44] It is symbolic how the last eighteenth-century contact between a Hungarian diplomat and the Swedish court took place: Pál Ráday was this time not sent to meet Charles XII, but rather to the *serdar* of Babadağ, one of the important leaders of the Ottoman armies in the European part of the empire. The main goals of the mission in 1710 were to win the Ottoman dignitary's support for those Transylvanian pro-Rákóczi nobles who had fled to Moldavia after the re-conquest of the province by the emperor's forces, and to transfer lucrative offers to the Sublime Porte for any assistance to Rákóczi, whose uprising was by that time clearly fighting for survival.[45] Ráday did not even have credentials written for the Swedish king; thus he did not get an audience, and could only discuss with some prominent members of the court living in exile in Bender.[46] Charles XII nevertheless informed the prince through Heinrich Gustav von Müllern, his secretary responsible for foreign affairs, that he held no grudges against Rákóczi for his contacts with Peter the Great, but politely refused the prince's offer for mediation with the tsar. He, in turn, promised to support one of the most important goals of Rákóczi by this time: the inclusion of the Hungarian cause in a universal peace that was going to end the War of the Spanish Succession.[47]

Earlier political contacts

The quest for finding a common enemy ended, as we could see, with very limited success: Ferenc Rákóczi II's diplomacy could not really find convincing arguments why it would serve the interests of Charles XII if he assisted the Hungarian cause. It is no wonder that the prince repeatedly turned to the past instead of discussing the present during the negotiations.

As he had to consider his actual aims and interests, when asking for the help of Charles XII, Ferenc Rákóczi II did not refer back to the Treaty of Radnót, which was more recent, but rather the Gyulafehérvár Agreement, because this was the one that stipulated cooperation against the emperor. This was, however, not the only aspect that made the treaty an excellent point of reference for Rákóczi. The document stated several times that it was also valid for the successors of Prince György Rákóczi I: if the prince were to die, his offspring were obliged to continue the war effort, and they also had to be included in the universal peace that would conclude the conflict.[48] This provided a good argument for György Rákóczi I's great-grandson, Ferenc II.

Ferenc Rákóczi II recalled in his *Mémoires* what an important role the treaties of György Rákóczi I from the 1640s played in the diplomatic activities at the beginning of his uprising.[49] The Hungarian aristocrat, as noted before, had a hard time getting himself accepted as a legitimate negotiating partner, because he had no princely authority. He held the title 'Prince of the Holy Roman Empire' but did not rule over any specific territory, and being a leader of the Hungarian uprising did not provide him the legitimacy necessary to participate in the European 'society of princes,' exchange letters with monarchs, and conclude treaties with them. Although the Transylvanian estates elected him as their ruling prince in 1704, he had to wait until 1707 for the ceremonial inauguration; furthermore, the deposition of the Habsburgs and the election of Rákóczi as Ruling Prince of Hungary also took place only in 1707. Thus, the mid-seventeenth-century treaties of the Rákóczi family served for a long time as the only argument for the prince to seek acknowledgement and support not only with the Swedish monarch, but also in the much more important relations with the French king.[50]

The Gyulafehérvár Agreement was used for the first time as an argument to mobilise Charles XII's assistance even before the start of the uprising. The wife of Ferenc Rákóczi II, Landgravine Charlotte Amalie of Hessen-Wanfried, referred to it in her letter to Charles XII, in which she requested support for her husband, who at that moment was under custody in Wiener Neustadt, with charges of lese-majesty committed against Leopold I.[51] Later the argument is used in the documents related to Pál Ráday's 1704 embassy; it was also mentioned in 1705, and again in the memorandum written to Rehnskiöld in 1707.[52] In the *Mémoires*, Rákóczi pointed out that his expectations concerning French and Swedish support were justified, because these treaties did not only stipulate military support to György Rákóczi I and his successors (with 6,000 infantry), but also a 40,000 Reichstaler stipend for the case that the Rákóczis lost their rule over Transylvania.[53]

There were, however, several problems with the treaty that had been concluded between the Swedish and Transylvanian rulers at Gyulafehérvár on 16th November, 1643. On the one hand, in the mid-seventeenth century, it was already disputed whether the document was also valid after György Rákóczi I concluded his separate peace with the emperor. The prince could point to an article in the text which specifically granted him the right to make this step if the consent of the sultan, the overlord of Transylvania, could not be gained for the anti-Habsburg war. The Swedish party, however, questioned the validity of the Ottoman threat, and the leading political personalities of the Nordic country accused the prince of ungratefulness, unreliability, and treason – if not publicly, then at least in their personal correspondence.[54]

It was also due to the lack of ratification in the 1640s that the Gyulafehérvár Agreement could not function as a proper basis of support. The text was not placed in the collection of Sweden's official treaties, and even today cannot be found in the relevant section of the Riksarkivet (state archives).[55] Chancellor Carl Piper told Ráday that they could not find the treaty in the archives and, although they did not question the credibility of Rákóczi's statements, could not verify the obligation of the past Kings of Sweden either. Thus, the chancellor requested that Ráday should bring the original copy next time, which was certainly not possible, since, as already noted, Rákóczi did not have it either. Thus, the arguments of the Hungarian prince based upon the earlier treaties remained ineffective.[56]

On the other hand, it was somewhat confusing what exactly the Gyulafehérvár Agreement prescribed. The Swedish–Transylvanian alliance in 1643 was created by several documents, some of which reached the regency government in Stockholm only in an abridged form, which did not fulfil their expectations of a formal treaty. Thus, they refused to ratify it, but – due to their lack of interest in formalising an alliance with the Transylvanian prince – they also did not make any serious steps to have a final version signed. What is more, in 1704, Ferenc Rákóczi II did not seem to have had access to the family's archives and the documents of the treaty preserved there. The document that Pál Ráday took to the Swedish camp to justify his statements survived among his personal papers, and from this it can be seen what Rákóczi based his arguments upon. In 1643, the Habsburg armies captured two documents that represented a specific phase of the negotiations between Prince György Rákóczi I and Lennart Torstensson, *generalissimus* of the Swedish armies in Germany. The texts were immediately published in order to unveil the secret plans for the alliance; in all likelihood, the Latin original was also printed, but there were also two German versions and a French translation.[57] The documents clearly did not fulfil the formal expectations towards an international treaty: Rákóczi's offer of ten articles, without any preamble, was published together with Torstensson's commentaries upon it. The formal shortcomings, however, did not prevent the publishers from presenting the text as a treaty between the Prince of Transylvania and the Swedish crown, and this must have been enough for Ferenc Rákóczi II to use this version to justify his claims.[58]

The question of religion

The other traditional argument for cooperation between Swedes and Hungarians, referring to the Protestant cause, seemed to be more promising than finding a legal obligation of Charles XII to assist the Hungarian uprising. The common interests of Protestantism played an important role in the justifications of each seventeenth-century attempt for cooperation between these two rather distant lands – even if, as in the case of the invasion of Poland in the 1650s, Protestant issues were not among the motivation of the political decisions.[59] Although confessional interests were for the most part no longer the determining factor of European foreign policy in the beginning of the eighteenth century, and the most important conflicts that Charles XII participated in were also not based on confessional issues, the young Swedish king was keen on maintaining the position that his predecessors held since Gustav II Adolph: that of the protector and promoter of European Protestantism.[60] Since the late 1620s, and especially due to the role given to them by the Peace of Westphalia, Protestants under duress often turned to the Kings of Sweden. In the 1670s, during a period of violent recatholicisation in Hungary, Swedish diplomacy tried to put pressure upon Leopold I: Bengt Oxenstierna, the envoy of the Crown of Sweden in Vienna, did not only file an official complaint with the emperor concerning the persecution of Protestants in Hungary, but also had the text published.[61]

For Charles XII, the role as a patron of Protestants was of high priority. Envoys of the Silesian Protestants had visited him in 1703 to summon him to stand up against the Catholicisation measures supported by the Habsburg ruler. Their common Protestantism was also regarded as very important in justifying the negotiations with the King of Prussia. The most obvious sign of the young king's dedication towards the Protestant cause was, however, the Altranstädt Convention, in which Charles XII forced the emperor to ensure that the Silesian Protestants' rights, specified in the Peace of Westphalia, would be respected and their churches returned to them.[62]

All these dealings should have provided Ferenc Rákóczi II with a good opportunity to use the defence of Protestantism in Hungary as an argument for winning Charles XII's support against the emperor. This had acceptable traditions: ever since István Bocskai's uprising between 1604 and 1606, confessional *gravamina* always played an important role in the resistance of the Hungarian estates against their Habsburg rulers, even if, admittedly, it lost some of its weight in the second half of the century.[63] As the majority of the participants in Rákóczi's insurrection was Protestant, they would have been ready to renew the seventeenth-century tradition of basing the legitimacy of the anti-Habsburg uprising on confessional *gravamina*.[64] Notwithstanding, Ferenc Rákóczi II, himself a Catholic, wanted to quit this trend. The manifesto to foreign powers, written by Pál Ráday in his name, had only one section, out of 21, which addressed church-related questions. What is more, even this was not related to Protestants, but rather to the question of appointing foreigners into Hungarian Catholic bishop seats.[65] Thus, the confessional question is practically missing from the text, the gravamina listed there are purely political.

The confessional issue was pushed to the back not only because of the personal conviction of Ferenc Rákóczi II, but also because the target audience of the manifesto was not the Swedish king, but it was supposed to make an impact in much wider circles. Even if confessional issues still provided arguments for justifying political action in the early eighteenth century, European alliances were very rarely concluded on the basis of religious adherence, contrary to the situation a century before. The most desired target of Rákóczi's hopes, the Crown of France, never considered repairing Protestant confessional grievances a valid cause for action. Sixty years earlier, in 1645, the reason to sign a separate treaty of alliance between France and Transylvania at Munkács (Mukačevo) was that the Gyulafehérvár Agreement, which theoretically was also concluded in the name of Louis XIV, had an article about defending the rights of the Protestants.[66] It would obviously have been impossible to win the support of the French king, who practised an emphatically intolerant religious policy, with the traditional discourse of grievances. Thus, the prince eagerly emphasised in his communication with French diplomats that instead of the serious confessional conflicts of previous times, the religious question did not cause much turmoil this time, and the motivations for the uprising were purely political.[67]

However, Rákóczi could not leave the traditions of confessional legitimation altogether untouched when specifically addressing the Swedish king: in Ráday's memorandum of 1704 to Charles XII, prominent place is given to the grievances the Protestants had to suffer from the Habsburgs; what is more, the text explicitly refers to the traditions of the late Transylvanian princes, István Bocskai, Gábor Bethlen, and György Rákóczi I.[68] The message was reinforced by the fact that in the company of Ráday, there was also a representative of the Protestant estates in Hungary, Mihály Okolicsányi, who gave the king a separate memorandum in the name of this specific group. There were no discrepancies between the requests presented in the memoranda of Ráday and Okolicsányi, and it is no surprise, since the latter was also penned by Rákóczi's secretary-cum-diplomat. It was, however, an important difference that the latter was much more liberal in using the terminology of common Protestant interests: for example, whereas the instructions of Rákóczi to Ráday requested Hungary's inclusion in the Swedish–Prussian alliance, Okolicsányi's memorandum mentions this as the 'league of Protestant powers.'[69]

Whereas Ráday and Okolicsányi travelled together in 1704, the diplomatic activities of the Hungarian Protestants, who were very active in the direction of Brandenburg in the previous decade, ran separately from, albeit conforming to, the princely foreign policy in the following years.[70] In June 1705, Ráday met Miklós Szirmay and Mihály Melczl in Rawicz, waiting for their audience with the Swedish king. Unlike Okolicsányi, this time the envoys limited the issues they wanted to discuss purely to those of the Church: they asked for financial support from Charles XII for the reconstruction of the Lutheran college at Eperjes (Prešov).[71] The king was once again visited with the same purpose by Daniel Krman and Samuel Podhorský in 1709, who – as it is known from the *Itinerarium* of the Slovak superintendent – stayed with Charles XII in the Ukrainian campaign, and returned from Bender after many adventures.[72]

Charles XII could only give a vague promise for sending funds for the college, although providing the Hungarian Lutherans with four stipends to Greifswald, the newly founded university in Swedish Pomerania. Nevertheless, it seems that the Swedish king found the common Protestant interest the most convincing part of the arguments presented by any envoy from Hungary. This is clear from the biography of Charles XII by the royal army chaplain, Jöran Andersson Nordberg. During Ráday's 1704 mission, he wrote that the only motivation for the king to intervene with the emperor for the Hungarian cause was to protect the religious liberties of the country. When writing of 1707, he devoted a long discussion to Charles XII's doubts, raised when he heard the news of Rákóczi's negotiations with the tsar: he was concerned whether the Hungarian prince had been following his own interests right from the start, instead of wishing to reinstate the rights of the oppressed denominations in Hungary.[73] It can, of course, be assumed that this purely confessional interpretation derived from Nordberg's position as an ecclesiast, but other sources also confirm that for the Swedish king this was the primary framework for understanding the uprising in Hungary. In early 1704, Charles XII sent word to Leopold I through Count Zinzendorf that if the cause of the rebellion was the religious question, the emperor should do everything in his power to remedy the grievances. He also justified his offer for mediation after Ráday's 1704 mission with his sympathy for the Protestant cause.[74] Even if Ráday, following instructions, gave the king Rákóczi's manifesto, which presented only those causes that were related to the estates' political grievances, Charles XII must have felt that he had no competence there. Thus, it turned out that stressing the traditional context of Protestantism was the only way to raise Charles' interest in Hungary.

Charles XII was not the only person towards whom this method seemed the most effective.[75] After Frederick IV of Denmark concluded an alliance with the emperor and Danish troops started to appear in the Hungarian theatre of war, Pál Ráday, as representative of the Hungarian Protestant estates, sent a long memorandum, although to no avail.[76] In Prussia, calls for confessional solidarity found more sympathetic ears. With Daniel Ernst Jablonski, the influential court chaplain of the king, Ráday maintained close contact, frequently informing each other about developments concerning the Protestant cause; however, no political cooperation between Frederick I and Ferenc Rákóczi II could be established.[77]

If Rákóczi's diplomatic attempts to mobilise Charles XII in the Protestant cause had been successful, it would have eventually caused serious problems in the prince's contacts with Louis XIV. However, Ferenc Rákóczi II did not have to face this conflict of interests, because the Swedish king was even less motivated to assist him than the French ruler, from whom he at least received some money and some well-trained military officers. There is little reason to be surprised over the outcome: even the diplomats with the best rhetorical skills had a hard time finding convincing arguments why the Swedish king and the Hungarian aristocrat should be allies, as they clearly had diverging interests and different adversaries. When assessing the results, however, it should also be considered that diplomatic contacts could be useful even if they did not directly lead to the conclusion of alliances. In 1704, when the emperor was in a difficult military situation, Rákóczi's contacts with Charles XII caused unease at the Viennese court, and the same could have happened at the turn of 1707 if the military situation in Hungary would have otherwise created a favourable position for the prince during the peace negotiations. The fact that it was not the case was not the result of Hungarian diplomatic shortcomings, but rather of the general European military situation after the Battle of Höchstädt, the turning point of the War of the Spanish Succession. As it is generally true for the outcome of the uprising in Hungary, the eventual gains of the Swedish connection depended primarily upon the outcome of the other fronts of the emperor's war effort. The defeat of the French and their allies eventually rendered this diplomatic contact little more than a curiosity.

Nevertheless, this curiosity is a useful tool for us to assess the power that traditions of co-operation between two players in the European theatre of war for the common Protestant cause had at the beginning of the eighteenth century. The attempt of Rákóczi to scale down the relevance of confessional issues in the legitimation strategies of his uprising, which may have eventually caused problems in his contacts with Louis XIV, could have logically produced the result that Charles XII, with whom he had practically no common interests, would have shown no attention to his pleas at all. The Swedish king, however, was one of the European monarchs who still liked to see themselves as champions of their religious group, an attitude well illustrated by his treatment of the Silesian appeals and pressuring the emperor into accepting the Altranstädt Convention. Not being interested in a closer co-operation and not even regarding Rákóczi as a legitimate member of the European 'society of princes', Charles XII seems to have corrected in his mind what he heard from Pál Ráday about the causes and aims of the actual uprising, and, based on his knowledge about the Swedish traditions of assisting Hungarian Protestants, concentrated upon the issue where saw himself competent. The messages he sent to Vienna however also should be seen as the limits of what he was ready to do: it is unlikely that more emphasis on confessional conflicts from the part of Hungarian diplomacy would have brought more success in gaining support from Charles XII. We can thus see this episode as an example of rare purity where the lasting legacy of the Protestant cause in early-eighteenth-century foreign policy can be observed, but also as a clear illustration of its limits.

Notes

* This chapter is based on an article first published in Hungarian: 'Kísérletek svéd szövetség biztosítására II. Rákóczi Ferenc szabadságharcához,' *Hadtörténelmi Közlemények* 126 (2013): 116–31.

1 See, with further literature, Johannes Burkhardt, 'Konfession als Argument in den zwischenstaatlichen Beziehungen: Friedenschancen und Religionskriegsgefahren in der Entspannungspolitik zwischen Ludwig XIV. und dem Kaiserhof,' in *Rahmenbedingungen und Handlungsspielräume europäischer Außenpolitik im Zeitalter Ludwigs XIV.* ed. Heinz Duchhardt (Berlin: Duncker & Humblot, 1991), 135–154.

2 For a general overview, see Géza Pálffy, *The Kingdom of Hungary and the Habsburg Monarchy in the Sixteenth Century* (Boulder: Social Science Monographs, 2009); Szabolcs Varga, 'Die katholische Kirche im Königreich Ungarn zur Zeit des Konzils von Trient,' in *Das Trienter Konzil und seine Rezeption um Ungarn des 16. und 17. Jahrhunderts*, ed. Márta Fata et al. (Munster: Aschendorff, 2019), 63–78.

3 Márta Fata, *Ungarn, das Reich der Stephanskrone, im Zeitalter der Reformation und Konfessionalisierung: Multiethnizität, Land und Konfession 1500 bis 1700* (Münster: Aschendorff, 2000).

4 Katalin Péter, 'The Golden Age of the Principality (1606–1660),' in *History of Transylvania*. Vol. 2: *From 1606 to 1830*, ed. László Makkai, András Mócsy and Zoltán Szász (Boulder: Social Science Monographs, 2002), 3–228; Graeme Murdock, *Calvinism on the Frontier: International Calvinism and the Reformed Church in Hungary and Transylvania* (Oxford: Clarendon, 2000); István Keul, *Early Modern Religious Communities in East-Central Europe: Ethnic Diversity, Denominational Plurality, and Corporative Politics in the Principality of Transylvania (1526–1691)* (Leiden–Boston: Brill, 2009).

5 Sándor Szilágyi, 'Gabriel Bethlen und die schwedische Diplomatie,' *Ungarische Revue* 2 (1882): 457–488; Michael Roberts, *Gustavus Adolphus: A History of Sweden, 1611–1632* (London–New York: Longmans, 1953–1965), vol. 1, 201–216, and vol. 2, 321–332; Gábor Kármán, 'II. Gusztáv Adolf és Erdély fejedelmei,' *Századok* 152 (2018): 717–769.

6 Sándor Szilágyi, 'Georg Rákóczy I. im 30jährigen Kriege,' *Ungarische Revue* 3 (1883): 237–260; idem, 'Georg Rákóczy I. und die Diplomatie,' *Literarische Berichte aus Ungarn* 2 (1878): 402–417; Gábor Kármán, *Confession and Politics in the Principality of Transylvania 1644–1657* (Göttingen: Vandenhoeck & Ruprecht, 2020), 53–86.

7 Kármán, *Confession and Politics*, 87–222; Sándor Gebei, II. *Rákóczi György erdélyi fejedelem külpolitikája (1648–1657)* (Eger: EKTF and Líceum, 1996), 166–73.

8 For a general overview on the history of the Rákóczi insurrection, see István M. Szijártó, 'The Rákóczi Revolt as a Successful Rebellion,' in *Resistance, Rebellion and Revolution in Hungary and Central Europe: Commemorating 1956*, ed. László Péter and Martin Rady (London: Hungarian Cultural Center–University College London School of Slavonic & Eastern European Studies, 2008), 67–76; Ferenc Tóth, 'Introduction,' in *Correspondance diplomatique relative á la guerre d'indépendance du prince François II Rákóczi (1703–1711)*, ed. Ferenc Tóth (Paris: Champion, 2012), 11–116.

9 The most recent summaries of Rákóczi's foreign policy are István Czigány, 'A Rákóczi-szabadságharc és a közép- és kelet-európai hadihelyzet 1703–1711,'

Hadtörténelmi Közlemények 124 (2011): 1013–31; János Kalmár, 'A Rákóczi-szabadságharc és Európa: Közjogi helyzet és külpolitikai törekvések,' in *Előadások a Rákóczi-szabadságharc történetéből. A Magyar Történelmi Társulat gyöngyösi konferenciája*, ed. Csaba Katona (Budapest: Magyar Történelmi Társulat, 2004), 7–16; Béla Köpeczi, *II. Rákóczi Ferenc külpolitikája* (Budapest: Akadémiai, 2002).

10 Specifically, on Rákóczi's contacts with Charles XII, see the following detailed but somewhat outdated surveys: Lajos Péterffy, *XII. Károly svéd magyar összeköttetései* (Arad: Aradi Nyomda, 1907); Aurél Wagner, *A diplomáciai viszony XII. Károly és II. Rákóczi Ferenc közt a poltavai csatáig* (Budapest: s.n., 1928). See also Gustaf Jonasson, 'XII. Károly svéd király és Rákóczi,' in *Európa és a Rákóczi-szabadságharc*, ed. Kálmán Benda (Budapest: Akadémiai, 1980), 61–4.

11 The best work to date on the foreign policy of Charles XII remains Ragnhild M. Hatton, *Charles XII of Sweden* (London: Weidenfeld & Nicholson, 1968). From the earlier literature, see also Otto Haintz, *König Karl XII. von Schweden*, vol. 1–3 (Berlin: de Gruyter, 1958). More recent titles are usually less detailed and written in a popular history style. See Jan Lindegren, 'Karl XII,' in Anders Florén, Stellan Dahlgren and Jan Lindegren, *Kungar och krigare. Tre essäer om Karl X Gustav, Karl XI och Karl XII* (Stockholm: Atlantis, 1992), 149–225; Bengt Liljegren, *Karl XII. En biografi* (Lund: Historiska media, 1999).

12 On the details of the envoy's activities, see Kálmán Benda, 'Le projet d'alliance hungaro-suédo-prussienne de 1704,' in *Etudes historiques publiées par la Commission Nationale des Historiens Hongrois*, vol. 1 (Budapest: Akadémiai, 1960), 669–93.

13 See the instructions in Kálmán Benda et al., ed., *Ráday Pál iratai 1703–1706* (Budapest: Akadémiai, 1955) (henceforth RPI I), 119–26.

14 On the military events in the first year of the uprising, see Tóth, 'Introduction,' 91–94. On the negotiations concerning the French assistance, see Béla Köpeczi, *La France et la Hongrie au debut du XVIIIᵉ siècle. Etude d'histoire des relations diplomatiques et d'histoire des idées* (Budapest: Akadémiai, 1971), 52–90; Ferenc Tóth, 'L'influence de la diplomatie française dans une region péripherique de l'Europe: Le cas de la correspondance diplomatique de Louis XIV durant la guerre d'indépendance hongroise (1703–1711),' in *Gouverner par les lettres, de l'Antiquité à l'époque moderne*, ed. Agnès Bérenger and Olivier Dard (Metz: Centre de Recherche Universitaire Lorrain d'Histoire, 2015), 74–94.

15 See points [II.]6, [III.]2, and [III.]1 in the instructions: RPI I, 123 and 125.

16 Actually, the document only secured cooperation at the Reichstag, and Prussian neutrality in the questions related to the Polish–Lithuanian Commonwealth in exchange for the acknowledgement of Frederick I's royal title. See Erich Hassinger, *Brandenburg-Preußen, Schweden und Rußland 1700–1713* (Munich: Isar, 1953), 87–102.

17 The Peace of Travendal was signed on 18th August, 1700, by the representatives of the Swedish and Danish kings. Charles XII received English and Dutch support because with his menace, Frederick IV broke the 1689 Treaty of Altona, of which these two powers were the guarantors. Haintz, *Karl XII*, vol. 1, 29–34; Hatton, *Charles XII*, 125–39.

18 As its inhabitants called the Noble Republic of Poland–Lithuania.

19 Haintz, *Karl XII*, vol. 1, 35–93; Hatton, *Charles XII*, 165–97; Robert I. Frost, *The Northern Wars 1558–1721: War, State, and Society in Northeastern Europe* (Harlow: Longman, 2000), 229–30, 263–76. On Charles XII's dilemma concerning Poland, see Gustaf Jonasson, *Karl XII och hans rådgivare: Den utrikespolitiska maktkampen i Sverige 1697–1702* (Stockholm: Almqvist & Wiksell, 1960), 168–260; id., *Karl XII:s polska politik, 1702–1703* (Stockholm: Norstedt, 1968).

20 Herman Brulin, *Sverige och Frankrike under nordiska kriget och spanska succcessionskrisen åren 1700–1701* (Uppsala: s.n., 1905), 160–62, 202–20; Jonasson, *Karl XII och hans rådgivare,* 200–28. French diplomacy also supported that Rákóczi should seek contact with Charles XII. See Wagner, *A diplomáciai viszony,* 22–25; Béla Köpeczi, *A Rákóczi-szabadságharc és Franciaország* (Budapest: Akadémiai, 1966), 51.

21 Jöran Andersson Nordberg, *Leben Carl des Zwölften Königs in Schweden,* [trans. Johann Heinrich Heubel], vol. 1 (Hamburg: Beneke, 1745), 490. See also Benda, 'Le projet,' 685–86.

22 Ráday's memorandum to Charles XII (Heilsberg, early 1704), RPI I, 135–40. On the Ottoman threat, see Ferenc Rákóczi II's secret instructions to his envoys (Miskolc, late January 1704), ibid., 129. Both the instructions and the memorandum emphasised that the leaders of the insurrection were not planning to apply for the sultan's help. At this moment, this was more or less true, although some negotiations had already been going on that Imre Thököly, the last Prince of Transylvania, who had been appointed by the sultan, would return to the country (which had already been under the Habsburgs' rule for some ten years) with Ottoman help. See Kálmán Benda, 'II. Rákóczi Ferenc török politikájának első évei 1702–1705,' *Történelmi Szemle* 5 (1962): 189–207; Sándor Papp, 'A Rákóczi-szabadságharc török diplomáciája,' *Századok* 138 (2004): 795–98; Gábor Vatai, 'Út az irrealitásba (Rákóczi török diplomáciája a szabadságharc idején),' *Keletkutatás* [38], fall (2011): 92–94. On the power of the 'Türkenkrieg' discourse, see Anuschka Tischer, *Offizielle Kriegsbegründungen in der Frühen Neuzeit: Herrscherkommunikation in Europa zwischen Souveränität und korporativem Selbstverständnis* (Berlin: LIT, 2012).

23 Carl Piper to Ferenc Rákóczi II (Heilsberg, 5th/15th April, 1704), RPI I, 142.

24 Ferenc Rákóczi II to Charles XII (Gyöngyös, 28th August, 1704), published in summary, RPI I, 166.

25 See Ferenc Rákóczi II's instructions to Pál Ráday for his meetings with Charles XII and Stanisław Leszczyński (Eger, 30th April and 1st May, 1705), RPI I, 251–58, 258–62.

26 Ráday's memorandum to Charles XII (early June 1705), RPI I, 277–80. On the military developments in 1704–1705, see Tóth, 'Introduction,' 94–97.

27 RPI I, 253–54, 278.

28 Hatton, *Charles XII,* 198–201; Nils Herlitz, *Från Thorn till Altranstädt: Studier över Carl XII:s politik 1703–1706,* vol. 1, *(1703–1704)* (Stockholm: Norstedt, 1916), 216–45.

29 On the Viennese worries, see Stig Backman, *Från Rawicz till Fraustadt: Studier i det stora nordiska krigets diplomati 1704–1706* (Lund: Gleerup, 1940), 340. The author suggests that Ráday's mission was motivated by the news that the tsar was planning to send troops to Hungary to assist the emperor. It is more likely that it was Charles XII's perceived threat upon Silesia that urged Rákóczi to send his envoy to the king.

30 RPI I, 256, 279.

31 On Ráday's audience, see his diary: RPI I, 295; Carl Piper to Ferenc Rákóczi II (Rawicz, 11th July, 1705), ibid., 281–82. On the mission in general, see Kálmán Benda's introduction to the edited sources and Backman, *Från Rawicz,* 338–45.

32 See the 10th July, 1705, entry of Ráday's diary: RPI I, 294.

33 Hatton, *Charles XII,* 193–94.

34 On the failure of the mediation attempt, see Péterffy, *XII. Károly,* 15–17; Herlitz, *Från Thorn,* 255; Backman, *Från Rawicz,* 345. It is worth noting that Stanisław Leszczyński showed much more enthusiasm concerning Ráday's suggestions. Although he deemed the invasion of Silesia untimely, he promised

that he would discuss the idea of the 'Hungarian–Polish league' at the diet. See the 4th July, 1705, entry of Ráday's diary: RPI I, 293.
35 Ferenc Rákóczi II to Pál Ráday (camp by Mocsonok, 29 July 1705), Kálmán Thaly, ed., *II. Rákóczi Ferenc leveleskönyvei, levéltárának egykorú lajstromaival*, vol 1, *1703–1706*, Archivum Rákóczianum I/1 (Pest: Akadémia, 1873), 380; Olof Hermelin to Pál Ráday (Warsaw, 15 August and 22 September 1705), RPI I, 317–18, 390–91. Rákóczi indeed mentioned the possibility of an Ottoman–Russian war in his instructions to János Pápai, the envoy he sent to Constantinople in October 1705; however, due to the pressure of the French ambassador at the Sublime Porte, this was eventually not mentioned in the memorandum submitted to the grand vizier. The impact of Rákóczi's diplomats upon the sultan's court remained rather limited; they did not even receive an official audience. See Benda, 'II. Rákóczi Ferenc,' 206–7; Papp, 'A Rákóczi-szabadságharc,' 803–812; Vatai, 'Út az irrealitásba,' 100–4.
36 On Grofey's actions serving Rákóczi's interests, see RPI I, 234–35. On his diplomatic activities and the contact with Des Alleurs, see Backman, *Från Rawicz*, 40–41; Gabriel Syveton, *Louis XIV et Charles XII au camp d'Altranstadt 1707. La mission du Baron de Benseval* (Paris: s.n., 1900), 15.
37 Charles XII answered to Grofey's questions that Rákóczi should rather take contact with the Swedish ambassador in Vienna. See Sven Olsson, *Olof Hermelin: En karolinsk kulturpersonlighet och statsman* (Lund: Gleerup, 1953), 470; Köpeczi, *La France*, 203.
38 The classic works on the Altranstädt Convention are Ernst Carlson, *Der Vertrag zwischen Karl XII. von Schweden und Kaiser Joseph I. zu Altranstädt 1707* (Stockholm: Norstedt, 1907); Norbert Conrads, *Die Durchführung der Altranstädter Konvention in Schlesien 1707–1709* (Cologne and Vienna: Böhlau, 1971), 3–50. See also Åsa Karlsson, 'Den tolerante enväldshärskaren? Karl XII och fördraget i Altranstädt,' *Karolinska Förbundets Årsbok 2008*, 203–13. According to Jerker Rosén, the contacts of the Swedish king with Rákóczi played a relevant role in the feeling of insecurity at the emperor's court. See his *Den svenska utrikespolitikens historia*, vol. II/1, *1697–1721* (Stockholm: Norstedt, 1952), 108.
39 Sándor Márki, *Nagy Péter czár és II. Rákóczi Ferencz szövetsége 1707-ben* (Budapest: Akadémia, 1913); Stěpan Tomašivskij, 'Adatok II. Rákóczi Ferenc és kora történetéhez (Dr. Márki Sándor monographiája kapcsán),' *Századok* 46 (1912): 113–27, 192–208, 758–72; József Perényi, 'II. Rákóczi Ferenc és I. Péter diplomáciai kapcsolatának kezdetei,' in *Magyar–orosz történelmi kapcsolatok*, ed. Endre Kovács (Budapest: Művelt Nép, 1956), 52–95; János Váradi-Sternberg, *Századok öröksége* (Budapest and Užgorod: Kárpáti, 1981), 7–47; Sándor Gebei, 'Az 1707. évi lengyel és magyar detronizáció politikai háttere,' *Hadtörténelmi Közlemények* 120 (2007): 1268–92.
40 Memorandum sent to Rehnskiöld in Pál Ráday's name ([Homonna], 22nd August, 1707) Kálmán Benda and Ferenc Maksay, eds., *Ráday Pál iratai 1707–1708* (Budapest: Akadémiai, 1961) (henceforth RPI II), 296–300.
41 II. Rákóczi Ferenc fejedelem, *Emlékiratai a magyarországi háborúról 1703-tól annak végéig*, transl. by István Vas, ed. by Béla Köpeczi, Archivum Rákóczianum. 3. osztály: Írók. II. Rákóczi Ferenc művei 1 (Budapest: Akadémiai, 1978), 397. As Kálmán Benda pointed out in his introduction to the memorandum's edition, this section of the *Mémoires* has several errors: contrary to what Rákóczi said, Ráday did not personally travel to the Swedish camp at that time: RPI II, 295–96.

42 Jöran Andersson Nordberg, *Leben Carl des Zwölften Königs in Schweden*, transl. by Johann Heinrich Heubel, vol. 2 (Hamburg: Beneke, 1746), 22–23. See also Olsson, *Olof Hermelin*, 470.

43 See the report of the unknown Polish mediator: RPI II, 302–3. On Charles XII's campaign and the failure of the Treaty of Warsaw between Peter the Great and Rákóczi, see Hatton, *Charles XII*, 231–60; János Váradi-Sternberg, 'Ukraincev, Péter cár követe Magyarországon 1708-ban,' *Századok* 93 (1959): 232–51; Vladimir Alekseevič Artamonov, 'Magyarország és az orosz–lengyel szövetség 1707–1712,' in *Európa és a Rákóczi-szabadságharc*, 45–51; Sándor Gebei, 'I. Péter cár és II. Rákóczi Ferenc fejedelem 1707. évi varsói egyezményének utóélete,' in *II. Rákóczi Ferenc, az államférfi. Tanulmányok a sárospataki országgyűlés 300. évfordulóján*, ed. Edit Tamás (Sárospatak: Rákóczi Múzeum, 2008), 98–119.

44 Árpád Markó, *XII. Károly svéd király és Magyarország* (Budapest and Stockholm: Svéd Intézet, 1970).

45 Rákóczi's instructions to Pál Ráday (s.d.) A Dunamelléki Református Egyházkerület Ráday Levéltára (Ráday Archives of the Danube Diocese of the Reformed Church, Budapest, henceforth DRERL), C/64 Ráday család levéltára 4d2–5, pp. 1–12. I am grateful to Sándor Papp for having called my attention to this source.

46 Credentials were written somewhat later (probably upon Ráday's request), but they reached Bender too late, and were not used: DRERL C/64–4d2–5, p. 89. Ráday entered into conversation with Royal Secretary Heinrich Gustav von Müllern, General Anders Lagercrona, and Stanisław Poniatowski. See Pál Ráday, '1709. Benderbe menő utazásomnak diariuma,' in *Rákóczi-tár*, vol. 1, ed. Kálmán Thaly (Pest: Lauffer, 1866), 410–14.

47 Pál Ráday to Ferenc Rákóczi II (Suceava, 13th January, 1710) and Heinrich Gustav von Müllern to Ráday (Bender, 3rd/13th January, 1710) DRERL C/64–4d2–5, pp. 72–73, 80–83. On the relevance of the universal peace in Rákóczi's foreign policy, see Ágnes R. Várkonyi, '"Ad Pacem Universalem." A szatmári béke nemzetközi előzményei,' *Századok* 114 (1980): 165–94; János Kalmár, 'La question de la Transylvanie aux traités de Rastatt (1714),' in *Európai szemmel: Tanulmányok Köpeczi Béla tiszteletére*, ed. János Kalmár (Budapest: Universitas, 2007), 61–66; Ferenc Tóth, 'Le traité d'Utrecht et la question hongroise,' in *La Diplomatie-monde: Autour de la paix d'Utrecht 1713*, ed. Lucien Bély, Guillaume Hanotin and Géraud Poumarède (Paris: Pedone, 2019), 343–56.

48 See articles 1 and 2 of the Gyulafehérvár Agreement, signed on 16th November, 1643: Sándor Szilágyi, ed., *Okmánytár I. Rákóczy György svéd és franczia szövetkezéseinek történetéhez*, Monumenta Hungariae Historica. Ser. I. Diplomataria 21 (Budapest: Magyar Tudományos Akadémia, 1873) (henceforth MHHD XXI), 106–7. The articles (without the preamble) were also published in Carl Hallendorff, ed., *Sveriges traktater med främmande magter jemte andra dit hörande handlingar*, vol. V/2, *1632–1645* (Stockholm: Norstedt, 1909), 539–42.

49 Rákóczi, *Emlékiratai*, 319.

50 Köpeczi, *La France*, 36, 54; Kalmár, 'A Rákóczi-szabadságharc'; Czigány, 'A Rákóczi-szabadságharc,' 1018–21.

51 Charlotte Amalie to Charles XII (Vienna, 15th October, 1701) Riksarkivet (Stockholm), Diplomatica Turcica bihang Transsylvanica, vol. 1, nr. 101.

52 Instructions of Rákóczi in 1704 (with the elaboration of the argument), RPI I, 124; Ráday's memorandum in 1704, ibid., 137; Ráday's memorandum from 1705, ibid., 277–78; the letter to Rehnskiöld, RPI II, 296–97.

53 Rákóczi, *Emlékiratai*, 318–19.

54 Kármán, *Confession and Politics*, 65–74.

55 The Gyulafehérvár Agreement should be in the Riksarkivet's following section: Originaltraktater med främmande makter: Bihang till Turkiet: Siebenbürgen. Two

copies, without the preamble, are available in the sections Diplomatica Turcica bihang Transylvanica, vol. 1, nr. 144; and Johann Adler Salvii samling, vol. 25, nr. 14. On the missing ratification, see Kármán, *Confession and Politics*, 54–64.

56 Benda, 'Le projet,' 685.

57 Rákóczi's declaration (Gyulafehérvár, 26th April, 1643) and Torstensson's commentaries (Dobitschau, 10th July, 1643), DRERL C/64–4d2-2, fol. 1–7. The German version, under the title *Vergleichung Zwischen Ihr Königl. Majest. zu Schweden Herrn General Feld-Marschalck Leonhard Torstensohn und Georg Ragotzky Fürsten in Siebenbürgen*, was later also republished in *Theatrum Europaeum*: Johann Peter Lotichius, *Theatri Europaei Fünffter Theil … [1643–1647]* (Frankfurt am Main: Merian, 1651), 403–5. The French version is known from later collections, such as Jean Dumont, *Corps universel diplomatique du droit des gens … Tome VI, partie 1* (Amsterdam: Brunel, 1728), 273–75.

58 The text was titled 'Puncta confoederationis' or 'Vergleichung' to make this point. The French edition was more realistic than the German and Latin versions, calling the text 'Sommaire/Acceptance des démandes.' This 'pirate copy' of the Swedish–Transylvanian alliance also misled modern historians: in his monograph about Transylvania's place in early modern international law, Gerald Volkmer presented this copy as the actual treaty and the November version (which was indeed signed by both parties) as the ratification document. See his *Siebenbürgen zwischen Habsburgermonarchie und Osmanischem Reich: Völkerrechtliche Stellung und Völkerrechtspraxis eines ostmitteleuropäischen Fürstentums 1541–1699* (Munich: Oldenbourg and de Gruyter, 2015), 373–5.

59 Kármán, *Confession and Politics*, 223–50.

60 Otfried Czaika, 'Carolus Redivivus oder der wiederaufwachende nordische Löwe – Das Bild Karls XII. als Retter des Protestantismus in der proschwedischen Publizistik,' in *Religia i polityka. Kwestie wyznaniowe i konflikty polityczne w Europie w XVIII wieku. W 300. rocznicę konwencji w Altranstädt*, ed. by Lucyna Harc and Gabriela Wąs (Wrocław: Wydawn. Uniw. Wrocławskiego, 2009), 56–83. Confessional justification strategies were still used in Sweden to explain the necessity of Sweden's effort in the Great Northern War. See Peter Ericsson, *Stora nordiska kriget förklarat: Karl XII och det ideologiska tilltalet* (Uppsala: Universitet Uppsala, 2002), 73–132.

61 László Makkai, 'Bevezetés,' in *Galeria omnium sanctorum: A magyarországi gályarab prédikátorok emlékezete*, ed. László Makkai (Budapest: Akadémiai, 1976), 7–28; Graeme Murdock, 'Responses to Habsburg Persecution of Protestants in Seventeenth-Century Hungary,' *Austrian History Yearbook* 40 (2009): 37–52.

62 Hatton, *Charles XII*, 198; Czaika, 'Carolus Redivivus,' 64–65.

63 Kármán, *Confession and Politics*, 251–58; Márta Fata, *Ungarn, das Reich der Stephanskrone, im Zeitalter der Reformation und Konfessionalisierung: Multiethnizität, Land und Konfession 1500 bis 1700* (Münster: Aschendorff, 2000).

64 This is how the point of Linda Frey and Marsha Frey should be understood, who also identified the Rákóczi insurrection as a confessionally based movement. See their 'The Confessional Issue in International Politics: The Rákóczi Insurrection,' in *R. Várkonyi Ágnes emlékkönyv születésének 70. évfordulója ünnepére*, ed. by Péter Tusor (Budapest: ELTE, 1998), 431–41.

65 RPI I, 92–110.

66 Kármán, *Confession and Politics*, 62–65.

67 Köpeczi, *La France*, 36. The religious policies of the prince indeed aimed at achieving peace between the confessional groups. See Tamás Esze, 'Rákóczi valláspolitikája,' in *Európa és a Rákóczi-szabadságharc*, 285–96; Sándor Ladányi,

'Ráday Pál vallásügyi tevékenységének helye II. Rákóczi Ferenc valláspolitikájában,' *Studia Caroliensia 5*, no. 3–4 (2004): 287–92.
68 RPI I, 136–37.
69 See the edition of Okolicsányi's memorandum in its full version, submitted to Frederick I of Prussia: RPI I, 148–50, and Rákóczi's instructions, ibid., 123. As noted above, the memorandum submitted to Charles XII made no mention of Hungary's inclusion to the Swedish–Prussian alliance.
70 On the envoys of Hungarian Protestants to Brandenburg, see Kálmán Benda's summary in RPI I, 145, n1.
71 See their memorandum in DRERL C/64–4d2–18, pp. 13–16. The mission's history was written, based on Szirmay's library, by Béla Majláth, 'Egy magyar követség Svédországban 1705-ben,' *Századok* 14 (1880): 785–95.
72 Daniel Krman, *Küldetésem története. Itinerarium (1708–1709)*, transl. by Zsuzsanna Szabó and Judit Nagy (Budapest and Bratislava: Madách, 1984).
73 Nordberg, *Leben Carl des Zwölften*, vol. 1, 505–6; vol. 2, 28.
74 See the summary of the offer for mediation: RPI I, 282. It is noteworthy that, similarly to the Silesian case, Charles XII referred to his role as guarantor of the Peace of Westphalia, although in the territories outside the Holy Roman Empire, such as in Hungary, this had no relevance. On the mediation offer, see Herlitz, *Från Thorn*, 253–55; Péterffy, *XII. Károly*, 15–16.
75 Tibor Fabiny, 'Rákóczi diplomáciájának egyházpolitikai vonatkozásai,' in *Európa és a Rákóczi-szabadságharc*, 301–5.
76 RPI I, 547–52.
77 Imre Révész, 'Comenius unokája. Daniel Ernest Jablonski születésének háromszázadik évfordulójára,' *Századok* 96 (1962): 1–24; Joachim Bahlcke, 'Die Rekonstruktion der intellektuellen Kultur Europas im 1700: Forschungen zu Leben, Werk und Wirkung Daniel Ernst Jablonskis aus drei Jahrhunderten,' in *Daniel Ernst Jablonski: Religion, Wissenschaft und Politik um 1700*, ed. by Joachim Bahlcke and Werner Korthaase (Wiesbaden: Harrasowitz, 2008), 40.

Bibliography

Archival sources

Dunamelléki Református Egyházkerület Ráday Levéltára [Réday Archives of the Danube Diocese of the Reformed Church, Budapest] (DRERL), C/64 Ráday család levéltára.
Riksarkivet (Stockholm) (RA), Diplomatica Turcica bihang Transsylvanica, Johann Adler Salvii samling, Originaltraktater med främmande makter.

Printed sources

Benda, Kálmán, Tamás Esze, Ferenc Maksay and László Pap, eds. *Ráday Pál iratai 1703–1706*. Budapest: Akadémiai, 1955.
Benda, Kálmán and Ferenc Maksay, eds. *Ráday Pál iratai 1707–1708*. Budapest: Akadémiai, 1961.
Dumont, Jean, ed. *Corps universel diplomatique du droit des gens … Tome VI, partie 1*. Amsterdam: Brunel, 1728.
Hallendorff, Carl, ed. *Sveriges traktater med främmande magter jemte andra dit hörande handlingar*. Vol. V/2: *1632–1645*. Stockholm: Norstedt, 1909.
Krman, Daniel. *Küldetésem története: Itinerarium (1708–1709)*. Translated by Zsuzsanna Szabó and Judit Nagy. Budapest and Bratislava: Madách, 1984.

Lotichius, Johann Peter. *Theatri Europaei Fünffter Theil ... [1643–1647]*. Frankfurt am Main: Merian, 1651.

Nordberg, Jöran Andersson. *Leben Carl des Zwölften Königs in Schweden*. Translated by Johann Heinrich Heubel. vol. 1–2. Hamburg: Beneke, 1745–1746.

Ráday, Pál. '1709. Benderbe menő utazásomnak diariuma.' In *Rákóczi-tár*, vol. 1, edited by Kálmán Thaly, 404–19. Pest: Lauffer, 1866.

Rákóczi, Ferenc, II. *Emlékiratai a magyarországi háborúról 1703-tól annak végéig*. Translated by István István Vas, edited by Béla Köpeczi. Archivum Rákóczianum. 3. osztály: Írók. II. Rákóczi Ferenc művei 1. Budapest: Akadémiai, 1978.

Szilágyi, Sándor, ed. *Okmánytár I. Rákóczy György svéd és franczia szövetkezéseinek történetéhez*. Monumenta Hungariae Historica. Ser. I. Diplomataria 21. Budapest: Magyar Tudományos Akadémia, 1873.

Thaly, Kálmán, ed. *II. Rákóczi Ferenc leveleskönyvei, levéltárának egykorú lajstromaival. Vol. 1: 1703–1706*. Archivum Rákóczianum I/1. Pest: Akadémia, 1873.

Literature

Artamonov, Vladimir Alekseevič. 'Magyarország és az orosz–lengyel szövetség 1707–1712.' In *Európa és a Rákóczi-szabadságharc*, edited by Kálmán Benda, 45–51. Budapest: Akadémiai, 1980.

Backman, Stig. *Från Rawicz till Fraustadt: Studier i det stora nordiska krigets diplomati 1704–1706*. Lund: Gleerup, 1940.

Bahlcke, Joachim. 'Die Rekonstruktion der intellektuellen Kultur Europas im 1700: Forschungen zu Leben, Werk und Wirkung Daniel Ernst Jablonskis aus drei Jahrhunderten.' In *Daniel Ernst Jablonski: Religion, Wissenschaft und Politik um 1700*, edited by Joachim Bahlcke and Werner Korthaase, 3–42. Wiesbaden: Harrasowitz, 2008.

Benda, Kálmán. 'Le projet d'alliance hungaro-suédo-prussienne de 1704.' In *Etudes historiques publiées par la Commission Nationale des Historiens Hongrois*, vol. 1, 669–93. Budapest: Akadémiai, 1960.

Benda, Kálmán. 'II. Rákóczi Ferenc török politikájának első évei 1702–1705.' *Történelmi Szemle* 5 (1962): 189–207.

Brulin, Herman. *Sverige och Frankrike under nordiska kriget och spanska successionskrisen åren 1700–1701*. Uppsala: s.n., 1905.

Burkhardt, Johannes. 'Konfession als Argument in den zwischenstaatlichen Beziehungen: Friedenschancen und Religionskriegsgefahren in der Entspannungspolitik zwischen Ludwig XIV. und dem Kaiserhof.' In *Rahmenbedingungen und Handlungs-spielräume europäischer Außenpolitik im Zeitalter Ludwigs XIV.*, edited by Heinz Duchhardt, 135–154. Berlin: Duncker & Humblot, 1991.

Carlson, Ernst. *Der Vertrag zwischen Karl XII. von Schweden und Kaiser Joseph I. zu Altranstädt 1707*. Stockholm: Norstedt, 1907.

Conrads, Norbert. *Die Durchführung der Altranstädter Konvention in Schlesien 1707–1709*. Cologne and Vienna: Böhlau, 1971.

Czaika, Otfried. 'Carolus Redivivus oder der wiederaufwachende nordische Löwe – Das Bild Karls XII. als Retter des Protestantismus in der proschwedischen Publizistik.' In *Religia i polityka: Kwestie wyznaniowe i konflikty polityczne w Europie w XVIII wieku. W 300. rocznicę konwencji w Altranstädt*, edited by Lucyna Harc and Gabriela Wąs, 56–83. Wrocław: Wydawn. Uniw. Wrocławskiego, 2009.

Czigány, István. 'A Rákóczi-szabadságharc és a közép- és kelet-európai hadihelyzet 1703–1711.' *Hadtörténelmi Közlemények* 124 (2011): 1013–31.

Ericsson, Peter. *Stora nordiska kriget förklarat: Karl XII och det ideologiska tilltalet.* Uppsala: Uppsala Universitet, 2002.

Esze, Tamás. 'Rákóczi valláspolitikája.' In *Európa és a Rákóczi-szabadságharc*, edited by Kálmán Benda, 285–96. Budapest: Akadémiai, 1980.

Fabiny, Tibor. 'Rákóczi diplomáciájának egyházpolitikai vonatkozásai.' In *Európa és a Rákóczi-szabadságharc*, edited by Kálmán Benda, 301–5. Budapest: Akadémiai, 1980.

Fata, Márta, *Ungarn, das Reich der Stephanskrone, im Zeitalter der Reformation und Konfessionalisierung: Multiethnizität, Land und Konfession 1500 bis 1700.* Münster: Aschendorff, 2000.

Frey, Linda and Marsha Frey. 'The Confessional Issue in International Politics: The Rákóczi Insurrection.' In R. *Várkonyi Ágnes emlékkönyv születésének 70. évfordulója ünnepére*, edited by Péter Tusor, 431–41. Budapest: ELTE, 1998.

Frost, Robert I. *The Northern Wars 1558–1721: War, State, and Society in Northeastern Europe.* Harlow: Longman, 2000.

Gebei, Sándor. *II. Rákóczi György erdélyi fejedelem külpolitikája (1648–1657).* Eger: EKTF and Líceum, 1996.

Gebei, Sándor. 'Az 1707. évi lengyel és magyar detronizáció politikai háttere.' *Hadtörténelmi Közlemények* 120 (2007): 1268–292.

Gebei, Sándor. 'I. Péter cár és II. Rákóczi Ferenc fejedelem 1707. évi varsói egyezményének utóélete.' In *II. Rákóczi Ferenc, az államférfi: Tanulmányok a sárospataki országgyűlés 300. évfordulóján*, edited by Edit Tamás, 98–119. Sárospatak: Rákóczi Múzeum, 2008.

Haintz, Otto. *König Karl XII. von Schweden*, vol. 1–3. Berlin: de Gruyter, 1958.

Hassinger, Erich. *Brandenburg-Preußen, Schweden und Rußland 1700–1713.* Munich: Isar, 1953.

Hatton, Ragnhild M. *Charles XII of Sweden.* London: Weidenfeld & Nicholson, 1968.

Herlitz, Nils. *Från Thorn till Altranstädt: Studier över Carl XII:s politik 1703–1706.* vol. 1, *(1703–1704).* Stockholm: Norstedt, 1916.

Jonasson, Gustaf. *Karl XII och hans rådgivare: Den utrikespolitiska maktkampen i Sverige 1697–1702.* Stockholm: Almqvist & Wiksell, 1960.

Jonasson, Gustaf. *Karl XII.s polska politik, 1702–1703.* Stockholm: Norstedt, 1968.

Jonasson, Gustaf. 'XII. Károly svéd király és Rákóczi.' In *Európa és a Rákóczi-szabadságharc*, edited by Kálmán Benda, 61–64. Budapest: Akadémiai, 1980.

Kalmár, János. 'A Rákóczi-szabadságharc és Európa: Közjogi helyzet és külpolitikai törekvések.' In *Előadások a Rákóczi-szabadságharc történetéből: A Magyar Történelmi Társulat gyöngyösi konferenciája*, edited by Csaba Katona, 7–16. Budapest: Magyar Történelmi Társulat, 2004.

Kalmár, János. 'La question de la Transylvanie aux traités de Rastatt (1714).' In *Európai szemmel: Tanulmányok Köpeczi Béla tiszteletére*, edited by János Kalmár, 61–66. Budapest: Universitas, 2007.

Karlsson, Åsa. 'Den tolerante envåldshärskaren? Karl XII och fördraget i Altranstädt.' *Karolinska Förbundets Årsbok 2008*: 203–13.

Kármán, Gábor. 'II. Gusztáv Adolf és Erdély fejedelmei.' *Századok* 152 (2018): 717–69.

Kármán, Gábor. *Confession and Politics in the Principality of Transylvania 1644–1657*. Göttingen: Vandenhoeck & Ruprecht, 2020.

Keul, István. *Early Modern Religious Communities in East-Central Europe: Ethnic Diversity, Denominational Plurality, and Corporative Politics in the Principality of Transylvania (1526–1691)*. Leiden–Boston: Brill, 2009.

Köpeczi, Béla. *A Rákóczi-szabadságharc és Franciaország*. Budapest: Akadémiai, 1966.

Köpeczi, Béla. *La France et la Hongrie au debut du XVIIIᵉ siècle: Etude d'histoire des relations diplomatiques et d'histoire des idées*. Budapest: Akadémiai, 1971.

Köpeczi, Béla. *II. Rákóczi Ferenc külpolitikája*. Budapest: Akadémiai, 2002.

Ladányi, Sándor. 'Ráday Pál vallásügyi tevékenységének helye II. Rákóczi Ferenc valláspolitikájában.' *Studia Caroliensia 5*, no. 3–4 (2004): 287–92.

Liljegren, Bengt. *Karl XII: En biografi*. Lund: Historiska media, 1999.

Lindegren, Jan. 'Karl XII.' In *Kungar och krigare: Tre essäer om Karl X Gustav, Karl XI och Karl XII*, edited by Anders Florén, Stellan Dahlgren and Jan Lindegren, 149–225. Stockholm: Atlantis, 1992.

Majláth, Béla. 'Egy magyar követség Svédországban 1705-ben.' *Századok* 14 (1880): 785–95.

Makkai, László. 'Bevezetés.' In *Galeria omnium sanctorum: A magyarországi gályarab prédikátorok emlékezete*, edited by László Makkai, 7–28. Budapest: Akadémiai, 1976.

Márki, Sándor. *Nagy Péter czár és II. Rákóczi Ferencz szövetsége 1707-ben*. Budapest: Akadémia, 1913.

Markó, Árpád. *XII. Károly svéd király és Magyarország*. Budapest and Stockholm: Svéd Intézet, 1970.

Murdock, Graeme. 'Responses to Habsburg Persecution of Protestants in Seventeenth-Century Hungary.' *Austrian History Yearbook* 40 (2009): 37–52.

Murdock, Graeme. *Calvinism on the Frontier: International Calvinism and the Reformed Church in Hungary and Transylvania*. Oxford: Clarendon, 2000.

Olsson, Sven. *Olof Hermelin: En karolinsk kulturpersonlighet och statsman*. Lund: Gleerup, 1953.

Pálffy, Géza. *The Kingdom of Hungary and the Habsburg Monarchy in the Sixteenth Century*. Boulder: Social Science Monographs, 2009.

Papp, Sándor. 'A Rákóczi-szabadságharc török diplomáciája.' *Századok* 138 (2004): 793–821.

Perényi, József. 'II. Rákóczi Ferenc és I. Péter diplomáciai kapcsolatának kezdetei.' In *Magyar–orosz történelmi kapcsolatok*, edited by Endre Kovács, 52–95. Budapest: Művelt Nép, 1956.

Páter, Katalin. 'The Golden Age of the Principality (1606–1660).' In *History of Transylvania. Vol. 2: From 1606 to 1830*, edited by László Makkai, András Mócsy and Zoltán Szász, 3–228. Boulder: Social Science Monographs, 2002.

Péterffy, Lajos. *XII. Károly svéd király magyar összeköttetései*. Arad: Aradi Nyomda, 1907.

Révész, Imre. 'Comenius unokája: Daniel Ernest Jablonski születésének háromszázadik évfordulójára.' *Századok* 96 (1962): 1–24.

Rosén, Jerker. *Den svenska utrikespolitikens historia. vol. II/1, 1697–1721*. Stockholm: Norstedt, 1952.

Syveton, Gabriel. *Louis XIV et Charles XII au camp d'Altranstadt 1707: La mission du Baron de Benseval*. Paris: s.n., 1900.

Szijártó, István M. 'The Rákóczi Revolt as a Successful Rebellion.' In *Resistance, Rebellion and Revolution in Hungary and Central Europe: Commemorating 1956*, edited by László Péter and Martin Rady, 67–76. London: Hungarian Cultural Center–University College London School of Slavonic & Eastern European Studies, 2008.

Szilágyi, Sándor. 'Georg Rákóczy I. und die Diplomatie.' *Literarische Berichte aus Ungarn* 2 (1878): 402–17.

Szilágyi, Sándor. 'Gabriel Bethlen und die schwedische Diplomatie.' *Ungarische Revue* 2 (1882): 457–88.

Szilágyi, Sándor. 'Georg Rákóczy I. im 30jährigen Kriege.' *Ungarische Revue* 3 (1883): 237–60.

Tischer, Anuschka. *Offizielle Kriegsbegründungen in der Frühen Neuzeit: Herrscherkommunikation in Europa zwischen Souveränität und korporativem Selbstverständnis.* Berlin: LIT, 2012.

Tomašivskij, Stĕpan. 'Adatok II. Rákóczi Ferenc és kora történetéhez (Dr. Márki Sándor monographiája kapcsán).' *Századok* 46 (1912): 113–27, 192–208, 758–72.

Tóth, Ferenc. 'Introduction.' In *Correspondance diplomatique relative à la guerre d'indépendance du prince François II Rákóczi (1703–1711)*, edited by Ferenc Tóth, 11–116. Paris: Champion, 2012.

Tóth, Ferenc. 'L'influence de la diplomatie française dans une region péripherique de l'Europe: Le cas de la correspondance diplomatique de Louis XIV durant la guerre d'indépendance hongroise (1703–1711).' In *Gouverner par les lettres, de l'Antiquité à l'époque moderne*, edited by Agnès Bérenger and Olivier Dard, 74–94. Metz: Centre de Recherche Universitaire Lorrain d'Histoire, 2015.

Tóth, Ferenc. 'Le traité d'Utrecht et la question hongroise.' In *La Diplomatie-monde: Autour de la paix d'Utrecht 1713*, edited by Lucien Bély, Guillaume Hanotin and Géraud Poumarède, 343–56. Paris: Pedone, 2019.

Váradi-Sternberg, János. 'Ukraincev, Péter cár követe Magyarországon 1708-ban.' *Századok* 93 (1959): 232–51.

Váradi-Sternberg, János. *Századok öröksége.* Budapest and Užgorod: Kárpáti, 1981.

Varga, Szabolcs 'Die katholische Kirche im Königreich Ungarn zur Zeit des Konzils von Trient.' In *Das Trienter Konzil und seine Rezeption um Ungarn des 16. und 17. Jahrhunderts*, edited by Márta Fata, András Forgó, Gabriele Haug-Moritz and Anton Schindling, 63–78. Munster: Aschendorff, 2019.

Várkonyi, Ágnes R. '"Ad Pacem Universalem." A szatmári béke nemzetközi előzményei.' *Századok* 114 (1980): 165–94.

Vatai, Gábor. 'Út az irrealitásba (Rákóczi török diplomáciája a szabadságharc idején).' *Keletkutatás* 38, fall (2011): 91–108.

Volkmer, Gerald. *Siebenbürgen zwischen Habsburgermonarchie und Osmanischem Reich: Völkerrechtliche Stellung und Völkerrechtspraxis eines ostmitteleuropäischen Fürstentums 1541–1699.* Munich: Oldenbourg and de Gruyter, 2015.

Wagner, Aurél. *A diplomáciai viszony XII. Károly és II. Rákóczi Ferenc közt a poltavai csatáig.* Budapest: s.n., 1928.

13 Afterword

Gábor Kármán

The Reformation introduced new phenomena into the functioning of diplomacy in Europe. Religious conflicts, which had until then only existed on the fringes of the continent, and in certain periods in relation to smaller territories that resisted the authority of the pope within Christianity, became a part of everyday reality in foreign policy and required, as a rule, constant attention in order to keep the system of relations between rulers functioning. Some scholars have even suggested that an international system was created as a consequence of the establishment of the various denominations: religious groups provided a stable framework that, to a certain extent, predetermined the place of specific actors in the system in a much more stable manner than the ever-changing dynastic preferences, which could be changed quickly and often without having to pay a substantial political price. By the end of the sixteenth century, most territories were confessionalised – that is, in general, rulers and their subjects belonged to a specific confessional group – resulting in adding religion and confessional issues as an important element to the factors determining political choices, and at the same time producing some problems that the culture of diplomacy had earlier not been acquainted with, such as the question of the embassy chapel.

Of course, through the establishment of various denominations and their connections to specific states, two spheres came into contact that were doomed to conflict, as is well illustrated by the chapters of this collection. Confessional adherence, based on accepting specific theological truths, logically led to the wish that these truths should also be accepted by others, or at least that those who had already been on the right path would not be misled by another party. The fact that these theological truths came into dispute with others produced a situation where it seemed obvious that the means of power controlled by politics could be used to access the ultimate goal: not allowing others to lead people into theological delusion. Contrary to the logic of power politics, where actors aim at maximising their profit, but should be ready for compromise if they face unsurmountable resistance, the logic of theological conviction was bound to lead people to conclusions similar to those of Melchior Khlesl, Archbishop of Vienna and main advisor of Emperor Matthias: that religious peace contradicted theology and conscience, and could only be accepted as a lesser evil to slaughter. As pointed out by Rubén González Cuerva in his chapter, some schools of thought (in this case, possibilism) helped to ease the conscience of those who in politics sometimes had to choose solutions that seemed morally dubious; nevertheless, the tension remained and resurfaced in various forms depending on the specific time and space – a phenomenon for which this volume gives an intriguing variety of examples.

The purest form of using political means for the sake of confessional interests can be seen by the example of the Holy See, as is clear from the number of essays related to papal foreign policy in this volume. In a Catholic environment, the nuncios enjoyed a high reputation, which made their task of promoting the interests of Catholicism (as interpreted by the Papal Curia) relatively easy. Even in mixed confessional contexts, the status of the pope as the sole representative of his creed provided him and his diplomats with a highly protected status: as Dorota Gregorowicz's analysis reveals, any Protestant critique on the nuncios' activities could be interpreted as a direct affront against Catholicism, and as such as a threat against religious peace, which provided the nuncios with a relatively wide space for manoeuvring. During the Polish elections, the nuncios seemed to have been able to realise their minimum programme – that is, fending off any challenge to Catholic dominance in the royal court – without any serious problems, which left them enough energy to look for the opportunities for further gains. The fact that their reputation was almost entirely based upon their spiritual position was, at the same time, obviously a serious disadvantage when facing Protestant powers. Even if they were present at their courts (which was far from given), they had little power to influence actual decision-making. As we see from the chapter of Cristina Bravo Lozano, the success of the most important task for the papacy in the British Isles, the protection of Catholics living in these territories, was highly dependent on the actual twists and turns of power politics. As a territorial ruler, the pope could certainly not wield enough power to threaten the English government; thus, if no major Catholic ruler put pressure on the British, there was little hope that the pope could gain any relief for his co-religionists.

Late seventeenth-century popes also had to face the dilemma of whether they should see themselves as the head of Christianity or of Catholicism. Innocent XI chose the wider framework in organising the Holy League for a large-scale anti-Ottoman war; his successors, among them Innocent XII, as presented in the chapter of Béla Vilmos Mihalik, had already started to doubt whether it would be wise to give financial help and political gain in the common endeavour to Protestant rulers, who eventually could use these against their Catholic rivals. The discussions around financial aid to the emperor highlights yet another relevant question: the channels of papal influence. Money was not the only means available to the Holy See to put pressure on other powers, and in the volume we have seen several further alternative tools as well, from simply relying on the reputation of the pope, as in the case of the nuncios at the Polish elections, to accessing the rulers through the 'way of conscience,' as practised by their confessors, who also guided and counselled monarchs in the realm of politics.

In the case of other powers, however, the hierarchy between confessional and political interests was much less obvious. Even if we accept the thesis that due to the confessionalisation process the beginning of the seventeenth century was characterised by a certain fundamentalist attitude, where the denominational choices of specific rulers also determined their political stance, by the middle of the century the situation became much more blurred. As is clear from Rubén González Cuerva's contribution, the idea of a Catholic block had its limits, and different confessor-counsellors at the imperial court represented the specific interests of diverging groups. Catholic minorities under duress, as presented by Charlotte Backerra, had to be cautious when turning to foreign powers for help. Due to reasons related to reputation and prestige (a very important determining factor in the functioning of the early modern society of princes), if one power had already consented to intervene on their behalf, the other would most likely not accept being only the second, but would rather withdraw any assistance requested by his co-religionists. Nevertheless, as my chapter presents, confessional solidarity also remained an important factor in the early eighteenth century – admittedly, mostly on the rhetorical level, no longer capable to overrule other concerns.

When political interests required making an alliance with a party of a different religion, this caused further conflicts, which sometimes produced significant obstacles to cooperation and required constant attention. Some powers under pressure, if they really needed the benevolence of another ruler, were ready to make concessions in the diplomatic sphere, even to accept such insults as to have a Catholic priest as a representative at a Protestant court, as explained by Ernesto Oyarbide Magaña. In the early eighteenth century, as presented by Charlotte Backerra, rulers could already be sure that if they tolerated some complaints concerning their attitude towards their subjects of a different religious group, soon political interest would again gain the upper hand and overshadow confessional conflicts. They could also rely on the certainty that religious minorities would also be found in the realm of their negotiating partners, and these would also be able to present gravamina, which could be used as counterarguments against incoming complaints. The idea of reciprocity, highlighted in the chapter of Martin Bakeš and Jiří Kubeš, made sure that confessional conflicts would not drastically influence political choices in this period after the mid-seventeenth century – but at the same time also that the scope of assistance religious minorities could expect from abroad remained limited.

Of course, foreign policy is not only determined on the level of the powers involved in it, but also on the level of people actually taking care of its administration – and this volume also provides some good examples of the confession-related conflicts that could occur related to persons with diplomatic status. I have already mentioned both cases of Catholic priests functioning as diplomatic representatives of secular powers, openly or latently, in both Catholic and Protestant environments, in the chapters of Rubén González Cuerva and Ernesto Oyarbide Magaña. Sometimes it was the addressee who motivated rulers to choose people from denominations that they were not happy to see in their own country: Robert Barnes, an envoy who had been declared a heretic in England, could be the best choice when accessing rulers who were turning Protestant, as suggested by Katharina Beiergrößlein's chapter. The Calvinism of Sweden's Scottish envoy was perhaps less of an asset in England in the first half of the seventeenth century; however, the local knowledge and good personal contacts of James Spens made him such an excellent candidate for the position of ambassador to London that the strictly Lutheran Swedish administration turned a blind eye towards his confession, as presented by Steve Murdoch.

This actor-based approach is what makes the question of the embassy chapel so relevant and intriguing. Contrary to what many would have assumed, no power seems to have curbed the rights of ambassadors stationed at their courts to have their own chapels and chaplains. The idea of extraterritoriality seems to have functioned well, and the reciprocity of diplomatic relations certainly contributed not only to the acceptance of the diplomats' immunity from the secular laws of the country they visited, but also from local restrictions in regard to following a specific creed. Conflicts, it seems, were in each case centred around the limitations of the chapel's functioning: the celebrations of religious events were not meant for the local population, but it was very hard to control who entered the chapel. This caused major problems in countries with a relatively well-developed public sphere, such as early modern England. As we learn from Roberta Anderson's chapter, even if the English court would have shown more lenience towards the missionary zeal of the chaplains at the Spanish embassy, the developments were followed with a keen interest by public opinion, and many angry responses were published against what pamphleteers experienced as a dangerous threat against their convictions. The problem was, however, not always caused by the diplomats themselves, but rather by their spiritual guides, the chaplains. As pointed out by Martin Bakeš and Jiří Kubeš regarding the priests attached to imperial embassies, these people had to deal with the problem of their multiple loyalties. On the one hand, they had to support the interests of the emperor and his representative, but, on the other, as ecclesiastics they felt just as much responsibility towards their Church and its current faithful, who were under duress, as well as its potential followers. The fact that the decision-makers of imperial foreign policy changed their initial attitude and started to exclude Jesuits from the service of embassy chaplains points again towards power politics gaining the upper hand on confessional interests.

This development seems to be a commonplace, it would have hardly been possible to maintain the fundamentalist attitude of the early seventeenth century in the long run, and some would say that even then it only existed in a very limited sense. Even for securing benefits for co-religionists abroad, it was necessary for each power to maximise the impact it had on others, which was only possible through ways that included political communication, and thus went against a seclusion of confessionally based blocks. This volume does not offer a precise chronology of when and how exactly this happened, but collections of essays are generally not designed to carve such conclusions into stone. Nevertheless, the chapters, by shedding sharper light on specific situations, help us to understand many facets of the intriguing issue of the conflict between the religious and the political in early modern Europe.

Index